YET MORE
SWEET DAYS

TOM SUTCLIFFE

YET MORE SWEET DAYS

Notes from a fly fisher's life

TOM SUTCLIFFE

'In his inimitable conversational story-telling style, Tom Sutcliffe is perceptive and insightful, and his matchless prose is enhanced by many of his arresting pen-and-ink sketches. He shows us that fly fishing is much more than the expected; it's also a way to view the world around us.'
– Peter Brigg

'I've been reading Tom's books since I was a teenager. They've kept me captivated and inspired. In my opinion, Tom is right up there with the Gierachs of this world. *Yet More Sweet Days* is a trip through the life of a legend.'
– Gordon van der Spuy

'Tom Sutcliffe has raised the bar yet again. *Yet More Sweet Days* has as much to do with life as with fly fishing. You will want to read and reread it. For me, his best work yet   and that's high praise!'
– Clem Booth

'Through his words and art, and in the images he provokes, Tom Sutcliffe will root generations to come – wherever they are – in what we love and what is beautiful: nature, places, people and trout.'
– Steve Boshoff

Published in South Africa by Mercury
an imprint of Burnet Media

•

Burnet Media is the publisher of Mercury and Two Dogs books
info@burnetmedia.co.za   www.burnetmedia.co.za
Facebook: Two Dogs / Mercury Books
Twitter: @TwoDogs_Mercury
PO Box 53557, Kenilworth, 7745, South Africa

•

First published 2019
1 3 5 7 9 8 6 4 2

•

•

Cover photograph: Tom Lewin on the upper Lourens River,
Somerset West, photographed by the author.
Cover flap photograph of author: Billy de Jong
All artwork by author

•

•

Distributed by Jacana Media
www.jacana.co.za

•

Printed and bound by Tandym Print
www.tandym.co.za

•

ISBN 9781928230717

Set in Adobe Caslon Pro 11pt

*This book is dedicated to my many friends and to my family,
all life's greatest assets.*

CONTENTS

FOREWORD

Tom Sutcliffe has been a literary and fishing presence in my life ever since I first picked up, read and re-read a copy of *My Way with a Trout* all those years ago. His subsequent publications have expanded the reputation established with that first book, and he has been an informative and imaginative companion to generations of fly fishers since then, not least myself.

Tom writes beautifully and accessibly. He has a rare gift for telling stories that are absorbing, entertaining and enlightening, and which impart substantial knowledge with the lightest of touches. This book winds its way through fly-fishing experiences ranging from the streams and rivers of Barkly East and Rhodes, which appear to have become something of a spiritual home for Tom, to the chalkstreams of England, float tubing for monster trout in sub-arctic temperatures in the Stormberg Mountains near Molteno in the northeastern Cape, double-handed casting for Atlantic salmon in Iceland, some brief flirtations with Tenkara, and much else. And along the way we learn about fly choice, stream craft, presentation, leader dynamics, and so on, in a way that is entirely germane to the narrative he is unfolding. We also learn about seasons, flowers, birds, friendships, meals shared, fishing trips wrecked by flooding – and all the other aspects that make fly fishing so absorbing a pursuit.

The well-known narrator of Herman Charles Bosman's Groot Marico stories, Oom Schalk Lourens, famously said that an important part of the art of storytelling was knowing 'which parts to leave out'. Oom Schalk was sufficiently gifted a storyteller also to know 'what to leave in', and this is something Tom understands well. The stories come to life because they take us into conversations with people met along the way, images of the wind flattening the grass, the build-up of storm clouds over the escarpment, the dregs in the coffee cup, or the banter between friends on the tailgate of a truck. The descriptions of landscape merit particular mention. Here is a sample:

> Further down the valley the scene was surreal. One half of the landscape was under a clear blue sky, the other half was under slate-grey clouds dropping sheets of rain that fell in scintillating silver pillars side-lit by sunshine.

Above all, a reader of this book learns to slow things down. This may be in the approach to a pool, in which we learn something of the art of holding back and watching, not wading into the more promising water near the head, checking even the unlikely looking spots that may surprise us with really fine fish. (It's a lesson I wish I had learnt earlier this year, as I spooked the biggest fish I saw all day on one of the upper stretches of the Bell, in water that I didn't think could even conceal a tadpole.) Or it may be in learning not to wish away the passing kilometres of a Karoo landscape in a flat-out rush to get to the fishing destination at the end of the journey. Tom takes us into the solitude of a roadside cup of coffee, in which the only sound is the ticking of a cooling engine and the only company the birds hungry for biscuit crumbs; or down a turn-off to a farmhouse, remarked upon in previous journeys but never visited – yet never missed – and the budding of an unexpected friendship.

In slowing things down, we learn to refine our powers of perception, and this is something Tom describes in fine detail. We also learn, through observation of movement, colour and the ways in which we pick up traces of which we may otherwise only be subliminally aware, just how much our own careless movement may cost us on the bankside.

Tom Sutcliffe is undoubtedly South Africa's leading fly-fishing author, and someone who can easily hold his own in the ranks of fly-fishing authors across the globe whom we all love to read. A new book from him is eagerly awaited by the many readers who have followed his work to date. This book will delight and inform those who pursue fish with the long rod, and will deepen and enrich our experience of pursuing trout in the many beautiful landscapes they call home.

Duncan Brown
Somerset West, June 2017

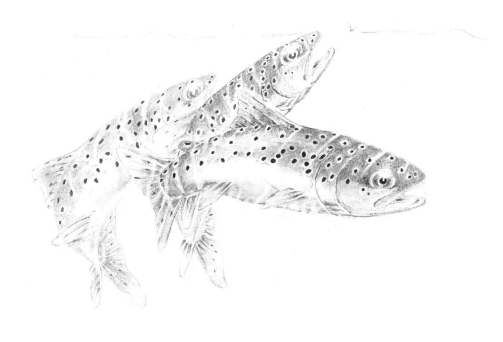

CHAPTER 1
THE PASSAGE OF TIME

*I'm a very ordinary woman who has had
a very extraordinary life through the magic of fly fishing,
and I wish that for everyone.*
JOAN WULFF

It's been fifteen years since I wrote *Hunting Trout* and a shade over seven since *Shadows on the Stream Bed* was published. The world has lurched through some dramatic political, financial and meteorological crises, and has changed radically. Discussing these changes perhaps isn't the expected way to start a book about fly fishing, but the condition of the world *is* important in that it forms the backdrop against which our fishing plays itself out. So it's not a bad idea, even just as a form of catharsis, to get the ugly side out the way first. Let's begin with the global picture.

Since I wrote *Hunting Trout*, the world, even to the most forgiving and optimistic observers, seems to have been on a slippery slide.

We've had wars, and many sad and atrocious terror attacks, and with the wars and the terrorism we've had human displacement on a massive scale. There is crime, sure, but like war, that's always been around; important perhaps is the relatively recent appearance of sophisticated cyber-crime – and that's scary in ways that go far beyond just getting mugged in the street at night.

There was one true-to-definition black swan event, the definition being something that is unexpected and difficult to predict, which comes out of the blue and has a profound effect – like breaking your fly rod at the end of a long hike up a river. This particular black swan was the financial meltdown on Wall Street in 2008 following the Lehman Brothers collapse. I'm not sure that it affected many fly fishers directly, other than the few who were the investors or bankers who happened to be deeply involved. But it generally left the rest of us feeling jittery about the global financial situation and the systems that underpin it, and that jitteriness has stayed. With it has come an increased wariness of man's irrational greed that leads to corruption.

Closer to fly fishing, there is growing evidence of the quasi-black swan reality of global warming, a phenomenon that in recent times accounted for, or at least contributed to, the severest droughts the world has ever recorded, storms on an unprecedented scale and mammoth bush fires that raged in places as far apart as California, Spain, the Western Cape and Australia. Linked to this is growing pollution through toxic spills. On the pollution front, these examples will keep you awake all night: the destructive effect of unmanaged and toxic mining waste, and the sewerage spills into many of our freshwaters and offshore estuaries. But seemingly taking first place of late, if just for the sheer scale of the problem, is the contamination of our oceans with plastics.

When it comes to man's irrational greed, two examples will suffice: the mindless slaughter of rhinos and the horrific incidental catches of pelagic seabirds, especially albatrosses, by longline fishermen. And I am not even mentioning growing government and corporate corruption and, here at home, the spectre of state capture.

That's the bleak side of our world during the last decade or so. But then, in a seeming paradox to a large part of the world's apparently inexorable slide into despair, war, decay and bigotry, a larger part of the world is now preaching a modern rhetoric that supports inclusivity, greater tolerance and the acceptance of diversity.

So the positives are there, even if we have to keep reminding ourselves about them – like the advances in technology that made your fishing easier or better or more comfortable or safer. It's interesting, or it's part of the condition of man, but we soon forget whatever it was that wasn't part of our fly-fishing lives and quickly adopt whatever is new and advantageous as if it were always there. Think of rotary fly vices, zingers, fly boxes that float.

As expected, fly fishing has changed over the past decade and a half, but unlike the mix of good and bad that we saw in the world's geopolitical dynamic, the changes in fly fishing have largely been for the better (if we exclude financial instability and global warming). Anglers in some countries have become innocent bystanders in generally depressed, almost rogue economies. For many South Africans, the crazy exchange-rate fluctuations and poor economic growth have challenged the affordability of the sport. It's reached the point where anglers, other than the very wealthy, now rate the financial cost of a trip – even just a day trip to a far-flung venue – as just as important as whether the actual fishing turns out to be good or bad. And I guess when you are spending more bucks than usual, it's not unreasonable to expect at least a few hatches to come off and a few fish to eat your flies.

But much of the change in fly fishing over the past decade was predictable. Certainly, the technological and design advances in tackle were, as was the appearance of a giddy heap of new tackle and some novel fishing techniques from a bunch of our deeper-thinking brothers and sisters.

You could safely have banked on better digital communication and you would have been right – but, like me, you would probably have underestimated its impact. I was way off predicting the scale of digital fly-fishing communication, potentially *the* major frontier of conquest during the past decade. As a result of wholesale subscription to fly fishing in the form of blogs, websites and a host of other computer-based applications, information flows on a cosmic scale, and fly fishing is now, more or less, a global community.

So, for example, I now count among my good friends a number of people I have never actually met yet still feel I know well – like fly tiers Leon Links and Hans van Klinken in Holland; Barry Ord Clark in Denmark; Hugh Rosen, a medical scientist and RAB and DDD dry-fly fanatic in California; bamboo rod maker Nick Taransky in New South Wales; Andrew Mackenzie, a prominent fly fisher in Sydney, Australia; Peter Hayes, supreme fly caster and guide in Tasmania; another Peter Hayes, the UK-based author of *Fishing Outside the Box*; and Simon Cooper, another UK-based fly-fishing author and chalkstream guide. Your list is likely as long.

An interesting side question is whether the vast selection of fly tackle now available is reaching saturation point, meaning reaching a level where a sort of angler retail fatigue sets in. On this point, I have to believe that the lives of retail fly-tackle dealers have become a nightmare of choices, just as the life of your everyday angler has become a nightmare of choices (never mind the beginners, who must be confused beyond belief). There are two sides to being spoilt for choice, and both don't necessarily face upwards.

The growth in yellowfish angling and the evolution of sophisticated tactics to catch them were more or less predictable, especially taking into account that there's no shortage of challenges with nine different species to hunt, and each behaves a little differently around flies.

What helped develop the sport was the quality of angling in places such as Sterkfontein Dam, the Vaal River and its tributaries, the Orange River (especially up- and downstream of the town of Douglas), and in the vast and beautiful expanses of the Richtersveld.

Over the same fifteen-year period there were advances in trout, steelhead and salmon fishing techniques globally, and though some were notable, none in my view was seismic. What turned out to be significant, and not unexpected either, was the growth in all aspects of saltwater fly fishing, including the increasing number of available destinations and, in keeping with the seemingly endless riches of the sea, the number of target species. More anglers now classify themselves as committed saltwater converts than way back when *Hunting Trout* came out.

One interesting change is the emergence of what, for want of a better term, I call *trends* in fly fishing. There's a trend to travel – often to far-flung, exotic destinations – as clients of the increasing number of destination outfitters, which offer fishing for a list of species that has grown as long as your favourite fly rod. And there's a trend towards inclusivity, meaning you now find increased diversity among fly fishers, certainly a healthier representation of anglers of different races and cultures and, with it, a welcome growth in the number of lady fly fishers.

The trend to use protective clothing is as expected as it is relevant, especially in still- and saltwater environments where the risk of damaging UV radiation is really high. For example, UV gloves are now almost as ubiquitous as sunglasses, and I am never without snake gaiters, even if they're mainly on my legs just for my own peace of mind.

There is also a trend, especially among farmers, to regard fishing waters as economic assets, and that has brought with it a growing awareness of environmental degradation, better farming practices and the need for vigilance and caution.

Then there are a few trends I call subliminal, because I'm not expert enough to comment on them with bulletproof authority. But I suspect they're real enough; like the minor renaissance in the art of tying traditional salmon flies, and tying dry flies or wet flies from traditional schools such as the Catskill and early chalkstream schools, all of them precise, intricate and exacting pastimes.

Then there's the increasing value of antique and collectable fishing gear, the resurgence of fly-fishing craftsmen and artists and, finally, the growth of new avenues of minimalistic fly fishing, not least Tenkara, which goes hand in hand with other interesting Japanese fly-fishing techniques. I'd also have to mention a host of other special techniques, be it French nymphing or the hand-to-leader methods people like Jeremy Lucas made so understandable and appealing.

Then there's the growing subscription to fishing bamboo fly rods, not a totally unexpected development after our headlong leap many decades back into all things graphite. Bamboo fly rods are now an unquestioned part of fly-fishing's mainstream tapestry, when not too long ago they were considered little more than the idle indulgence of a small bunch of eccentric, hard-core fly fishers who were either slow on the uptake or glued in the past, or just devoted to bamboo for the sake of tradition, poetry and romance. But the realisation came, as it inevitably had to, that *good* bamboo fly rods, far from being brittle, sloppy to cast and heavy (common and often undeserved labels of the past), are in fact extremely strong and responsive instruments that, importantly, are more forgiving in the casting stroke. Nobody asks why you fish with bamboo any more.

These are some of the main trends as I see them. There are many more, but we can rest with this lot for the time being.

If there were any downsides to fly fishing over the same period, and there were, they were mostly not insurmountable. Some, though, are concerning – like the altering weather patterns I mentioned that are exacerbated by climate change. The denialist lobby around this developing disaster is of particular concern. So many industrialised nations still see the risk of climate change as no more than an inconvenient truth – or, worse, the wacky theories of a bunch of misguided, radical left-wing climatologists.

The anti-trout lobby in South Africa, noticeably less vocal in other countries where trout are alien, like New Zealand, Australia and Argentina, has been well countered by the brave and dogged efforts of the Federation of South African Flyfishers (FOSAF), where people such as Ilan Lax and Ian Cox (both lawyers), Dr Bill Bainbridge and many others have tirelessly presented a cogent case in support of sanity or, if not sanity, at least common sense and pragmatism. Pronouncements I've heard of late from assorted reputable sources suggest that invasion biology is becoming if not an outdated postulation, at least one that is being revisited. As the obvious fluidity of the world's species unfolds, it becomes more and more apparent that the xenophobic approach to life on earth needs to be questioned, as it ignores the simple fact that the world is in a dynamic, ever-changing state of flux as far as species distribution is concerned. I don't need scientists to tell me this.

Rather than trying to rid our country of its lovely trout or trying to limit the stocking of our trout waters through reams of strangling legislation, let's focus on preserving the ecosystems that sustain trout – our rivers and streams. We'll be doing a lot more good than chasing our tails trying to oust a fish that has already been here well in excess of a century. Besides, trout do no measurable harm, add vastly to the economy and provide untold joy to the thousands of devoted disciples who regularly stalk them.

Overcrowding on fly waters is a minor problem in South Africa. It's a problem at times in the USA, where there's so much fishing available I feel little sympathy for anglers who bleat because they happen to end up standing cheek-to-jowl on some famous blue-ribbon trout water – and then only at certain times of the season. It would be understandable if they had nowhere else to throw a fly line, but the truth is these same anglers are free to fish elsewhere, and the choices in the USA are sumptuous. Anglers may end up fishing little-or lesser-known streams, but the truth is little-known streams are fine when you learn to make the most of them. We're masters at it in South Africa; I suspect, many anglers in parts of Australia are as well. As it happens, I actually *prefer* to fish little-known streams – and that goes for most of my fishing pals. In fact, the less well-known and the smaller the stream the better – and we don't mind if that sounds a little weird to a lot of folk.

As we said, affordability, and with it accessibility, to really good fly-fishing opportunities remains a problem for all but the wealthy, but that's not limited to fly fishing, and it's not limited to South Africans either. Getting a ticket on an English chalkstream, or on any recognised salmon or steelhead river worldwide, is never a cheap ride. But you don't have to be on prime water to have fun. As a friend once said, 'You don't need to drive a convertible Ferrari to feel the wind through your hair.' He drives a '90s Landy, and says he gets plenty of wind through his hair with the windows down and the dash vents wide open.

I live near the bottom of the fly-fishing affordability chain, so exotic destinations haven't featured too high on my list of experiences. I've been lucky to have a few friends who occasionally invite me as a guest to fish the Hampshire chalkstreams, and once a salmon river; I've been invited twice to fish the Skeena River system for steelhead as well as some famous streams in Montana and Wyoming on the way to the Skeena. The chalkstream experience was particularly wonderful in ways that aren't that easy to describe without sounding like a real snob. Perhaps I could say the fishing is so different from the rough, freestone-stream fishing I'm used to, with its fast-flowing, crazy cross-currents and often fleetingly snappy rises, that it makes chalkstreams seem remarkable if only by contrast. I enjoy our tall, craggy mountain landscapes, our sweeps of russet-coloured veld, and the remoteness of most of our better streams and rivers, but I'll admit that it was comfortably easy, for a while anyway, to swap all of this for gently-flowing chalkstreams with their manicured banks, smoothly laminar flows and slow-rising trout. When I think of chalkstreams I think of comfort, of purposeful trout, of cottage pie and a stoup of ale served in a cosy pub. Here at home, I think of dust, bumpy roads, tangled riverbanks, snappy trout, roughly sliced sandwiches and lukewarm coffee. Different, sure – but still two sides of the same gold coin.

My friend Mike Harker dropped in for coffee the other day on one of his rare visits to Cape Town. I hadn't seen him in ages, and he told me he hadn't fished in three years, save for a week-long saltwater trip to Alphonse. I asked him what the trip had been like. He said it was nonstop casting to sighted fish, torpedo-fast attacks, slamming takes, a delicious continuum of heart-thumping, reel-screaming, rod-bending, super-heavy-fish kind of angling. In fact, it was like nothing he'd ever experienced. He said he had a triggerfish bite straight through a heavy hook, lost a fly line, snapped a rod… It cost him a small fortune, but when I asked whether he would do it again, he said that if he had no other responsibilities he'd stay fishing on Alphonse until his funds dried up.

The next question I could ask myself is, what will the following decade bring? More of the same for sure – the use of virtual reality, augmented reality, artificial intelligence; maybe even super-saturated, real-time satellite imaging and more use of drones for augmented imagery in fly fishing. And with self-drive cars on the map, what about self-casting fly rods? I suspect there's a point where futuristic imaginings might cut so deep into the soul of fly fishing that most of us would rather roll over and say, 'Keep it.'

In contradistinction, if fly fishing were suddenly to revert to the fishing of the 1960s, my life in the sport would be different, sure, but on balance *no less pleasant*. Much of what has changed has certainly made life easier and more convenient, but in some ways it has also made life more complicated – or more complicated than it needs to be just to catch a fish, and no more pleasant in terms of the fun we used to get out of that simple act. So while I would not like to trade my present truck for a '60s model of the same make, I wouldn't care if a lot of other aspects of fly fishing reverted to what us oldies easily slip into calling 'the good old days'. Meaning if fly fishing *did* revert back to, say, the 1960s or the '70s model as we lived it back then, I guess that since I don't feel discernibly happier now or any less crazy about my fishing than I did then, nothing much would be different, if that makes any sense.

From student days, through the age of hype and humbug
In my student days, I fished the town water on the Eerste River in Stellenbosch with the bare minimum of gear and only a tenuous grasp of what I was doing. But I was happy. I celebrated every fish I caught, and was secretly confident that I was becoming something of an expert. The fact that I wasn't didn't really dawn on me. After all, I was catching trout – so what more was there to know? And if I didn't catch trout, I'd think someone must have poisoned them, or that they'd all temporarily migrated downstream for some unknown reason. I had many of those dark kind of thoughts.

Later, when I got to fish with people who *were* a lot better than me, I realised I had a lot to learn. I became hungry for knowledge, and hung on to every word my new-found expert friends uttered as though each statement was a decree straight from the Vatican. They reeked of wisdom so, naturally, I copied every nuance of their various techniques, began investing in better tackle and unashamedly took heaps of flies off them.

Back in class, while my lecturers droned on and on, I found it difficult to take my mind off the riffles and runs that had challenged me the week before. I was suddenly spending as much time thinking about fly fishing as learning about medicine. I even took to sketching in the margins of the notes I took in class, because I found it therapeutic. Yet in a strange way that I can't explain to this day, I was somehow able to follow the thread of the lectures. My notebooks ended up cluttered with small ballpoint sketches of trout and trout streams. I once left a notebook in a lecture theatre overnight, and the next morning it was handed in to the lecturer, presumably by a watchful janitor. Holding my notebook in front of the class, our lecturer remarked sarcastically that he couldn't recall discussing fish, and that we should please draw his attention to it if he ever did. I suspect he handed my notebook to me with some exaggerated ceremony, but it was a long while back so I can't be sure. He was definitely no fly fisher – that much I *can* tell you.

And so, yes, we make progress and there are changes and new discoveries and new developments, but the happy truth is that the core elements of our fly fishing – the inner peace, the solitude, the transient disappointments, the moments of exquisite joy – remain the same regardless of the steady procession of intervening years and all the hype and the humbug and the progress. Which is not to say that progress hasn't also been welcome.

You can talk of great tipping points in fly fishing, be they in tackle (as in the arrival of graphite) or in fly tying (the arrival of CDC feathers), or the flood of great books from great writers, or the added scope that new and modern techniques have offered. But let me cut to the quick and suggest that none of this, in your fly-fishing life or mine, holds a candle to the influence friends have on your enjoyment of angling. Personal view, but I can defend it if I have to.

Perhaps you haven't been well blessed with pals but, by the grace of God, I have. I thought I should mention some who have influenced my life one way or another, because they're interesting people, or eccentric, or brilliant exponents of technique, or great craftsmen or artists, or just plain ordinary folk who have offered me unconditional friendship, all in the context of our parallel love of fishing.

But compiling a list of friends sets you on a road as potholed as a wedding invitation list invariably gets, in that some people will be left out who don't expect to be or deserve to be. So I won't travel that route. Some I will mention in the passages of this book, some in the acknowledgements; the rest I hope will understand the confines that a work like this imposes on you, as much as your budget ultimately prescribes your choices in tackle, even your fishing destinations.

In my own life, I have lived by the simple principle that it is better to share than to receive, a sentiment that has sometimes morphed into an obligation to share. I have studied this not with a psychologist's wisdom or insight, but as a plain fly fisher who just wants to go about a life of catching fish, especially trout – although I soon realised that I would fish for frogs in a roadside reservoir deep in the Karoo if that was all that was left, but then preferably with a fly. (The latter would not be an exclusionary clause.)

The answer I've come to about obligations to other fly fishers is simple. I am no blindly altruistic, ultra-benevolent do-gooder at all. There have been times, many of them, when I've purposefully dodged communion with fellow anglers, and when I haven't felt the slightest inclination to share any aspect of what I know or have.

But there are more times when I *am* inclined to share than when I'm not, and the important part is that I happen to enjoy sharing. At the same time, I understand that other anglers may hold different views, and I'm not going to suggest they conform to mine. We're made differently, after all.

Insofar as my sense of *obligation* to share is concerned… Well, there are more and more days when I can confidently say I got over it as a pressing need, do it still when I'm inclined, and always enjoy it just as much as I ever did – which is a lot. That's most of the purpose of this book.

Storm over Birkhall

CHAPTER 2

BETWEEN THE STORMS – BARKLY EAST, NOVEMBER 2009

I no longer want ideal conditions of weather and water,
though I look for both within reason. But a bright
and pretty day, a day when one is free to go, is the
day to go fishing, even if the fish do not think so.
RODERICK HAIG-BROWN, FISHERMAN'S SPRING

There was a time on my frequent fishing trips to Barkly East when I drove straight through from Cape Town in a day and ended up on Basie and Carien Vosloo's farm, *Birkhall*, road-scorched and tar-crazed – the highway equivalent of jet lag, I guess. You could put it down to old age or just to a steady falloff in my need to rush, but I've at last arrived at the point where the drive up on any long-distance fishing trip is almost as enjoyable as the fishing once I get there.

At first on these road trips I just leaned heavily towards taking my time, but later I began making a real point of it – and once the countryside stopped flashing by like the blurred-green scenery you see from one of Europe's bullet trains, I began to notice how much I'd been missing. In fact, I noticed three things; the first being how interesting and beautiful the countryside is when you actually take the time to look at it, especially the deep Karoo. Then I got to understand that the prospect of fishing can somehow seem all the more enticing just for the waiting. Finally, after one or two encounters you could call close shaves or near misses, it dawned on me that I was rapidly increasing my chances of getting written off in a head-on collision, a point when you naturally start considering a more defensive lifestyle.

And so my trips to *Birkhall* jumped from around twelve hours of solid driving interspersed with hurried stops for coffee to something like twenty-four hours with a relaxing overnight stay and plenty of unhurried stops at various points along the 1,100-kilometre route.

*

The R61 is the dead-quiet, flagpole-straight, endless and seemingly boring stretch of road between Beaufort West and Aberdeen, and I love it like no other highway in South Africa. It passes through 150 kilometres of its own vast void of apparent nothingness. But that's deceptive, because I discovered the R61 is actually varied and interesting when you take the time to look around.

The first half *is* unremarkable. It's almost featureless; just flat, treeless Karoo scrub country with mountain ranges too distant to be distinctive. But the closer you get to Aberdeen, which is the village at the end of the R61, the more the road takes on the character of the Camdeboo Karoo, meaning impressively tall mountains to the north and a distant, pastel-blue range to the south, both ranges running the whole length of the highway. Vervet monkeys congregate in the thorn trees that line the dust-dry riverbeds, small herds of springbok graze the veld, raptors are plentiful, especially the Pale Chanting Goshawks that classically sit in wait on treetops. And then, in the colder months, fields of blood-red aloes light up the drab veld like Chinese lanterns.

I begin Route 61 with my mind numbed from the soulless five-hour, truck-dodging drive up the N1 to Beaufort West. But halfway from Beaufort West to Aberdeen, I begin to feel free and comfortably alone. I relax, count goshawks, monkeys, kestrels, antelope, the rarer shy and cleverly camouflaged bustards and korhaans, and suddenly I don't notice those sleep-inducing white lines slipping relentlessly by under the bonnet any longer. And if I pass more than a dozen cars on this ninety-kilometre section, the road feels busy.

I always pull off the road near a bridge over a dry riverbed, where a stand of thorn trees throws a pool of shade onto the edge of the highway. I stop as much for a cup of black, sweet coffee and to stretch, as to suck deep breaths of Karoo air into my lungs.

This trip, the truck was half in, half out of the shade. It's not the deepest shade and not the coolest. The countless different birds I'd seen from the truck were strangely absent, as if alerted by my stopping. But somewhere in the trees along the riverbed I eventually heard the sound of birdsong. In the far distance, a small troop of monkeys crossed the road in loping, taunting strides, stopping on the white line to stare at me. Only a single car passed with a whoosh and a toot of its horn. I sipped the last of my coffee and left. Moments later, through a hallucinatory heat-haze, I saw a silvery-blue lake shimmering just below a distant line of mountains. It was hard to believe it wasn't actually a huge, sparkling piece of water.

About thirty kilometres from Aberdeen, and close by the road, there's a lovely old farm called *Kariegasfontein*. Its tin roofs and white-washed buildings are set in a stand of trees, edged by tall palms and prickly pears. The farm spans both sides of the highway; farmhouse one side, outbuildings and sheds the other. I have liked the look of this farm ever since I first saw it seventeen years back, and I always slow to a walking pace here to soak in its sense of remoteness and its rustic, timeless, deep-Karoo atmosphere. In the vast sweep of bone-dry Karoo country, the palms and the surrounding trees lend the aura of an oasis to the place.

Over the years I had wondered who owns the farm and pondered its history, and was frequently tempted to drop in and announce myself as a passing visitor in need of a cup of coffee and a history lesson.

On this trip I actually did turn off at *Kariegasfontein*. I took a drive along a side road that swung around the back of the farmhouse, parked off and busied myself taking photographs of the scrub veld and thorn trees and the nearby range of tall mountains. The only sound was the silky click of my camera's shutter. Then a farmer drew up in a truck. I suspected from the look on his face that he was about to ask what the hell I was doing on his land, but instead he lifted a hand in greeting and said, 'Okay, I see you're just taking a few photos.' I told him I had admired his farm for years, that I'd kept telling myself I'd drop in one day, but somehow never had. He introduced himself as Philip McNaughton and I introduced myself. He looked at me for a long moment, then asked, 'Do you do any fly fishing?'

'When I get the chance,' I said.

'Are you the guy who wrote a book on it?'

'For my sins I did,' I replied.

'Small world,' he said. 'It's back in my house right now. Can't recall the title. My uncle passed it on to me.'

'Is it *Hunting Trout* maybe ?'

He said, 'Could be.'

And that, roughly, is how we became acquainted, and how I learned a little about the history of *Kariegasfontein*.

*

I've got into the habit of breaking my trips to Barkly East at a place called *Mount Melsetter*, Mike and Candy Ferrar's guest farm midway between Middelburg and Steynsburg, though you might need to consult a map to get a bead on exactly where that is. I'm usually there at about 5pm, when it's a relief to unpack, stroll around, then sit on the veranda with a glass of white wine looking over a vista that starts with a wide sweep of garden and a stand of thorn trees hiding a dry riverbed, and ends in the wavy, purple outline of a range of distant mountains.

This part of the Karoo is a birding paradise, so I picked up my binoculars and strolled up the riverbed with Mike. We spotted a few interesting birds, didn't find the Namaqua Sandgrouse Mike had seen the day before, then came across what I thought might be fossil remains. Mike confirmed it and took me to a few more pieces, carefully wiping the dust off one particularly large specimen to expose the stark-white remains of a ribcage embedded in grey rock.

'Palaeontologists think this is *Lystrosaurus*,' he said, 'the precursor to mammals on earth, around 250 million years ago.'

Standing in that dry Karoo riverbed, holding the remnants of the ribcage, made mankind's history on the planet seem remarkably recent – and my own existence in the wider picture of the universe remarkably brief, never mind insignificant.

*

From *Mount Melsetter*, the drive to *Birkhall* is just a lazy roll through folding grassland country and then into mountains. Along the way the weather changed. In Burgersdorp the sky was blue and laced with clouds, but by the time I stopped to fuel up in Barkly East, the clouds were low-lying and slate-bellied. The clouds were reflected in the pools of rainwater that stood in the streets. When I asked the petrol jockey for his forecast on the weather, he just shook his head, as if implying some dark portent, then added, *'Maar, meneer, jou bakkie lek rooiwyn.'* (But, sir, your truck's leaking red wine.)

I walked around the back. Sure enough, a wide swath of dusty-red cabernet stained the tailgate and bumper, and the inside of the load bed smelled like a shebeen. I had packed the back of the cab with my fly-fishing gear, float tube and five boxes of Shepherd's Cottage wine – a couple of cases each of reds and whites, and a case of rosé. The wine was a gift for Donie and Juan-Marie Naudé, who run a fly-fishing lodge on their farm *Vrederus* in the Pitseng Valley. Then I remembered hitting one of the noxious speed bumps on the outskirts of Aliwal North. They remind me of the ski-ramps you see in the Winter Olympics. Even at 40km/h, I was launched into space. Everything on the floor lifted, then crashed down with a bang that I could feel through my spine, but I hadn't given a thought to the wine. One of the boxes of red hadn't quite survived the fall. At least half the bottles were cracked and emptied; thankfully the rest were intact.

I checked everything in the cab. All was good. Rod bags, rod tubes, fly vests, the airless carcass of my float tube, folded waders, fly-tying kit, nets. All were free of wine stains. Not that it would have mattered.

*

The drive from Aliwal North to Barkly East had been pleasant, the dams along the road all full, the aloes decked in red blooms, and the prickly pears sprouting flowers of pastel pink and pale yellow. In one field I counted more than a dozen Blue Cranes. That was pleasing, because not many years back we saw few enough of them to be concerned. And since I've done this road trip on average at least twice a year for many years, I'm in a position to notice changes like this, and it's good when they're for the better. Some years, certainly 2005 comes to mind, Blue Cranes were as rare as honest politicians. I wondered what had changed in their favour, but long may it live, whatever it is.

*

The real nature of this trip, though, revealed itself as I crossed the Kraai River at Moshesh's Ford, forty kilometres from Barkly East and only six kilometres from *Birkhall*. The river was a thundering, bank-high, coffee-coloured torrent. By the time I pulled into the farmyard it was raining, and Basie said more rain was on the way. Plan B was already going through my head.

*

When the rivers in the lowlands are rained out, you have to head into the hills to catch fish. In the headwaters, the flow in the streams will be high, and the water may look like ginger beer, but that's no problem. In normal conditions, these headwaters are mostly thin, fragile and exquisitely clear places, where you walk on eggs, use hair-fine tippets and tiny flies to catch trout. But give them a day or two to run off after rain, even after a heavy storm, and they suddenly become as sweet as a summer peach.

*

My friend Tony Kietzman drove across the next morning from Rhodes where he lives and works. We decided on fishing the Coldbrook on my friend Theuns Botha's farm. It's a tributary of the Sterkspruit River about thirty kilometres upstream from *Birkhall*. We enjoyed a pleasant hour catching up with each other on the gravel road that heads into the mountains and crosses the Sterkspruit three times. At each crossing, the flow was still churning with fullness and colour, but turning onto the side road leading up the valley the Coldbrook runs in, the water changed. It was still fast-flowing, but clear enough to be fishable. We stopped just short of the first drift above Theuns's farmhouse. He owns this section of the Coldbrook and, over the years, has become a good friend of mine.

The stream is interesting up here – mainly swift pocket water, but there are deeper, slower-flowing runs and a few pools where the water takes on a soft, jade-coloured tinge. We drifted dry flies through the better pockets and runs, each drift triggering the lovely anticipation of an imminent take, but nothing rose to our offerings. But there is plenty of stream up here, so we kept moving, casting a dry fly over likely-looking spots, and if it didn't raise a trout, quickly moving to the next. In an hour's fishing we never saw a fish. In fact, we didn't even spook one, which was ominous. I told Tony I'd fished this same stretch with some pals a few months back when we lost count of the number of fish we caught by the time we got around the first two bends.

We changed to small nymphs hung under chartreuse poly yarn indicators and fished with the fly occasionally bumping riverbed pebbles, our eyes following the indicator, waiting for any hint of unnatural movement, and when there was, lifting our rods smartly. It wasn't as poetic as dry fly fishing, and it wasn't how we'd have chosen to fish a stream like this, but we got a few trout. They were the sort of rainbows that are typical of most little-fished, upland tributary streams: startled-looking fish, all small and ice-cold to the touch, all iridescently bright with rose-coloured flanks heavily spotted, as if scattered with the drifting soot of a campfire.

Along the riverbank there were stands of bright-yellow irises, *Moraea huttonii*, and the surrounding valley was looking beautiful. It was enough just being there, but the fishing was fun in the old-fashioned sense that upstream-indicator nymphing for small trout always is. In the end I fished the leader naked, without an indicator, just watching for the glint of a fish, or for the leader to move or tremble or slow. We weren't short of trout, but they weren't in every run either, and none was longer than a ruler.

Mid-afternoon a wind got up, with an icy edge to it. We were about done and a long way above the truck. We headed out, following convenient sheep tracks along the side of the stream, then hugged a fence in the last paddock where a bull lifted his head to stare at us, his jaws rolling rhythmically on the cud, his eyes vacant with indifference. At the truck we poured a mug of warm coffee, wondered why this hadn't been another sixty-fish dry fly day and, in the end, put it down to the weather. It had seemed a certain bet we'd catch a heap of fish off the surface; but then one of the lessons you learn in fly fishing, after mastering casting and some of the other circus tricks the sport is known for, is that you can't second-guess wild trout.

The drive back was beautiful in its own way. Huge plum-coloured clouds heavy with rain lay low-sprawled across the horizon, but here and there we saw thin patches of blue sky, and splashes of sunlight lit lucerne fields a neon-green. At times the mountains on one side of the road were golden with treacle-coloured light, while on the other side they were deep in shadow. It was a strange, surreal landscape: the southern Drakensberg in one of its grander guises, a gentle beauty in a landscape that under the fast-approaching storm was becoming faintly menacing. Yet this sort of scene is no more out of place this time of the year in these mountains than a London cab in Oxford Street. We stopped the car to take photographs. I could smell the rain coming on the cold wind – the dank, earthy smell of wet leaves newly turned. Suddenly the petrol jockey's silent shake of the head came to mind.

*

That evening on the *Birkhall* veranda, Basie grilled steaks as thick as roof rafters. He did them on a steel wok connected to a portable gas cylinder. The white-marbled meat was good in ways it's hard to put your finger on, other than to say you can't lose sight of the fact that it hadn't come from a fridge in some city supermarket, but from a grass-fed animal slaughtered on the farm.

*

The storm went through and the morning sky was a huge blue dome. I caught trout in the lake on *Birkhall* using a standard pattern that I tie to imitate hatching midge pupae. The abdomen is an amber-coloured Nymph Rib, which has a lovely resinous quality and thins out as you stretch it tighter. The thorax is peacock herl, and the breathing gills are white filoplume fibres. I tie them unweighted on grub hooks in sizes 14 and 16.

The wind was light, and swallows and martins swooped around hawking insects off the surface, their beaks leaving only the tiniest marks on the water. If a fish rose within casting range I'd drop a fly alongside it, leave the fly dead still to sink, then lift gently, wait for the bow wave as the fish swung to intercept, pause that crucial fraction of a second, then, as the leader straightened, set the hook with no more than a gentle lift of the rod tip. The fish weren't big. Well, not as big as trout *can* get in this piece of water. But then I reminded myself they were big enough to have eaten the fish we'd caught the day before in the Coldbrook, meaning the size of any fish you catch is relative; at least to your, and the fish's, circumstances.

It began to rain way out north over the mountains, the rain falling in grey columns that immediately left a liquid rainbow across the skyline. It was nearly as pretty as the rainbow that appeared some years back when I fished this same lake with Chris Bladen. Not to gild the lily, but that day the mountain above *Birkhall* was white with snow and the light as clear as diamonds.

*

A day later I sat on the *Birkhall* veranda, tying flies in the soft rays of the early morning sun. I'd given Carien's handsome chickens the eye as a potential source of hackles, then thought better of it. Later I strolled across to the shed where shearers were deftly flicking ewes onto their backs; in one long, uninterrupted run they'd shear the wool off an animal, then casually toss the shorn pelt intact onto the sorting table as if it was a complete duvet.

*

I checked the Sterkspruit at the Lindisfarne Bridge. The river could have drowned you. Basie asked if I'd mind going to Barkly East to collect feed for his rams. On the way I took care to avoid a tortoise crossing the road, an uncommon sight in this part of the world, then came across another nearer town. On the road back I threaded around another tortoise crossing the road on a blind rise and got out of my truck to save it. It was making for high ground,

39

so that's where I put it. Then it struck me that *all* these tortoises had been making for high ground.

*

There were deep rumbles across the hills that night, and lightning lit the black sky. There was one momentous clap of roof-rattling thunder that seemed to explode inside my skull, and we were in darkness. For a moment, every feature of the garden and every tree was floodlit by a lightning strike, and I saw rain sweeping across in nearly horizontal waves, shafts of silver water blown on winds that seemed to buckle everything. I went back to bed and read by candlelight, enjoying the storm's sudden electric flashes of light, the steady sound of rain on the roof and the slowly receding, deep drumrolls of thunder – the exhibition of primeval power. It made me wonder whether tortoises know a lot more about weather patterns than we humans do.

*

The next day was as quiet as a dove in a tree, the sky laced with feathery clouds. Things felt innocent enough down on earth; in contrast, the long vapour trails left by passing jets were blown apart in seconds, a clear sign that something less innocent was going on up there. Once again Tony joined me. The rivers were still out, so we waded into weed patches in *Birkhall* dam until we were up to our waist, casting short lines into emerald-coloured buckets of deep water in front of us. We'd driven past a Black Stork on the way in, and an African Spoonbill was feeding quietly in the shallows on the far side of the lake.

I was back on my midge pupa imitation. It was small – say, size 16 – but then the natural is often small, and it somehow felt right.

The water looked inviting in the way lake water does when it falls straight off weed banks into resinous-green caverns full of clarity and depth, and where the surface is winking with light. There was plenty of lake and there were plenty of trout. The weather was good, and I felt comfortably confident. I fished the midge pattern dead slow, like a natural, just under the surface, almost on a gentle wind-drift. I had greased a few inches of the tippet to stop the pupa sinking too deep. I had one hard pull and lost the fish, then landed a rainbow hen of around three pounds.

Sometime that morning I left my rod lying on a patch of weeds floating on the surface to search my vest for something. While I was searching, the palest green damselfly nymph came wriggling towards me, just beneath the surface. It crawled up a stalk of weed and hatched in front of me into a flimsy, waxy-winged adult. Then it climbed onto the handle of my fly rod to dry out. I photographed the whole process, and then, with that remarkable piscatorial insight we fly fishers are occasionally known for, I changed to an imitation of a slender, pale-green damselfly nymph and fished it slowly in gaps between the weed-beds. I hooked and landed a few rainbows, one of them a brute of a fish well over six pounds. Tony had a heavy fish break him clean off. Then way down the bank, I saw him lift a dripping landing net that bulged deeply under the weight of a bucking fish. Against the sunlight Tony was briefly surrounded by a sparkling halo of spray.

You might say the cue to change to a damselfly imitation came as a blessing of sorts, but the fact is we don't often crack the code in fly fishing quite this easily. The point you need to remind yourself of is that the code is mostly waiting there to be cracked as long as you keep watching and thinking – or, like me, just get plain lucky.

*

YET MORE SWEET DAYS

It's a reassuring sign on any trip – and fishing trips especially – that things are going well when you lose track of the days, and it's even better if you aren't exactly sure of the week. I'd had a day wandering up a tiny stream that handed over its trout quite easily, but none of these fish was as impressive as the pair of prancing Crowned Cranes I came across on the drive back, or the little White-throated Swallow that refused to fly off its perch on the railing of a bridge until I got so close I could almost have touched it.

I had been fishing a tributary of the Sterkspruit, petite and not open to the public, a bright stream that I guessed we would actually never bother fishing if the better-known rivers were even in half-good nick. So it's rarely fished, and trotting a size 16 RAB through the runs proved the point. The trout were either off guard or they were as trusting as house pets. Maybe both. Whatever, getting in some fishing like this once in a while strokes the ego. And you couldn't turn your nose up at the size of these fish either. Okay, they averaged out around nine inches, but that means the occasional twelve-inch fish showed up.

*

I spent an afternoon on *Birkhall* dam again, this time experimenting with different patterns. Things were getting to feel comfortably familiar. There isn't much better than a small damselfly nymph on most trout lakes in this country, but it's pleasant, in a contrary sort of way, to do something different, so I tried a size 10 DDD that bobbed nicely on the surface but remained untouched. I changed to a sunken midge pattern and had a trout take it in mid-water straight away. This pattern mostly does best in the evening, and mostly up in the shallows, but here the pattern was suddenly working on a bronze-bright day in deeper water when the dry fly wasn't. It was one of those counterintuitive revelations that happen

fairly often on stillwaters – although when I think about it, you don't so much work out these revelations as stumble on them.

Part of stumbling on things in stillwater fly fishing has to do with common sense, empirical learning and the percentage game. The percentage game says that from about, say, 10am to 4pm, the odds are loaded on the trout feeding in mid- to deep water. It works, but it discounts the propensity stillwater trout have to rise at any buggy-looking dry fly when you least expect it, and often from deep down. I've traded on that for a long while – especially when the water is clear, a west wind is up and there's a nice chop on the water. And if it needs a lot of faith and patience, a solid rise to a dry fly bobbing over deep water in the middle of the day has a lot more going for it than a solid take to anything else fished deep-sunken and unseen. Just a personal view.

A lot of the empirical experience comes second-hand from countless, mainly UK-based stillwater fly fishers, who over the years have increasingly experimented with small midge patterns, often fished static, never mind what time of day or how deep the water.

*

Carien reminded me that we were due in Rhodes the following day to look at a couple of houses that were on the market. My wife Kathy and I had this dream of moving up there, and on one occasion we nearly pulled it off, but the seller turned down our full-asking-price offer at the last minute. I took some pleasure in telling him to get lost.

Apparently it was Thursday, though I couldn't quite get my head around that because it felt so much like it was the weekend. Had we not been in the market for a small cottage in Rhodes, I might just have headed back into the hills on my own. As well I didn't.

We took the back road through the Bokspruit Valley, where from the debris lying around it was clear the river had come over the bridge a few days before. When you have recent memories of a section of river, even in its detail, then arrive back there expecting to see what you remember, it's a shock when you find an entirely different-looking river, with not much you can recognise outside of the broadest detail. It was wide-flowing and discoloured, but I still wasted time looking into the water from the bridge. I don't know exactly what I hoped to see, but the habit is too ingrained to shake off.

We ran into a squall before Rhodes that quickly turned into a minor hailstorm, and although stormy weather isn't anything unusual up here in November, this was a day that got me thinking a lot more about climate change than before.

*

In Rhodes we had coffee with Tony Kietzman in his cottage with its red-slatted veranda. Tony wants to put the flora of this whole area on the tourist map and, when he isn't guiding visiting fly fishers, he's often out hunting for rare plants, particularly orchids.

It's not a bad idea to have a plan B up here because guiding is a hard business, even with hundreds of kilometres of river on your doorstep. Again, it's the uncertainty of the weather that unhinges the prospect of anything like a regular run of fishing clients. Tony stepped off the conveyor belt of business life in Johannesburg a few years back, packed his bags and moved to Rhodes; since then he's lived a quiet but interesting life and hasn't looked back, at least as far as I know.

He lifted a pot of coffee off the stove, lit his pipe and said, 'You know, this life is working for me. I have a pleasant job, I know where the trout are and I know where to find orchids. That's enough for the moment.' Compared to a hectic pace of life in the Big Smoke I thought it made plenty of sense, and I was happy for him.

*

Carien and I looked over a few houses in Rhodes. I saw one that might suit, made some notes and took a few photographs. It's perhaps a romantic dream that I have an 80 percent stake in, my wife hovering at around 20 percent but to me living in Rhodes would tick many boxes. To her, those same boxes would likely stay empty. I just thought it would be nice to settle here, to write, to paint and do a spot of fishing, maybe even practise a little medicine. Kathy wasn't opposed to the idea, at least not to the point where I had to drop it altogether, so I was soldiering on. That property I told you about that I lost out on at the last moment was ideal: a basic, rustic but charming cottage without electricity, on four plots with plenty of fruit trees and birds in the garden.

After seeing the houses, we popped in to greet Dave Walker at Walkerbouts Inn. This place is something of an institution in Rhodes – as is Dave himself, I suppose – at least in the sense that if you visit the village and miss out on popping in here, you'd have to admit you had toured the city of Agra in India but missed seeing the Taj Mahal.

We left Rhodes a little late, around 4.30pm, after Carien had been tapping her watch and pointing at the heaping banks of dark clouds. Five minutes out of town, the godfather of all storms hit us, rain driving in violently like bullets from machine guns. The road turned to mud, raindrops hitting the soaked ground so hard the muddy water bounced back into the air, leaving a hovering brown haze as high as the front bumper. I could see nothing beyond this liquid-brown veil, couldn't pull over – we'd have been in a ditch all night – couldn't stop because I had this vision of someone smacking into the back of my truck. At times the storm lifted its intensity and I relaxed, but as quickly as it lifted, heavy rain would come in again. I did have time at one point to stop and engage four-wheel drive, but it was a long, slow, slippery twenty minutes of tricky driving before the rain settled to just being very heavy.

As we came back along the road to *Birkhall* the storm eased, but the tiny rivulet running down the hill alongside the farmhouse had grown into a braided torrent of fast-flowing water all of fifty metres wide. It left tiny green islands with newly shorn sheep clustered on them like shipwrecked survivors clinging to rafts.

Below us the Sterkspruit had burst its banks.

The farmyard was bedlam. Neighbours had poured in to borrow canoes, rafts, tubes, anything that floated. They were going out to rescue their sheep. Philip Gush's wife swept past me, soaked to the bone, with a canoe on her head. And the rain was still coming in showers that hit us like nails. A lot of sheep drowned that afternoon.

In the evening people gathered in Basie's lounge. Sarel Steenekamp, Basie's neighbour, was there, unable to get home even though you can see his house from Basie's front veranda. The Sterkspruit was a metre over the Lindisfarne Bridge, effectively cutting him off. He eventually left after midnight when the bridge was safe to cross.

*

This was the evening I got to meet two young fellows from Cape Town, Gavin Schneider and Gavin Duveen. They had turned up at *Birkhall* rain-soaked and hoping to get some advice – and maybe some moral support as well – on the best route to *Welgemoed*, a farm only twenty kilometres away up the Bokspruit Valley. They got the advice they needed from the farmers gathered around Basie's pub, and then in the fashion of typically crazed fly fishers, the three of us put the storm aside and made plans to fish the Bokspruit on *Gateshead* once the rivers had settled. For the rest, they sat around waiting, just like Sarel, for the water coming over the Lindisfarne Bridge to drop.

Two days later I drove across to *Welgemoed* to show them *Gateshead*. 'We might even be able to fish it,' I said.

*

Gavin Schneider, a young Cape Town-based businessman, bought *Welgemoed* on the banks of the Bokspruit River and converted the old farmhouse into a neat fishing lodge. I knew the house from years back, so I could appreciate the changes he'd made. He'd knocked down inside walls, creating open-plan spaces. Now the kitchen flowed into a dining room and on into a lounge, then onto a patio looking out over the river and the mountains.

On the drive up to *Gateshead* we saw signs of storm damage; branches, even logs, trapped against fences and against the mouths of bridges where they threatened to block the flow, flood the bridge and cause the lands on either side to wash away. We saw land-slips on mountainsides, and deep crevices washed out in open fields. We drove up past the *Brucedell* beat of the Bokspruit where you see a wonderfully tall waterfall from the road. It was pumping. I'd never seen it more beautiful.

Naturally the river was up, but at each bridge we crossed the water got clearer until after the long haul up to *Gateshead* we came to the first concrete drift where you could say the water was fishable – just. A section of the concrete drift over the river was missing, but we threaded past it. At the second drift there was a massive cavity on the upstream side of the concrete crossing that could have swallowed the truck's left front wheel. So we stripped off our boots and socks and waded in, carrying rocks to fill the hole. We felt like dentists filling a large cavity in a big tooth. Then I inched the truck across the drift, the two Gavins slowly walking backwards through the water ahead of me, watching the left front wheel, at the same time giving me nervous hand signals that weren't difficult to interpret except when they gave contrary instructions as to where my wheel should be. It might seem like going to a lot of trouble just to catch a few small trout, but what made it worthwhile is that *Gateshead* in many ways is an unspoiled fly-fishing paradise, and we wouldn't lightly give up on fishing it just because a little bridge-work was needed to get there. Conditions like this call for a developed sense of adventure and, as it turned out, for a sense of humour as well, because later, as we were tackling up, I realised I'd left my boots and socks on the far side of the drift. But I had wading boots and a spare pair of socks.

*

The river was wide and running full, and the current pulled hard on our legs. In the deeper runs, the flow felt like it could carry you away. Gavin D went for a hike just to see the countryside. Gavin S put out a dainty dry fly, and a rainbow took it on his first cast. By the time we reached the corner pool above the old settler's cottage, he'd taken half a dozen more. I was supposed to be giving him a little help, guiding him, if you like, but there's not much advice you can give someone casting a short line upstream with trout jumping on his dry fly in every likely hole. So I joined in the fun with a size 16 Elk Hair Caddis and we had a dry fly bonanza.

The fish seemed crazily hungry from days of not eating in the high flows and cold water. Also in our favour was that the river had lost its usually absurd clarity, and I'm talking the cut-glass clarity that so easily gives your game away. *Gateshead* is usually one of those places where if you don't dress drably, lengthen your tippet to four feet at least and slow down your body movements, especially arm and hand movements, you will go home with a light creel. I once fished up here with a fellow who pulled on a pair of white sun-gloves. I told him that unless he kept his hands in his pockets we wouldn't catch a fish. I lent him a pair of my gloves; a dark pair, in camouflage greens and greys. Even they worry me at times, but they're better than bare hands.

*

We had fished our brains loose, but the weather was changing, and when the tall mountain behind the cottage on *Gateshead* suddenly disappeared in cloud, we took a precautionary hike back to the truck. The drifts had been fordable, but only just. Up here in the catchment an inch or two of rain would lift this river like a freed helium balloon and we'd be stranded for who knows how long. Of course, that would have had its attractive side, but not without enough provisions and beer for a protracted stay.

Gavin D joined us after what he said was a spectacular hike. We were chewing on apples and swallowing the last of the fruit juices when the clouds miraculously lifted, the sky dissolved to a wash of soft blue and the wind dropped. The change was so sudden it seemed surreal. So we hiked downstream and fished back to the truck, all of us catching trout on dry flies from the green-tinted places where the water had depth, until none of us was sure how many fish we'd actually landed. We were fished out, as they say, and didn't miss the occasion to celebrate. I opened a bottle of Springfield Estate's Life From Stone. After all, this was the kind of day when the fishing, if we were to get any at all, was in the lap of the gods, and could easily have been more moody than electric. We sipped the cool Sauvignon Blanc from enamel mugs, and it didn't taste the worse for it.

My boots were where I'd left them on the far side of the drift, and the drive out was a stroll.

*

On streams like this, dry flies and emergers add some sparkle to the fishing and, without wanting to sound elitist, it is the purest way to catch wild mountain-stream trout. Some days it can feel like it should be the *only* way, but when the fish hold fast, a small nymph is actually just as attractive to fish.

This time we fished RABs, Klinkhåmers and Elk Hair Caddis patterns on 7X tippets, but I noticed that one fussy trout refused them all, then rose nicely to a size 18 spinner pattern. If ever there was a dry fly pattern worth trying on difficult fish this is it. Art Lee, in his book *Lore of Trout Fishing*, refers to spent-spinner patterns as 'your clarion angels'. But I'm not suggesting there's just one pattern for fussy trout. The arrival of CDC feathers, alone, changed that horizon forever. Nor is it to say there will ever be a 'single pattern' that can be put into the bracket of a panacea, though we all tend to contrive elaborate personal theories that we believe head us in the right direction when it comes to dry fly selection. And so it should be. The best attribute any pattern ever had is your own deep faith in it.

*

Back at Schneider's place, we poured beers and sat on the veranda. I brought out a stick of Basie's beef biltong, and Gavin rustled up a plate of assorted cheeses and biscuits. Sitting there, we couldn't quite see the Bokspruit River running behind a stand of willows, but we were close enough to hear it. We relived the day's fishing against the river's swiftly flowing sounds, and then got a little more serious about trying to solve some of the world's pressing problems. Politics came into it, as did climate change, sport and the precarious state of the world's financial systems. It was pitch-black by the time I left to head over the mountains to *Birkhall*.

*

After a while on a trip to this part of the world, your pulse slows to the pace of the place, and I was feeling settled, even though nothing about the weather had changed other than its unpredictability.

Someone once told me that a wise local from these parts said you never get a wet autumn and spring in the same year, which I guess is one of those myths that last until they finally get blown out of the water. But I had an uneasy feeling the place would turn into a fly-fishing paradise as soon as I left – which is more or less what happened.

*

The morning was cold, but a shaft of sunlight lit the barn roof outside the kitchen where the dogs gather like rock rabbits in the warmth. I discovered again that *Birkhall* is a hard place to leave, but at least it wasn't a beautifully sunny day with the Sterkspruit running clear as a spring creek, bugs hatching, swallows swooping and fish rising. I suppose this is the one positive side to a recent flood. It makes leaving easier.

*

There was rain on my drive back through the Karoo, with headwinds so strong I had both hands on the wheel most of the way. At Aberdeen I dropped in on Phil McNaughton, and we leaned against his truck, chatting. It was cold and the clouds were low. It looked like he was also about to get rain. Twenty minutes later I hit a storm, and in no time I was driving past lakes of water on either side of the road. The last time this happened on the R61 I came across what I thought was a pig. It turned out to be an aardvark. It's a burrowing, nocturnal animal and a very rare sight during the day. I guessed its den must have got flooded.

At *Melsetter*, I collected my copy of *Roberts Bird Guide* – a really useful, more compact, workhorse version of the well-known *Roberts Birds of Southern Africa* – that I'd left on Mike and Candy's bar counter, and the rest of the trip was one long spell of tar bashing, truck dodging, drinking dubious coffee at roadside takeaways and watching out for speed traps. Somewhere along the road, Basie called to say the weather had cleared and the Sterkspruit was dropping fast. It felt strangely as if this trip wasn't actually over, that if things kept getting better I'd have to give in and head back, within the month maybe... although I guessed Kathy might turn down my visa application for that trip.

The Bokspruit River

CHAPTER 3

BARKLY EAST, MAY 2011, AND BRIEF FLIRTATIONS WITH TENKARA

It has often been remarked by trout fishermen that when they are about the affairs of stream and rod, the events of yesterday and the necessities of tomorrow are singularly dwarfed in importance.
BEN LAMPMAN, *A LEAF FROM FRENCH EDDY*

I was about two hours into the trip and deep into the heart of the Karoo, the back of my truck loaded to the gunnels with fishing gear, boxes of booze, a float tube with accessories, assorted cooking paraphernalia, including two enamel kettles with matching mugs, and a gas stove for brewing coffee and heating soup or beans when, for some unknown reason, I got this sudden heart-chilling thought that I'd left my orange-coloured Orvis rod caddy propped up against my study wall back home. Why our minds suddenly slip off along anxiety-provoking tangents like this I don't know, but it happens. In fact, the more tortuous the notion, the more your mind seems to select it. In keeping with this distressing syndrome, the more I thought about it, the more I became convinced I wasn't wrong. Before long I just knew I had left all my fly rods at home, which is an end-stage symptom of this condition.

Naturally, my first impulse was to stand on the brakes, pull over and check through the back of the truck, but I was sandwiched between two eighteen-wheelers and there was no way I could stop right then. I sat for ages behind the leading truck, locked in worry, my doubts feeding on themselves and growing all the while. At times I was almost able to pass the truck, but not without taking a risk. When you're on the N1, deep into a road trip and worrying that you've forgotten your fly rods, you're not in the right frame of mind to take high-speed risks.

The rig ahead of me had a red canvas tarpaulin covering an obviously empty trailer, and on the downhill runs, when the driver was nudging 120km/h, the tarpaulin flapped like a giant flag in a storm. Also, he was not one of those polite guys who pulls over onto the shoulder to let you through. When I did eventually overtake him, ten long minutes later, it was on a long, dead-straight section of a steep hill when he'd slowed to a walking pace. I could see clear tar for miles ahead and floored the pedal. As he came into my rear-view mirror I felt ready to pull this imaginary lever on my dashboard that would release a pile of razor-sharp builder's nails onto the road, puncturing both his front tyres. It's a sort of James Bond-type fantasy I use to help relieve attacks of road rage.

Look, I have arrived on a river before, desperately keen and ready to fish, only to find I'd left my rod behind. Or my reels. In fact, most of us have done it more than once. On one occasion I was with Ed Herbst. I purposely hadn't taken a rod because I wanted a few really good close-up photographs of fins and skins, so I'd loaded a camera and wading gear and nothing else. Ed hauled out the single rod tube he'd brought, unscrewed the cap, shook it, stuck two fingers deep into its throat, got a really worried look on his face, then upended the tube and shook it. An empty, emerald-green Sage rod bag fell limply to the ground. That's when he remembered he'd put the rod out to dry the night before. We got over it, climbed out of our gear and headed to the nearest café for a coffee.

But to leave *all* your rods behind on a two-week-long fishing trip is, as they say, a horse of an entirely different colour. In fact, it's not compatible with an extended fishing trip, full stop, unless wherever you are going has a conveniently useful reserve of fly rods – and some do, like the better fishing lodges, but most places I stay don't. In fact, at best, I'd be fishing a few ancient two- to four-weights of varying pedigree and condition. Certainly no bamboo.

After I'd put plenty of distance between myself and the flapping red tarpaulin, I pulled over at an abandoned railway siding called Konstabel, a siding that had obviously been important enough in the heyday of rail traffic to cause trains to stop here. Now the small cluster of railway houses was sad and dilapidated, but at least I was well off the highway and in a pool of shade under peppercorn trees.

I stepped out. It was strangely cool; I felt road-stiff and not sure I even wanted to open the canopy door. Countless chirping sparrows were noisily going about life in the trees. I reminded myself to crush a few biscuits for them before I left.

It's been said that Murphy's Law applies to most things in life, and that one of its tenets is that if something can go wrong it will always be the worst thing. But my more sage friends tell me that the real world is governed by O'Reilly's Law, which simply says Murphy was an optimist. So you will believe me when I tell you it took me a full heart-thumping minute of shifting boxes and assorted gear before I spotted a corner of the orange canvas of the rod bag. It was lying in the last place left to look. I heaved a long sigh of relief, punched a fist in the air, poured a mug of coffee, crushed a generous portion of biscuits for the sparrows, stuck my mug in the cup holder on the dashboard, and was just pulling off when the red tarpaulin roared by. I cursed him out loud and lifted a finger. In my rear-view mirror I saw the sparrows swooping from the tree to the crumbs on the ground, and that at least pleased me.

*

It wasn't the best way to start a two-week, 1,100-kilometre fly-fishing trip to the Eastern Cape, but there was some solace in knowing it could have been worse. Also, in an obscure, roundabout way, this sort of thing is strangely pleasant – after a shock like this, the sweeping sense of relief you get is satisfying. I slipped a disc into the CD player – Herbert von Karajan conducting Beethoven's *Symphony No. 4*, a gift from my musician friend Dulcie Kirby – and within ten kilometres I had chilled enough to enjoy Karoo landscapes sliding slowly by, trying from time to time to guess how far it was to the top of the next hill on ruler-straight pieces of highway. In the Karoo it usually works out at anything from ten to fifteen kilometres, but you can be wrong when there's a midday heat haze, and find it's more like twenty.

*

I'd left Cape Town pretty much on schedule, which was late in the day for a long drive like this, but then I'd had plenty of loose ends to tie up. So I booked a room at a B&B in Graaff-Reinet instead of pushing on another 150 kilometres to Mike and Candy Ferrar's farm on the far side of Middelburg.

I took a brief stroll around Graaff-Reinet, noticing that this attractive town was showing a few signs of becoming a tourist trap, then sat down to dinner on a pleasantly cool outside veranda adjacent to a small swimming pool in a lovely garden. They served leek and potato soup, followed by a leg of lamb cooked as I think lamb should be (meaning not underdone and bleeding, but well-roasted). The gravy had a hint of rosemary in it, and I added a generous spoonful of tart-flavoured mint jelly to my plate. My only companions were a couple of French tourists who were locked in deep conversation, other than when they complained to the young waitress that the wine they'd ordered should have been uncorked in front of them, not brought to the table ready to pour. They had a point, I know, but I was glad they hadn't started this conversation with me. I was tired, with a hovering dose of road rage, and I just might have reminded them they were eating in a charming, unpretentious little restaurant in a tiny Karoo town, not at Les Jardins de L'Espadon in the Ritz Hotel on the Place Vendôme in Paris, to where, I would have added, they should hastily return.

The waitress brought another bottle to their table, and opened it with exaggerated twists of the corkscrew and a flamboyant yank of the cork that made a more than the usual muted 'plop' as it left the bottle. She got her point across, no doubt, but I also guessed her tip disappeared right then like a spooked trout in a glassy stream.

Instead of waiting for dessert and coffee, I decided to head to bed early. I did sit awhile in the courtyard outside my room with a mug of coffee, and was reflecting on the beautifully starlit night sky when the French couple strolled past. They didn't look up at the sky, and I wasn't about to point it out to them. Blind as bats, I thought ungraciously. My road rage was apparently still hovering.

But I was back on the road early the next morning as the first rays of sunlight lit the sleepy town. There were clouds around, and they slowly built into banks as the kilometres clicked by. When I drove through Burgersdorp two hours later, a few drops of rain hit the windscreen, but that was the last of it, and the clouds melted away.

*

From the bridge over the Kraai River at Moshesh's Ford, roughly forty kilometres from Barkly East, I looked down onto a river running high but clear – clear enough to make out the stones in the riverbed. In time I saw a trout in a pebbled depression near the far bank. It held a still station, moving only with the slowly lifting and settling thrusts of the current.

Judging from the puddles along the road there had been a good fall of rain. I'd driven through the odd slippery patch where, for reasons I don't fully understand, the harder shale surface suddenly gives way to short stretches that are more a soft clay than gravel, and where you can find the back end of your truck starting to waltz if you come in too quick or aren't that careful. The weeping willows on the banks of the Kraai were turning gold, but the poplars were already leafless and starkly bare. The air was icy on my face, and I saw no bugs hatching. I thought the river was certainly fishable; moments later, the trout I'd spotted rose confidently. It drifted in a lazy arc at least a metre downstream in a swinging rise, suggesting that whatever it had come up for was worth the effort.

*

At *Birkhall*, Basie and Carien had kept lunch for me, and within an hour I felt at home, almost as if I had never been away. Packed on my bed in a neat pile were the clothes I'd left from my last visit, plus a couple of items of fly tackle, including a pretty Hardy Marquis reel I'd somehow never really missed or, in truth, never knew I owned. Basie convinced me it was mine. It passed through my mind that when you own too much tackle you get a sort of collective fly-gear amnesia that includes everything except the fly rods. When you forget those, it's time to see someone professionally.

The wind had died and the late afternoon was mild. I took a drive to the Lindisfarne Bridge. In the deep pool below the bridge, trout were gently touching the surface. So I set up a rod, tied on a CDC midge pattern, skirted the tail of the pool and then moved up on it quietly. Whatever was hatching was small – I guessed a mayfly or maybe a midge – but from twenty paces in fading light you can't be sure, other than that any small grey insects coming off an evening stream are mostly either *Baetis* mayflies or midges. I have run into late hatches of tiny flying ants, and micro-caddis hatches aren't uncommon up here either, but they're more likely to hatch in warmer, sunlit day. Not that it matters much what you think is actually hatching, because you can always rely on the trout to tell you if you've got your fly selection right – or horribly wrong.

In the slanting sunlight the 7X tippet glowed on the surface and, within seconds, a small trout took the fly and leapt like a salmon when I hooked it. The trout came in quivering, but then lay still in my hand with a look of deep resignation on its face as I freed the hook. I caught a few more until they stopped rising; that happened, as it does so often, when a cold wind arrived, lifting leaves from the riverbank, scattering them like confetti, the gusts flattening sweeps of veld. You might ask why rises stop so abruptly when a cold wind gets up. Perhaps the bugs stop hatching because the wind ripples the surface, but I doubt it. Delicate midges and most species of mayflies hatch in rippled water precisely because in rippled water the meniscus is easier for them to break through. Or is it that the emerging insects somehow sense the dangers of hatching in cold, windy weather where, if they break the surface and hatch, they will get swept away on the wind before they get a chance to get out of their shucks? Or is something else at play here? Like, does a sudden drop in air temperature threaten the survival of newly hatched adult bugs? Or perhaps the bugs actually *don't* stop hatching in the wind at all; they just get harder for trout to grab because they're blown away as soon as they hatch. I guess the answer, to try to be helpful, is *all of the above,* qualified by the word 'depending' – the panacea term for the many events we can only guess at in fly fishing.

*

That night Basie said it was too cold to snow and I offered to light the fire in the lounge. He quickly said, 'Don't worry, leave it to me.' I suspected this was a deep survival response that got embedded in his mind when I lit the fire in his lounge one particularly cold evening on a previous trip. The wood then was slightly damp, and the flames just wouldn't take hold. Basie suggested I add a little 'starter', a turquoise-coloured, high-octane inflammable gel. I poured a little gel onto blackened embers that I could have sworn were nowhere near still smouldering. Bad call. The bottle burst into flame in my hand, and I reflexively tossed it straight into the fireplace. There was a massive whooshing sound, and the entire chimney lit up in a blinding sheet of orange flame. For a few long moments it looked like the Taliban had scored a direct hit on Basie's lounge with a petrol bomb. No serious damage was done, but Basie needed a stiff drink before the colour came back into his face and he could speak.

*

Tony Kietzman drove across from Rhodes the next day on the back of my reports that the Sterkspruit looked good – high, but dropping. He knew that if there's ever a great time to fish it's when a river or stream is falling and clearing. We went into what we loosely call the gorge, a section on the farm *Branksome* a few kilometres upstream of *Birkhall.* It was a day that looked good for the moment; meaning the weather could switch either way in minutes. At least wind wasn't a problem, and we thought if it rained lightly the fish might come on.

We parked in a paddock alongside the river, slipped over the fence and crossed the river. The flow here is normally wide and shallow enough for an easy crossing, but this day the river was running higher than I'd expected and the weight of the current dragged heavily on my legs. The water was clear and flowed brightly over pebbles in the shallows. In the riffles it tumbled, leaving lattices of white waves and bubbles. The deeper reaches were opalescent-green. Everything about it looked perfect – perfect in ways you will find few people can actually put into words, but which is something anglers recognise instinctively if they've been programmed on rivers for long enough.

We walked downstream on the far bank through *ouhout* bushes where the tangled debris of dead branches cracked under our boots and raised a fine dust that smelled strangely of honey. The veld swept up the hillsides in rust-coloured waves, in some places reaching to craggy ridges. Although the valley is generally narrow in the kilometre or two of this section, it's not really a true gorge; nothing like those on other streams hereabouts, like the Swith or the Joggemspruit, and certainly not like some Western Cape streams, such as the Witels or the Jan du Toit's, where in places the rock faces on both banks reach upwards like the spires of a cathedral.

Further downstream we crossed the river again at a place where it is wider and shallower, but its pull was still strong. You cross a river like this with care because it drags at your legs and the rocks are smooth, round and slippery. And that's not only because you'd rather not end up soaked to the skin, but also because any river crossing takes on a special meaning when you have enough unprotected camera gear in your backpack to make a down payment on a small apartment. So you wade carefully, never moving a leg forward until the other foot is secure. It's one of the secrets of safe wading.

We walked down the south bank until we had a comfortable morning's fishing back to the truck, then we slid quietly into the ankle-deep water at the tail-out of a run, where the breeze was gently upstream. Tony is a dry fly man when conditions allow for it, or when there's even a hint that a dry fly will work. He had on a RAB and I used a bushy CDC dry fly that I fished on my corn-yellow Dugmore bamboo rod. In this first run we got a fish apiece, both sturdy trout in good condition.

We were in no rush. Tony lit his pipe, filling it from the crumpled Ziploc plastic bag that (for as long as I've known him) doubles as his tobacco pouch; not quite in the Dunhill league, but then we weren't on the Houghton Club water of the River Test either. With his pipe in his mouth, he dropped a dry fly near the head of the run and hooked a third fish that zigzagged around between us till he reached for his net, rod high, and landed it. I got lovely photographs of him landing that fish, the angler backlit with the water sparkling like diamonds. I took a fourth trout from the same run and we realised the fish were really on. They were all around fourteen inches.

The fishing was constant after that, meaning if any presentation in good holding water was right, most often a trout would lift to our dry flies. Sometime during the morning we noticed mayflies hatching, but not in profusion. They were dull-coloured insects and tiny and didn't bring on much by way of rising fish, at least not that we could see. But later I noticed a good head come up in the tail of the run we'd waded through when we crossed the river on our way downstream not an hour before. This trout rose in a narrow, deep slot near the bank. It took my dry fly and raced downstream. I finally checked the fish and played it into the net. It was all of sixteen inches. Tony was about to press the shutter on his camera while I was posing with the fish when it bucked in my hand and was gone. It's not the first time I've dropped a fish at that critical moment, and it won't be the last. I think the secret is to lift the fish cradled in your hand and not held tight. That is if you are going to lift it out of the water and, more and more, I am of the view that because it's risky for fish to be exposed to air, we shouldn't be doing it for more than a second or two, if at all.

As happens some days on rivers after a busy start, the fishing just went lame for an hour or two, only the occasional fish coming from the best-looking places in the best-looking runs that we knew held a heap more fish than we actually got from them. And we only got those on deep-fished nymphs. They weren't interested in the dry fly any longer. Well, not for the moment at least.

Midway along this lovely section of the Sterkspruit there is a wall of sheer rock that drops steeply into the water for about a hundred metres. It's on your right as you're going upstream. The rock is dark-grey, almost black, but it's patterned with bright patches of red and orange lichen, like God's graffiti. The water running along the wall is deep and inviting, and suddenly we were catching fish again with ease. In fact, they were taking so confidently we switched back to dry flies and trout rose to them all the way along the rock face and even up in the bubbling whitewater at the inlet.

Upstream we came on a place where the river widens on a corner and then braids into a series of shallow, quick-flowing runs. It was not far from where we'd parked the truck, and suddenly we were hooking small fish at will, the biggest maybe ten inches.

It was after 3pm when I dropped the tailgate on the truck and lit the gas burner under a kettle of river water. I added a few spoons of coffee grounds and left the kettle until the lid boiled off. The coffee tasted good, even in the absence of milk and sugar – and despite my chipped enamel mugs. Or perhaps it was good for all these reasons. Tony, anyway, takes his coffee black, and always seems to enjoy my sub-standard brews despite only drinking the proper filter stuff back at his home.

We were drinking the coffee sitting on the tailgate of a truck parked alongside a trout stream with birdsong drifting in on the breeze, in the same paddock where years ago my friend Mario

Cesare and I stopped for a late lunch after fishing this beat. I remember him asking me how long I'd fished my Orvis 4-weight Western Series graphite rod (it turned out to be ten years from the date on the butt cap). I also remember that I'd climbed over that barbed wire fence a lot easier back then. But I'm not concerned about taking a few extra minutes crossing barbed wire fences – especially not in a high-priced pair of Simms chest waders. And, as if in a replay of what transpired all those years back, Tony reached over, picked up my Dugmore bamboo rod and flexing it said, 'Nice stick. Feels like a 4-weight.' I said it was, and I could have added that in many ways its action reminded me of my old Orvis 4-weight Western Series, just that the Dugmore is a little smoother on long casts, and a little more forgiving on bad ones.

We left the paddock and headed upstream to the bridge that roughly divides the farm above, *Broadford*, from *Branksome*. This is pretty water; the river is wider and shallower but full of structure, including a bridge and a weir. The fishing can be interesting in that the trout are, if a little smaller on average, quite discerning at times. In the hour we had to fish we proved neither of these points. Not a single fish rose and we couldn't get a take from even the tiniest of trout until, in the run below the weir immediately above the bridge, we did hook a few finger-long rainbows on a dry fly. By then the weather was closing in and the temperature was down. But if we hadn't at least tried this lovely piece we would have died wondering that night.

It was dark when we got back to *Birkhall*. We had dinner with Basie and Carien and I easily persuaded Tony to take one of the spare beds for the night. I told him we'd fish the lake in the morning. Around midnight I awoke to the sound of thunder. Through the lace curtains of my bedroom window lightning lit up the night sky, each of the flashes followed by a deep rumble of thunder. With the window open I could hear and smell the rain, and I took a torch and padded through the sleeping house to the porch. Rain was falling in slanting sheets that bounced high off the stone wall that skirted the veranda. The storm's omens might not be good for the fishing, but this was pure oxygen for the rivers.

*

Next morning we sat around the table in the kitchen eating bacon and eggs and toast thickly coated in marmalade, and kissed the prospect of fishing goodbye. I was comfortable with that, but only because I had a heap of flies to tie. Tony left to check on his indigenous nursery project in Rhodes, and we loosely agreed to fish the Bokspruit as soon as the weather cleared. It was May, and we argued that it couldn't rain that long up here in May. But since when can you second-guess the weather? As it happened it rained for two days, with the sun coming out in patches that suddenly changed the vistas off the veranda from scenes of impending storms into pretty pictures of sun-soaked pastoral peace. But they never lasted long.

*

I met Agostino Roncallo on the Internet. He ties flies in Genoa, Italy, and he's a magician with CDC. He'd sent me a box of his patterns, about three of each, and I sorted through them on *Birkhall* during a truce in the weather, choosing his Mirage dry fly to copy. After a few attempts I got one to look roughly the same as his, if a little clumsier, but good enough to try on the local trout. The note he'd sent with his gift of flies asked a particular question. Roncallo wanted to know if his patterns would catch trout in Africa. I ended up tying half a dozen size 14s and 16s on grub hooks, using grey 8/0 UNI-Thread and dun-coloured CDC feathers. I was as keen as he was to find out if they worked, but I kind of knew they would.

*

The weather cleared a day later, turning to blue skies attractively laced with wispy clouds. The clouds were splashed across the sky in beautiful patterns, making for as lovely a day as I've ever seen up here. But it felt fragile; as if the weather was hiding behind a thin veil; as if the last two days of bruised skies and lightning were not quite gone; as if more bad weather was waiting just around the corner, ready to pounce.

*

I love the upper Bokspruit where the river is swift, stony and quickly forgiving of storms. Tony and I decided to fish the *Birnham* beat, upstream of some other well-known beats you may recognise, like *Hillbury, Welgemoed* and *Knockwarren,* but downstream of possibly the best of the upper Bokspruit, *Gateshead.*

I met Tony along the road. He parked his truck in a lay-by, then moved his fly gear across into mine. There wasn't much to move because we hadn't unpacked my truck that well after our trip into the gorge and there was plenty of his stuff still in the back. You may have noticed that it's not unusual for fly fishers to leave gear lying around. In fact, on a fly-fishing trip if you don't end up with bits of gear spread around the place you probably aren't fishing hard enough. Tony is pretty good at spreading gear, and so am I.

The other thing I noticed is that Tony and I share a love of bridges. Not just as in slowing down and having a look at the water from a dawdling truck, but stopping, getting out and having a long inspection – both sides. The first bridge on the road up the Bokspruit is on *Welgemoed*, where Gavin Schneider has his house. The water looked pretty here, tinted a pale-green, clear and flowing briskly. A bunch of branches and logs had washed up against the mouth of the bridge. I made a mental note to tell Gavin about them before the water broached the bridge after another storm.

There were fish about at the bridge, dancing nervously in and out of structure: small, delicately-coloured trout that were almost transparent they were so close in colour to the riverbed itself – slippers of glass I call them. And there were plenty, at least twenty trout each side of the bridge.

*

The road up the Bokspruit Valley is lonely, all the way to *Gateshead* where the road ends. The traffic is light, only the occasional tractor, now and again a farmer checking on something on a farm he owns but doesn't actually live on. I don't think a farm up this valley is actually occupied. It can be quite eerie. Some years back I locked the keys in my truck up here after we'd fished the *Knockwarren* beat, and in the two hours we waited in the dark hoping for some passing traffic, not a single car went by. It's a long story, but we eventually got a message through to Basie, and his manager drove across. He arrived with a long face and my spare key. I guess he wasn't expecting to leave his warm bed to come to the aid of a bunch of idiots stranded in the dark on a remote country road.

The absence of traffic up the Bokspruit Valley is nothing we complain about. I sometimes wish all the world's roads were as quiet as this one, but it's probably enough just knowing there *are* still a few places like it, and that you can escape to them when you want a little solitude and to shake off as many reminders of the real world as you can, like the constant heave of heavy traffic and the persistent packs of pressured people. Come to think of it, the search for solitude is a big part of why many people go fishing in the first place. This may sound a little like some homespun philosophy, but in today's world, solitude has become a priceless commodity.

*

We crossed under a fence spanning a culvert and were on the Bokspruit in two minutes. The streambed on this beat is mixed: sheets of pale-green, sometimes apricot-coloured, sandstone alternating with stones, pebbles and fine grit that looks like the coarse volcanic silt you find in rivers in Iceland. But it's the colour of the sheets of sandstone bedrock on *Birnham* that sets it apart from other beats: a light ice-green. There are stretches immediately above this beat where the bedrock changes colour, to anything from a pale yellow to a deep honey. You find sheets of tinted sandstone in many streams in this area, like the Bell on *Dunley* and the Karringmelkspruit, but on *Birnham* the extent of the bedrock sheets and the relative intensity of their colour is extravagant.

We had two objectives this day, outside of just wanting to catch a heap of trout. The first was to take a few underwater photographs of fish sitting over the green sandstone and the other was to try out the Tenkara kit I had brought along.

Tenkara is the application of an ancient Japanese style of fly fishing, with the emphasis on simplicity and minimalism. In the modern Japanese idiom, Tenkara is more than that. It is the perpetuation and faithful rendition of a deeply traditional method of catching fish on a fly. Nowadays it's used not only as a smart method to fish, but I suspect also to revive or revere, or both, a branch of angling with deep roots. Without falling into the trap of overly sentimentalising the art, it's an attempt to arrive at a philosophical high point where supreme simplicity, effectiveness and even the poetry in fly fishing all converge – though I doubt this was necessarily the goal the Japanese forefathers had in mind when they developed and described the various techniques. To the ancients, I imagine Tenkara was just a clean, quick and easy way to harvest fish. We've maybe since added a little hype and bunkum.

Okay, so where are we in all this? Tenkara is ultra-minimalist, but its benefits derive more from its convergence with the poetic than with the practical. At least that's what I tell myself. It has serious limitations, but it also offers interesting new horizons. For example, there is no reel. You attach the twelve foot braided line to a permanent loop built into the tip of the fly rod. The rods are telescopic, collapsing down to something about as long as your forearm, but extending out to anything from ten to fourteen feet, depending on the model. They are mainly graphite and very light. I say mainly graphite, because I suspect that Tenkara glass rods, if they aren't already here, will soon show up – glass rods being a fraction more traditional than plastic rods.

You attach the leader to the end of the braided line as in regular fly fishing, add a tippet and a fly, and you're ready to go. Here's where the technique borrows a little from my understanding of dapping, and a little from what we call 'high-sticking'. The cast is an easy figure-of-eight sweep, like a roll cast at times, at others like a conventional cast, but always dead simple, and you can get amazingly accurate. Casting distance is limited so you have to fish close in whether you like it or not, something most experienced fly anglers have preached for the past forty years anyway.

The long rods offer amazing leverage, enough to 'walk' a fly through runs or to drift it close along those dark, cave-like recesses under banks, or to play the fly on its toes in the twisting twirls of current that hold around jutting boulders or at the foot of falls. The fly is carried only by the leader, and sometimes just by the tippet. At first it all feels a little strange, but later when you work it out, when you understand the dynamics of it, you can land a fly on a sixpence, hook trout under your nose, and it starts to make its own sort of perfect sense.

Just to add to the traditional way we were fishing, Steve Boshoff had made me a Tenkara net. It is beautifully crafted from cherry

YET MORE SWEET DAYS

wood, with a long, straight handle and a perfectly circular opening, and it looked just right in the underwater shots I took that day.

*

So we began the day with nothing more vital to decide than what fly to add to the Tenkara outfit, settling on one of the Mirage CDC patterns I tied. It was enlightening. The flow on *Birnham* was perfect, and the first three casts produced solid rises that we missed because we struck too soon. When we measured the strike, we landed eight small trout from one run and missed two others, many fish taking the fly right under the tip of the rod not more than four feet from us.

And so it went all the way up to the stand of poplars near the top end of the beat. We'd fished less than a kilometre of water and had taken a heap of trout, I guess between forty and fifty – best not described in numbers but simply as non-stop action. Typically the trout took close in, and if you sat down to analyse what we were doing with the Tenkara rod that was different, it probably came down to fishing very close, almost totally drag-free and covering more water in every run and pocket than we would have with a conventional fly rod. And there's a general lesson in this. Most of us tend to rush up streams instead of slowly combing through every part of a run, probing every inch of water with the fastidious care of a forensic auditor.

At the poplars we would normally have carried on fishing upstream until the river meets the road, where we can climb out easily and walk back to the truck. This day, on a whim, we decided to fish back downstream over the water in which we had just hooked a heap of trout, and we took at least another half-dozen we'd somehow missed on the way up. Tony muttered something about starting a new article of faith that would go along the lines of, 'You don't just *walk* back, you *fish* back!'

We tried nymphs as well, but they somehow didn't add much to the catch rate or the poetry, and little to the fun of drifting a bobbing dry fly on a downstream current a few feet from you. It's as deadly a way to fish close in as any other, and I wondered why we didn't do more of it.

Where we had started that morning there was a deep, narrow run with a long undercut bank that had a decent sweep of current running alongside it. I set up the camera under a willow, and Tony crept to the tail end. We had run out of Mirages by then, but I had proved a point for Agostino Roncallo. His flies work in Africa. (I let him know once I returned to Cape Town.)

Tony ties a good, buggy-looking RAB. He fished the fly up the run until, near the neck, in the sweetest part by far, a really decent trout took hold of it. It was fifteen inches, a hen fish that showed all the signs of having spawned early; she was brightly coloured and there was no sign of eggs in her belly. And a little higher up, I caught one of the most colourful cock fish I have ever seen in a river. Its gill plates were a neon-lit tapestry of dazzling purples and pinks all laid out on a flame-orange background, with flanks as red as a late evening sunset. You can't easily take the beauty of any trout for granted, but some are so magnificently coloured they can get you wondering about the meaning of life. Mostly these are browns, but when a wild-river rainbow really gets dressed up, everything else can take a back seat.

*

Tony's early-spawning-trout theory is interesting. He believes that in the Rhodes district trout spawn when the conditions are right, not necessarily on or about the date they were spawned themselves, the latter being a generally accepted hypothesis for salmonids worldwide. And he may have a point, given that flows and temperatures in this part of the world can be so different on any given date of each year.

On this point, it's a fact that brown trout spawn earlier in our rivers than rainbows, sometime in May for browns and more like mid-June for rainbows. And since rainbows spawn after browns they obviously mess up the brown trout redds, which could partly explain why the two species rarely coexist in the same stream.

*

It was around mid-afternoon when we left the river under a bruised sky heavy with cloud. We needed coffee and a bite to eat before heading up to the higher reaches, so we drove up to the now-vacant old *Birnham* farmhouse and parked under a canopy of trees that had layered the yard with a carpet of yellow leaves so evenly spread it was clear there hadn't been a vehicle up this way in days. I boiled coffee on the tailgate and Tony produced a range of cheeses that we spread on dry crackers. We each ate a tomato like an apple, sprinkling it with salt. There's no better way to eat a tomato.

We had planned to move on upstream to fish the *Brucedell* beat and were just about to pack up when a few drops of rain fell. By the time we got into the truck it was raining hard. We took a drive upstream in case the rain stopped, and got out of the truck where the river flows shallow and wide over honey-coloured sandstone. The wind was strong and the raindrops hit us like bullets. I said to Tony that when we were a lot younger we probably would have pushed on and fished this stretch. He nodded, blowing a plume of blue pipe smoke into the air and said, 'For sure. In shorts and a T-shirt, with a fly box in one pocket and a spool of nylon in the other.'

'That's about it,' I said, 'except for the sandwich in the back pocket that we'd have already sat on a few times.'

He knocked out his pipe and we headed back.

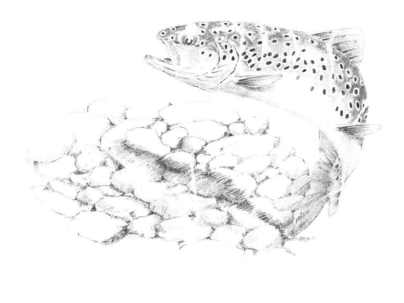

*

Another day of rain. More fly tying. I was starting to get a mild dose of farmhouse fever when Tony called to say the weather was due to clear the next day and asked about going to *Brucedell* to fish the steeper-gradient water from the causeway up. 'I've got about enough flies now,' I told him, 'so let's do it.'

At the *Welgemoed* bridge the water was fishable, but there was rain about and the wind was cold. I looked at the clouds and they told a story. It was likely to rain again sometime in the day. I might not be a meteorologist and I can't second-guess the weather, but sometimes you just get a feeling about things. We slid back into the truck and headed for the causeway that crosses the river at the start of the water on *Brucedell* a few kilometres upstream.

Brucedell is divided into two beats separated by a tall waterfall. The best water is the mile or two *below* the falls, where the top half is the best of all, simply because the river develops more structure and runs have more substance the higher you go. But the mile or two of river *above* the falls is also attractive. There are plenty of places to park to fish the piece above the falls, and then it's best to first hike downstream to the bottom end of the beat where the falls are, and where you get to a point where you start believing the earth must be flat after all, because you're watching a wide river falling right off the edge of the earth apparently into nothing. I never get too close to the edge because water mesmerises me and I don't do heights when there's no firm railing around the dangerous parts. If there's one secret to fishing this upper stretch, the piece above the falls, it's that the tiniest pockets can hold big rainbows.

The fishing was slow, even the pretty runs producing only the occasional fish. Nothing of size hooked, though plenty of small trout flashed at the fly and missed it. We were using the Tenkara rod again, sharing the runs. Midway up this section you come to a few long, aquamarine-tinted pools that are deep and glass-clear. At the first big pool I drifted a size 12 Yellow DDD near the inlet, letting the current carry the bobbing fly downstream. As it hovered near the end of its drift, a big rainbow casually rose up to it. We followed the fish all the way from the riverbed to the fly, which seemed to take an age. I let it turn on the fly, then struck. It felt solidly hooked and it felt strong, a deep-sided rainbow of around twenty inches that briefly flashed silver under the surface then fought deep with plenty of head-shaking. The fish wasn't easy to handle without a reel. Eventually it broke free as Tony was trying to slip a net under it with the leader in his hand. He stood silently for a long moment, the empty net dangling at his side. He had that thousand-yard stare in his eyes, as if hoping for some redeeming intervention from on high.

A lovely thing about Tony is that he takes his fishing, and yours, as seriously as a surgeon operating on someone's head.

I said, 'Don't worry. We'll catch another one.' It was a reckless invocation to the gods, and we paid the price for it.

The storm moved right in, and the fishing went right off.

Further down the valley the scene was surreal. One half of the landscape was under a clear blue sky, the other half was under slate-grey clouds dropping sheets of rain that fell in scintillating silver pillars side-lit by sunshine. We fished back to the truck in light rain, taking two small trout from shallow runs, and none from the deeper places we knew must hold plenty. The frustrating part about this sort of situation is that you know the trout will come on again, just that you don't know quite when: in the next few minutes maybe, or the next hour… or not for a week. These are wild, freestone trout, well beyond a century from their ancestral gene pool in some American hatchery, and there's no way of being too sure how they'll behave. They are perfect that way though, if you agree that 'perfect' includes little by way of predictability.

On the trip out, the weather lifted and we were under blue skies again. We drove up the Riflespruit Valley out of idle interest and found the river looking good. The Riflespruit is much like the Bokspruit in ways that count in the river's favour – clarity, lovely stream textures (meaning a variety of features), and an abundance of insect life and trout. We marked a few places we needed to come back to fish. The top reaches of the Riflespruit are really good, but there's not much wrong with the lower and middle stretches either.

*

Next day the weather looked fine and I tried to get to what Ed and I used to call Tank Pool on *Birkhall*, but the road was a lottery after the rain. I was alone, hoping to catch the river for an hour or two while it was still in good shape. I closed the farm gate leading to a track that goes down into the valley, and for the next few hundred metres it felt like the steering assembly on my truck had come loose. The vehicle just slid wherever the deep ruts and the mud led it. I got out and checked the tyres. I could see no tread at all, just a thick layer of caked mud on each tyre. I guessed I could probably slither down the steep hill into the valley, but getting out, never! So I turned back. The approach to the solid wooden pillars supporting the gate was on a slight downhill, and the truck began to slide. I stood on the brakes. Nothing. The truck just kept sliding towards the gateposts as if all four wheels were on roller skates. I braced for the crunch. The truck finally stopped inches from a post. I stepped out to open the gate and saw just how close I'd come to a deep bumper dent. You couldn't have squeezed a size 22 ant pattern between the front fender and the gatepost. Okay, make that a size 12.

Later that morning Carien and her mother waltzed off the road coming back from Barkly East. They put their truck through a fence, followed by a full 360-degree spin, fortunately with little by way of damage other than losing some rubber trimmings and scratching the paintwork. They managed to drive back onto the road through the hole they'd left in the fence and in less than a minute they were on their way home again.

The day stayed bright, and I grabbed my pocket-sized Zeiss binoculars to do some bird watching. I got what I thought was a first sighting, a tiny, bright-blue kingfisher with a rust-coloured chest that was hovering nervously around the reservoir next to Basie's house. I thought it was an African Pygmy Kingfisher, and was as excited as a twitcher until I got back to consult the bird books. They suggested I was wrong, and that if it was an African Pygmy Kingfisher it was on the very limit of its range, meaning I was either lucky to see it, or else long on imagination and in need of field practice. It turned out to be a Malachite Kingfisher. (The only reason I name-dropped my fancy field glasses, by the way, is that they were given to me by Mario Cesare fifteen years ago, and they were pretty special in ways that go well beyond the fact that they were made by Zeiss. I eventually destroyed them in bizarre circumstances, but that's something I'll tell you about later.)

The reservoir in the *Birkhall* garden has a steady stream of water feeding it, and Basie has used it at times to grow out trout. In fact, I hooked a monster on a dry fly in it one day that I never landed. But the presence of fish and frogs and tadpoles means that kingfishers aren't uncommon visitors.

*

I left *Birkhall* and drove to Rhodes to fish the Bell with Tony and to spend the night at Walkerbouts, where I had some business to discuss with Dave Walker. At the Lindisfarne Bridge the Sterkspruit was running high and discoloured, and in the next valley, so too was the Bokspruit. But the Bell at Rhodes was pure glass, so we tried it with dry flies and caught small trout. They were rising to a hatch of tiny *Baetis* mayflies, and they took a size 18 RAB, but inconsistently. We had added a longer leader to the Tenkara line and were getting more distance with the rig, landing the fly pretty accurately, yet in their own purposeful way these fish were either strangely fussy or unquestioningly gullible, depending what fish you were casting at. In some cases a rising fish would take the fly immediately, but another fish rising a rod-length away would ignore it. We ordinary fly fishers would say, 'That's fishing,' but the technocrats might say something like, 'In some drifts you probably missed the micro-drag,' or 'If you'd been observant you'd have seen some fish were taking emergers, not adults.' I think the first assumption – micro-drag – was probably the cause for the refusals, but it was puzzling as any micro-drag was seemingly undetectable.

Then a cold front came through, and if we hadn't been out fishing we'd have been glad of the rain. We enjoyed watching its sudden arrival. The clouds formed a deep-purple bank about ten kilometres to the south, suggesting serious celestial forces were at work up there. As fronts go it was spectacular, but it ended our fishing. We left before the rain, in a landscape way beyond spectacular, with purple skies and patches of barley-coloured sunlight flooding the autumn veld where the sun's rays sneaked through gaps in the clouds like the spokes of giant golden wagon wheels.

In the tiny, cluttered lounge at Tony's cottage in Rhodes, we cleared his table of reels, rods, landing nets and a pair of waders, set up a laptop and started going through the underwater pictures we'd taken that day. As always there were plenty of shots of trout with their heads or tails out of the frame, and in the poor light of the frontal weather, most of the better photographs were sombre. We ate rusks and drank a pot of coffee, then drove to Walkerbouts.

That night I recounted the story of the two trout I had drawn with a black permanent marker on a wall of the Walkerbouts pub in 1996. I know the year exactly because I dated the sketch – okay, graffiti. Dave had since done alterations to the bar area, taking down a few walls to add space, but he framed the sketches in a wooden mount under glass and left that wall intact. Back before 1996, the walls in the pub were covered with the impressions left by various guests, male and female, who had daubed their bums and other body parts in paint then pressed them against a wall, often at amazing heights. One evening, Ed Herbst and I suggested to Dave that we could maybe lift the tone of the place by adding a few sketches of trout to counterbalance the assorted anatomical imprints. He was in the kitchen at the time and hadn't heard more than that I needed a Koki pen, which he arranged, and then carried on cooking. I was just finishing the date on the sketches, when he came out of the kitchen, looked mildly surprised, scratched his beard and said, 'Okay, I'll learn to live with that.'

But our discussion in the pub this last visit added some interesting dimensions to my graffiti. Say I went into the bar in a really upmarket place – like the Mount Nelson or the Cellars-Hohenhort, two of the most prestigious hotels in Cape Town – asked for a Koki pen, then scribbled trout sketches on a vacant wall. The difference came down to a beard-scratching observation from the owner of Walkerbouts that he'd learn to live with it, to immediate arrest and a jail term, suspended at best, if it had been at the Mount Nelson or the Cellars-Hohenhort, depending on whether counsel for the accused could argue mitigation on the grounds of a severe dose of fish fever.

It rained heavily that night.

*

I had a note from a young man called Byron Grant a week or two before I left on this visit who said he was planning a trip to Rhodes in May and wanted some advice on a 'must do' bucket list of sorts. I did my best to tell him where I thought he might enjoy himself, and to sensitise him to the fact that there had been plenty of rain and that more could be on the way. He wrote back to say he'd made up his mind to go, and hoped he'd bump into me on a river somewhere.

The day after I got back from my night in Rhodes, Byron called me. His fishing, like mine, had been dogged by rain, and looking out from the veranda on *Birkhall* I didn't have much good news for him. Skyscraper-tall clouds were already building up. But he and Tony drove across to *Birkhall* anyway and, with the rivers out, we tied a few flies. As for the chances to get in some fishing in the next few days, we were hanging on thin shreds of hope. The forecast was for solid rain, and I found myself with the dilemma of having to decide whether to make a break for home or just sit it out, hoping the forecasters were wrong. In the end I headed home. Tony and Byron reckoned they might try the top of the Bell on *Boarman's Chase* the day I left. I didn't make it. Byron cut his stay short and left for home a day or two after I did.

*

The trip back was uneventful, and I reached the Karoo National Park in Beaufort West in time to see a few red hartebeest cross in front of me in the last light of day. The best thing about stopping overnight at this place is that you are six kilometres off the N1, meaning you get away from all the road noise and diesel fumes from the serial rows of trucks.

Speaking of modern highways, I haven't mentioned the gradual proliferation of speed traps on the N1, set up in places you would least expect to find them and, I suspect, aimed more at bolstering the revenue of local municipalities of small towns than making our roads safer. On a deep country highway, when you spot more traffic police crouched behind artfully disguised cameras than Pale Chanting Goshawks, something is fishy.

That night I was able to phone my long-suffering wife and to learn, happily, that she hadn't left home or run off with a billionaire from Monaco.

Early the following morning I sat on the veranda of my rondavel with a cup of coffee and one of Carien's home-baked rusks, watching the birdlife and in no hurry to leave. A pair of Cape Robin-chats were doing their best to peck morsels of fat off the braai grid I'd used the previous evening, and sparrows chattered expectantly until I threw them some crumbs.

I decided to make the run back to Cape Town a slow one, and to stop for a quiet lunch at the Laird's Arms, a small pub in the Victorian village of Matjiesfontein. An hour out of Beaufort West I noticed an orange warning light on my dashboard. I pulled over and nervously paged through the owner's manual to find that it was a fuel filter warning light. It was a Sunday, and I had no idea whether the truck was safe to drive, or if there was a risk the engine would suddenly give up on me. I called Basie. No reply from *Birkhall* or his cell. I got hold of Ed Herbst and asked him to Google it. Ed couldn't comment on what the cause or the prognosis was, so I called Basie again. This time I got him. He was more confident and said, 'Drive through to Cape Town. You should be okay. They can change it next week.' Which they did.

I enjoyed the snack at the Laird's Arms, and a short drive later I pulled into the shade of the same peppercorn trees I had parked under on the way up. A gentle breeze rustled the leaves. Scrub grasses, small bushes and succulents all growing on stony ground formed a seemingly endless expanse of flat grey flora that ended in a distant mountain range. Other than the passing cars and trucks, the place was silent. I poured a mug of coffee and pondered the coincidence of two nasty surprises on this trip. First, on the way up, the sudden fit of phobic panic that I'd left my orange-coloured Orvis rod bag at home, and now, on the way back, an orange warning light burning menacingly on my dashboard – both, by strange coincidence, events that had sprung on me at roughly the same place, in the heart of a remote corner of the Karoo. I swilled out the coffee and crushed the last of the biscuits to feed to the sparrows. Again they swooped to the ground. It felt good to feed them. No doubt a legion of well-meaning scientists out there will howl a disparaging chorus of criticism about how feeding wild sparrows threatens their existence in some convoluted way that, in the end, would likely be hard to argue against. Except to say that life on earth is ever-changing, ever-adapting, and that some of today's apparently rock-fast theories on conservation – and on medicine, for that matter – often become tomorrow's trash ready for instant recycling.

I binned the empty biscuit packet, slipped some music into the CD player and was home a few hours later. And I'll keep feeding those sparrows.

*

I should wrap up this chapter with a few more observations on Tenkara, as long as you understand I'm hardly an expert on the subject. And there aren't many of those, at least not in South Africa. Craig Thom, who owns a fly shop in Cape Town, is one, and Steve Boshoff, the bamboo rod maker, is another. Neil Rowe, whom I fished with briefly up at Highland Lodge some years ago, was apparently the first South African to get into Tenkara (and no doubt is still at it). Outside of them, to my knowledge, the sport has limited subscription, unless there's a heap of practising converts who've stayed under the radar.

The occasional flirtations with Tenkara that Tony and I enjoyed on this trip would hardly qualify us as more than mildly experienced, and certainly not true disciples; maybe enthusiastic dabblers is how you could best describe us. But we were both in agreement that Tenkara fly fishing, at least as we experienced it, is a lot more like ballet than conventional fly fishing – a hard point to get across that should become more obvious as we go on. And we were in agreement that it's fun and mighty effective, perhaps even an easy way to catch trout in small, fast-flowing streams, which, as it happens, is also where our brief experience with Tenkara began and ended at the time – that is, on small, fast-flowing mountain streams. Since then Tony has carried on with Tenkara, in a roundabout sort of way, and I've occasionally lapsed into using Tenkara on Western Cape streams, but without the regularity needed to pronounce on its virtues and limitations with any real authority. At best you could say I have tried my hand with Tenkara, rather than fished it seriously.

The question is, why not more dedication than that?

One of the likely reasons is that Tenkara fishing has limitations (I'll get to these later), and the other is that I enjoy casting fly lines on conventional fly rods. There's a challenge in it that, in a way, touches on one of the most pivotal aspects of the sport of fly fishing – casting a virtually weightless fly and fly line with enough accuracy to qualify as a decent presentation. Tenkara does that to an extent, but differently. The casting stroke is limited, which means easier casting with less room for error. The rods are long, allowing you to *place* the fly as much as *cast* it. And while this is productive, and there's no doubt it is, the cast is infinitively less challenging.

Getting distance is sometimes a problem in that you are limited to the length of braided line, leader and tippet off the end of the rod. But if you want to cast long distances, you're missing the close-up and minimalist intention of Tenkara.

Finally, there is no reel. I don't need to tell you there will be times that you won't easily check a long run from a strong fish. Certainly you will not have a fish run into the backing, because there is none.

As far as the limitations of Tenkara go, I'm understandably at times staggered by the reports I read (or occasionally hear about) of large fish being taken on Tenkara rigs – not giant saltwater GTs and such, but certainly big trout and yellowfish.

I touched on the advantages of Tenkara at the beginning of this chapter: dainty drifts, less drag, less mending, easier casting and, above all, a certain poetry that you can only reliably describe once you've been behind a Tenkara fly rod, especially on a small, well-stocked, quick-flowing and averagely tricky trout stream. Some have said it's as exciting as your first date. That depends. My first date was a mess; nothing like my first Tenkara outing. But, look, if the simile strikes a chord with you, you'll have little difficulty understanding Tenkara.

The River Itchen

CHAPTER 4

CHALKSTREAMS

*The driftless area, like the English chalkstreams and indeed like
a great many spring-creek landscapes, has a kind of gentleness
about it. A pastoral place of small farms nestled in hollows
between wooded hills, the countryside is settled but not settled
out of existence, a compromise of sorts between the civilised
and the wild that gives the land an intimate, domestic quality.*
TED LEESON, *JERUSALEM CREEK*

The first time I fished a chalkstream was in the 1970s, when my
wife Kathy and I were in the UK on our first overseas holiday. Near
the end of the trip, my friend Tony Biggs joined us in London,
and we headed south to Hampshire. Tony and I were regular
companions in the mountain streams of the Western Cape long
before steam was invented.

On this trip we fished three streams: the Hampshire Bourne, the
Wallop Brook and the Test (though the Test is really more a river
than a stream). The Bourne and Wallop are tiny and delicate – true
streams by any definition.

The Test and Bourne are steeped in angling history, and over the years I'd read everything about them I could lay my hands on, so that when I finally stood on their banks I had mild waves of *déjà vu* tinted with an inexplicable nostalgia – a strange emotion, since I'd never set foot on the banks of a chalkstream in my life.

Our first good look at one was a stretch of the River Test near the village of Houghton. The river was clear, flowing gently over a porcelain-coloured streambed that was in striking contrast to the patches of emerald-green weeds that seemed to sway seductively in the pull of the smooth-flowing current. The banks were manicured, much like a formal garden, with mown lawns and scatterings of wildflowers like dandelions, and a backdrop of leafy trees. Little wooden benches and thatched huts for resting anglers dotted the banks, and here and there a wooden bridge spanned the broad river. It was all very English in a Constable painting sort of way, and the fishing seemed a little dreamlike, I guess because the Test is possibly the most hallowed trout stream in the world. And here were two hicks from the southern tip of Africa about to fish it in jeans and American-style fly vests, not in tweeds and neckties.

The trout lay in depressions scooped in the chalkstream bed. These holding stations were surrounded by bottle-green weed-beds of water crowfoot (*Ranunculus*) and starwort. Most of the smaller pockets held one or two trout, sometimes a pod of grayling – especially on the Bourne. The bigger pockets on the Test were long, linear strips of bare chalk gravel, alternating in colour from white to straw to honey-coloured. In these you could count five or six fish, some up to twenty inches.

The water was anything from knee- to waist-deep, with the occasional really deep hole, usually where the river took a tight bend. We were on a beat where wading wasn't allowed, so our fishing was strictly from the bank, and on rivers like this, breaking rules doesn't even enter the outer fringe of your thinking.

Occasionally a fish would rise, and we got most of those to come to a dry fly – using small RABs – without much fuss or any real mystery. At a deep pool on a bend I took two fish in quick succession on a deep-sunk PTN, the first a brown trout of nearly two pounds, the second a brook trout not much smaller. We had struck the Test on a good day, even if it was August – the time of year the famous chalkstream fly fisher and author Oliver Kite described as 'the dog days', when hatches are rare and activity is minimal.

We were staying at the Fifehead Manor, a comfortable country hotel in the village of Middle Wallop. Part of the hotel had once been a medieval monastery, and reputedly the birthplace of Lady Godiva. The manor house extended from an eleventh-century Saxon church, a fact of such seeming antiquity that I had trouble getting my head around it. The hotel was in the heart of chalkstream country, so for ten days we fished from this base, covering glorious water and catching a heap of trout, never once packing bags to move.

*

I'm not sure how we managed to afford all this fishing back then, but the pound was only about twice the value of the rand, and we had decided to splurge out. We also had a lucky break. On the first evening we dropped into a pub for a beer. It was called The Boot, and by chance we fell into conversation with a couple of off-duty river keepers. Three ales later we were friends, and they understood we were fly-fishing-crazy South Africans who weren't rich. For a few pounds they opened up waters for us – a morning here, an afternoon there – and before long we had fished a few beats of the Test, including the famous Longparish section (where we caught some heavy trout on tiny PTNs) and the Houghton water.

On a day when our keeper friends had run out of the limited beats they had access to on the Test, they offered us a morning on the Wallop Brook, a chalkstream they warned us would be difficult. The fishing may have been 'difficult', but for reasons we couldn't work out it turned out to be the best day's fishing of the trip, at least if you go by the number of trout we landed. Having said that, it was also a charming, natural stream, with none of the manicured banks we'd seen on the Test. It was tiny, heavily weeded and ridiculously clear, the pockets seemingly brimming with medium-sized wild brown trout. The fishable holes in the weed-beds were not much bigger than hatboxes, but with the large blankets of weed we had some cover and could get in close enough to drop a dry fly on target with ease. Perhaps it was the tightness of the stream that made the keepers hint that we'd have a battle, or else we just struck a good day, because difficult or not, those Wallop trout rose to our RABs all morning. I'd be guessing, but we must have returned upwards of thirty fish.

The loose hold on our tight budget finally cracked when it came to fishing the Hampshire Bourne. There was no way we would have got onto this well-known stream other than by paying a full rod fee, but then it was a stream we both wanted to fish if only for its deep history and its universal acclaim as an ultimate piece of trout water in the writings of the late Oliver Kite and Harry Plunket Greene. We were in awe of this water, and I don't use the term lightly – maybe even more so than of the Test itself.

In the end we drove into Winchester and bought ourselves tickets from a fly shop called The Rod Box that is still there to this day. Look, it wasn't unaffordable, but at that price you wouldn't be fishing this stream every week of the season, any more than you would be eating a regular lunch at Restaurant Le Meurice in Paris. I remember the ticket costing roughly as much as a meal for two in a fancy restaurant, with a bottle of good wine thrown in.

It was one of the loveliest streams I had ever seen, a tributary of the Test and the subject of Harry Plunket Greene's minor angling masterpiece, *Where the Bright Waters Meet.* The stream runs through Hurstbourne Priors, a village dating back to the eighth century. All the landmarks we'd read about in Plunket Greene's writing, as well as in Oliver Kite's books *A Fisherman's Diary* and *Nymph Fishing in Practice*, came to life: the cemetery in St Andrew's Churchyard where Plunket Greene is buried, Long House (Plunket Greene's home), the red brick viaduct, the cricket field, Buttercup Meadow, the Bee Hive. I'm not too moved by history nor do I hold overly romantic notions about places, but I admit to some deep emotion seeing all the landmarks I'd read about probably a dozen times on another, far-removed continent. Now I was standing in these very places and, clearly, not much had changed.

The fishing on the Bourne was tricky. The stream was exquisitely clear and generally shallow, running briskly over almost chalk-white gravel between bright-green patches of starwort weed. Brown trout held nervously above the gravel, often ahead of a grayling or two. But with the water surface not as smoothly laminar as the Test, we naturally got into a spot of trouble with drag and, as I recall, we managed only half a dozen trout in the morning, mainly on small RABs.

We left the river at midday and strolled over to the village pub for a slow lunch and a glass of ale. It seemed a strange but very civilised way to go about a day's fishing. By early afternoon we were back on the Bourne, trying the lower beats.

Here the small grayling were a nuisance, darting upstream and spooking the browns. We took a few small trout, then found a decent fish rising in a tight hole under a bank, where the roots of an old oak hung just far enough over the stream to make casting difficult. Eventually Tony got a RAB to settle perfectly and hooked the fish. It was the best of the day, a brown trout over two pounds.

*

We were on the Test on our last day's fishing, stretched out on the grass at the end of our beat, eating a sandwich, dressed as usual in jeans and American-style fly vests. A Rolls-Royce drew up silently and parked on the other side of a fence not twenty metres from us. A uniformed chauffeur stepped out, opened the trunk of the Rolls and took out a collapsible table. He set it up, decked it with a red-chequered cloth, knife and fork, a wine glass, condiments and a porcelain plate. The passenger in the back seat slowly emerged. He was elderly and overweight, dressed in a tweed jacket and a brightly striped regimental tie (or maybe it was an old-school tie, I don't know, but it was a tie you couldn't miss; alternating stripes of purple and red). The old man sat down to a lunch that appeared from a copious wicker basket. While he was eating, the chauffeur set up his bamboo rod. The old guy patted his lips with a table napkin, swallowed the last of the wine, slipped into a pair of thigh waders and strolled off downstream. We later saw him throwing impressively smooth loops across the river. It was a reminder of how the other half live. Well, at least how *a few* of the other half live. He'd given us no more than a passing glance, but it was a look that suggested he'd quickly written us off as a pair of foreigners invading one of England's most sacred streams, unsuitably attired and not worthy even of a polite nod. In his defence, though, we were probably staring at him with our mouths wide open.

*

I left England with no real hopes of ever returning to fish the chalkstreams. As it happened, I was wrong, and I'll explain how that slice of piscatorial good fortune struck me. It's a long story about a friend of mine, Robin Renwick, but I'll make it brief.

I met Robin thirty years back when he was the UK ambassador to South Africa. We happened to share a pleasant weekend on the lakes at Inhlosane in KwaZulu-Natal, got along well and remained friends, fishing together one or two days each year in the Cape when he and his wife Annie make their annual December visit to South Africa. He's done well on the Holsloot, the Smalblaar, the Molenaars section of the Smalblaar, the Lourens and the Elandspad, and I don't think we've missed fishing together any one year since I moved to Cape Town in 1993.

A few years back, a good friend of Robin's, Clay Brendish, bought the Kimbridge estate in Hampshire with seven miles of the Test flowing through it, and Robin persuaded me to come over and join him for a couple of days on the Test and a few other chalkstreams. All I needed to do was pay for my plane ticket.

*

Chalkstreams have had their challenges over the years. People will tell you they aren't what they used to be, and the further back any chalkstream angler can remember, the better the streams will have been. A few serious droughts didn't help, and neither has increasing water abstraction. Pollution has also played a role. For example, watercress farmers – you will see a typical farm below the viaduct on the Hampshire Bourne – have expanded their operations, and at least once I was told that the use of chemical defoliants had temporarily wiped out weed-beds in some sections of the Test.

Poaching is on the increase. Water weeds need regular trimming. So looking after chalkstreams is costly and labour-intensive, and I guess you could say the fishing on any particular beat ends up about as good as the river keepers are at doing their job, and how interested the owner is in keeping the river optimally fishable.

Then, finally, leasing a rod on a good chalkstream costs plenty, and anglers buying tickets or leasing a share in a beat expect to catch trout. So over the years, stocking hatchery-grown fish, including rainbows, inevitably became a major part of the management of some beats, the Test and the Avon among them. I guess purists will always see this as a capitulation to the needs of the moneyed, and a dangerous regression from the ideals of purity and wildness. Which may be so – only, in the modern world, we know that purity and wildness are not always attainable, never mind sustainable.

All this said, I have made two recent trips to fish chalkstreams in Hampshire when they seemed in perfect condition. I never felt a hint of indignation catching a few big rainbows, some over six pounds, on the Test, nor any superior elation catching the pretty wild browns that I got from the upper Itchen.

*

My wife and I arrived in London with two missions: to visit my son Robert and his wife Tammy, and to take up Robin Renwick's invitation to fish the Test, the Lambourne and the Itchen.

I took a cab to Robin's Chelsea home. We left for the Test, his car loaded with gear. I was relying on my Winston 2-weight to see me through most of the fishing, but I also had a Sage 3-weight with me and a Sage SPL 0-weight, all with matching floating lines on a bunch of Orvis CFO reels. I had a heap of fly boxes crammed with newly tied dry flies and nymphs, and more spools of fresh nylon than I needed. In fact, I was completely over-gunned for the simple act of fishing, but you know the story because you've probably been there often enough yourself. I'd somehow forgotten Oliver Kite's appealing philosophy of minimalism, where in even his most complex chalkstream fishing he carried a rod and reel, a snuff box with a 'pinch of flies' in it, and a spool of nylon. But then, I notice it all came to him relatively late in his career, and he had the advantage of living so near to the banks of the Avon that he just had to walk across a paddock to fish it.

It was late June, but we still hoped the Olives or Pale Watery Duns would hatch, with a few Iron Blues and Blue Winged Olives in the evening. I'd tied up a few BWO imitations and a couple of Kite's Imperials, all on size 16 hooks, just in case we did bump into a hatch, but I also had a tin of wispy RABs and a few caddis and midge imitations, because they're patterns that have become part of my DNA and I don't feel easy on a stream without them.

We passed through the village of Stockbridge, where the Test divides into five shallow streams that cross under the main road. You can add a rare dimension to any shopping trip here by watching trout from the sidewalk as you cross little bridges between stores. I noticed an Orvis sign in the high street, and the Grosvenor Hotel, forever a part of the famed Houghton Fly Fishing Club's history. But other than that there wasn't much to suggest the town was so central to much of England's fly-fishing history or so near to so many well-known chalkstreams, like the Test, the Anton, the Itchen and the Bourne. It had none of the fly-fishing capital-town buzz of, say, a West Yellowstone or Livingston in Montana. As far as Stockbridge goes, you'll only find evidence of its deep fly-fishing history in books, not in the high street. Like English fly fishing generally, the town is somewhat understated, at least in relation to its great fly-fishing past.

From Stockbridge we headed south along the Test River Valley, then swung off the main road onto a typically English lane that ran through a leafy umbrella of trees: a narrow, winding lane with hedgerows either side and wooden gates that offered fleeting views of wheat fields or sheep-studded pastures and the occasional stately mansion. The lane eventually crossed the Test on a small bridge that I instantly recognised. Tony Biggs and I had stopped at this exact spot all those years back. I remembered we had found a decent trout holding just downstream of the bridge, and we had tossed tiny pebbles into the water a yard behind the fish. It had swung around to inspect the 'plops', until it got tired of the game, sat tight and ignored us.

Clay Brendish's home turned out to be less than a hundred metres from that same bridge, a lovely old mill cottage straddling tight on the winding lane. He took us through a gate, then over a small bridge alongside the old millwheel he said he was going to restore, then to a sweep of lawn lined with bright flowerbeds, the lawn running straight down to the banks of the Test not twenty metres from his front door.

I strolled to the edge of the river running quietly by. On the far bank, a swan and her cygnets drifted with the current, the mother with her head held high and alert. In mid-stream a trout rose, then rose again. Against the light I saw a sprinkling of insects lifting off the water. Fifty metres upstream another river, the Dun, joined the Test on the far left bank, wide and smooth-flowing and every bit as attractive as the Test, but not a true chalkstream I was told, though how you tell the difference is anyone's guess. To me the Dun looked every bit as marvellous as the Test. (I have since checked its pedigree with Simon Cooper, author of *Life of a Chalkstream*, and he said he regarded it as a true chalkstream. That somehow felt very right. But Clay was adamant. I spoke to him after writing this piece and he said it is a spate river that rises and falls just like a freestone stream. So be it. To me it will remain one of the loveliest trout streams I've ever had the privilege of fishing.)

Clay is a fit man in his early fifties, and I discovered he's also a sharp fly fisher. We didn't mess about with pleasantries, other than a cup of tea, before we set up our rods. Kimbridge is dry-fly-only water, so there was no need to angst over whether to use a nymph rather than a dry. I tied on a RAB, gave a few to Robin. Clay had enough faith in Royal Humpies not to bother with anything else. We went our separate ways, and I didn't see either of them all morning, which will give you an idea of the size of the place.

I walked along a neatly mown bank and crossed a footbridge where I stopped in mid-stream to take a long look into the water. It was slightly cloudy, but I guess if you had been on any river other than the Test, you'd have said the water was near gin-clear. The Test, and chalkstreams generally, lift the bar on the meaning of clarity in running river water.

There had been weed cutting upstream a day before, something Clay apologised for, as if it made the slightest difference to a South African fishing the Test for the first time in God knows how many years. I watched the occasional untidy clump of weed float by, but standing for a long while on the bridge, I saw no rises and I saw no trout.

I crossed the bridge and followed a path that brought me to a carrier-stream of the Test called the New Stream. Now this stream really *was* gin-clear, and there was no floating weed in it. I cautiously crossed a wooden footbridge, then stalked up the left bank to keep my shadow off the water. Two fish were rising a long way ahead of me. They were coming up in the middle of the stream, and I marked their positions. I would get to them in good time.

Close by, a big brown rose so boldly and so suddenly that it startled me. The fish darted out of a weed-bed in the centre of the stream, then, once positioned, it lifted deliberately to take a drifting dun with a soft gulp that I could actually hear. And then, silently, it was gone. The fish's timing was immaculate. So, obviously, was its eyesight. It must have spotted that dun from two rod-lengths away.

I threw a couple of casts, trying to mimic the drift path of the dun, but got no interest. Eventually I dropped the RAB against the top end of the weed-bed, with the fly running alongside the very edge of it, the tip of the fly line resting on the weeds. A trout rose confidently and languidly took the RAB, and when its head turned down I lifted the rod and set the hook, and the fish fled downstream straight under the footbridge. It was a strong fish, and

I couldn't check him for fear of snapping the 7X tippet. In seconds, the line was well downstream of the bridge and the tippet did snap.

The two browns I had spotted earlier were still rising; I caught one but couldn't interest the other. Moments later, while I was drifting the RAB blind along the far bank, I hooked a brown of twenty inches. It put up a magnificent fight, including a leap when it bucked in mid-air, loosening a shower of silver droplets, then bore deep into the weed. I kept even pressure on the fish, and gently moved it into a clear, white-pebbled channel of shallow water where I was able to slip a net under it. The trout was thick through the shoulders, not deeply spotted and more olive-green than brown.

I came across a moorhen fidgeting around on the far bank just ahead of me. As I moved upstream, so the bird moved with me. It probably had a nest or was hiding chicks, but it sure as hell wasn't improving the fishing. I strolled back to the Test, comparing the neatly mown paths I was now on to, say, the average going on the Holsloot or the upper beats on *Gateshead*, which by comparison seemed like training grounds for paratroopers.

Back on the Test, I found a fish rising and hooked it first throw, a pretty brown trout sharply etched with vermilion spots. It could have been a brown from anywhere in the world, remarkably like those you get in the Willow Stream in the Eastern Cape or in the Witte River outside Wellington.

It was late in June and it was hot, certainly for this part of the world – hot enough for my Polaroids to start fogging up. I found a sliver of shade and took a packet of boiled sweets from my vest pocket. I was on a wide path of mown grass running up the side of the main river with a stand of tall trees behind me; ahead, a smooth-flowing expanse of river was lit with the reflections of clouds. Beyond the river there were scattered trees in rolling-green pastures, with a few quaint buildings peeping through the distant foliage. There wasn't a sound to be heard, other than birdsong.

I could not have been anywhere but in England, and probably nowhere on earth but on the banks of the River Test. It was such a rare privilege that I felt a strange responsibility to get up and fish so as not to waste a moment of it. I walked slowly back to the cottage, taking three small brown trout on a RAB that by then was hardly floating – when, as you know, this pattern can become just as deadly as when it's fresh and dry and daintily stands up on its toes vibrating and weaving on the curls of the currents.

On a table on the Mill Cottage lawn, glasses of Champagne and sandwiches were laid out, and we drank a toast. Clay had taken trout on the Royal Humpy and so had Robin – but only, Robin said, until his RABs had run out. I took out my fly box and replenished his supply.

I think of myself as something of an egalitarian fly fisher, or at least a firm member of fly fishing's proletariat, but I noticed I was slipping into the life of the landed gentry with remarkable ease. With Champagne in my hand and the bright waters of the Test running just about under my elbow as I lifted the narrow glass, I wondered if hunting trout ever got more comfortably sumptuous than this.

In the afternoon, I passed on the Test because of the weed cutting and fished the Dun. It was a dead-easy river to fish; clear banks, smooth, laminar-flow surface, trout rising here and there to a sporadic hatch of mayflies that came off nearly all afternoon. There were browns, rainbows and blue trout in the mix, some far bigger than I expected, but I guessed these were stocked fish that had grown well. The blue trout is a hybrid of the rainbow, stocked because of its excellent fighting abilities.

A small green Land Rover pulled up next to me, and I met Clay's two young river keepers. They told me that the blue trout is a strong-fighting novelty, almost electric in its silvery blueness, bred in hatcheries by crossing really dark rainbow trout, though it struck me as not worth the trouble given that rainbows are pretty enough and as strong as they need to be. They said the river would fish well all the way around the corner a few hundred metres ahead, but after that it would fish even better. As it happened, I didn't catch a blue trout that afternoon, but around the corner I did land a rainbow of twenty-three inches and a brown of twenty, along with a heap of medium-sized and feisty brown trout. The fish all came freely to the RAB on a 6X tippet, until I lost the last of my RABs and had to fall back on a variety of scruffy-looking dry flies I plucked off my vest patch. I'd left my fly box at the house. That's probably one of the downsides of quaffing Champagne at midday, but my fly patch was well enough stocked not to bother returning to fetch the box.

I also tried a side stream of the Test called the Coldbrook. It was a narrow stream about a rod-length wide and gentle-looking, but flowing in a tight avenue of leafy trees. The water was clear and the trout, mainly browns from what I could tell, were spooky and hard to spot in the shade. I took a pretty brace on a tiny, black One-Feather CDC Midge. I couldn't be certain, but the last time that particular fly landed on a stream was probably on Beat 6 of the Smalblaar.

In the evening we went to a restaurant in Stockbridge, the Greyhound, a warm place full of charm and atmosphere, where I had one of the best meals I can remember. The restaurant was in an old building on the high street, with a stone doorway you had to duck your head under to get through. The food was prepared to perfection. I had a rack of lamb with vegetables done *al dente* and a salad of garden-fresh herbs and lettuces in a piquant Roquefort dressing. Every box scored a tick, and the wines were excellent. When we eventually got back to Mill Cottage it was still light enough to sit outside watching trout swirl at the surface of the silent river while we sipped on a slug of single malt whisky on ice.

That night I fell asleep while writing the pencil notes I keep in a small wire-bound exercise book. I woke some hours later wondering at how hard the pillow felt, slipped the book out from under my head and was asleep again in a wink.

*

Robin, Clay and I had an invitation to spend a day on Roger and Victoria Harrison's water, a section of the upper Itchen that is kept wild – meaning no stocked fish and obviously no rainbows. From what I gathered, Roger keeps his water private.

We travelled over early on a bright day when the world seemed to glow in warm sunlight. The rolling, hedge-lined landscapes, the quaint villages we drove through, the tightly winding lanes all looked clean as if freshly scrubbed. We ran a while alongside the Itchen where it was marked by a bordering row of trees, and crossed the river once, where I had a fleeting glimpse of a silvery stream flowing under a low, brick bridge. The road followed close by the river for a hundred metres and ended at the Harrisons' farmhouse.

Even among chalkstreams as celebrated as the Test, the Avon, the Hampshire Bourne and the Wylye, the upper Itchen is special. Many hold that it's the best chalkstream on earth, something that, if difficult to prove, is equally difficult to contest.

Unlike freestone streams, chalkstreams are silent. You don't hear them flowing. They seem to glide at a gentle pace, no faster than a brisk stroll. This is exactly how I would have described the piece of the Itchen I was looking at that morning – silently gliding, the only rider being that it was coming straight from under the Harrisons' house. We'd parked the car in their driveway, and Robin and Clay went ahead to knock on the front door. I stayed back to take in this extraordinary sight. From an opening in a chalk-stained, red-brick wall of this rambling old farmhouse, the Itchen appeared suddenly like a train from a tunnel, then quietly flowed past me into a tree-lined field. It turned out that their home had once been a watermill, which provided an explanation but did nothing to lessen the charm and appealing novelty of what I was looking at right then.

Inside, the house was a long maze of rooms with low, wood-beamed ceilings connected by equally low-slung doors. The kitchen window looked out over a long sweep of the Itchen that ended up flowing right under our feet. You could feel the mild tremor of its flow. The water, pale amber in colour and clear, was threaded with patches of white chalk, bright green starwort weed and the water crowfoot.

'That's some view to have from a kitchen window,' I said.

'It's a lot better from our bedroom upstairs,' Roger replied, and you had to believe him.

On a wall in the study there was a framed collection of artefacts with a handwritten inscription in fading, sepia-coloured ink that read, 'James Standerwick, Ovington House near Alresford, 1795'. Behind the glass was a cluster of flies, mostly winged wet flies around size 14, attached to loops of gut. There were two ochre-coloured wedges marked 'Bee's wax' (presumably for dressing fly lines), a packet of hooks marked 'Mayflies' and a crumbling leather fly wallet. Roger told me he had come across them by accident in a distant corner of the house, believed they belonged to a previous owner and had decided to frame them, as such old and interesting fishing artefacts rightly deserve.

Out front, the Itchen flowed through a bright English garden. Near the house, two wooden footbridges spanned the river just before the flow slipped under the house, presumably at the point where the mill had once stood. Flowerbeds, clusters of rambling roses and apple trees gave way to hedges and paddocks and distant woods. The river flowed through the garden and then, beyond the garden, it flowed straight and smooth and glinting in the sun for at least another half a kilometre before it disappeared around a bend.

Roger and Victoria had no fix on exactly how old their home was, only that a part of it was recorded in the Domesday Book, dating it back to at least 1086. The main body of the house looked Georgian, suggesting a part, at least, was built somewhere between 1720 and 1800. President Roosevelt had visited the house, as had the American writer, artist and fly fisher James Prosek. He went on to produce a short DVD of his day here, doing a watercolour painting sitting on one of the wooden footbridges outside the kitchen window. While we were drinking tea in the shade of some apple trees, William Daniel, a local fly-fishing guide who runs an operation called Famous Fishing, arrived to join us.

From the house, across a wooden footbridge, a path led to a paddock, and a few hundred metres beyond that, to a carrier stream of this section of the Itchen. I decided to try the carrier, and Robin and Clay each took a section of the main river with William.

The carrier was the most sublime small stream I have ever seen in my life; crystalline water running over the palest riverbed imaginable, almost pure chalk it seemed, dotted with occasional clumps of bright-green starwort that in the clear water almost seemed to have a neon-like, emerald-coloured glow – a stream no wider than a country lane, running knee-deep for just a few hundred metres more or less straight through open pasture, before disappearing around a corner into a leafy thicket.

The stream made me think of my small-stream-fanatic friends; Ed Herbst topped the list, but Billy de Jong, Steve Boshoff, Tom Lewin, Stanton Hector, Pete Brigg, Gerald Penkler, Tony Kietzman, Mario Geldenhuys and Leonard Flemming came to mind, and a few others besides. They would kill to be on this water, and I wanted to be sharing this stream with them because it was that magnificent. And to be alone on it somehow didn't feel right, or at least made me feel slightly guilty in an obscure way. It was as if there was too much joy and too much perfection wrapped up in this little gem to be fishing it alone. I needed a few like-minded companions to celebrate it with me, maybe to pinch me from time to time to remind me this wasn't all a dream.

Roger walked with me to the edge of the carrier. He described a few of its quirks and sketched out something of an approach to fishing it, but added that I'd be fortunate to take a brace of trout. He said I should move slowly, walk on eggs and make for the top of the beat where it was treed-in and where, he said, the fishing would get a lot easier.

I re-rigged my rod when I saw the clarity of this delicate stream. I say 're-rigged', but all I did was add a few extra feet of 7X tippet and dress the tippet lightly so it wouldn't sink. I stepped into the water where it was ankle deep, feeling its coldness and the soft crunch of chalk pebbles underfoot. I waded gently upstream, scanning the water for trout. Roger had said there weren't many trout in the carrier, that they were wild brown trout and that they were always nervous. I kept my rod low and behind me. The sun was bright and I knew rod-flash would be a problem. Other than the rod, I had nothing that would flash – no forceps, no silver zingers, and I had taken off my watch.

The first fish I saw was holding in a pocket near the left bank, and as I watched it, trying to measure an approach, a second fish drifted down from upstream like a phantom and took up a station just ahead of the first fish. They were both around fifteen inches, lying between trembling fronds of starwort on a scoop of caramel-coloured gravel. I loosened a few yards of line and tried to drop a dry fly, a size 16 RAB, a little ahead of the leading fish, but long before the fly landed, even before my abbreviated back cast had unfolded, both fish quivered, then darted off. It was going to be a tough morning.

I tried a few more trout with the same result. I knew changing flies wouldn't help, and I couldn't lengthen the tippet much because the downstream breeze was already a challenge. But in the end, it was the breeze that got me the first trout I caught in this section.

Halfway up the carrier and still fishless, I was at a point where the stream broadened with deeper water along the right bank and a pocket in the middle. I cast blind into the pocket just as a gust of wind came through. It hinged the leader, sending it off to the right, and landing the fly as gently as a feather falls inches from the deeper water along the bank. The RAB only drifted for a second before a trout swallowed it, a decent fish of fourteen inches and as beautiful as an artist would paint a wild brown trout. It was a quintessential, small-stream jewel of a fish. I took a second trout in a similarly improbable way a few moments later. I'd like to say I made the wind-hinged-right-angle cast part of my small-stream repertoire that day, but the truth, as you guessed, is that getting the second fish was as much plain luck as the first.

Once I got into the thicket of trees, the fishing changed. The stream banks were rougher, despite a path of sorts along the left bank, and the water was deeper but just as clear. In places, branches

hung low over the stream. I found a decent cock fish holding in an opening, but he ignored the RAB and several changes of dry fly, so I ran a PTN right across his nose and hooked him firmly. He put up quite a display, including a jump that landed him in the grass on the far bank for a brief moment before he flopped back into the stream. I netted the fish and guessed him to be sixteen inches. He was darkly coloured and discreetly spotted.

From this point right up to where the carrier joined the Itchen proper, I saw no rises and spotted no fish. But I had a few trout on the PTN, and at the junction of this carrier with the Itchen, I found a trout rising. I covered it with a RAB and hooked it just as Robin joined me.

'Nice fish,' he said. 'I got one rising at *exactly* this spot earlier this morning. Could be the same fish… I also got it on one of your RABs.'

If I hadn't just released that fish I'd have checked its mouth for signs of a previous hook-up. I said it was about sixteen inches, Robin agreed and we settled for it being the same fish. It seems that even trout with the most aristocratic pedigrees on earth can at times be curiously incautious.

'Right, let's break for lunch,' Robin said. It felt more like he should be saying 'Let's tear ourselves away for lunch' because I was getting into my stride and enjoying myself, at least as much as I have done on any of the few places where I might have said, 'This was the best fishing of my life.'

We strolled back along the riverbank, our eyes on the water, sometimes passing sizeable trout that were rising in full view, and here and there we saw small schools of grayling, and one lone fish of considerable size lying deep and exposed. I just had to drift a PTN over this fish, and Robin understood. I got it to take the fly, but the tippet snapped like straw at the end of its first run. Now whose fault was that, I wonder?

The lunch in Roger and Victoria's garden topped a few previous high points in my life for remarkable lunches, never mind that it was a riverside lunch.

*

I worked up the main stream that afternoon, catching brown trout between one and two pounds, and a brace of iridescently coloured grayling that sipped the dry fly off the surface so gently you could hardly notice the take.

I was fishing only to rises with a variety of patterns, including a Goddard Caddis, an extended-body mayfly pattern that Stanton Hector had given me, and an Arpo, a single-feather CDC caddis imitation that an Italian fly fisher, Edoardo Ferrero, introduced me to. For some reason the fish weren't interested in the RAB, perhaps because I had run out of smaller sizes. The first refusal to the RAB, though, was spectacular. I had spotted a chunky brown rising close by and dropped the RAB ahead of it. The fish rose slowly, hung under the fly as it drifted downstream towards me and, for a moment, we were on a collision course. It turned away less than an arm's length from where I was standing, dead still in the middle of the river – from which you will deduce that this is a beat of the Itchen you can wade and, further, that the RAB was refused. It's not the first time a trout has done this to me.

Midway through the afternoon, Robin fielded a crisis business call and had to leave in a hurry. We had been booked to spend the night in a nearby village, Teffont Evias, and to then fish the Lambourne, a smaller chalkstream in Berkshire and a tributary of the Kennet, but in a wink that was all washed down the sink for Robin. He left, and Clay and I fished on with William Daniel.

William, as I said, has an outfit called Famous Fishing, focusing on chalkstream trips. His then-partner Bill Latham is a friend of mine from way back, and it was good to be fishing with William. Together we caught a few sturdy brown trout, and I got some fair underwater photographs of them. When we finally left the Itchen after farewells to Roger and Victoria, Clay headed back to Kimbridge, and William agreed to drive me to my hotel. Along the road, William's interest in the angling history of this part of England came through; legends like Walton, Halford, Skues, Marryat, Plunket Greene, Sawyer and Kite were all mentioned. We were, after all, in the centre of their respective fishing universes.

We stopped at the Bourne and visited Plunket Greene's gravestone, decked, as always, in fly boxes left by visiting anglers paying homage to the great man. Then we drove up the winding lane especially to look at the viaduct that carries the rail link from London and spans this pretty chalkstream. It's a tall structure known as the St Mary Bourne Bridge, with seven or more towering arches, and seen in the distance from the road bridge over the Bourne. When viewed upstream, the Bourne meanders through a meadow for at least a kilometre before it passes under the viaduct. It's a famous sight in English fly-fishing history.

*

I was told Teffont Evias is one of the prettiest villages in England. At least that's what William said, and even allowing that he lived in the village himself and might carry a little home-town bias, I wasn't inclined to argue the point when we got there. Rows of quaint cottages with thatched or red-tiled roofs lined the high street. They had stone-dressed walls, some draped in rambling roses or ivy, and each had a tiny strip of garden out front, edged in bright flowers. Most of the cottages were built from local stone hued from the same quarry used to build Salisbury Cathedral. Running just in front of the cottages was a stone furrow, easily a metre wide and equally deep, with chalkstream-clear spring water flowing through clumps of green starwort weed. The furrow had all the hallmarks of originating in chalkstream country, and I couldn't help thinking that if you owned a house in this village you could rightfully lay claim to having a chalkstream as a pavement.

I took a long walk, until I was well below the town. The sun was setting, and the countryside glowed in yellow light. The furrow water crossed under the road, flowed along the edge of a sidewalk, then headed into a pasture, where I suspected this little stream became fishable before it ended in the Nadder, another well-known chalkstream. Walking back, I found a house in the village that had a small chalkstream running through the garden. If it wasn't for English winters, I'd not have minded retiring in this house. I studied it carefully until the grey-haired head of a woman appeared at an upstairs window. She was eyeing me with some suspicion and probably saying to her husband, 'Bert, I'm a bit worried. There's an unshaven old man dressed like a hobo loitering outside. I think he's eyeing our TV set.'

I was staying at Howard's House, a boutique hotel in the village, with spreading lawns and long views. I seemed to be the only person at the hotel. I shaved for dinner, then sat outside at a comfortable table with a beer, watching the thread of birdlife as the light slowly faded. It struck me that the stream I had just fished, the upper Itchen, is by reputation the most beautiful piece of chalkstream water in the world, and I lingered comfortably with my thoughts on that, and of the day, not unhappy to be alone.

At dinner in the tiny dining room, I had the company of an American family celebrating their son's birthday, and we got talking. They weren't that interested in fly fishing, so our conversation was limited to the sort of polite pleasantries you exchange with strangers who aren't concerned about where you fished, what you caught or what flies you used. But the old man did say he would have loved to have done some fly fishing himself if he could have. I never probed why he didn't, because you can find yourself listening to a sad chapter of someone's life that really doesn't interest you and that will mainly come down to too little time, which when you read between the lines probably boils down to being too busy making a lot of money.

*

Bill Latham and I were due to fish the Lambourne the next day, but in the end we skipped it, simply because on the drive to the Lambourne, Bill was keen to show me Frank Sawyer's water on the Avon and I was keen to see it. The river here looked good, running a hundred metres or so from a palatial-looking estate called Heale House, owned by Guy Rasch. Although the property was grand, Bill was not sure it was actually a manor house. The house was in Middle Woodford, and its history intrigued me.

Heale House was built in the latter part of the sixteenth century by Sir William Greene. The house was given to his daughter and son-in-law, Sir Gerald Errington, in 1553 as a wedding present, passing from them into the hands of Lawrence Hyde of Hatch, and given again as a wedding present to his son. The house was considerably enlarged by the son, covering very much the same area as it does today. After about a hundred years, the Bowles family bought the property; it remained in their ownership until 1813, when it was sold to clear the debts of the bankrupt owner William Bowles. It changed hands twice more in the 19th century and was occupied by various tenants, suffering considerable fire damage in 1835 when it was reduced by two-thirds. It was bought by the Honourable Louis Greville in 1894, the great-uncle of the present owner. Mr Greville was soon to set this right, building to the east and north on the foundations of the earlier house. The whole place was enlarged, with a taste and sensitivity so often lacking in the extensions to houses at the beginning of the 20th century.

A moment of pride in Heale House's background came in October 1651, when Charles II secretly took refuge here for six nights before riding on to Shoreham, where he fled by ship to France with a bounty of £1,000 on his head.

That nicely set up the background for our fishing that day. We were pretty much just off the front lawn of Heale House.

We parked alongside a hedge where a narrow carrier of the Avon flowed, and where I watched two trout holding in a gravelled gully between the weeds. A path took us through an avenue of deep shade to an old mill house, where the main river channelled alongside a crumbling building with a signboard that read, 'Piss off I'm busy'. There was a black weather vane on the moss-covered roof depicting two men in a boat, one holding a deeply bending fishing rod.

The water surged into a deep pool below the mill, where I saw the shadowy-green shapes of big fish moving nervously in the tail-out. Further on, the river spread as wide as a long cast, flowing lazily through hedged paddocks. The far bank was dotted with enormous trees. Through the trees I got glimpses of the beautiful red-brick Heale House. Sheep grazed under the trees, their reflections caught in the surface of the stream. On the other side of the paddock there was a scattering of white-walled, thatched cottages running along a country lane, and behind them a tree-clad hill.

In so many ways it was a typical patch of rural England – pastoral, peaceful, rustic: an opulent and elegant mansion within sight of modest but brightly-decked cottages, the two divided by hundred-year-old trees, hedged paddocks and the clear, weed-laced waters of one of the world's most prestigious trout streams. If there was a clear divide here between the gentry and the middle class, you'd have to say neither side was likely to be that unhappy about it.

*

The fishing was good, and I learned a number of valuable lessons from Bill. You can't wade this part of the Avon, but you can use nymphs. Fishing from the bank was no problem because our side was treeless, and the slight elevation above the river made spotting trout quite easy.

It's interesting how each day's fishing unfolds in its own particular way, never mind whether it's the same river you're fishing two days in a row or yet another chalkstream for the first time, or the same farm pond week in and week out. This was a day where you would say the water could have been clearer, but the fish were active; we caught so many I can't remember the exact tally. The first was a brown, nymphing in a clear pocket that took a Zak in a sweep. Then a couple of rainbows followed, also nymphing, all the fish strong and all easily over sixteen inches. It was much the same for Bill, who was also using a Zak.

Then I found a good-sized brown sipping in mid-stream that refused the two drifts I put over it with a parachute dry fly Bill had given me.

'Your drift's too long,' Bill said. 'Smack the fly right on its nose and he'll eat it.'

I did just that, and the fish smoked that dry fly. I had heard about this stunt before, but it wasn't something that would have struck me as a tactic for a chalkstream like the Avon.

Chalkstreams are known for mayfly hatches in May and June, including the *Ephemera danica*, and we ran into an unseasonably late spinner fall of these big bugs – not dense enough to bring on a feeding frenzy but lovely to see, even just for the sake of tradition and history, because this is the most iconic bug in fly fishing. The insects spun like falling leaves as they dropped, their slow, spinning descent being where the name 'spinner fall' comes from.

*

Later that afternoon I got on a train in Salisbury, arriving in London in time to take Kathy and the kids to dinner. We went to a place on the high street in Dulwich; the food was good, but the noise level was so high we had to speak in a kind of sign language, which left me no chance of describing the more interesting nuances of three days spent fishing on chalkstreams. Not that my family cared. They're just glad when I get a few fish and they're happy to leave it at that.

*

Farlows at 9 Pall Mall in London is a high-end fly shop by any standards, with two floors of cosmic tackle and clothing, and a fair stock of books. A friend was one of the managers in the store at the time, an ex-South African who, it struck me, lived in a perpetual haze of hovering homesickness, even if he loved his job. I'm not sure if he still works there. I browsed around the large store, eventually bought some stuff, and got the best discount I ever got in a fly shop. Never mind that I probably didn't need what I bought – fly-tying materials and books, mainly. But since when is a top-grade honey dun cape or good quality CDC, including some natural, undyed CDC feathers, anything you can easily resist at a third of the going price?

From Farlows I took a walk to the Orvis shop, maybe two blocks away, hoping to look up another South African fly-fishing friend, Jim Boyd. I got hopelessly lost. Not that I mind getting lost in London: it's a city so full of the atmosphere of itself that every minute in it is a pleasure. In the end, when I did find the store, Jim was out of town, but the manager, Katerina Blake, an attractive ambassador for Orvis, offered me a cup of coffee and didn't mind that I sat drinking it in one of their comfortable leather chairs with a hefty Farlows shopping bag right alongside me. Eventually I did buy a book from them – Gierach's latest – even if I could have got it back home for a lot less. I just wanted some reading for my twelve-hour flight later in the week. Before that, I had a day booked to fish the Anton and the Test with my son Robert. Kathy and Tammy had shopping planned, so Rob and I got an official nod from the ladies to go off fishing.

*

If you asked my son what dry flies he prefers to fish with, he'll quickly say 'RABs' – but then he'll lapse into a long silence and scratch his chin trying to think of the name of a dry fly other than a RAB. There was a time when he tied fantastic RABs, because at ten years old you unconsciously make the sort of mistakes that produce nicely untidy, buggy-looking flies. His RABs really caught fish – and I didn't just use them to please him, believe me.

We carried a heap of gear – and a good supply of RABs – onto a train at Waterloo Station, and headed south for Andover, where we took a cab to the Mayfly Inn, a pub on the banks of the River Test. By the time we had set up our rods to fish the Anton, a chalkstream tributary coming into the Test just below the inn, it was raining, and after an hour's fishing we were soaked. We hadn't expected rain, and although we had lightweight rain jackets on, our pants got wet in the long grass.

The Anton was grey in the rain, and its fish were impossible to spot. The weed-beds were dense, and we saw only the occasional rise. Two fish came to the fly, both small brown trout; in the end we decided that fishing the Test above the Mayfly Inn would be a better bet.

We stopped at the inn and ate a tasty shepherd's pie; I ordered a pint of warm ale. We sat out on a wooden deck edged with pots of blood-red geraniums. By now, a watery sunlight bled through the clouds, and the deck was filled with diners. Below the deck we watched brown trout milling in a deep pool. They looked huge, and in moments we understood why. People watching them from above would toss scraps of food to the school of fish. Nothing drifted on the surface longer than a few seconds before it was gone.

After lunch we found the trout really dancing on our beat of the Test. This was one of the most beautiful sections I had seen on this river, and with the sun shining again, we soon spotted feeding trout. Robert got a brace of sixteen-inch browns – on a RAB, what else – and then hooked a cow on one of his lazier back-casts. The cast travelled low over a barbed-wire fence where a bunch of cattle had silently gathered to watch us. The cow kicked out viciously and broke him at a brisk trot.

A red metal bridge spanned the river, throwing a shimmering crimson reflection onto the water surface. Then, as suddenly as the sun had broken through the clouds, it began to rain; a steady, soft, soaking rain that wet us as perfectly as if we'd stepped into a barrel of water. We called it a day and took a cab from the Mayfly Inn to the Andover railway station.

Travelling back by train, we were still pretty wet from the knees down. Small pools of water gradually formed around our boots. It looked as if we'd both been struck with sudden incontinence, but nobody gave us even a half-interested glance. The English are so inscrutable, so private, so, well, English, I guess.

As the train approached London, it was rocking gently with speed. Monotonous rows of semi-detached houses, factory yards and small tenement gardens flashed by. The soft rhythmical click-clack of the train would seem to pick up as it rushed through a cutting and out of it, the tightly bordering trees turned to a green blur. My eyes were closing, and I guess I might have drifted off if it weren't for the numbing cold in my feet.

It had been a great father-and-son day, and I was impressed with how well Robert had fished considering his enforced two-year layoff after moving to London. This was the first time he'd ever fished a chalkstream, and chalkstreams can be intimidating to novices, if only by reputation. But he could have been on the Sterkspruit or the Smalblaar, he was so confident in what he did. I also wondered at how smooth and elegant left-handed casters can look – and my son is no exception.

*

We spent the evening at an Indian restaurant only a short stroll from our tiny hotel room in Dulwich, where the food was authentic and the atmosphere superb. The next day was a nightmarish rush to Heathrow, followed by a series of slow passages in seemingly endless queues until, at last, over the banking wing of the aircraft, we saw the lights of London slip away. I settled back, opened Gierach's book and had a pleasant enough flight home.

I returned for another week to the chalkstreams the following year, which I'll tell you about later.

Bridge over the Sterkspruit River on Branksome

CHAPTER 5

BACK-COUNTRY BRIDGES

Ask anyone who has driven in a car with a freshwater
fisherman what happens when the fisherman spots
any sort of moving water. The answer is invariably
a sudden change in focus from road to water. With any luck,
the driver will pull over to keep the passengers safe.
PAUL MILLER, *SECRET CREEK: FRIENDSHIPS,*
PHEROMONES AND FLY FISHING

I'm a sucker for bridges – at least for bridges that cross back-country trout streams – and many of my fishing buddies share the same sentiment. We love them and, within reason, we stop on just about every one we cross, at least on the way in to fish some river, as opposed to on the way out, when we're maybe less driven to stop and keener to get back home to a can of beer.

But as with most things that fall under a single heading, no two bridges over streams are entirely alike, though they share commonalities, and we stop at them for roughly the same reasons: out of curiosity and for the fun of it – and not necessarily in that order. Which doesn't fully explain the level of fascination a lot of anglers have for bridges, I know. My sense is that it goes well beyond the curiosity and fun bits. In fact, some people I know – myself and my pal Tony Kietzman included – have a love of trout stream bridges that may border on being mildly obsessive. But let's leave deep psychology out of this. Let me just say that the longer I keep company with my close circle of fly-fishing friends, the more I'm inclined to believe that a healthy love of bridges is an inevitable outcome in most anglers' lives in fly fishing.

But there is one important supplementary explanation for our attraction to bridges that I probably should mention, and it's that they offer us heaven-sent opportunities to get the same voyeuristic pleasure we get standing in a clear trout stream, cautiously peering around boulders and into runs in the hope of unearthing an unsuspecting trout. In fact, spotting trout is one of the great pleasures of fishing a stream, and standing on a bridge gives you the same pleasure, only magnified and augmented by the added advantage of height.

Some bridges have a certain appealing atmosphere due to their old-world architecture. Generally, most bridges built in the 1800s have a lot more style than their modern counterparts, which tend to be plain, unattractive blocks of concrete rather than anything graceful and artistic. In the Eastern Cape Highlands – a part of the country known for its pretty bridges, by the way – the Loch Bridge is a good example. It's a tall, handsome bridge designed by English civil engineer Joseph Newey and built, like many others in the area, from locally quarried sandstone. It was opened in 1893 and spans the Kraai River on the road from Barkly East to New England. The view from it into the river is worth a whole morning's fishing. I once stood for an hour or so, early in the season, on a sunny day, transfixed as I looked down from it onto yellowfish moving upstream in their hundreds. And there are equally pretty bridges in Maclear and Ugie, though they are nowhere near as high as the Loch Bridge.

*

But to strip all the romantic hype out of it, we actually stop at bridges for a number of practical reasons: to see what the flow is like; to establish whether the river has changed from the day before or over the week, depending how far you are into a particular trip; whether the water is running clear or discoloured; if any trout are on show; where the wind is coming from, and at what strength; whether bugs are hatching and, if so, what bugs; whether any fish are eating them… I could go on. So bridges have their uses, but in a strange sense, there's also something homely and intimate about deep-country bridges, something that I haven't quite put my finger on yet.

*

It dawns on most anglers over time that when they stop at a bridge and find there *aren't* any bugs hatching or any fish on show, it's almost a given that if they hang around long enough they *will* eventually find either or both. This is the main reason why bridge breaks gradually develop into more protracted stays. And, in occasional and joyful contradistinction, we sometimes do arrive at a bridge and discover a couple of decent fish out feeding in full view, maybe in the height of a nice hatch or plumb in the middle of a clear run. But that doesn't happen often, at least not in my experience – certainly not often enough to dull the exquisite thrill of the experience when it does.

Of course, trout often sit *underneath* bridges – often the better trout, as it happens – and to locate them you have to get down onto your stomach and hang precariously off a parapet to peer under it, something that over time we've become moderately practised at doing. This obviously looks odd to people who don't fish, and we've fielded some strange looks from passing motorists over the years. I've also got a standard answer in case I'm asked any of the usual questions. So a typical dialogue might go along these lines:

'So what are you guys peering under this bridge for?'

'Swallows' nests.' A half-truth, by the way.

'Okay. The wife and I thought one of your mates had fallen in.'

I suppose we could have a lot more fun if we got a little contrary, along these lines:

'So what are you guys hanging off the bridge for?'

'Well, I'm a priest and we're just checking how deep the water is before we baptise our flock.'

*

The time we typically spend on the bridges varies from a minute or two (rarely), to a full ten minutes (commonly) or even longer. It depends on the river or stream we are crossing, the amount of time on our hands, how much coffee we've brought along and, occasionally, who we're fishing with. It's also happened, though not often, that we've used a deep-country bridge on the way in to tackle up on, or on the way out as a smooth, dirt-free place to get out of wet gear and brew up a pot of coffee. And I can't recall that we ever felt guilty about using an integral part of a provincial road system as a convenient change room or makeshift kitchen, or both, which will give you an idea of the amount of traffic the bridges I'm talking about averagely carry.

I once had a long lunch on a bridge with a friend. It lasted over an hour and ended in us eventually spotting, and then catching, a really nice trout – but not from the bridge, of course. We climbed down onto the bank and caught the fish on an easy downstream drift. Fishing in the South Island, New Zealand, Fred Steynberg and I caught more than a few trout this way.

*

Some anglers don't do bridge delays at all. They'll step out, have a pee, glance at the river, and look tellingly at their watches, even tap them, to signal they want to move on. But they're rare. The majority of anglers I know can't get enough of bridges, which suggests to me that bridge fever is endemic among fly fishers – and, by implication, probably also contagious.

For example, Tony Kietzman and I once fished with an upcountry client of his who was new to fly fishing – well, relatively new – and when we stopped at the first bridge (it happened to be the one that crosses the Bell River near Moshesh's Ford), he thought, okay, this is it, this is where we're going to be fishing. When we told him we were just checking on conditions, and pointed out a few interesting features in the riverbed far below, he went off to fetch his camera. Then a kilometre or two down the road we stopped at the old iron bridge over the Kraai; we got out once again, and had another long, voyeuristic encounter with a couple of decent trout and a few yellowfish on show. We pointed out that the Sterkspruit wasn't as clear as the Bell, but that it *was* fishable. Tony's client was intrigued. He said it reminded him of opening a book, and I said, 'Yes, and you'll read a different version of the same chapter every time you open it,' meaning that what you see from the same bridge will differ from day to day and week to week – mainly only marginally, but sometimes catastrophically, like sweet-flowing one day, mud the next.

Later that afternoon on the way back from a good day's fishing, Tony's client automatically reached for his camera each time we slowed down at a bridge. He was clearly showing signs of becoming a convert.

*

I'm often tempted to fish off a bridge, but I haven't succumbed (with one exception, which I'll come to), either because I didn't have rightful access to the water, or because I surrendered to the wave of moralistic high-ground stuff that says catching fish off bridges is seriously unsporting. Whatever your view, you'd have to agree that hooking a fish from a bridge is one thing; landing it humanely after that is another, unless you can easily get down into the river, which mainly you can't. And even without fences or steep banks to negotiate, getting off a bridge into a river after you've hooked a fish will take your mind off all the other important things you need to be doing in order just to land it.

And while we don't need to rethink the morality around not catching fish off bridges, I will confess to a trout I once hooked casting off the Lindisfarne Bridge on the road from *Birkhall* to Rhodes. The fish in question was around twelve inches long, holding to the side of the main current just a metre or two upstream in a hatbox-sized hole that had a minor logjam ahead of it. There was also an awkward counter-current in the hole that swirled like a spinning top. It was obvious that there was no way I could drift a fly over this trout standing anywhere *in* the river, upstream or down. Well, at least that's what I argued, perhaps in an attempt to attenuate the feeling that what I was about to do was an act of minor deceit. I also argued that, with the barbless hook I was using, and given enough slack, the fish would get off anyway, and that the *dry fly* I had on was somehow more sporting – a belief now

Lindisfarne Bridge

well beyond just doubtful. The trout had the fly in a wink. The take and the brief zigzagging run were, just as I had thought, quickly followed by a long-line release that came with a minor sense of comfort and relief.

*

On the subject of the Lindisfarne Bridge, it is one of my favourites. From upstream, there's a pretty run coming in, around fifty metres of narrow-flowing, knee-deep water, and downstream of the bridge there's a huge, slow-swirling, cavernous pool where we nearly always see large trout or yellowfish or both, gliding like phantoms in the bottle-green water. For years I spelled the bridge with an 'e', as in Lindesfarne, and no-one pointed out that I was wrong. Google will tell you that Lindisfarne is an island off the north-eastern coast of England, very near Scotland, with a castle dating back to 1550 and a population of 162 people, that it is spelled with an 'i' not an 'e', and that it is sometimes known as the Holy Island. Whatever, how this particular bridge in the middle of the Eastern Cape Highlands got its name is a mystery, and one that I'd love to unlock, but according to an authority on matters concerning the history of the Rhodes district, Dave Walker, the surveyor-general, had it down as Lindisfarne. So if we now know how to spell its name, we still don't know how it came by it, which is actually far more important really. What do they say – a bridge by any other name would be as sweet…?

*

What for want of a better name I call the 'bridge-cluster phenomenon' is an important if intermittent feature in the Eastern Cape Highlands. It comes down to congregations of many small trout that hang around in large but loose-knit schools around bridges, often both sides of the bridge. Mostly they're out on show – less hidden, I'd say, rather than plain obvious – always dancing nervously, and when they get spooked they somehow move in unison, as if the whole school is not made up of individual trout but is a single, amorphous mass.

You typically see these clusters from bridges, simply because bridges provide good vantage points. But in times like this you can bet there will be clusters of small fish in any decent pool upstream or downstream of that bridge.

It's a variable thing, but I always look on these mass gatherings of trout with a level of foreboding. As someone up here once said, you could be fooled into thinking the trout were ganging up on us. And in a sense they are, because the clusters are a clear signal that the trout have bred well, and decent lies for fish are so scarce that they take refuge in numbers rather than holing up alone in concealed places. And it's also a signal that if you don't catch anything decent that day, you'll at least catch a bucketful of fish where each is as long as your outstretched hand.

It's only when you've been up to this part of the world a few times that you start to recognise bridge-clusters for what they are. You see them when there have been preceding years of plenty, meaning good summer and late-season rains, and useful winter snowfalls – the conditions that are ideal for breeding and that lead to a general overpopulation of the rivers with small-sized trout. And the converse is true, in that in years preceded by below-average rain and snow, the cluster phenomenon is rare. So the actual importance of the clustering fish is that it's a pointer to what you can expect of the fishing in a particular season, or in a particular year, to be like. But you'll discover that soon enough anyway when you actually start fishing a river and after an hour realise you've landed and released a few dozen trout, all of them tiny.

People will tell you that in times of plenty you should throw all the tiny trout you catch into the bushes, but I never felt quite right about that. Besides, conditions like this make good dry fly practice.

So, speaking generally, we don't like years when the bridge-cluster phenomenon is pervasive because it means an abundance of small trout. And we all want to catch bigger trout, including the hard-boiled, small-stream addicts, no matter what they say. And even if we agree that 'big' is a relative term when it comes to small-stream trout, we all agree that we at least want to catch a few fish longer than our middle fingers.

*

It was a cold morning on a bridge high up in the Bokspruit River Valley. The bridge was littered with a carpet of autumn leaves spread like yellow confetti. There was no wind, and the falling leaves dropped slowly in gently twirling gyrations. The flow of water spilling under the bridge made the steady, softly sibilant, sucking sounds of a stream in good flow. We stepped out of the truck and could smell the water and the leaves, a compressed mix of cold freshness, wet loam and mulch, the air so saturated with fragrance that it made you want to breathe in deeply. Above the bridge there was a long pool of clear, thigh-deep water; below it, the stream ran white and rough.

A trout weaved in the pool above, at first not easy to see but later so obvious it seemed strange we hadn't spotted it straight off. But that's often how it happens on bridges. You have to wait and watch and keep a low profile, to be more careful than if you were actually in the stream itself. Because your profile is raised on bridges, stealth is even more important. I was with Billy de Jong, and we'd taken the trouble to park well short of the bridge before we stalked it.

We watched the fish for some minutes. It changed position slightly at times, disappearing into the shadow of an overhanging branch near the top of the pool. Then it would drift out into a patch of sunlit water again, just a matter of inches from the shade, when it was visible in liquid, semi-translucent colours that left the unmistakable, yet somehow ethereal profile of a hovering trout dancing with the currents. We celebrated the trout with a cup of coffee and kept our eyes on it, watching how its watery outline changed between the light and the shade, until our eyes got tired of looking and our mugs were drained. I told Billy that such are the blessings that reward the devoted bridge-stalkers among us.

On a more carnal note, we were tempted to put a fly over that fish, but we were on our way somewhere else a lot further upstream after other trout – a lot of other trout, we thought. Besides, neither of us really felt like unpacking the back of the cab to get to our gear. We looked at our watches. We were running late. On some small bridges time seems to stop… We reluctantly moved on. In a strange way, I guess we felt as satisfied at just finding that fish as we would have had we actually hooked it. Well, almost.

We drove slowly across the bridge, but from the passenger window Billy said the fish wasn't evident, and we discussed the value of not just slowing down on bridges but actually stopping, getting out of the vehicle, and stalking them. Crossing bridges at a crawl and peering out of the open window of a slow-moving vehicle just isn't reliable enough, not if you are a convert.

On the trip back, later in the afternoon, when the sun was low and the light was like liquid brass, there was no sign of our bridge trout. So much that concerns finding trout is a matter of light, a matter of chance and a matter of dance. Sometimes the fish just aren't out and dancing. But that can change by the hour.

*

I spoke of the Lindisfarne Bridge as *one* of my favourite bridges, which prompts the question: which is my favourite? It's the old iron bridge over the Kraai River near Moshesh's Ford, and I'd be guessing, I know, but among anglers who love fishing in the Eastern Cape Highlands, I'm sure it's the favourite bridge of many more.

It's an imposing structure: two flat-topped, roughly wagon-shaped spans of crisscrossed steel girders set on a thick metal platform, each around fifty metres long, that meet in the centre of the river where they're supported by a single, massive concrete pillar rising roughly twenty metres above the water. The abutments are set deep into the banks on either side.

Standing *in* the river looking *up* at the bridge, you get an impression of great size, strength and permanence. But *from* the bridge, looking upstream over the Kraai and to the confluence of the Bell and the Sterkspruit rivers that form it, or downstream along a long sweep of the Kraai, you could be forgiven for thinking your GPS was faulty and you had landed on some lovely river in the heart of Patagonia.

The Kraai here is impressive, not only because you're looking at it from a giddily high position but because of the river's imposing breadth. The rugged surrounding landscape adds to the illusion of grandeur and it's likely to strike you, as it always does me, that it's somehow out of keeping with our rough notion that bridges over deep-country river crossings are supposedly tiny, compact and intimate. The Kraai bridge is nothing like that. It is big, long and so high that it took me a while to conquer the mild rush of vertigo I got just leaning on the railings to scan the riverbed – never mind leaning over them to look straight down below.

Coincidentally, the bridge over the Bell River, not more than a kilometre back up the dirt road towards Rhodes, is a similar structure. The only real difference is that the central column is not made from concrete but from cut sandstone blocks, and it's even higher.

*

On the subject of favourite bridges, my friend Robin Douglas, his son Keith and I have for the past few years got hooked on visiting a tiny bridge over the upper Lourens River in Somerset West, to the extent that even if we're booked to fish a different beat than the one flowing under it, we still drive the extra ten or fifteen minutes just to check out the stream from it, and then drive back to park where we're supposed to be fishing.

It's a simple metal bridge that crosses the stream where it's less than two metres wide, and the railings are painted red. So, naturally, we call it the Red Bridge. Maybe we make a point of visiting it because it's within easy reach, but we've noticed we don't feel quite right fishing anywhere else on this river until we have stood on it and gazed into the flowing water below. I'm not entirely sure why this is, other than for a few slender but pragmatic reasons – like, the view of the stream gives us a hint about our prospects for the day's fishing, through aspects like the clarity of the water, the presence (or not) of hatches and rises. Or maybe it's because a really decent trout once held station here right under our noses for two seasons in a row. That fish mesmerised us, but then it suddenly disappeared like a passing gleam and, of course, we were convinced some devious bastard had poached it. So now a part of the reason we keep visiting this bridge is in the hope that we will find this fish has somehow miraculously returned, even if we know there's a better chance of getting tickets on Elon Musk's planned mission to Mars than ever seeing it again.

*

There's a bridge I could never end this chapter without mentioning. It's the smallest of them all and the most remote, and the most filled with intimate atmosphere, perhaps more than any other bridge I know. To put it in perspective, this is a bridge I have written about, if mainly just in passing, but always with some passion. I love this bridge because of what it means to me, where it is and how it is – because of its secreted trout, because of the memories I have of it when it was the centrepiece to all that played out in a remarkable spell of fishing. It is the bridge over the Swith Stream at the very foot of the Naude's Nek Pass: a tiny strip of worn concrete, a single, shadow-filled arch carrying a babbling flow of crystal water that, both sides of the bridge, is darkly overhung and full of mystery and small trout.

The first time I stopped here was before I knew Ed Herbst, other than by reputation as a journalist on the *Witness* newspaper in Pietermaritzburg; long before I knew Donie and Juan-Marie Naudé, who live nearby and run the guest farm *Vrederus*, and before I had met Dave Walker, or Basie and Carien Vosloo. In fact, it was back when I described Rhodes in one of my early books as 'a ghost town', when it actually *was* a ghost town. A bunch of us were on an extended fly-fishing trip in a battered VW Camper Van I owned at the time (and write about later), somewhere in the mid-1980s, when we were just discovering the delights of trout fishing in the Eastern Cape Highlands. We missed stopping at this bridge on our way over the pass, probably didn't even notice it, but we spent some time on it on the way back. I remember the stream looking so good we came close to poaching – or we did, I'm not sure any more.

Since then I have crossed this bridge going in one direction or the other around a hundred times, and only once have I failed to stop – when I happened to be crossing the pass in the dead of a night wrapped thick with fog.

CHAPTER 6

STILLWATERS IN THE DEAD OF WINTER

I do not know whether it ought to be so, but certainly
silly things do cease to be silly if they are done by sensible
people in an imprudent way. Wickedness is always wickedness,
but folly is not always folly. It depends upon
the character of those who handle it.
JANE AUSTEN, *EMMA*

We left Cape Town just as the first shards of sunlight lit the high mountains that cup the city; the truck's heater on, the tank full and the coffee flowing. It was midwinter, and I was with my friends Darryl Lampert and Chris Bladen, all of us on our third or fourth trip to Highland Lodge, a stillwater venue between Molteno and Dordrecht in the Eastern Cape. The owners, Vicky and Luke Bell, have a few productive lakes and access to a few more on nearby farms.

Nine hundred kilometres later, we were driving into Molteno ahead of a setting sun. It was August, a month still hovering with its feet in winter, a month when the landscapes up here are typically bleak and the weather is cold, dry and windy. We stopped to refuel and to stretch stiff muscles. Chris bought a jumbo packet of potato crisps, and we cracked a beer as diesel ran into our near-empty tank.

On the way up we had pulled over near Graaff-Reinet to take photographs of a distant, snow-capped mountain range. It was the first time I'd seen a snowfall in the heart of the Karoo, a strangely contrary sight in a part of the country that is mainly hot, bone-dry scrub country. In Graaff-Reinet, where we bought takeaway burgers, the wind felt like ice, and a friendly local told us the cold weather was far from over.

Midwinter trips to Highland Lodge are always cold. They lean heavily towards the spartan side of life's spectrum, in the sense that although the lodge is comfortable and has a wood-burning fireplace and an old AGA stove that warms the kitchen, the days can feel as cold as the Arctic and the nights just get a whole lot worse. At least there's electricity (until we turn off the generator at about 9pm) and gas-heated hot water in the two bathrooms. But coming across a snowfall in the middle of the Karoo pointed to this trip being even colder than our last one a year or two back. And that was cold, even by Highland Lodge standards. I remember spoons freezing solid in any dregs of coffee left overnight; I also once sketched an image of an Adams dry fly on the back window of my iced-over truck using a goose quill for a pen.

But we enjoy the winter fishing up here, not in any perverse sort of way that says if you're not actually suffering the fishing can't be good, but because in winter the water is comparatively clear, at least clearer than it is in high summer. The trout are just as big – and there are some real hogs up here – as they are at any other time of year, and the fishing *is* usually good, even though the water is cold and the hatches aren't as abundant as they are in spring and summer. Or else the fishing is usually good *because* the water is cold and hatches aren't as abundant, which goes along the lines of the overly simplistic theory that the colder it is and the less the natural food, the hungrier the fish are. It might have a compelling ring to it, but it's not an entirely watertight hypothesis.

Also, the trout are in spawning colours, and given the clarity of the water, conditions for photographing fish under the surface are cosmic, even if submerged fingers holding the camera get frozen to what feels like one step off frostbite. Bear in mind that the coldest winter temperature in South Africa was recorded on a neighbouring farm. So we also smugly believe our winter battles are harder-won here, and any trout caught is somehow more deserved, no argument.

I suppose you could also rightly read a little pseudo-masochism into all of this, and none of us regulars who visit here in midwinter would argue that's not part of it, except to say it's more a dual diagnosis, really, where the main part is plain big-fish fever. That, and the fact that there is no fly fishing quite like in the dead of winter in South Africa.

*

Rather than keep a diary on this trip, I made rough notes that, when I read them over, gave more of an impression than anything like a detailed account of the fishing. But a few things made this trip more remarkable than most, and one or two of the diary entries I made confirmed the 'dual diagnosis' I just touched on.

*

To get one thing out of the way, the fishing on this trip was superb, even by this lodge's standards, where the angling is usually on the slow side, but productive enough to keep you awake and interested all day. I guess that goes for the outcomes you can expect on most extended fishing trips anywhere around the world, other than a few high-octane destinations, such as Jurassic Lake in Argentina or Alphonse Island in the Seychelles.

On previous trips here, most days the trout were sporadically on the prod; on a few the fishing was one long, dreary battle, punctuated by occasional hook-ups. I guess what I'm saying is the fishing at Highland Lodge is never consistently hectic. I'm talking of the winter months – June, July and August. I've never done a trip in one of our more traditional stillwater months, like October or November, when the water is warmer and, I guess, the fishing is a little better. Then again, much depends on the amount of rain they've had, because droughts are not uncommon in this part of the world, and once the lakes start losing water and bare earth shows around their edges, the angling falls off. In fact, in really bad years I've known Vicky and Luke to close their lakes altogether.

The main point about Highland Lodge is that in good seasons you are always in with a chance of catching fish of between seven and ten pounds, as opposed to just a 'good' stillwater trout of four to five pounds. There have been years when trout over twelve pounds have been caught but, again, that's not anything you can bank on happening more than just occasionally. The mere fact that it *is* on the cards, though, adds a nice edge of anticipation to every cast you make, and probably accounts for why we stay out fishing until the sun sinks below the hills when, by loose medical criteria, we are probably hovering on the fringes of hypothermia.

*

When we arrived at the lodge on this trip, the snow had followed us from Graaff-Reinet. Hilltops were capped white, and the branches of the old pine trees around the house sagged under the weight of snow. Vicky said more bad weather was on the way, and added that she and Luke had been snowed in for a week before we arrived, unable to move out of their house.

*

So we geared up in the usual midwinter Highland Lodge way, meaning we wore multiple layers of technical clothing, fleece-lined gloves, beanies, UV-protecting buffs, chest waders with chest straps locked tight. Our float tubes were pumped to just the right pressure for the icy weather, and we all carried on-board flasks of hot coffee or soup. I could go on. It's a performance. By the time we get everything done, we somehow feel that when we do eventually hook and land a fish we deserve it – more than any trout caught wading a small stream with a light stick on a sunny day.

We've built up something of a routine to our fishing on these trips, and it's now almost cast in stone. We leave the house after a good breakfast, each with a thermos of coffee and maybe a few rusks or biscuits, then come back for a late brunch, boil up more coffee or maybe soup, add a roll or two, then go out again, possibly changing from one lake to another, depending on how we're doing. We press on until the sun starts to sag, then pack up in the last of its light. It's usually dark when we're done.

During the day we beach our tubes for regular breaks to warm up, fix rigs, change flies, always sitting in the lee of a vehicle if there's a wind blowing, and on most days there is. Often we need to add air to the tubes because they soften as the temperature drops. We sip hot coffee, maybe snack on something, maybe check leaders and tippets, always interrogate strategies. We scroll through the LCD screens on our cameras to see what pictures we got right – or, with the underwater shots, more often where we got things crazily wrong because, to the last, we are all SLR fans.

By the time the sun has dropped and we've beached – *never before* – sipping Old Brown Sherry or adding a dram of whisky to our coffee feels more like a necessity than a pleasant ritual. In the end someone will lift the float tubes onto the truck's roof racks and secure them with rope. We leave our small forest of fly rods set up and carefully tie them down on the soft surface of a float tube, then head home, hoping not to be the guy who has to get out to open and close the gates. (By the way, I say 'never before' we beach our float tubes, because liquor and float tubing make dangerous companions.)

Back at the lodge we set the rods up in a safe corner of the lounge, hang our waders off a curtain rail and lean the float tubes against a wall in the dining room so they don't freeze solid overnight. Then we light the log fire, pull off wet waders, shed damp clothing and get into a pair of sheepskin slippers. With the fire lit, wet clothing gets draped around the fireplace. Someone pours drinks, and two or more of us will be on kitchen duty preparing the evening meal, mostly a simple stew or a hot, filling pasta, always with plenty of buttered bread and maybe a salad. The dining-room table is cleared of fly-tying stuff and prepared for the meal. Dishes of food are brought in, dinner plates are heaped alongside uncorked bottles of wine, and a vast array of condiments appears, mostly hot.

Before going to bed, we boil water on the AGA stove in a huge, battered kettle, fill hot-water bottles from it, pull on headlamps, turn off the generator and hit the sack wearing as many layers of night clothes as we can fit into. By then the temperature will be minus something. In fact, it's often around -10°C.

The only thing I haven't mentioned are our regular evening calls to family or friends. We have to make them from a particular spot on the far corner of the wooden deck that extends off the dining room. It's the only place where you get an erratic sliver of cellphone reception, unless you drive a few kilometres down the road until you are in line with a certain fence post. I am not making this up.

As for the fly fishers we invite to join us, we don't like moaners. We also don't do people who aren't bothered to contribute a little work for the collective good of the rest, like laying the fire, cooking a meal or generally tidying up the place. We also don't do people who aren't interested in fishing on account of the weather. We like committed fly fishers, because the more people go out fishing, the more likely we are to find out what the trout are doing and where any new hotspots might be.

On this trip, Gerrit Redpath travelled down from Bloemfontein to join us. He's just the sort of cheerful and optimistic fishing buddy you want to have on these trips. Even better, he's a really great fly fisher.

*

I wouldn't describe Highland Lodge as being in breathtaking scenery. It's surrounded by the distant Stormberg Mountains, which aren't strikingly impressive. The setting is rolling grasslands, typical of high-lying, semi-Karoo cattle- and sheep-farming country. If it has a beauty, then it's more in the sense of its sparseness and isolation, rather than the sort of rugged grandeur you find in some fishing landscapes in this country. But we like it as it is, and the sunrises and sunsets on winter days when there's been a lot of wind and there's dust in the air are spectacular. The other blessing is you won't see any anglers other than those in your own party.

*

The details on trips like this tend to blur when it comes to catching trout, unless you're keeping a diary, which as I said I wasn't, at least not in the strict sense. But in the final analysis, it would be fair to say we caught a heap of lovely fish, all but one of them rainbows.

The brown trout here are mostly confined to Bernard's, a large lake around three kilometres from the lodge, and one other stillwater called Syd's, a little further down the road from Bernard's. We fished Syd's one day until a storm drove us off, but none of us caught a trout, let alone a brown trout. From recent reports the lake had been off, and we consoled ourselves by saying we had just confirmed it. (I've since heard Syd's, which for a long while was an enigma in that it didn't produce any trout at all, is again producing really good trout.)

When you fish for six days on the trot and end up being uncertain what day of the week it is, all you remember later are the highlights, and that often boils down to a few particular fish that were memorable for one reason or another, not just because they happened to be big. Then, of course, you remember the string of notable events that always seem to surface on extended trips.

On this visit, the snow around the house helped to make the trip memorable, and we put it to good use with our cameras. We photographed rods, landing nets and flies in the snow; then, being snow-struck South Africans, we ended up throwing snowballs at one another. Then there was my kiddies' boat, a bright-yellow canoe-shaped inflatable craft that I brought with a view to transporting my cameras and lenses alongside my float tube. The theory was I would have easy access to my camera equipment (two DSLR cameras and three lenses on average), given that the pouches on my float tube aren't really roomy enough for what *I* consider essential stillwater camera gear (but that most people would describe as extravagant overkill). Worse, the pouches aren't waterproof, and in choppy conditions they soon become worryingly damp.

We named my new craft 'Worms for Sale', and wrote the name in bold letters along both sides with a black Koki pen.

The third notable thing about this trip was the dunking of two seriously expensive cameras and lenses in one day, first by Gerrit then, hot on his heels, by Darryl. The latter's was the result of a leaking camera case that he stows behind the backrest of his float tube. How it leaked is anyone's guess, but when he beached and opened it, a small waterfall poured out of it. Gerrit's was due to a problem I will describe later. Both sets of gear were dried back at the house in the oven. Sadly, Darryl's lens didn't survive. Gerrit was luckier, and recovered both his lens and camera. Then, later in the week, I dropped my Zeiss binoculars into the shallows on Bernard's, and warmed them in the oven thinking they would come right. They might have, had I remembered to turn the oven off. They got cooked beyond repair. 'Nuked' is the term Chris used.

The final theme of this trip, which was particularly cold and harsh even by Highland Lodge standards, with winds that cut through our jackets like iced nails, was an expression Chris came up with, a statement that had to be viewed in the dire circumstances of the weather. The version edited for younger readers was, 'Hey… Harden up a little!'

Picture the scene. We would arrive back at night frozen to the bone, and someone might complain a bit about having to haul ice-covered float tubes off the truck, and Chris would quickly be in with his chirp, 'Hey… Harden up a little!'

The prevailing conditions gave him ample opportunity to bark out his command, though always with a wry smile on his face. Soon we all took to it – in no time we were chanting the instruction to anyone who showed the slightest hint of weakening, or offered any suggestion that conditions were getting more than usually rough.

*

I do remember one fish from this particular visit among the many I was lucky to land. It happened to be the first fish of the day on the first day of the trip. We'd all just launched and were bobbing out in the bay on the northern edge of Spurwing, a large lake a kilometre from the lodge. The water was clear, and the wind was strong enough to put a smooth swell on the surface and make my kick-boat rock gently. I'd set up my default stillwater rig, the product of habit, laziness and some empirical experience. It's worked for years more often than not, and when it does work, it's more fun than catching a fish on a fast-stripped streamer on a sinking line. It boils down to a 5-weight floater, a 12-foot leader, plus three feet of 3X fluorocarbon tippet with a size 12 neutral-density Red-Eyed Dragonfly Nymph on the end, meaning the fly is unweighted, but it has an under-body of wool that gradually soaks up water, so you can control the sink rate. When you squeeze water out of the fly it's fairly buoyant; when it's soaked it sinks, but not unnaturally fast.

I was in water about two metres deep. Scattered islands of weed showed at the surface. From where I was sitting, the lake ran from the far shore towards me in a long, ever-deepening slope of water laced with weed-beds. It was the sort of place to position yourself to intercept trout traffic coming in from deeper water to feed in the shallows, or the other way around; I'm not sure that it matters.

I had made a few casts and was settling in, adjusting and arranging various items around me, making myself comfortable, much like a dog fidgets its way around its bed in seemingly purposeless circles before settling in. 'Worms' was tied to the left of my float tube, and I could see already the lightness of the craft was going to be a problem. I kept having to readjust the attachment to the tube to prevent the wind swinging her in front of me. In the end, I worked it all out and fished the water in a fan-shaped spread of casts, with my back to the wind and the anchor holding. That's when I saw a decent-sized fish swim up lazily to within a foot of the surface, and then slowly turn and sink, moving from my left to my right about five metres off, leaving a small, dome-shaped depression in the water. It was as clear as daylight.

The trout had obviously taken something just below the surface. It's not often in a lake that you get to see sub-surface feeding like this so clearly. I gently lifted the fly line and dropped the nymph two metres ahead of the fish's path and left it to sink. The leader winked with light as the fly slowly drifted down. I steeled myself not to retrieve too early. When I imagined the fly was around a metre deep, I straightened the leader until the fly line was moving, then gently lifted the rod tip in a slow, even, upward arc, dropped the tip once more, then lifted again and actually saw the fish take the fly just a foot beneath the surface and not more than four metres from me.

It was a deliciously strong, visceral pull that you instantly know is a good, well-hooked fish. To my delight it turned and made straight for the deep water. The fight was first the long, dogged, far-out, head-shaking struggle that I thought was a cock fish, but then it ran and left the water in two lovely leaps. I heard Chris shout something from a distance that sounded like the muffled words of congratulation, but when I looked back I saw that his rod also had a deep bend in it. In the net my trout was a green-backed hen fish, with red flanks and gill plates as bright as a sunset. It was not quite seven pounds, but near enough not to matter. It was the way that fish had started my trip that mattered more.

*

'Worms' was saved a day later by Gerrit. We were on Bernard's. I had beached, wanting to make some adjustments to the small craft. I say small, but it was all of four feet long and about one-and-a-half deep; still, no more than a cheap kiddies' canoe. I carefully packed the cameras away and untied the craft from the float tube, and was pouring a mug of coffee on the tailgate of the truck when a sudden gust got under 'Worms' and sent her tumbling bow over stern across the lake. It stopped for a moment about two hundred metres away as it hit the far bank where Gerrit happened to be anchored. Then it took off again and was blown up a grass-covered hillside. Gerrit quickly beached his tube and went in hot pursuit of the tumbling canoe until he pinned it down with a flying tackle.

It was at this same spot, a day or two later, that Gerrit hooked a decent trout close to the shoreline. He had his camera around his neck, a Canon 7D, with a serious lens on it. He was leaning forward to net the fish when a gust of wind got under the back of his float tube and upended it, depositing him and his camera into the water. Fortunately, he was only a metre or two from the shoreline where it was shallow enough – if only just – for him to get onto his feet and not have to swim. In waders and in a full set of thick clothing, with the water at about eight degrees, his life would have been a lottery. Like a wet fowl in a thunderstorm, Gerrit paddled back to the parked trucks. We happened to be on the bank at the time drinking coffee and saw the accident happen. Through chattering teeth, and standing in a pool of water slowly spreading around his wet legs, Gerrit said he was lucky the water was shallow enough to stand in. He muttered something about being cold and needing hot coffee, which I think is when Chris said, 'Hey… Harden up!' But I can't be sure, other than to say it would have been such an irresistible opportunity to get the chirp in that he's hardly likely to have missed the chance.

It was a sobering lesson, and one you might want to keep in mind the next time you lean forward in your float tube with your back to a strong wind. Think about it.

*

One of the real problems with long leaders on lakes – or, for that matter, on rivers with sizeable fish – is that the knot connecting the leader to the line can get stuck in the tip-eye of the rod when the fish is still too far out to net. It is possible to overcome this by using Super Glue Needle Knots, where the end of the leader is coated with glue, then pulled up the tip of the fly line by at least a centimetre. The protruding stump of leader is carefully trimmed with a scalpel and the joint is covered in a layer of Loon's UV Knot Sense, providing a smooth surface that easily slips through the eyes of a fly rod. This allows you to get a big fish close enough to your tube to net. If you don't trust a Super Glue Needle Knot on very large fish, and some people don't, you can coat a standard Nail Knot or a Needle-and-Nail-Knot combination, with a tapering layer of Knot Sense.

*

We revisited Spurwing, and caught enough fish on and off all day not to bother moving to another lake. But we did head back for brunch. Sometimes these are modest meals, but mostly they are extravagant enough to suggest we pay little attention to our respective cholesterol levels when we're up here. Besides, we argue that you burn fat rapidly in cold weather. But then it also strikes me that in all the years we've been fishing this place we've never returned after a week's fishing without a mountain of leftover food. We always end up over-catering, mainly because we don't plan things like meals as well as we plan the fishing. But we do understand that running out of food up here would be a serious hardship, so we don't take any risks.

*

One morning on Bernard's, the wind blew so strongly that it pulled up my anchor often enough to become an irritation. Yet we caught a heap of decent fish, Gerrit's the best, a near double-figure trout. There's something about high winds on lakes that often seems to improve the fishing. It's a combination of things. The wave action dislodges nymphs from weed-beds, high winds blow terrestrials onto the water, and waves add oxygen. Finally, to help shore up my hypothesis, trout feeding at the surface in choppy conditions have more cover from predators. You want to fish the windward shoreline though. Whatever, you don't want to miss out fishing a lake because the wind is too fierce.

*

Spurwing is marginally more protected from the wind than Bernard's, and on this trip it was particularly productive, so we spent more time here than on the other lakes. But there was a day when Vicky said she'd lead us out to a small lake about twenty kilometres west of her farm that, from recent reports, promised great fishing. It seemed no colder than usual when we left the house that morning, planning on meeting Vicky fourteen kilometres away where the dirt road from Highland Lodge joins the R56 highway. But for some reason we couldn't get my truck to move at anything more than walking pace, even with my foot flat on the pedal and the gear lever in high range. I thought the turbocharger might have blown, but a passing farmer stopped, wound down his window and after hearing the problem said, 'Just let her warm up. The diesel's frozen to jelly in your tank. Or maybe light a few coals under the tank to warm it up.'

Look, I can't exactly vouch for the accuracy of the farmer's diagnosis, but I do have three witnesses. We did eventually make it to the highway with the truck gradually picking up speed – and we never gave a moment's thought to putting burning coals under the gas tank. Nor should you.

We followed Vicky to the promised lake. It looked magnificent: islands of healthy green weed in water as clear as a spring creek, certainly the clearest lake I've ever seen in this district. It was one of those bright-sky windless days when you wouldn't be surprised to see a hatch come off, even in midwinter. The lake was relatively shallow, just four metres or so at its deepest near the wall, and averaging around two metres for the rest, so I figured I'd find a few trout if I walked its entire length looking for them. I did the walk, but I didn't see a fish. That worried me. And in two hours of fishing, when we tried every trick in the book, none of us had so much as a follow. We called it a day and were off the farm and back at the house in time to fix ourselves a late lunch. We wondered if a flock of cormorants hadn't cleaned the lake out, even wondered whether we'd maybe fished the wrong lake, but Vicky had left us right on the water's edge saying we would have a marvellous day. So the mystery of that lake remains, more so because the water looked so promising. Vicky could hardly believe her ears when she came over that evening and heard the news.

*

There was an afternoon on Spurwing when Chris and I took a few trout from the bank. It was an ice-cold, cloudless day, but the sun was warm on our backs. It was so unusual that, at one stage, it felt as if there was someone standing behind me ironing my shirt.

We had found a promontory, a narrow slice of land just beyond the wall that ran twenty metres out from the shoreline. On either side there were lovely expanses of water, with large, bottle-green holes edged with walls of thick weed. It looked like perfect holding water, and Chris and I both believe we know the real thing when we see it. Sometimes we're right, and a good-looking stretch produces fish and confirms our faith in our ability to be the hunter-gatherers nature intended, but sometimes we fail, mostly, if not always, for reasons we don't fully understand. I've learnt that no matter how good a piece of water looks, how good the day is, whatever the reputation of the water, a large slice of what will happen when you fish it is in the lap of the gods. Or, put differently, it's only decided when you finally put a fly in the water.

We rigged bloodworm imitations under large DDDs, and did well enough from the pier to draw the attention of Darryl and Gerrit, who had either seen our regularly bent rods or heard our frequent whoops of delight. They came paddling over in their float tubes like hyenas homing in on a kill. And they were both soon into fish. So for the rest of the trip we often made for this spot. We either fished it very well, or it was full of hordes of hungry trout that would eat anything – I'm not sure which, but it scarcely ever disappointed. There were times when it went quiet, sure, when we gave some thought to changing flies, and times it went so still that we actually did change flies. But for the most part, the spot continued to perform as well as, if not better than, any of the other hotspots on this particular lake – like the gently shelving bay on the northern end of Spurwing where I had caught that first fish I spotted on day one, or those corners of deep water on either end of the wall on Spurwing that hardly ever fail.

*

We could start a long, serious discourse about hotspots on lakes and say they exist because that's where fish like hanging out, or they exist because that's where anglers have been told most fish are caught and so fish them to exclusion. Given the laws of probability, the more anglers fish a so-called 'hotspot', the more likely they will catch fish and perpetuate the conviction that they were right. But, on balance, I'm a firm believer that trout do like certain spots in a lake, even if we can't always understand why, though the availability of food must be a commonality. It's a topic that reminds me of an interview I once watched years back on television, in which a lady psychologist was trying to get behind a hardened bank robber's inner thinking. After a long discussion, she finally wrapped up by asking the most telling question of her whole show. Leaning forward and looking serious, she asked, 'So, Fred, tell us, *why* do you rob banks?' And he replied, straight-faced, 'Well, lady, because that's where they keep the money.'

In general, though, hotspots are the places of *interface*: where deep water meets shallow; along the rocky edges of the wall; where weeds abut clear water; where deep water is backed by reeds; where stony outcrops drop off into depth; where quick water meets still water, as at inlets; or where the water is cooler, say at a particular depth or, less commonly, where an underground spring comes into a lake.

So it was that we came to like the pier on Spurwing, fishing the two bays each side of it or the deeper gutters straight ahead of the pier, from tubes or off the bank, it didn't seem to matter.

One evening, as the sun was setting, I got a few good photographs of Chris on the pier, landing a fish in a pool of water lit gold by the setting sun. He then held the fish high out of the water so I could shoot a close-up of it against the background of a full moon in a pink evening sky. We quickly released the trout. The air temperature was dropping rapidly and, later, when Chris picked up his landing net, it was frozen solid. For a laugh he held the net upside down above his head where it stood straight up, as black and as pointed as a witch's hat.

By then our lines were frozen in the guides of our rods. And we felt just as frozen. Bouncing back to the house, we had the truck's heater blowing gales of hot air through hissing dashboard vents, air that smelled vaguely of coffee grounds and wet waders, a sort of humid, sun-baked smell but not unpleasant. Someone moaned about having to get out of the warm truck to open a gate, and as we drove through, Chris dropped the window and shouted, 'Hey… Harden up!'

*

I was in a tube fishing around the pier one afternoon when I had two follows from decent fish, and I hooked them both, something that doesn't happen as often as it should, mainly because of technique. When I see a fish following my fly, my rule is to immediately stop the retrieve, but not for more than a second. I figure that the sudden halt gets the fish wondering and momentarily puts it off balance. The next step is then to immediately accelerate the retrieve using the rod tip, not your line hand. You want to get in a quick but long and smooth acceleration of the rod tip and, importantly, you don't want the fly to *lift*. If it does lift, the fish will look up and see you. So don't accelerate the fly by lifting your rod straight up. That will bring you and, importantly, also your moving arm and the rod, into the fish's field of vision. Bring your rod tip back flat, quick and low, almost parallel to the water surface and off to one side. That way the fly also changes direction *away* from you. Chances are the fish won't see you or your rod and will be inclined to take what it interprets as fleeing prey. Well, that's the theory.

*

We were leaving the next day, and I'd say it was one of the coldest nights I remember up here. We took time that evening to pack up, prepared an eclectic mix for dinner from most of whatever was left over, drained a few bottles of wine, and staggered to bed far later than usual. Needless to say, we didn't leave on schedule the next morning.

A return trip to forget
We were back again the following year, also in August, along with the rest of the party. This time a young fellow called Jean Bence, a friend of Darryl's, drove up in a BMW – a sleek, low-clearance, three-litre model. How he made it over the rough-rutted dirt road to Highland Lodge in that thing I'm not sure. But out on the highway Darryl told me that Jean apparently hits the pedal in a big way. In fact, he had to head home early on this trip; he left just after sunrise and made the 900-kilometre drive back to Cape Town in time for late afternoon tea.

*

I was determined to take the best photographs I ever had up there, but trout were less plentiful than the previous year, though on average bigger. It didn't snow, but a local resident we fell into conversation with in Molteno on the way home said it was way too cold and dry to snow. I'm not sure about that; it's not the first time I have heard it said, but I do know that I have never had a worse trip to Highland Lodge from a fishing point of view. I also didn't get many memorable photographs, caught fewer trout than ever and picked up a bug. It was one of those trips where the more I tried, the less I succeeded – reminiscent of the saying that you can't squeeze a tomato ripe. To make matters worse, I started to get a sore throat on the drive up. I convinced myself it was a figment of my imagination but a day into the trip I realised it was the real thing. I even spent time not fishing at all, just soaking up the winter sunshine that filled the lounge while I tied flies and swallowed medicine. I didn't even feel that up to tying flies at first, but eventually I did produce a few size 16 Soft Hackles that never hooked a fish.

The first time I felt well enough to get out fishing, I parked my tube right behind Chris's. In fact, we connected them with a piece of light rope. I had my camera at the ready, intending to get the perfect wide-angle shot of an angler with a leaping trout. My Canon was set on a fast shutter speed, and I had the wide-angle lens on it. But the trout Chris finally hooked just wouldn't leap, though I did get a lovely picture of him in his floppy hat, hunched forward, arm held high, his rod deeply bent and his line straight and tight into a huge up-welling of water in the middle distance that the hooked trout had left behind.

Only two other photographs from this trip really stood out. One was a backlit shot of Jean playing a fish near sunset, where he's standing in his own glowing reflection; the other was of Darryl, again just before sunset, seemingly in deep meditation or asleep, I'm not sure which, on Bernard's. He was lying back in his float tube just off the bank in water as flat as glass and coloured gold by the last light, the reflections of his float tube and his two fly rods all in seemingly perfect and tranquil symmetry.

*

We tried the long drive up to Greywing, a small lake high in the hills above Spurwing. The track ends in a small upland dale that holds this pretty piece of water. Gerrit attached a GoPro camera to the front fender of his Land Cruiser. It gave a surreal, otherworldly perspective to the drive up. Travelling into the mountains through grasslands, we are always on the lookout here for Rudd's Lark, endemic to the area and rare – but we weren't in luck.

We've had plenty of lovely fish from this lake over the years, and it's small enough to lend a cosy feeling of intimacy. But when we arrived at the lake we immediately realised it had 'turned', a term used for an inversion, when the lower level of water lifts to the top, bringing up clouds of silt from the lake bed. It's not something I know much about, but this normally crystalline lake was now dishwater-grey. We threw a few desultory test casts, then poured mugs of coffee that we sipped sitting on the faded-yellow hull of an upended rowing boat. We swilled out the mugs, loaded our gear and headed out. We decided this lake would come right, but not for a few months.

*

The person who excelled on this trip was Darryl, using a few interesting fishing techniques applied with his usual dogged determination, and when he did take time out to warm up with a mug of hot coffee, it was never for longer than it needed to be.

The fishing was tough compared to previous years, and catching fish with anything like regularity – meaning one or two fish every few hours – needed commitment and studied concentration, as much as sound presentation and the right flies for a variety of stillwater techniques. I decided that it was the kind of fishing where you needed a lot of faith in yourself, and mine had temporarily deserted me. It was generally tough going and cold, and as the sun

YET MORE SWEET DAYS

sank and the air temperatures fell through the floor, our fortifying slugs of Old Brown Sherry or hot, black coffee, laced or otherwise, again seemed even more like essentials for survival than comforting indulgences that I referred to earlier in this chapter.

*

The essence of success in stillwater fly fishing is finding fish – or, to be more precise, finding the depth at which they're feeding. In winter it varies more than it does in summer, when on hot days they tend to sit deep and move into the surface layers only when the day cools. In winter they can be anywhere from right on the bottom to feeding on the surface or, more often, feeding a metre or so below the surface in what I call the 'mid-water'. In winter, the mid-water is one of the main target depths for me, especially near weeded areas.

Darryl tried a number of different techniques that we soon all latched onto because his success was contagious, proving yet again that fly fishing is at least in part a communicable disease. It's not that he threw conventional methods out of the window, like fishing a single size 6 streamer with a variable retrieve on a floating line or on an intermediate line – even, at times, a sinking line. He did. He also used dragon- and damselfly imitations, and other nymph patterns, fished on a floating line with a long leader and slow retrieve. He also used a New Zealand rig with, say, a DDD trailing a bloodworm imitation, or a Flashback Nymph. He did all those things, the things countless stillwater anglers worldwide have done before, and will do forevermore.

The only thing I'd say about Darryl is he isn't as keen on fishing a large dry fly as a prospecting pattern on stillwaters, at least not as keen as I am. Before this trip he'd been pretty conventional in his approach or, put differently, as technical as the conditions dictated he needed to be. But now a few modern English stillwater tactics appeared in his arsenal. He used teams of really small flies and, occasionally, added Boobies and Blobs. But his 'wash line' of three patterns, either tiny nymphs or a mix of soft hackle patterns, or a combination of both, was intriguing for the *size* of the flies on which he was catching really decent-sized fish. They were anything from size 16 to 18, even 20.

There was a time back in the late 1970s and early '80s when we experimented on stillwaters in the Dargle lakes in KwaZulu-Natal with small nymphs, mainly olive-coloured Gold-Ribbed Hare's Ears and midge pupa imitations in sizes 12 and 14. We fished these singly and as naturally as possible, and although we had some success using these patterns, especially the suspended midge pupa, I don't think we followed through or pursued the minimalist, imitative, stillwater option anywhere near as fully as we should have back then. This was partly due to the effectiveness of the Red-Eyed Damsel Nymph at the time, various dragonfly nymph imitations, including the Neutral Density (ND) Dragon, the DDD and, before that, a host of attractors and streamers like the John Beams Woolly Worm and the Red Setter.

Years back, English stillwater anglers, led by the likes of Tom Ivens, Dick Walker and Arthur Cove (who popularised a deep-fished PTN-like nymph and using teams of flies) and, less far back, competition anglers like Brian Ledbetter (a two-times world champion), incrementally changed the approach to stillwater fly fishing. They used smaller flies, often in teams, including nymphs, soft hackle patterns, egg patterns and a wide variety of midge pupa imitations, often in varying weights and on variable but controlled drifts, so as to tick all the depth and movement boxes. Then there was the arrival of a sort of fault line in stillwater patterns that came with the use of 'aberrant' flies (if you'll excuse the term because I can't think of any better) that in some quarters were – and still are – frowned upon, and these included the use of Blobs and the Boobies.

I think these views and pronouncements are unwarranted or, worse, just reflect self-serving bias. Blobs (spun yarn on a hook, rather like a large, elongated egg pattern) and Boobies (nymphs, often with bright marabou tails and two large foam eyes to keep the fly buoyant) are every bit as legitimate as Woolly Buggers or Strip Leech patterns, and for the same reason – namely that all fly fishing is a simple act of subterfuge, and subterfuge is not easily or comfortably subject to any moralistic pronouncements on its grades of decency or legitimacy. Subterfuge is subterfuge. Full stop. In other words, fishing a size 22 Parachute Adams or, conversely, a Blob or a Booby to a feeding stillwater trout – or any other fish for that matter – is still subterfuge. You have to get over yourself if you believe otherwise. That closes that sermon for the day.

But the teams of small flies did especially well, and for a while on this trip there was some frenetic tying of micro-sized nymphs and soft hackle patterns during the mid-morning lulls when we were back at the house for brunch or, less often, after dinner.

Also popular on this visit was a bloodworm imitation I came up with, tied on a grub hook with UTC's red Vinyl Rib, augmented with a few turns of red holographic tinsel and with a turn or two of peacock herl at the head. It seemed to work well enough on the previous trip fished static a metre below a buoyant dry fly, like the DDD, but for some reason if it worked for the others on this trip, it didn't do much for me. I remained with poor score cards, comparatively speaking, the entire time we were there.

What crosses your mind more than once on trips like this with plenty of blank sessions is, when is the right time to change a fly? Given my poor showing, I thought about it a lot as I was bobbing fishless yet again on those wide expanses of well-stocked trophy waters. At the time, I was also reading one of Ted Leeson's books, *Inventing Montana*, in which he raises this very question. Should you change flies after twenty minutes of not catching, or after an hour?

He comes to no answer – except to point out that it's a question that doesn't really have an answer. Well, not technically speaking. As he so skilfully describes it, it is something that depends on the person rather than on the fishing, meaning there are anglers who change flies at the drop of a hat, and those who resolutely hang on to the same pattern come what may. But he recognises, quite rightly I believe, that most of us fall into a group between these two extremes, though the longer we fish, the more we tend to lean to the side of measured persistence. But there is one exception.

During spells when the fishing is slow, we immediately attach huge importance to the fly that any angler nearby catches a fish on. It's almost a given. Think of the most common question you're asked by a neighbouring fly fisher when you catch a fish. It has to be, 'What fly did you get it on?' If you answer 'A Gold-Ribbed Hare's Ear', you can bet that nine out of ten anglers will make the change.

This rule holds good for most of us, but as we gain experience, we learn to look at *how* someone is fishing that fly, *what line* he's using, *where* he's fishing, *how deep*, exactly what *size* Gold-Ribbed Hare's Ear he's using, his *leader and tippet dynamics*, his *retrieve technique*, and more. It's one of the reasons that, when I'm fishing up at Highland Lodge, I take breaks when other people take a break, so I can get detailed information from them. And it's just as important to ask what anglers are doing when they *aren't* catching fish – because that's as vital to know as what they're doing when they *are*.

There are of course days when many different strategies will be working at the same time, sometimes wildly disparate strategies, which underscore the fact that successful fishing frequently doesn't involve just a single successful formula but a multiplicity of them, especially in stillwater fly fishing.

All of this has to be balanced against the consistently better performance of some individuals, not only on a particular day or on a particular trip, but season in and season out. This, I think, has less to do with particular fly patterns than with countless other skills – like aspects of presentation and retrieve, including the ability to quickly establish the right depth to fish at; long experience that lends a deep, empirical understanding of just what you should be doing, where on a lake you should be doing it and why. Then there is something some anglers have – and some never acquire – that we can safely call 'fish sense', which speaks to the fact that there is a lot about success in angling that is the result of natural intuition and the right temperament (but especially the intuitive bit).

*

On the western bank of Bernard's is one of those 'hotspots' I was talking about. It's a submerged platform of rock halfway on the bank opposite the wall and not far from where you have to park. It runs about two metres off the shoreline at a gentle angle towards the shallows, suddenly dropping off into deeper water all the way along. You can wade to it through water about mid-thigh to waist-deep, and can end up fishing off a rim of solid stone in ankle-deep water, which you don't want to do. Best is to cast from behind the cover of the wall of rocks into the water that drops off just beyond; or to anchor your float tube near this spot so you can fish parallel to the rocks in the corridor of deep water running just off them, casting as close to the rocks as you can without hanging up. I lost a heavy fish there from my tube on this trip, and watched Chris land a honey not ten metres from where I was fishing, both of us using bloodworm imitations. Then late one afternoon, Darryl anchored his tube at this spot. He wasn't three metres off the shoreline, and he sat there fishing a bloodworm imitation until the evening light ran out. I'd be guessing as to how many fish he hooked in the patient two hours he stayed in exactly the same spot, but it wasn't less than three, and all of them were well over five pounds.

*

There was a bright, sun-filled morning when we loaded gear into my truck and into Gerrit's Land Cruiser filled with optimism for what the day promised, only to find the Land Cruiser as dead as a shot duck. Jump-starting from my Hilux would be a minor formality, we thought, but it turned out to be anything but. In fact, we got nowhere until we read the instructions in the Land Cruiser's handbook. It happens that the negative lead attachment for this Land Cruiser is a very specific and somewhat obscure little bolt, and unless you do things exactly by the book you won't charge the battery. We got his engine running and had a pleasant, relatively wind-free day's fishing; for a change I took some nice trout. We planned on leaving the water early to pack before heading home at first light the following morning. In the end we just fished as usual until it was dark, and had a later-than-expected start the next day.

*

Darryl was back at Highland Lodge the following year, also in August, with Gerrit and Jean. Chris and I had to miss the trip for family reasons, but from what we heard the fishing was not up to standard. In fact, they caught very few trout. When you have missed out on a trip, in a strangely selfish way this can sound like good news – well, at least better than hearing you missed out on a trip where the trout ate dry flies all day and averaged ten pounds.

CHAPTER 7

BARKLY EAST, SEPTEMBER 2011, AND FURTHER FLIRTATIONS WITH TENKARA

Rivers, like women, have a personality all their own,
and on the whole they run true to form.
Of course, it takes time and intimacy to weigh this up,
and the process is both interesting and instructive.
OLIVER KITE, *A FISHERMAN'S DIARY*

The drive up to Barkly East from Cape Town was characterised by a lot more than just the rote boredom of sitting behind a wheel as endless kilometres of highway belt by. This trip was punctuated by multiple stop-and-go hold-ups for ongoing roadworks between Laingsburg and Beaufort West, where the irritating delays inevitably exceeded the ten minutes the signboards optimistically announced. In fact, people got out of their cars, stretched, and generally looked tired and irritable. At one stop, a lady stepped out of her car with a pair of binoculars and enthusiastically scanned the Karoo veld for birds. I took note. It beat sitting in the heat, staring into space.

It was spring, and the Karoo was alive with wildflowers. They decorated the roadsides in bursts of colour that compensated for the tedious processions of heavily laden trucks that rumbled past at each of the forced delays. I wondered what birds the lady had spotted; taking her cue, I slipped my binoculars out of the cubby hole just as the long row of cars I was stuck in got waved through. But the binoculars came in useful later.

I had a pleasant overnight stay with Mike and Candy Ferrar on *Mount Melsetter*. We had a customary glass or two of cold white wine on the veranda while a pair of White-throated Swallows watched us from the same nest they'd used the summer before, and then enjoyed a slow dinner of a perfectly done leg of lamb.

I was about to leave the next morning when Mike remarked that the roads were in bad shape and said I should drive carefully. He was right. Just beyond Steynsburg the R66 crumbled into a scattered mosaic of potholes. I saw an upmarket German sedan abandoned on the side of the road fifty kilometres out of Steynsburg, both its low-profile front tyres blown out. I'd come across potholes on this route before, but they had since multiplied to the point where they turned the road into a lottery. I stopped at a lay-by for a mug of coffee and, on a whim, stood an Orvis CFO fly reel upright in one of the potholes to get an idea of its scale. The hole was a ragged-edged cavity the size of a tea tray, and it dwarfed the CFO for height by a good few centimetres.

The potholes, scattered like confetti, continued all the way through to Lady Grey. And there were more than a few on the road from Lady Grey to Barkly East. So by way of a break from pothole-dodging, I took the long route to Rhodes, turning off the R58, taking the dirt road through the Wartrail and New England

Districts, crossing some lesser-known but beautiful trout streams such as the Diepkloof, the Vlooikraalspruit and the Joggem.

After a comfortable evening at the Walkerbouts Inn, I crossed over Naude's Nek Pass early the next morning along with Tony Kietzman and Michelle Rogers, and we found sheets of ice on the hillsides at the summit. We were on our way to spend a few days in Ugie, where they were hosting the Ladies' Fly-Fishing Festival.

Michelle Rogers and her husband were at the time popular doctors living in Rhodes, practising in Barkly East and running the clinic in the district. They've since taken up jobs elsewhere, which was a sad loss for the community.

From the top of Naude's Nek Pass, the view out towards Maclear and Ugie was hazy but still spectacular, in that you are 2,500 metres above sea level on one of the highest road passes in South Africa, and at the lay-by, you look out over a 180-degree view. It seems like you're looking out over the whole world.

For a change, the gravel road down the pass was in good shape. Some years it's a nightmare. At the foot of the pass we stopped for coffee at the bridge over the Swith and found the stream running clear. The water was dark with shade, and there were no trout to be seen. Michelle opened a hamper of food and uncorked a bottle of Rosé, meaning the brief stop lingered on into a pleasant stay. Further on, in the rolling grassland countryside on the eastern slopes of the southern Drakensberg, we came across a few hundred Crowned Cranes in a cornfield that had recently been burned to stubble; a mile or two later we found a second flock, smaller but still impressive.

*

The festival is a fun event that has been going for years, where the contestants are treated like royalty for two-and-a-half days. They get to fish some of the fine streams in this part of the world,

165

like the Mooi, the Pot and the Little Pot. The arrangements were immaculate, with plenty of volunteer guides and good food, and to top it off, the rivers were in good shape. Tony and I were put up in a vacant, fully furnished house belonging to a forestry company.

*

The tree industry was a fairly recent arrival in this part of the world; when I had visited the area a few years back, it seemed every square inch of land was suddenly under pine. It was forestation on a massive scale and it came as a shock – like when you make a nostalgic return to a place of your roots and find the house you grew up in is now an ugly ten-storey office block. Mile after mile of once-familiar grassy hillsides were transformed into plantations of sapling pine trees, not quite overnight, but that's what it felt like. To the north of Ugie there's a massive timber mill employing hundreds of people. My first thought was that it wasn't good news for the fishing, but the fishing has stayed as good as ever. In defence of the forestry company, they saw to it that none of the wetlands were destroyed and that the trees were kept away from the banks of the many streams.

Somebody mentioned, though, that the rare and endangered Blue Swallow had been all but wiped out as a result of the tree planting, or rather due to the loss of the mistbelt grassland habitat these birds need for their survival. We said a solemn prayer for this rare intra-African migrant, of which there are less than a hundred breeding pairs left in South Africa, cursed forestation, then later discovered that the Blue Swallow had never been endemic to this area in the first place. Not that it changes my view that what happened to this lovely part of the country in the name of agricultural development wasn't far off large-scale environmental looting.

I mentioned this to one of those tree-hugging anti-trout lobbyists who came to my home to interview me about trout. I asked what he thought about grasslands being wiped out by forests of alien pine, since he was clearly on a mission to rid the land of all alien species (especially trout) and was, you could say, following the siren call of environmental sanitation. He didn't know about the forestry situation around Ugie and Maclear – or if he did, he pretended not to – but he did get a little glassy-eyed. When they're on a mission, irksome questions make environmental zealots uncomfortable because they can't provide cogent answers without blowing their cover, or exposing a distinctly vulnerable underbelly in their argument.

*

I guided a few ladies on the Mooi, the Pot and the Little Pot and, by some good fortune, those handed over to my doubtful care never blanked once. And there were a few interesting moments. Just before lunch on the first day I was walking back along a bank on the Pot when I saw a lady standing alone, knee-deep in the tail end of a perfect-looking run. She was reeling in and was obviously making to leave. I asked how she'd done. 'Nothing so far,' she replied in a disconsolate tone that suggested there was no justice in the world. I asked her to stay where she was, and studied the run for a few moments. It was around twenty metres long, with whitewater washing into the throat through a tight inlet. Then it widened slightly, and on the left a nice curl of current flowed around a suitcase-sized boulder with a nice patch of smooth, slack water behind it. To the right, the water sloped up gently to a shallow pebbled bank. And near the throat, just off to the left, was a green-tinted deeper pocket half the size of a bathtub. The water was a misty-green, so you couldn't bank on spotting trout, but it was the sort of run that you would back your last dollar held at least a couple of nice fish. I climbed down, waded in and joined her. The flow was colder and stronger than I thought, and the run seemed the more promising for it.

I added three feet of 7X tippet to her leader, and tied on a size 14 weighted Zak. She took the rod and with three or four false casts, sent the fly line right up the centre of the run, landing the nymph in the tumbling whitewater at the throat. She could cast beautifully. Then she lifted the rod tip and started a quick retrieve.

'Okay,' I said, when she had the fly in sight, 'now try a short cast into that slack water behind the big boulder.'

'Really?' she asked. 'Isn't that too close?'

I assured her it wasn't, and she dropped the fly into the patch behind the rock.

There is something about certain runs that makes them look way beyond just promising. In fact, on some runs, your anticipation of catching a fish almost borders on certainty. This was one of those runs, and its promise was fuelled by the fact that less than an hour earlier I'd seen trout being landed higher upstream from water not half as nice-looking as this.

She landed the fly in the right place with a neat cast, but she immediately started a quick retrieve. On the next cast I asked her to give the fly time to sink, to take up the slack in the fly line, to hold her rod tip high to keep the line off the water, and to fix her eyes on the indicator. She did it perfectly. Seconds later the indicator moved and I screamed, 'Strike!' She hooked and landed a ten-inch rainbow. I was a little embarrassed at yelling at her; I should have left her with that decision, but the shout is too ingrained in me.

Then she missed a second trout in the same spot through striking a fraction late, perhaps because this time I *did* manage to keep my mouth shut, then hooked a fat twelve-inch fish in that pocket of deeper, emerald-coloured water we'd both been eyeing near the inlet. She was delighted and generous in her appreciation, but she was reeling in, clearly making to move on. I suggested she try the deep pocket once more, and again she said, 'Really?' I nodded, and three or four casts later she hooked, but sadly lost, a fish that for a few brief moments put a really deep bend into her rod as it tore off upstream. We finally waded out of the run with her bubbling on about the size of the fish she'd lost, and the number she'd hooked and landed – and all from the same run, she reminded me, shaking her head in disbelief. Her emotions were a nice combination of excitement and maybe a little enlightenment. She has since gone on to become a gifted fly fisher.

I left the river feeling there are days when I just can't get enough of fly fishing.

*

One evening we were fishing on the lower reaches of the Pot. The light had turned honey-coloured; a local guide, Richard Viedge, told me that a hatch was about to come off and that I should switch to a dry fly. Richard is one of those gentle people who speaks no ill of anyone and who does all he can to help. No hatch came off, and finally the sun sank behind the hills and the air turned cool. It was all I could do to stop Richard from apologising for the absence of a hatch. I told him God decides these things, and that no matter how good they are, guides can't second-guess God. By then he'd uncorked a bottle of wine, and we drank a toast to absent hatches.

*

There was a day on the Little Pot, a slip of a stream flowing below a surrounding bowl of pretty mountains, when we were gathered in the mid-afternoon on the bank of the stream where the organisers put on a braai. To join the party I'd had to cross the same stream higher up, and spotted a decent fish rising. After lunch I told one of the ladies that I'd found a fish rising earlier, and we went off to try for it. She hooked it first cast. Later we came to a long, shallow, glass-clear run where another trout was rising in full view. Secretly I rated her chances of hooking that fish as scanty, but she got it with the gentlest presentation you could hope for, and then, as the afternoon unfolded, she took a few more trout besides.

I managed to take some interesting photographs with my charge that afternoon, a young lady from upcountry somewhere, including one of a leaping trout that the camera froze in a circle of droplets at the height of her waist. The other photograph worth pressing the shutter button for was of the same angler hooking a fish in a glassy run against an amphitheatre of surrounding mountains bathed in late-afternoon sunshine. Again the image was perfectly timed, the shutter opening precisely as the trout mouthed her dry fly, more a matter of chance and luck than good camera work. All that aside, though, I'm not sure who was guiding whom that afternoon. That lady could fish.

*

I did get a chance to try the Wildebeest River briefly one evening with Tony Kietzman when the festival was done. A year or two back we had had some fun on this pretty little stream, fishing higher up where it weaves and tumbles between boulders, forming runs and pools the length of a kitchen table and pockets the size of a kitchen sink. One side of the stream is bordered by imposing mountains, with buttresses that seem to reach up to the ceiling of the sky.

You could have bet your house the fish would eat dry flies in this stream on this day. Mind you, when we arrived, there was a hatch of tiny, straw-coloured mayfly duns that bobbed like tiny sailboats on the stream, and the trout were after them. Tony handed me a pale, size 18 CDC dry fly pattern that looked buggy and the right colour and said, 'That'll fool 'em' – and it did. We caught fish with ease on his pattern, fishing it on long, limp 7X tippets, the trout no more than nine to ten inches at most. In our hands they quivered as if an electric current had just run through them. All were rainbows, all were as colourful as a spring garden, and in the fading half-light of evening they seemed to sparkle as if scattered with jewels.

When the sky turned from rich a orange to a deep rouge, we trudged back to the truck not twenty minutes away. We swung the tailgate down and poured mugs of coffee. I told Tony you didn't need to be an Oxford don to work out a game plan to catch a mess of fish up here. He agreed that fishing doesn't get much easier or more pleasant for its relaxed rhythm of cast, drift, rise, strike. He said the only way to have gone wrong on this stream on an evening like this was to slip on a wet rock. It had been a brief and charming spell. And as I sipped my coffee, I thought, who could ask for anything more? I suppose we could have wanted more challenging fish, fair enough – but every now and again life is just perfect when it arrives in one of its simpler masks.

*

After the Ugie festival, I dropped Michelle Rogers and Tony in Rhodes and headed for *Birkhall*, where I spent a week fishing the Sterkspruit, trying to really understand this lovely river. For the most part I was alone and fished it lazily, taking as many trout on dry flies as on nymphs. When the Sterkspruit is like this, it's fishing well.

*

On my way to *Birkhall*, I had stopped at the bridge over the Kraai. The Bell and the Sterkspruit looked good, but I couldn't help noticing there was more flow in the Sterkspruit. It goes like that up here. You can get rain, good rain, but often it's patchy. It will sometimes fall well in one valley, but miss the next one completely.

171

Below the bridge, the Kraai was a picture of perfection. As I looked downstream into a long sweep of the river, I spotted a lone fisherman in the distance. He was busy landing a trout.

*

The first morning at *Birkhall*, Basie took me to the site of a lake he was repairing in a valley above the farmhouse. The wall had broken twelve years back in a flash flood. The repairs were well under way, the new wall nearly complete. Huge trucks were loading earth scooped by bulldozers from the old lake bed. The trucks trundled back to the wall belching clouds of diesel fumes. Dust and smoke and the noise of heavy machinery filled the air. It was an impressive operation. Basie went off to chat to the contractor, so I took a hike up the tiny feeder stream to look for trout. I wasn't hopeful because the stream is no wider than a runner carpet and, in most places, no deeper than a bucket, and there was only the lightest flow.

But I eventually found a school of tiny fish not half a kilometre from the work going on downstream. I could see the spots on their semi-lucent bodies. They were trout fry; nervous fish that darted for cover at any hint of danger, the whole school vanishing swiftly in a mass so tightly packed it seemed they were a single living organism. The water was as clear as any mountain spring gets, and just above the spot where I saw the fry, I found two adult trout, both of them around ten inches. They were holding side by side, as still as fence posts. They were close to a bank, well camouflaged and half-hidden in fingers of dappled shade. As they breathed, the white of their mouths was momentarily visible and gave them away. Sitting side by side and so still made me guess they had spawned in this stream. I took a few photographs and then went back to photograph their fry. I wanted to convince Basie this stream was a gem and that he wouldn't have to stock his lake when it filled.

I decided to hike a little higher, and the further I went up the stream's narrow course, the more fry I discovered. It's a slip of a stream, sure, but at a push, I reckoned it would fish well enough with a 0-weight fly rod and size 20 dry flies, providing you did a lot of ducking and belly crawling. It was very closed in.

*

My sortie up the feeder stream made for good discussion over lunch. Basie was intrigued at the prospect of not having to stock his repaired lake. Stocking comes with a heavy price tag and needs plenty of organising, not to mention the vexed question of deciding how many fish you should stock in the first place. And it will inevitably seem that you've only just stocked a lake when it needs to be stocked again, at least if you believe, like I do, that lakes should be stocked at least twice a year to maintain variety in the size of the fish.

So this little stream's trout were a blessing; even better, they were obviously a hardy strain of heat-resistant rainbows that had probably been in the stream for more than seventy-five years. I was surmising this simply because this little beck drains into the Sterkspruit, and this is probably the route the ancestors of these wild trout took to be here. Their new home would have offered few comforts, rather just hardships, like otters, flash floods, droughts, heat, low oxygen levels, challenges that would be prevalent more often than not, winter and summer. But when these trout eventually drop down into the lake, as must happen, they will quickly pack on weight and end up close to bulletproof.

You can have a day on some big-name Alaskan river catching super-sized rainbows, or a day fishing the flats on some atoll in a far-off ocean when giant-sized triggerfish or GTs tear line off your reel all day, or a day when you wade waist-deep in a famous steelhead river, like the Kispiox in British Columbia, when latching onto a fall-run twenty-pound fish that would feel like hooking a passing train. All would be memorable experiences or memorable fish, or both, though the outcomes would probably have largely been expected, or at least not unexpected. But a day like I had up this tiny creek, swooning over the totally unexpected discovery of a brace of small trout, neither of them much longer than a pencil, felt as wonderful as any fishing experience I can remember, as though I'd just unlocked something deep and mysterious – some nascent treasure of the universe unexpectedly revealed.

*

One dreamy day on the river followed another where, save for an afternoon when catching trout was like drawing teeth and I managed only two small ones, the fishing was the Sterkspruit as I like it best. Trout came happily to dry flies like RABs, Para-RABs or Mirages, among others, but only when the drift was right. And when the dry flies drifted well but went unnoticed, the fish took nymphs, like Zaks in various weights, PTNs, Brassies, sometimes suspended under a dry fly or a poly yarn indicator, sometimes just fished on a bare leader. All ordinary, all variably effective. I sometimes think about the seeming timelessness of some of the old familiar patterns, like the PTN, the Elk Hair Caddis, the RAB and the Para-RAB, and wonder whether their appeal will ever wane. I suspect we are too set in our ways and in some of our deeper beliefs for their demise to be anywhere near a foreseeable reality, at least in the near future.

*

On the second day I parked the truck on the edge of the Sterkspruit under willow trees, where sunlight caught the branches and threw parcels of shade onto the grass below. There's a run here: a long, straight, continuous hundred-metre run on a nice gradient, so the flow is quick and just right for the dry fly to come back to you at the perfect speed, not slow enough to invite any close inspections, not fast enough for the fish to occasionally miss the fly altogether or not bother to rise. It's a series of knee-deep riffles interspersed with the occasional slick-surfaced pockets and, in places, the banks are cool with shade and nicely undercut. I took a dozen or so trout, starting with a dry fly, but when the fishing slowed on the dry I switched to a small size 16 Zak with a brass bead. There wasn't any need for an indicator. The flow was too good and the fish too quick and strong in their takes to miss seeing the abrupt halt in the leader, or the sudden line-tip movement, or the tippet slipping away unnaturally as if the fly had just got heavier. It was the sort of fishing when you can use a nymph and rely entirely on leader and line-tip messages to signal takes. But for this to work best, you want to start by first dressing the fly line well with something like Mucilin so that it floats high – something I notice many of us, myself included, are lax about.

I landed the first trout using my new Deon Stamer net, tried to take a photograph of it and ended up briefly submerging the front of my camera's lens, but it survived after a night packed in dry rice.

I was near the top of the run and was just returning a fish when I heard the muffled sound of clapping. I turned to find two ladies sitting on a log not too far behind me, kitted in fly gear and with rods. They said they'd been there for some time, watching me. But I was lost to the world following leaders and trying to land casts tight against banks, and hadn't noticed them. I remembered meeting one of these ladies, Denise Hill, at the Ugie festival. I invited them to try the next few runs and stayed long enough to watch one of them take a nice trout on a dry fly from it. Then I crossed the river and hiked over a field to another run I know, leaving them enough good water to get on with.

*

I was testing trout stomach contents almost every day and, as usual, it was a mixed soup of small mayfly nymphs, caddisfly and midge larvae, and the occasional beetle and ant. Among the mayfly nymphs, a dark *Baetis* species, around size 18, seemed more prolific than the others. Absent were stoneflies that at one time were fairly common around here (but never prolific), and it was probably too early for inchworms or sawflies. They tend to appear around mid- to late October and hang around until the end of March. During this time there are four breeding cycles, the adult sawflies laying their eggs on willow leaves. Eggs hatch into pupae or, as we know them, inchworms, with a lifespan of around fourteen days. There was a time when they would fall off the crack willow trees into the rivers in their hundreds, providing a continuous meal for waiting trout.

The species of inchworm that fed off crack willows (*Salix fragilis*) was imported from the USA in 1993, apparently into Lesotho, and then spread south into the Eastern Cape Highlands. They thrived on the crack willows until the willows were eventually eradicated; then that particular inchworm disappeared.

There is another species of inchworm around this area that lives on the weeping willow (*Salix babylonica*), a larger insect though less abundant than the inchworms that once fed on the crack willows. The weeping willow is also alien, by the way, and despite its name, originally came from China.

*

I left the river late enough each day to sometimes get a decent hatch. What interested me, and still does, is how rarely these hatches bring on a rise when they first appear. Mainly you need to wait until the sun is slipping behind the mountains, or until the river is set alight by the colourful glows of sunset, before the fish really get down to throwing circles on the surface.

One morning I crossed the Bokspruit River on my way to visit Dave Walker in Rhodes and, as usual, I parked on the far side of the bridge under the shade of a willow tree and strolled back to scan the water. Upstream I saw more trout than I could count, many holding in exposed positions over open bedrock in bright sunlight, others milling in equally exposed positions over a sandy stretch of riverbed. They were all around ten to twelve inches, and although they were sitting ducks for any passing kingfisher or cormorant, they didn't look nervous; rather they were restless, judging by their constant and seemingly aimless shifting and swapping of positions. I have often seen schools of trout in the Bokspruit, sometimes up to ten or twenty fish, but I had never seen this many, particularly not trout well beyond fingerling stage. Downstream of the bridge I didn't spot a single fish. What accounted for the huge gathering above the bridge I don't know, but the scene certainly made for some interesting can-you-count-all-the-shadows photographs.

*

I spent an afternoon with Tony Kietzman and his friend Stephanus Klopper, a young man I hadn't met before. As we drew up at the entrance to the gorge section of the Sterkspruit on *Birkhall*, a juvenile Jackal Buzzard stared down at us from its perch on a road sign just long enough for me to drop my window and photograph him with a long lens. Then the big bird opened its wings, lifted gracefully, swooped low over the river and was gone on the wind. Nice way to start a spot of fishing.

Tony was using my Tenkara rod, and Stephanus and I were sharing my Winston 2-weight. He was new to fly fishing, and we began the day on the sort of run your mind would drift to if you were hemmed in by four walls in some city office block, bored to the marrow and looking for an escape. The run was at least fifty metres long, not too deep but deep enough, the water tinged a glassy green, with nicely undercut banks on both sides and a backdrop of high, grass-covered hillsides with rocky crevices near the top.

Stephanus took a couple of tidy and spirited trout from this run, fishing a nymph suspended under a large indicator that every now and again would dart upstream when a trout took the fly. The water was a beginner's heaven, and I couldn't help thinking that if he didn't become a convert to fly fishing after a day like this, he never would. A convert, too, to the general joys of this part of the country, its rivers, its landscapes and, of course, the village of Rhodes.

But to get back to the mouth-watering run I mentioned, it was possibly the best on this section of the river that season, and always worth the extra ten-minute walk downstream along a pretty rough riverbank to get to below it. What makes it even better is there's a easily wadeable gravel spine running up the centre, so it's easy to fish both the left and right undercuts standing in knee-deep water in the middle of the run.

Actually we had started out with a dry fly, but when it went untouched through the length of the run we climbed out at the head, took our time retracing our steps back to the tail, changed to a nymph, eased back into the water and immediately had some action.

It was interesting that in runs that produced a number of fish on conventional fly gear, Tony winkled out one or two more on the Tenkara outfit, even when we thought a run had been thoroughly fished. He was also on a nymph by then, but it was suspended under a dry fly that didn't get any attention. And again we were attracted to the sheer simplicity of Tenkara fly fishing, and at the top of the gorge where the river slides along sheer, lichen-patterned dolerite walls, I tried the Tenkara rod myself. I couldn't interest a fish until I got near the head of the run where the flow was swifter and as bubbly as soda water. Here I took two nice trout in quick succession.

We were back at the truck by late afternoon, having landed and released more than a dozen trout on each rod, and I don't think we saw a rise all day. The Sterkspruit can be like that. It can fish well even when you haven't seen any bugs hatching, never mind so much as a hint of any surface-feeding trout. Even the swallows and martins weren't showing, and the fish we got were holding deep. Isn't that so often a pattern to a day? The fish are flatly uninterested in a surface fly but they're active on deep-sunk nymphs. And, of course, the reverse can hold true.

*

I have a special affection for the Sterkspruit on *Birkhall*, given my close friendship with the Vosloo family. I know it as well as you can know a river, even taking into account how rivers change, not only from season to season but week by week, day by day, even hour by hour. Over seasons, rivers change in form: a bend smooths out here, a run deepens there – though, barring catastrophic events, the essential character remains constant. By day, rivers may change slightly in level, dropping on hot, windswept days or lifting as a result of upstream storms, even colouring as you watch. By the day, even by the hour, rivers can change in mood, from being generous and forgiving to stubborn. These are subtle changes where, as often as not, the edges are that blurred that unless you keep fishing you are never certain how the fish in a river will respond at any given hour, even from cast to cast, no matter what's gone before.

My opinion of the Sterkspruit is probably biased in its favour, but based on empirical evidence gained over years of fishing in this part of the world, I have found it to be more constant, and its trout more eager, fatter and stronger than in neighbouring rivers and streams. I've also been lucky to see the Sterkspruit in all its guises: in its times of abundance and in its times of dearth. If there are occasions when the fishing isn't that good, believe me, there are enough times when it is. And other than seasonal nuances in colour and texture, its immediate landscapes remain attractive and distinctive in their own special ways. With the deepening familiarity that comes over time, I now think of the Sterkspruit, as you should think of all the good trout streams you get to know really well, with a combination of affection, respect and forgiveness.

*

I set aside an afternoon to pack my truck so I could leave early enough the next day to drive through the sunrise on the road back home. Heading south from *Birkhall*, the morning sun is behind you and it lights up the landscapes in ways you don't want to miss.

In the morning I had driven down the slope of the hill that hides the wall of the *Birkhall* lake where I set up a rod, then strolled to the lower section of the Sterkspruit on *Birkhall* where willows crowd the banks. It was a final fling before facing the inevitable departure.

I find it best to get straight into this lower section and wade up the centre so you can cast to both banks. The bank water is deeper here than in many other sections of the Sterkspruit, and better fish aren't uncommon.

Sunlight filtered through the willow fronds, lighting the far bank. I focused on the deeper slots and on the shaded ones, fishing a weighted nymph with no indicator, getting the fly to drift into the runs from a metre or two upstream so that the nymph travelled through the best parts as deep as possible. At times I felt the light touch of structure through the fly,or felt the fly-tapping pebbles, and as the nymph drifted through a run, I left it to swing upwards as the line straightened in the pull of the current. That's when the first fish took the fly. My diary notes of that morning's fishing are scanty, but there's the number '12' with a circle around it and the words, 'None on dry. All deep. Snake crossed river way ahead. Wind NW. Strong at times.'

There's no mention of the exact size of the fish I caught, but I remember them being twelve to fourteen inches; put differently, I don't remember getting any twenty-inch fish so, by deduction, I figure I didn't get anything of size. But I do remember the fish were shaped like rain barrels.

The snake, by the way, was too far off to guess at, though from its length, easily over a metre. From its litheness, I took it for a cobra and carefully marked where it left the run to slither silently up the bank.

Just to dwell on diaries on fishing trips once again, they are invaluable, because on long trips, events have a way of running into one another in your mind. Even the important ones. You can end up not remembering much more than a conflated overall impression, and that can even distil down to no more or less than, 'Good trip' or 'Bad trip', which is of no use to anyone.

At times I carry a tiny wire-bound notepad that easily fits into one of the smaller pockets on the average fly vest, though the downside is that you eventually lose either the pencil or the diary itself, or forget to take both. This particular morning's fishing is taken from just such a diary, a wire-bound, shirt-pocket-sized notebook with entries in pencil, that I discovered by chance some weeks later when I was tidying out the portable fly-tying kit I take with me on long trips. It's a beautiful, leather-bound case with multiple drawers that was once my medical bag when I was a GP.

More often I write up the events of a day last thing at night, when not only the fish I caught or the flies I used but also the impressions of the day are fresh in my mind, and when I'm less likely to suffer short-term memory loss than if I write them up even a day later. The sparse days, or the days when I fished clumsily, also need to be recorded with as much honest detail as the less frequent days when I was blessed with plenty of fish, when my casting worked and when I couldn't put a foot wrong. Recording the nuances operates on a sort of honour system, where if things get too favourably distorted or plainly dishonest, the only one to lose out is yourself.

Just one other observation on diaries: they keep better earlier in a trip and tend to fall off to brief and sloppy towards the end. It's understandable, because when you first arrive you are fired with enthusiasm, and everything that happens takes on an importance that outweighs its actual relevance. All quite logical, really.

But there is one final entry in the diary I was talking about, the one covering this last day on the Sterkspruit, and it simply says, 'Huge bulge under willow left bank. Threw everything. Zip.'

I don't always have the strength of character to quit on a good fish, even when I know it's high time I did, and in this particular case, my diary entry (if not my memory) still serves me well. The emphasis was on the word 'bulge'. This fish moved a bucket of water, and I felt it was a given that I'd hook it on a nymph. I changed to a 5X tippet, wiped it with a rag soaked in mud so it would sink, and tied on a weighted nymph. Twenty casts later, and after a considerable number of fly changes, I eventually gave up, reeled in, bit off the fly and hiked up the hill to my truck.

*

I reached Beaufort West safely after successfully dodging the potholes, and had a restful night in the Karoo National Park. I phoned Kathy to tell her where I was, then bought a few lamb chops to braai on the veranda of my rondavel. I did that under a black, star-scattered sky. Early the following morning, the Cape Robin-chats were on cue cleaning morsels of fat off the braai grid not a rod-length from where I sat.

*

It's been a long while since I bit that last fly off my tippet and trudged up the Sterkspruit's grassy banks to my truck parked in the paddock below the *Birkhall* lake. But still, back here in the hustle and rush of city life, the memories of the river's resinous runs, its slow-flowing, green-tinged pools, its riverbanks lined with willows and poplars, and its spirited trout are a daily comfort. My feet still feel the coldness of the water, my legs the drag of the currents, and in my mind I still see the long sweeps of brightly lit water, the pockets, the corrugated riffles, the still flows though jade-coloured pools. I am here, but I am partly still there.

The trip held no great surprises, no real high points. The fish were as bright and as wild as ever; the weather was, well, the weather; my friends were a blessing. It was enough, in its own peculiar way, to be carefree in that wide-horizoned, blue-skied part of the world.

CHAPTER 8

SMALL STREAMS, THEIR TROUT AND THE NOTION OF INNOCENCE

But the skills I learned on those little high mountain streams
have worked for me pretty much everywhere I've fished,
while skills I learned on classic waters don't transplant
into the mountains worth a dip of snuff.
JAMES R BABB, *CROSSCURRENTS: A FLY FISHER'S PROGRESS*

Straight off, let's settle what we're talking about here. By small streams I mean really small streams that are mostly, but not always, in mountain country; and by 'really small', I mean streams that, in places, you could just about straddle, or lay the butt of your rod on one bank and have the tip resting on the other.

As a rule, they tend to be near or in mountain country, and flow quickly down the gradient the slopes provide, though obviously that's variable. Equally, the degree of gradient ultimately shapes the nature and character of any small stream. Not that small streams are limited to mountain country; you will find more than a few in low-lying areas, where they meander sinuously through grassland plains. For the purposes here, I want to deal with quick-flowing mountain streams *and* meandering pastoral rivulets.

In steep gradients, small streams are often a series of tiny waterfalls that, more romantically, some would call liquid staircases. These waterfalls mostly run into small cascade pools where there's a lovely combination of slick and churn and bubble and sparkle. Near the throats of these pools, the churn and the bubbles often extend from the streambed right to the surface, offering cover for the trout, but the cover quickly dissipates when the flow slows down as it enters the body of the pool, and where riverbed stones and pebbles become clearly visible.

Some anglers call a series of small cascade pools *pocket water*, rather than just small pools, and there's really no right or wrong answer to that, except that where a small stream runs in longer, flatter sections that go well beyond just being a small confined pool, you can also find pockets. These are discrete, irregularly shaped depressions that are deeper than the surrounding water. Their depth is given away by two important signs: they have a smoother surface and there's a hint of colour to them, anything from a pale green to an amber or a misty grey, depending on the overall colour of the stream you happen to be fishing.

So what's in a name? Why the fuss over what is or isn't pocket water? Well, small pools are obvious targets for anglers, but many fly fishers, even experienced ones, miss spotting the pockets in shallower, flatter water. The most important part is that these pockets are prime holding lies in small streams, and because the flow is averagely less turbulent in them than it is in cascade pools, they often hold better fish.

When the gradient flattens out in the middle reaches, small streams start to look more like any river – just smaller, downsized versions of the real thing. So you'll have pools, runs and riffles and, of course, pockets, but there will be a little less swiftness, swirl and unevenness, and maybe fewer contrary currents. Some runs will be smooth, relatively shallow and glassy-clear, and these will be notably trickier to fish. This is where it pays hands down to first spot your trout so you can size up just the right cast.

When small streams run in pastoral settings they typically meander, as I said, but they are also invariably deeper and often have undercut banks that are overhung with grass or scrub. Depending on the size of the stream, you can feel more comfortable calling small pastoral streams like this brooks, or maybe becks or burns, but none of these terms gets much traction any more, at least not in modern writing. The term 'creek' is a lovely one, but it's more in use in America and Canada, where it applies to any small stream, no matter whether it's bouncing down through high country or twisting lazily through flat, pastured farmlands.

Regardless, these streams are tiny, so they're the kind of waters you sneak up on rather than wade; where you drop a fly onto a target rather than lay out a line; where a long drift is more like one metre than two. And they're often *tight*, not only in the sense that they're maybe bushed in, but also in the sense that the sweet spots are anything from the size of a hat box to not much bigger than the back seat in a small family sedan.

The charm of small streams is not locked in their grandness of scale, but rather in their diminutiveness; not in any celebration of the size of their trout, because these are mainly small, but with the caveat that small trout are every bit as beautiful and often just as difficult to fool. I suspect what draws us anglers to small streams is the chance to introduce minimalism, delicacy and even a kind of poetry into the usual subterfuges that make up fly fishing.

So it's no surprise that small-stream addicts are often caught up in a few predictable and parallel passions, like bamboo fly rods, custom-made landing nets, silk fly lines. In fact, with some I'm never quite sure whether we're dealing with a narrow, bona fide subset of fly fishers as much as a fanatically minimalist, ritualistic and tradition-seeking cult. Which is to say that while bamboo fly rods, custom landing nets, silk fly lines and so on aren't absolutely necessary to the authentic small-stream experience, they do add a lustre to it and they feed into its aura. To some small-stream anglers these trappings are essentials, to others they aren't, and there's no exact point that you can define as the unshakable middle ground in small-stream fanaticism. We just accept that all anglers are different, small-stream anglers more so, and if some of us do tend to get overly quirky and a little romantic about the gear we use, well, it's become such an accepted part of the small-stream scene that we just let it ride.

*

Look, you either love small streams or you don't, and those of us who do can get a little carried away by their charm, obsessive about light tackle and delicate casting, and defensive and guarded about the location of the better ones we know. The *perfect* ones can become sacred, and most small-stream addicts have at least one or two special places, holy places if you like, that we keep quiet about; places we'd rather fall on our swords for rather than spill the beans on. Secret places. Hidden honey-holes. You've heard it all before. They are still out there, but there are fewer of them now, thanks to the growing number of fly fishers and the inherent inclination among most anglers to share. Google Earth, one of the most powerful instruments of the modern fly-fishing era, hasn't helped, and keeping a secret in this digitally connected world is a lot more difficult. You need added help to keep things under the radar.

For example, a friend and I share a small stream flowing from the mountains between two tiny villages in the Western Cape. It's well hidden and protected; to get to it, you need to turn off a minor tar road onto an even more minor side road that travels through an established, well-tendered fruit orchard (never mind what kind of fruit) – an orchard that runs the entire length of the stream almost to its banks. So workers are often around, and the farmer himself is often there, meaning any poacher is likely to have a limited shelf-life. It's a known fact that this guy doesn't do poachers.

But let me name a few small-stream gems that I *am* happy to share with you.

*

First off, the upper sections of most of the Western Cape's trout streams fall into this category, but there are some stars among those: the Jan du Toit's near Worcester; the Kraalstroom, a tributary of the uppermost reaches of the Elandspad; the beat of the Lourens River near Somerset West where it runs in a steep gorge; the headwaters of the Witte River in Bainskloof; and the Kaaimansgat, a tributary of the Holsloot River. And there are many others besides.

In the Eastern Cape Highlands you have streams such as the Coldbrook, the upper section of the Willow Stream, the Kloppershoekspruit, the Bokspruit from *Gateshead* right up to its source in the Drakensberg, the Koffiehoekspruit, the Swith, the Wildebeest, the Hawerspruit, the Bradgate, the upper Luzie and the Tsitsa. I could go on. And KwaZulu-Natal is full of them too, again often in the upper reaches, or as tributaries of trout streams such as the Bushman's, the Umzimkulu, the Mooi and the Tugela.

But, as I said, there are some that we keep to ourselves, for no other reason than they couldn't handle much traffic without showing signs of damage, or they're private, or they're so tiny that most people couldn't be bothered hearing about them anyway. As you'd expect, these are among the most prized and the most jealously guarded. So there are some small streams I'm sworn to secrecy on, and that, of course, raises questions about the morality of secrecy when it comes to trout streams that don't belong to us in the first place, but that we want to keep hidden. We argue that in these places we acquire an unwritten *right* to non-disclosure, equivalent to the laws that apply to things like intellectual property rights, for the very reason that we 'discovered' them – by whatever roundabout route – and therefore assume that by some sort of plebeian common law we have earned the sole rights to their use, even if we know that our case wouldn't stand scrutiny in the lowest courts in the land.

And it's not a matter of selfishness. It's just that we don't want these places swamped with throngs of anglers who might not visit the same care and concern on them or their trout as we do. Written down like this it actually doesn't sound like an unreasonable position to hold.

Then there's often plenty of bush clearing to be done to get a route into a stream in the first place, and this, along with the ongoing streamside clearing and pruning that's needed, heightens the sense of deserved sole ownership. We've even gone to the lengths of cryptically disguising the paths into streams and, at convenient points upstream, marking equally cryptic and carefully disguised routes out, all of which is not only hard work but adds fuel to the belief of 'ownership'.

Anglers, I have discovered, are as good as sniffer dogs at finding out most of our secrets and, as I said, we are prone to sharing hidden gems with buddies we can trust – always, of course, under the strict mantle of sworn secrecy. But even then the message somehow spreads, slowly and incrementally, like the ripples from a pebble tossed into a pond. Just the other day I was sharing a cup of coffee with a new acquaintance who, leaning over the table and looking around to check who might be listening, whispered the delights of a new-found stream while swearing me to the sort of secrecy you'd expect from a national intelligence operative. I didn't have the heart to tell him I'd been fishing the place for years, nor that his estimates of the number and size of the fish in it were exaggerated to the point where I wondered if we *were* actually talking about the same place. And I also didn't tell him that the last time I fished it with a friend I *can* trust, we variously found the clear imprints of size-10 wading shoes, along with a few discarded pieces of fluorescent-red poly yarn indicator material.

*

Why us devotees like small streams so much is a fascinating question. Is their diminutive charm the same sort of charm that draws us to small villages more than to big cities, to tiny cobbled lanes rather than tarred highways? Or is it that they offer particular challenges, or particular opportunities – like fishing really light or really tight, or fishing so close in that the delight of searching for, and occasionally finding, trout in tiny crystal-clear pools becomes a sort of pleasant form of angling voyeurism?

Speaking for myself, because you will certainly have your own views, the joy of small streams is in their tightknit intimacy – the sort of intimacy where the fly fishing is under a microscope rather than splashed on a big screen. That said, I admit to being no less happy fishing a river; I just have a preference for small streams, though it's not an exclusive, all-or-nothing issue for me. With some anglers it does get pretty close to that; it's as if their default setting is for small streams and everything that encompasses them. Small streams predominate their thinking and eclipse all else, and I have little argument with it. After all, some of my best friends… Okay, let's just leave it there.

Another obvious joy of most small streams is their beauty. They are invariably prettier than rivers – certainly prettier than those really large rivers that motor past you like big, wet freeways, where if you wade just one metre too far you risk drowning. But that's a long way from saying there aren't pretty rivers out there, and maybe there's even an argument for saying no trout water is anything less than pretty; just that each is pretty in its own particular way.

Back to that 'intimate' story again. Many of the small streams I fish somehow give the impression of being framed like a painting, by mountain folds or maybe by bushes or trees or scrub or rock faces. And the fact that they are often on steeper gradients adds a swiftness to them, flowing as if hurried, often dancing, or slipping silver over stepped cascades, or swirling around rocks, or sweeping into snug, leafy, often mysterious-looking spots. But it's a manageable swiftness, not something that can drown you. And their prettiness doesn't border on anything like an inspiring grandeur, but rather just on a sort of welcoming cosiness. And, anyway, most small streams are invariably packed with the best features of a river, only in miniature, and we happen to like that.

One last point: I cut my teeth fishing a small stream, caught my very first trout from one – a tiny, pretty brown trout – so my love of small streams is perhaps partly a throwback to youth or some sort of epigenetic evolution, not that I fully understand the concept.

*

On the point of the charm of small streams, there was a day not too long ago when Billy de Jong and I fished a mountain stream small enough to step over. We were showing two Danish guests the place; it took us half an hour to walk in. Much of the time they could see the stream from the path along which we were hiking, but they were too polite to say much about it being bushed in and small and an

192

unlikely place to be hunting trout. They did ask about snakes a few times; we reassured them that while there might be a few around, we couldn't think when we last saw one, which was only partly true.

Eventually, we cut off the path and dropped into the stream where it's so overgrown with indigenous trees that you can't even get a bow cast in. Our guests fell into silence. Thirty metres later, the verdant canopy opened, as we knew it would, to reveal the most delightful stretch of high-mountain trout water. It's not the longest section, but it is clear and pretty, and our guests caught fish on tiny dry flies, one or two of them quite decent fourteen-inch trout. Near the end of this section, where the stream gets unfishable again, they remarked on its exquisite beauty, how brightly coloured the trout were, how the walk in was worth it – and they added that even if this was the tiniest stream they'd ever fished, it was also one of the nicest fishing experiences they'd had in a long time.

This is about when Billy and I spotted the puff adder, all of a metre long and as thick as your arm, drifting down the run in which we were standing, heading straight for us. The snake maybe sensed the presence of humans because, a rod-length away, its autumn-leaf-patterned body slithered in sinuous folds up the far bank, and in a moment it disappeared. That's when I noticed that one of our guests had literally climbed up Billy like he was a stepladder. He was sitting on Billy's shoulders.

*

With notable exceptions, small streams are fished less, and the normal conclusion that derives from this is that they're probably too easy to offer any real challenge. Some small streams are an easy touch and productive, maybe because they hold a lot of naive, little-disturbed and perpetually hungry trout. If you stop off at one of the bridges crossing the uppermost reaches of, say, the Bokspruit on a sunny day with a gentle breeze and a reasonable flow of clear water, you'll likely spot a few trout. They'll mainly be small, but you know that's only because the bigger fish are not on show. They'll be under the banks – or maybe under the bridge you're standing on. I mentioned the gentle breeze because riffled surfaces often make trout bold enough to come out on show.

But the general notion that all wild, small-stream trout are a soft touch is shaky – even in streams that aren't fished that often. Small-stream trout can be ridiculously easy to catch, but it's not a rule you want to bank on.

The telling thing is that no matter how easy the fishing on any particular small stream is, experience has shown me that there are always a few anglers who regularly catch more trout in small streams than others. This points to the fact that small streams and their trout have a lot to teach us, as do those gurus who consistently do better than most at figuring them out.

The small-stream soft-touch bit goes around the obvious fact that small-stream trout do live in more confined spaces; meaning you can cover the water more completely with short casts that show little or no fly line. Add to that the wobbly assertion that the holding water is often more turbulent, so the fish won't spot you quite as easily. This holds good as far as it goes, but as one of my friends Fred Steynberg once said, 'Some small-stream trout are an easy touch, sure, but in the same stream on the same day I'll find you half a dozen trout that are geniuses at not getting caught.' The linear logic in this suggests that you always know plenty about the fish you hooked and landed, and next to nothing about all those you missed, spooked, couldn't interest or didn't even know were there.

Selectivity, turbulence, smartness and gradient
It doesn't take rocket science to figure out some of the challenges small-stream trout face.

To start with, food is less abundant and insects mainly pass by at speed, certainly in the small streams with gradient. So these fish are more often hungry opportunists than fussy gourmets.

Finding trout feeding selectively on the sort of small streams that fit the definition for inclusion in this chapter is relatively uncommon, outside of the occasional hatch of mayflies, or hatches of net-veined midges or micro-caddis that are sporadic and invariably short-lived. Having said that, selectivity is not uncommon on somewhat bigger streams, like the Smalblaar and Holsloot in the Western Cape, or the Sterkspruit and Bokspruit in the Eastern Cape Highlands, and in KwaZulu-Natal, the Mooi, the Little Mooi and the Bushman's. It's obviously also common on the chalkstreams, no matter their size.

I've also heard anglers say that wild trout in swift-flowing mountain streams don't, on average, live as long as trout in rivers, so they don't end up as street-smart as any highly experienced five-year-old veteran you might find, say, in a famous spring creek or a chalkstream. But that's also shaky. Wild trout are *born smart*. It's part of the contract of being 'wild'. And if they live out a year, they'll be *ultra-smart*. In any stream that isn't fished a lot or where the fishing pressure is comparatively low, the only thing they might lack is the basic experience of the high levels of subterfuge we anglers are increasingly capable of. And to me this is a major point in this particular debate, together with just one other – the level of the gradient the stream flows in.

Here the basic rule is the steeper the gradient, the faster the flow; and the more the stream is a necklace of small, contained cascade pools and pockets, the easier the fish are to catch. The most you can say about this rule is that it applies most days, but not all.

*

Talking about wildness, I remember years back visiting the Kamberg trout hatchery when the late Rob Karssing was running the place. He had fingerling brown trout in two small, vinyl-sided pools, and he invited us to walk up to one of them. At the first pool, the fish were mildly alarmed at our presence but soon settled. In the second pool, the fingerlings vanished before we got within a short cast of them, and they stayed hugging the bottom while we were nearby. The difference was incredible. Rob explained that in the first pond he had brown trout fingerlings bred from his usual brood-stock taken over years from the upper Mooi River, so maybe there was a little inbreeding at play. In the special pond he had fingerlings that were from the eggs of two totally different strains of brown trout that he had collected separately after hiking to the source of two tiny, little-known Drakensberg trout streams. Talk about street-smart!

Fishing small streams

From the angler's point of view, casting into small pockets of running water requires no deep understanding of rivercraft, and if you add the fact that most mountain streams are less often fished than grander big-name rivers, you start to piece together a scenario where anglers are going to find fishing them easier, as long as they stay out of sight and don't slap the water. Okay, I know there are exceptions to the stereotypical easy-to-fish, high-mountain trout stream. The *Boarman's Chase* section of the Bell on Naude's Nek Pass is one that comes to mind. But that's because many anglers fish that stretch, and it has as many runs that are smooth and glassy and tricky, as runs that are tumbling with the gradient and easy.

On the other hand, relatively few people fish streams like the Bokspruit where it runs right up on the summit of the southern Drakensberg or the upper Luzie near *Vrederus*, or the upper Tsitsa, the Swith or the upper Riflespruit high in the mountains between

Rhodes and Barkly East. In streams like these, you could say the trout will likely be naive and not be wrong. But these are also places where the only footprints you see will be your own, and where catching trout can get as easy as picking apples off a tree. What's more, we have plenty of them in this country. But even on these 'easy' streams, I can name a raft of anglers who on any given day would quickly out-fish most others. The point I'm making is that some level of naivety in trout will serve you up to a point; thereafter, a heap of other skills needs to come into play if you really want to get to the front of the pack.

Much boils down to how you approach wild trout in small streams, and the best is not to rely on them being overly forgiving or naive just because they live in a less prestigious address than, say, the upper Itchen or a crystalline spring creek in the South Island of New Zealand.

Finally, if trout happen to live in turbulent water (and most high-gradient small-stream water is turbulent), the view they get of the outside world is similar to looking through the rippled glass of a shower booth, so obviously they won't be alerted to an angler's presence as easily as a fish holding in a smooth-flowing, limpid stream, such as a carrier of the upper Itchen. The flip side of that coin is that, in turbulent water, *you won't spot them easily* either.

On this point, a few years back Leonard Flemming and I were on a tiny Cape stream that never gets fished – which sounds Irish, I know, but I can't exactly explain this without blowing our cover. Where we climbed in the runs were quick, broken and threaded with whitewater, and the fishing was easy. As soon as we got to sections where the runs were smooth and long and glassy and slower, all the usual demons kicked in: we got spotted, the fish picked up micro-drag and they had time to inspect our flies. But we still took a few startled trout. They'd been willing risers as long as our flies landed gently and rode without hindrance, and as long as we stayed hidden. We caught enough fish that day to feel we'd done well, but I'm willing to bet that if we fished this stream regularly for a season or two, we'd get better and these trout would get smarter.

*

There was an occasion when I got to fish a stream that last saw an angler sometime around World War II, and I'm not making that up. My friend Donie Naudé introduced Ed Herbst and me to one such stream, the upper Bradgate, on a day when there was a slight breeze, the sky was blue and the birds were singing. But with the water as thin as cellophane, that little stream was as challenging as any tough place you know about. We got a few fish from the tumble-water, but the glassy runs were testing, even though we were fishing long leaders and 7X tippets, lying in the grass as flat as snakes, and generally being as cautious as accountants.

*

Then there was the first sortie Billy de Jong and I ever made to the Lourens River near Somerset West, where the stream cascades down a tightly hemmed kloof high above *Lourensford* farm, and where Gerhard Compion, the fishery's manager, told us few people get to fish. We caught trout, but I've never known more discerning small-stream fish, particularly as far as micro-drag is concerned. We've since been back a few times and it's always the same. You can take fish with ease where the water is boiling, quite often from holes or pockets no bigger than a prayer rug. But as soon as you get to the middle section where the valley flattens a little and the stream slows down, opens up and is crystalline and smooth as satin, all the usual curses immediately creep in – drag and micro-drag, rod flash, even selectivity once or twice.

198

Fly rods for small streams

One of the curses of some little mountain streams is they are often bushed in, which no doubt started the myth that you mainly need short rods to fish them. Perhaps this is a good time to start talking about the rod you use to tackle these tiny places.

I don't like a really short rod, say 6' to 6'6", on a small stream, for three reasons: I lose the added leverage I use to avoid drag; most really short rods don't load as easily close in; most of the small streams I fish are open in many places when I feel thankful for the extra length I have above the cork handle. Take the Kraalstroom, a tributary of the Elandspad in the Western Cape, a really small stream I have occasionally fished with my friend Ryan Weaver. Much of the riverbank has dense growth, and standing in some places it wouldn't be difficult to sell an angler a 6' fly rod. But then there are places where the stream suddenly opens up and casting a 7' or 8' rod is a breeze. Also, if you are of average height, by simply dropping to your knee to cast you lose three feet of rod length. You lose even more by dropping your elbow while casting in a kneeling position, or by tilting the rod into a flatter casting plane.

(By the way, Peter Hayes, the ace Tasmanian caster, showed me a neat trick for casting in tight, bushed-in places. You hold the end of the fly line and leader in your hand while you make the back cast, then release the line and leader in the forward cast. The principle is that a closed loop of fly line hitting vegetation behind you won't get hung up the way a leader and fly will. It was so simple that it made me wonder why I hadn't thought of it a decade ago.)

But 'short' and 'long' are relative terms with fly rods. I consider a short rod to be anything under 7', and on small streams, especially bushed-in streams, the outer limit is probably 8'. But in modern fly fishing, rods up to 10' or even 11' are becoming more popular on streams that aren't bushed in. In fact, this is the way many stream

199

anglers are going. Fishing Tenkara rods of 11' and over happened to point me in that direction, but the modern trend was towards longer rods on small streams, wherever this is practical. It's the one – and only – downside to fishing bamboo. Split cane (or so a few serious makers have told me) has an outer range of 8'6" for 3-weight rods, after which they just get too heavy or skate too close to the edge of the specification limits of bamboo, or both.

Bamboo makers might differ. Steve Boshoff, a serious rod maker, has some interesting thoughts on the subject. But before I get to them, here's a point he makes on the term 'rod maker' as opposed to a 'rod builder'. Steve says 'makers' make from scratch – in any material. 'Builders' assemble, again from any material. 'That issue,' he says, 'appears to have been settled, at least among the rod makers.'

Steve's points of view have to be seen in the context of him being a bamboo-rod maker in the first instance, and a small-stream fanatic as a secondary but important personal persuasion. Reading what he says on this subject makes you realise – well, it did me – that there's more to rod length choice than meets the eye. I quote from him:

'Offhand, I wouldn't say that 7'6" is short. For tiny streams that would be long. The original Sage "Ought", at 8', was certainly long for a 0-weight rod.

'So, for small streams I would say that short is below 7', say 6' and a bit, or 6'-something. That certainly has a short, small-stream ring to it. The problem is that if you go to 9' (in graphite) in a 1- or 2-weight, you could say they aren't really 1- or 2-weights, but more like 3- or 4-weights.

'Great small, freestone stream rods in bamboo were generally below 7'. Vincent Marinaro worked in 6' and 6'6". The Paul Young Midge is 6'3". Garrison's small stream rod was 6'9", and Payne's 95 and 96 were respectively 6' and 6'6". Lew Stoner's small-stream

3-weight ranged between 5'6" and 7'. I have never agreed with the 7'6" for a 3-weight theory. I think that the ideal is closer to a 7' for a 3-weight.

'So, for bamboo and glass, short and "midge-like" is certainly below 7'. In graphite, it is perhaps 7'6". The Sage 000-weight to 3-weight rods for small streams were all 7'10", but they've since been replaced with the Sage One. It has to do with the nature of the material. Different materials have different possibilities, although some push the possibilities in one direction or another – through hollowing (in the case of bamboo), stiffer butts (in the case of graphite), and so on.

'The length of Tenkara rods has to do with the fact that there is no "shooting" of additional line. One cannot handle a reasonable length of line continuously with a short rod without a reel.'

See what I mean? Nothing is written in stone. And we haven't even spoken much about the crucial aspect of line weight. Here we open another can of worms.

I only use 0- to 3-weight rods on mountain streams, but other scribes differ. I do have a Steve Dugmore 000-weight bamboo rod; it's on loan to Tony Kietzman in Rhodes at the moment, because the joy he got out of using the stick was so infectious I simply had to hand it over to him before I headed home after my most recent trip up there. I had no choice. I just said, 'Look after it, and when either of us drops off the perch, it goes to my son Robert.' He agreed. Perhaps too readily.

I said other scribes differ about small-stream rod weights. Tom Rosenbauer, in *The Orvis Guide to Small Stream Fly Fishing*, maintains it's difficult to cast a size 10 dry fly with a 2- to 3-weight fly line. I had to read that sentence a few times to make sure I wasn't suffering from some sinister cognitive disorder. He goes on to talk about 4-weights being good on small streams and 5-weights being *maybe* too heavy. I think the issue at stake here is in what we and the Americans interpret as small streams. Their definition of a small stream is obviously a lot bigger than ours.

I believe that you shouldn't approach small streams in ways that lose sight of the poetry there is in just fishing them. To my way of thinking, 0- to 2-weights, and even 3-weights, will do pretty well anything I ever want on small streams and, at the same time, serve the more poetic need for lightness. Not that lightness in small-stream fly rods is all about poetry. It's not. There's a practical side to it as well. Lighter fly lines land on the water more gently, full stop.

But above a 3-weight I feel I'm missing the point and getting decidedly over-gunned. My favourite small-stream rod for years, before the truck door ate it, was my five-piece Winston 7'9" 2-weight. It's been a while, but I don't like to trouble Steve Boshoff, who has an eye to repairing it, because like so many of his ilk, he is up to his eyes in bamboo dust and smeared in glue most days.

My Sage 8' SPL 0-weight, my Sage Circa 2-weight and my bamboo rods – Boshoffs and Dugmores, all 3-weights in 7' and 7'6" and built more or less on original Paul Young tapers – are all I need for small streams at present, barring a wish list a mile long of rods I can't afford and don't really need. Yet one of the sweetest rods I ever cast on a small stream was a 9' 1-weight that Steve Boshoff built from a Scott graphite blank about five years ago.

But here's an interesting point. After many years, I discovered I take more fish from small streams with my 8', medium-action Sage SPL 0-weight and Sage Circa 2-weight, and that I *lost* more with my medium-fast action Winston 2-weight, as lovely as it was. It had to do, I now realise, with a simple truth. If I was fishing for trout of less than twelve inches, the extra weight and stiffness in the butt of the Winston lifted them in the strike and, as they fell back, this often allowed the barbless hook to drop out. My slower-action Sages and my bamboo rods all 'give' with the fish in the strike; they don't lift the fish as you strike, and so they stay hooked. I hope you read this carefully. It took me some time to figure out, and there was a moment of revelation when I did. The first three times I fished the upper Lourens I used my Winston 2-weight and, each trip, I lost as many fish as I caught. On the fourth trip, I happened to use my Sage 0-weight and never lost a fish. And it's been pretty much the pattern ever since. That, in a nutshell, is the advantage of a slower rod in small mountain streams with six- to twelve-inch fish in them. When the fish in a stream average fourteen inches my 2-weight Winston is right on the money.

Leonard Flemming arrived for a cup of coffee one day and told me he had experienced exactly the same thing. Does this benefit improve as you drop from 0- to 000-weight? I don't think so. I like to think that Sage's SPL 0-weight was the point of ultimate perfection in small-stream fly rods – at least as far as graphite is concerned. It's a pity Sage sort of lost the plot after that, but I think they worked it out pretty well, doing a full circle and arriving at where they had begun with their lighter range of rods. As Sage put it, '…in search of *advanced* slowness…' (their words, not mine). Ian Douglas was kind enough to build my Circa, a 7'9" 2-weight, and it's as close to the perfect small-stream fly rod as you'll find, unless you're cluttered by a few unreasonable prejudices.

Fishing the Avon and the Itchen one year in England, I noticed my friends William Daniel and Bill Latham were using 4- and 5-weight medium-to-fast-action rods, not neat little 2- to 3-weights as I imagined. They said they hook and hold the bigger browns in these streams far better on a quicker, heavier rod. More importantly, they can check the first run, or quickly turn a fish's head before it ends up buried in a weed-bed on the opposite bank. But we're talking big river browns and rainbows here, say sixteen inches plus – deep, robust fish. And the Avon, for example, you'd describe as a river and not as a stream, let alone a small, tumbling mountain stream.

We've been talking about light, quick-flowing, minimalist streams with modest-sized but honest fish in them that you can catch with gentle casts, and if that's the largest part of the charm of streams like this, it's probably why 000- to 2-weight rods were invented in the first place. On this kind of water, a 0- to 2-weight rod feels like you slipped your hand straight into a neat-fitting glove. The ideal state of balance, the philosophical point you can call perfection if you like, is when you're on a tiny stream and unaware there's a fly rod in your hand. You're just aware that you're looking at sweet spots in the stream, doing something with your wrist, and mostly landing the fly right where you want it to be.

You need to keep trying different rods, different makes of line and different line weights until you reach this state, I guess, but you don't want to get too glued up in science trying to get there either.

Here's a last thought on rods. Since small-stream fly fishing is also a percentage game, where every little nuance has a place, when I fish with a good pal we'll often only take one rod along. Apart from the appealing economy in this, it cuts the risk of rod flash in half and frees up one of you to really concentrate on watching the water – or, in my case, to do some camera work, for which I'm gaining a growing reputation as a pain in the arse on trout streams.

The food chain

I base my findings on the food chain in small streams on the hundreds of stones I've lifted from riverbeds right around the country, and on the stomach contents of the occasional trout I have checked. On the stones there's a predominance of tiny *Baetis* mayfly nymphs, varying in colour from dark to light straw-coloured, followed, in no order of importance, by cased- and free-living caddis larvae, and mountain midge and black fly (*Simuliid*) larvae. Occasionally I find a dragonfly or damselfly nymph, but stonefly nymphs are rare.

The incidence in stomach contents is much the same, though ants and beetles make an appearance. Here and there I've found dragonfly nymphs three to four centimetres long, and damselfly nymphs around two centimetres long, but they're uncommon.

In a nutshell, if there is no real abundance of food in most fast-flowing mountain streams, there is also no real shortage either, even though it's true enough to say that the higher you are in a stream and the faster the flow, the lower the density of aquatic insects per square metre of riverbed compared to the wider, slower-flowing pastoral reaches. And the vast majority of the insects are small, as in size 18 to 22.

So what affects the average size of small-stream trout is not so much the relatively low density of insects in small streams, but the relative difficulty trout have in retrieving them. That, coupled with higher fish populations and the constant, energy-sapping flow of the currents these trout have to contend with, collectively accounts for their averagely smaller size.

Three almost immutable facts so far
First, small-stream trout are more eclectic and opportunistic feeders than their downstream cousins. And that goes for surface, surface-film and sub-surface feeding. As far as dry flies go, some people like the term 'free-rising' to describe trout in certain streams, but personally I think it says too much, or it's only partially reliable.

Second, these trout are smaller because they live life against currents, and the insects they feed on are in general less abundant, smaller and more difficult to harvest. Look, that small-stream trout are small is not the law of the Meads and the Persians, but it is something you will mostly be right about. I have taken sixteen- and even seventeen-inch fish from little brooks, but it's not something I'd go around betting will happen that often, or with any great certainty, in South African waters. That's why a big fish from a small stream is such a cause for celebration. As an aside, if you can call, say, the Smalblaar River a small stream, although it doesn't really fit the description we've given for this kind of water here, then fish up to twenty inches plus are not rare.

Third, far from being easy to spot, small-stream trout can be notoriously difficult to find. Part of this stems from the often-broken surface under which they live, but it's also because, in shallow and relatively exposed environments, they become masters at remaining well concealed in the deepest slot they can find. And they are mostly perfectly camouflaged against the mosaic of tiny, multicoloured pebbles you find in small streams, especially in the Western Cape. This applies, of course, to both browns and rainbows. They seem to slot almost invisibly into whatever surroundings they live in.

Small-stream holding lies, mistakes, waiting and watching,
and your approach

There are exceptions to finding small-stream trout that are important to note, but let me say that these principles hold good for both rivers and streams. Primary lies are easy. They are the deep slots anywhere in a stream, but especially where boulders or overhanging vegetation offer additional cover. But the secondary or feeding lies are often where you'd least expect to find a trout, such as right at the very back end of runs or pools, even where the water is ridiculously shallow; or in the slips of current right up against the banks, especially where there's a little overhanging vegetation. When the water is low and conditions are warm, shade is important, and I always look carefully into shaded areas. In fact, trout often migrate during the day from sunny to shady spots in a stream as the sun changes position.

Finally, one other spot I've noticed trout love, not necessarily only as a feeding lie but also a holding lie, is immediately *ahead* of a waterfall – but again, this applies to rivers as much as to small streams. The fact is trout, and often the better trout, frequently hold just below the lip of waterfalls, especially ones that have some depth, because there's a pushback effect here that slows the current just before it cascades over the waterfall. The pushback effect creates a comfortable cushion ahead of the rocks forming the waterfall, where not only the current slows down, but where drifting bugs arrive more slowly and become more accessible.

Two mistakes people make fishing small streams stem from trout holding in unusual positions. The first is that people don't take enough time or enough care approaching a run to scan it properly before fishing it. Instead, they walk right up to the back of a run or a pool, fly rod in the air. I've yet to find a way of cursing the people who do it without losing the few fishing friends I still have.

You must *stalk* up to the back end of runs, not only on small streams but approaching any holding water – rod down, crouched, moving slowly with no rapid movements, eyes scanning all the time. It's doubly important on small streams because if you spook a fish, it's likely to blow your chances on the whole of that run or pool. Bigger waters provide more room for error after you've spooked a fish simply because there is more space and therefore less chance that the trout you spooked will spook others.

Having arrived at the back of the run, many anglers don't stay crouched to wait and watch. Remember the old idiom, 'Given time, nature will reveal herself.' It never counted more than when you're fishing small, clear-flowing streams.

I may have written before about the experience I want to relate to you now, but it's worth repeating. I was on a typical, gin-clear Western Cape mountain stream with a friend of mine, Gerhard Laubscher. Around midday we got to a really nice section, a pool of braided water with two separate waterfalls at the head, which I'd fished often before and knew held good fish. But a quick scan revealed nothing more than that it was indeed an interesting and likely-looking piece of water. So we parked off and had a bite to eat.

After five minutes of idle chat, we spotted a nice fish. A few minutes later we spotted a second, even nicer, fish, and maybe a full 10 minutes into our break we saw a third, a honey, in a really unlikely (and, as it turned out, awkward) spot. Gerhard caught the first fish with a single cast, missed the second and rose the one in the tricky spot at least four times before it got wise to us. I walked over to the lie and found it was a narrow, pebble-bottomed depression with a thread of current coming into it from a tiny bushed-over and cool tributary. In all the years I'd fished this stream I'd never noticed the little tributary. The trouble with this fish was micro-drag caused by a thin thread of cross-current. Later, with the wisdom of hindsight, we decided we should have added another three feet of 8X mono to the leader, but that's another story.

The whole point of telling you this is to illustrate how much we saw that we would have missed if we hadn't spent time really studying that pool and the various current tongues in it.

We've handled one obvious error you can make on small streams; here's another: people won't fish the tail-out of pools and runs, the very lips of them; that's where the water leaves the run or the pool, often over a small waterfall. For some reason, many anglers prefer to put the first cast straight into what looks like the best spot; the plump, deep belly of the run, the heart of the run. That's normally around the centre in a small stream run, or two-thirds of the way up it, where they imagine the best holding water is – which is mostly right, but it misses the point, in that any trout holding in the back end run for cover and often aren't even seen.

So you have to fish the back end first, by high-sticking it to avoid drag, first covering the centre, then both right and left sides, with short casts that show only the leader or, at most, very little fly line. And in doing this, let me say again, you want to be low, crouched, creeping, whatever, not standing on your toes like you're trying to peep over a garden wall.

By the way, this is where the modern drive to use longer rods comes in. They provide extra reach, as in Tenkara fishing, or a kind of quasi-Czech nymphing in miniature, or even fishing in the style of Jeremy Lucas's hand-to-leader methods with no fly line at all. This is also where the new minimalist fly lines like Snowbee's Thistledown or Rio's Euro line and ultra-long soft-action rods found their origins. But I am not going in to all these techniques. They are mainly methods for bigger streams, although I read more and more these days of leader-only fly fishing on all kinds of waters, including small streams, and also of the joys of Tenkara.

But just on the subject of these ultra-thin fly lines, the Thistledown and Euro line are rated rather contrarily for those of us who believed the old AFTMA scale was sacrosanct. They market an AFTMA 2 to 5 in one fly line! Apparently, the idea is that when the rod is held high, the line is so thin that it doesn't come running back down the rod guides. Food for thought. I haven't tried these lines, and I am not an expert on these methods.

The curse of the telltale crease

There's another mistake in small-stream fly fishing I see often, surprisingly from anglers who really ought to know better. Because small-stream trout live in relatively tiny, almost encapsulated environments, they don't miss much. So you never want to give your presence away, and I don't mean by wearing bright clothes or wading like a buffalo. I take it for granted you won't do that. I mean something as innocuous as creasing the water surface when you lift your fly line off to cast again. It's a seemingly minor fault, but most often it's the kiss of death – more so on any flat, calm, clear surface where you might as well throw a rock into the run. When you lift a fly off, it should be so gentle it leaves no trace. In fact, as gentle as a feather dropping on a windless day.

For this very reason, leader-to-line connections should preferably be super-glued needle knots – never loop-to-loop connections that are stiff, that induce drag, and that increase the chance you will crease the surface as you lift the fly off the water to cast again.

Further thoughts on rivercraft in small streams
I often pick up technical books that describe a section of a typical trout stream with its banks, runs and boulders, either in the form of a diagram or a photograph that has the likely location of trout superimposed on it, as if the distribution of trout in a stream was close to some law of physics or the product of a mathematical formula. Look, it's helpful, except that a formulaic approach ignores one important reality: in a small stream, trout can be anywhere. In a large stream or river as well. That's a truth that dawns on you after years of spooking trout from ridiculous places, or catching a fish where no trout had the right to be, at least not the way you've been taught to understand things. When that's happened often enough, you start to fish a stream differently. You take more time to cover the water and you don't rely on what the books tell you about likely lies – but, at the same time, you don't totally ignore it either.

I was fishing the upper section of a small stream with Billy de Jong. We weren't catching much, but were not yet wondering if we had the right flies on, or whether the fish had moved off to spawn. We were using a dry fly that covered most bases (probably an Elk Hair Caddis), lazily fishing mainly the sweet spots – the throats of the runs and the undercut banks – and we took the occasional fish. Then, by chance, we hooked two trout in quick succession from water so shallow it only just covered our wading boots, and that pretty well remained the pattern of things for the rest of the day.

The question was, why? In the end we put it down to maybe a hatch of mountain midges that prefer hatching in shallow water when the temperature is, say, exactly x degrees, and the water level is just exactly *so* high, or at least some argument along the lines of, 'Fish will be where the bugs are at any given time.' In fact, we weren't even half-sure why the trout were in such shallow water on the day, except that the presence of bugs is often the answer.

But the reason is not as important as knowing that you can never really tell where trout will hang out in a small stream, other than they're not always only in the sweet spots. The difference between small streams and bigger waters is that the feeding lies in small streams often end up being in ultra-shallow water. In that sense, the science of rivercraft often loses its relevance on them. In fact, an interesting exercise to try on a stream is to spend an hour fishing all the 'wrong' spots. I do it occasionally if only to remind myself that our linear thinking on how to approach trout streams, especially smaller ones, is never a watertight science. The number of fish that show up in unusual places shouldn't be surprising me any more, but somehow it still does.

Last word on books on small streams: in my experience, they're good for the basics. But fishing small streams is much the same as fishing bigger ones, only you have to do a lot more creeping, crawling and crouching, short casting and fetching flies off branches. In most other ways they're actually as easy, or as difficult, to fish as rivers, and their trout are every bit as forgiving or as unpredictable, only on average smaller. Something small streams do teach you, and something you won't need a book for, is that catching big fish isn't the only way to have fun fly fishing. Naturally, we all want to catch big trout, and most of us agree that a real hog from a small stream is somehow more momentous than one that came from a river with a pedigree. But having said that, small trout have never disappointed me.

A few Coldbrook lessons

There was a day up on the Coldbrook Stream a few years ago when Billy and I took trout after trout in one pretty run after another, all on dry flies. The fish were everywhere, often coming up to the fly from dark, hidden corners, sometimes taking them as they landed in ankle-deep water. We got as far as a fenced cattle camp when the sun was setting behind the hills. Bugs began appearing, lit in shafts of sunlight like sparks from a campfire, and then the fish went crazy. This was not a day on a stretch of stream to write a learned treatise on rivercraft, other than to say you could have left all the textbooks at home. It reinforced my growing view that book knowledge is not the only way to understand reality.

And this was the same stretch where, some months later, Tony Kietzman and I couldn't buy a trout in a whole morning, but that's a contrary enough story that perhaps goes a long way towards explaining why we go fishing in the first place.

It's also the stream where Ed Herbst and I had a good day just before he got ill, fishing a stretch further downstream of the top sections we normally make for, where in many places the water is flat and the runs are as smooth as satin. The stream was low and clear, and with it being a bright day, most of the fish we caught we'd sighted. We didn't get that many or, put differently, we didn't get as many as we could have, but then we weren't fishing as if our lives depended on it either. We were just taking our time. One of my friends would say we were fishing 'properly'. He's also been known to describe some rocks in rivers as 'ideal beer perches'…

When you spot more than one trout

Most trout sort out a pecking order, even in pocket water, but in pocket water my impression is the pecking-order positions are not as obvious. Just the other day, my friend Stanton Hector and I were on a really delicate stream in the Western Cape when we came to a tiny, glass-clear hole that was a clearly super-sweet piece of holding water. There was a little undercut on the right bank, and one or two big rocks on the left to add cover and to slow the currents, but the whole of it was not much bigger than the rug in your den. Three fish were holding in this spot, and they were as easy to see as a red traffic light. The best spot in our estimation held the smallest fish, and the biggest fish was sitting on an exposed gravel bar with only a thread of current flowing over its dorsal fin. That's not unusual in small streams, and we've seen it often enough in this particular stream to always check a run carefully before pounding away at the first fish we happen to see.

The next event wasn't unusual either, and it's interesting. Naturally you want to hook the best fish first because, for sure, you are only going to hook one of them before a little spot like this gets shaken up. The trick is to hook the bigger fish and then take careful note of where it runs. It'll usually head straight for where it lives when it's not in a feeding lie. In this case, I hooked the better fish first and it made a straight line to the undercut bank; a moment later, when we released him, he shot off to the exact same place. That's where he lives when he's not out shopping for bugs, and we made a note of it.

We watched for a while, more in hope than out of any real conviction, in case the other two fish came back, but they stayed under the rocks. Sometimes they return, even moments later, even start feeding again, even get caught, but it's rare with fish that are visible in a stream this small and this clear.

Having said that, on small streams with depth, cover and a nice surface twirl, you can take a raft of fish just starting at the back and delicately working your way up a run. Some days it feels as easy as walking down an aisle in a supermarket picking goods off the shelves. But it depends on the stream and the run, the weather, what mood the fish are in, and maybe how much wine you left in the bottle the night before.

Some streams are made for serial trout picking, others are not. In one small stream we fish, occasionally even just missing a take puts the rest of the fish on high alert. Then there are streams where even if you've spooked a pod of fish, you can still tease them to take a weighted nymph fished deep and with movement. I don't know what the reasons for these differences are, but they are there and, eventually, this is how you get to know a stream. But it's not something they cover much in books, perhaps because it's awkward to write about things that have no real answer.

The three four-letter words in small-stream fly fishing:
wind, drag and false-casting
Wind makes ultra-light rods frustrating instruments to use, no matter in what direction it's blowing, but when it's downstream straight into your face, casting with ultra-light rods becomes a lottery. Then you're better off with a quicker 3-weight rod.

But a bigger problem in strong wind is you easily lose control of leader and tippet placement. In rivers it's less of a problem because there are generally fewer limitations to putting in a good cast than on tight streams where wind, especially gusting wind, can get embarrassing. You aim at a sweet spot, miss the water completely and suddenly your fly lands two metres up the opposite bank. It's like driving a car with a loose steering wheel. In gusty conditions the obvious trick is to wait for a lull before you cast, and the strange part of that is how few anglers do.

The problem with drag on small streams is you have less time to do what you have to do to avoid it because the drifts are shorter and swifter. But you should study not to over-correct your mends. Correcting drag, no matter how quick or ruffled the surface, should be done as *gently* as you stroke a sleeping cat, and as *accurately* as you flick a speck of ash off the sleeve of your jacket. I occasionally see anglers wildly over-mending a line, creasing the water and alarming every fish, even before drag actually sets in. The art of drag correction, in its highest Zen-like form, is to study a run before you cast, to anticipate where and when drag will happen, and, having cast, to mend the fly line with light, precise movements introduced at the very last second. It should be pretty to watch. And drape your fly line over any convenient rock – it can help eliminate drag naturally. Dry fly purists will tell you that's why God put them there.

Micro-drag is hard to detect, is a real curse and deserves a hot place in hell.

False casting? Don't. Not on small streams.

Final thoughts on small streams

I love them. Their smallness adds intimacy and charm. Hills or vales or remoteness often keep them hidden and conveniently less known, and their lack of trophy trout helps to keep them less fished. The relative absence of the signs of recent human passage is a bonus, and if there's a sense that a little stream has freed you from the rigours of the world, even briefly, well, that's just added cause for celebration.

But underlying this all is a minor mystery. And the mystery is the opiate-like hold that small streams and their trout have on so many anglers, despite their trout being naive, easier to catch and averagely not much longer than a size-eight shoe. For their hold is real. And the fact that it is a minor mystery – or at least that it can't be fully explained, not even by us fanatical fans – is not a matter we lose any sleep over.

CHAPTER 9
RIVERBANKS

Elevated banks increase the amount of water
that can be visually searched.
RENÉ HARROP, *TROUT HUNTER: THE WAY OF AN ANGLER*

I want to touch on the subject of riverbanks and their role in fly fishing, using the streams in the Eastern Cape Highlands as a kind of model, simply because so many of them have undulating banks that are often high enough above the streams or rivers to be pretty useful. And, as it happens, they're conveniently threaded by sheep and cattle paths, so the going along them is generally a lot easier for anglers than it is on many streams around the world.

But why bother about doing a piece on banks in fly fishing at all? Well, I'm not going to make a huge issue out of it but, in a nutshell, when banks are well above a stream they can provide convenient and sometimes super-effective vantage points. This is mainly because the elevation helps to cut the glare off the water, meaning you can better study the tapestry of a streambed, identify the best holding water, see where the main current flows are, and maybe also spot a fish or two. And the more you establish things about current flows and potential holding lies and so on, even if you don't spot any fish, you can at least sort of work out where the *better* ones are likely to be. And, in turn, you can get a good idea of what casts or presentations will be most effective and where you should position yourself in a stream to start fishing.

Sometimes fish sit too deep to find easily, or the water won't be clear enough to find them at all, but as a general rule, scanning a stream from an elevated position gives you a better chance. There's also the happy chance you'll actually spot a rise – and rises, especially the more cryptic ones, are also easier to see from *above* than when you are in a river looking upstream from a flat plane, especially if you are battling against glare.

*

Thinking of all this reminds me of one of the first times I fished with my friend Stanton Hector back when he was a student and long before he'd done his PhD. We covered a lot of water fishing up a pretty stream in the Western Cape, and spotted and caught a fair number of trout on dry flies, none much longer than twelve inches. Later that afternoon we headed out on a hiking path above the stream, and from time to time we would stop to inspect some of the runs we'd fished through. I'm not sure how many trout we spotted from the path walking out (I'd say at least six, which was nothing special), but what was of interest were the two big fish we spotted, each at least fifteen inches. On this stream these are notable fish and we realised, perhaps a little shamefacedly, that we must have missed them altogether while we were fishing. From the path they were sitters to find. And let me tell you that even back then Stanton was no slouch at finding trout in fast streams, and I was getting better.

I don't want to harp on too much about the value of elevation, but on the other hand, why not?

*

If you take a stroll along streams like the Sterkspruit, the Bokspruit, or the upper Willow on *Balloch*, to name three I know reasonably well in the Eastern Cape Highlands, you will find yourself well above the water from time to time. The only risk is getting spotted yourself, even standing well downstream of the water you're scanning. The basic precautions are all routine: avoid sudden movements, especially when your profile is above the skyline, don't wear any light-coloured clothing and be careful not to cast a shadow over the water when the sun is behind you. All straight up and down as a starched shirt.

If you're in the river and you don't have someone on a bank to spot for you, you will catch fish anyway. After all, fishing *in* a river is part of our holy grail, and the majority of the fish we catch didn't need, or get, any bank climbing. But the fact remains that taking time to study water from above will increase your chances of sighting fish, which in turn may even help you catch *better* fish. When you come to think of it, this turns riverbanks into prime, tactical fishing tools. In an ideal world, you want to fish with a pal up a bank scouting the water for you, providing he can recite by heart all the rules on how not to get spotted himself.

*

There will be times when you find yourself at a spot in a stream where the water looks good and where there's a conveniently high bank on one side, and since height offers advantages, you'd imagine a few anglers would consider climbing out of the river to scan the water from up there before fishing it. But mostly we don't, and

I'm including myself in this. Well, let's say I don't know anyone who makes anything like a routine of it, I suppose because it's a hassle to get out of a river to haul your body up some steep bank when you feel pretty confident you'll catch fish right where you're standing anyway. After all, you've done just that for years. Once in a while, though, I do climb a bank, but only when the bank is conveniently adjacent to a really pretty, deep-flowing run, and it's relatively straightforward and easy to climb – and nicely elevated.

But the truth is that, most times I end up peering off a usefully high bank simply because that's where the path I was hiking on happened to take me. And it's also why on a downstream hike along a riverbank to get to wherever I'm going to start the day's fishing, I make every use I can of all the elevated spots that afford me a good view into the river. In fact, in the Eastern Cape Highlands this is one of the advantages of walking downstream to begin a day's fishing – at least on some streams. It depends on the path and the lie of the land.

The high incidence of useful banks in this part of the world relates to the topography of the riverbeds and valleys. They run in conveniently uneven and hilly country. I can't think of many other places where finding a long enough piece of flat ground to make a landing strip would be more difficult than up here – not forgetting you'd also need a longer runway to compensate for the altitude.

Many streams in the highlands flow well below the level of the surrounding lands, in what amounts to deep dongas that I can only guess are the result of aeons of natural erosion – and in some cases, perhaps a few decades of more recent erosion. So the banks are mainly bare earth or, far less commonly, just plain rock.

*

Most runs under banks are good for fishing, and they often hold better fish too, I guess because the flow along them is mostly deeper and slowed by the bank itself, making insects more easily available, and the water is conveniently shaded, at least part of the day. The same applies to banks formed from solid rock, but obviously these are permanent structures, whereas the earthen banks, being a mix of sedimentary rocks, small stones and compacted soil, are fragile and tend to crumble and deposit silt and soil into the water. As far as the fishing goes, there's little difference between earth and rock banks.

In some places banks are really high, and the earthen ones can hang precariously over the water like huge hollowed-out caves. You always want to remind yourself that the tops of these overhangs are unpredictable as far as supporting your weight is concerned, and standing too close to the edge risks a sudden collapse that will drop you and a load of soil straight into the water. But earthen banks collapse often enough anyway, mainly from rain, erosion and the passage of livestock, and only rarely through the weight of an overly bold angler who isn't scared of a little risk-taking. So coming across clods of earth lying in streams up here isn't uncommon, more so in a wet season. Mostly the clods are no bigger than a wheelbarrow, but some are big enough to do serious damage to the river course. Occasionally, a big slip will add some value to a run.

For example, one year a bank the size of a two-car garage collapsed into the river on *Birkhall*, and when I got to fish this spot a few months later – a place I happened to know well and had fished many times – I found that the rubble and rocks had converted a relatively uninteresting, knee-deep stretch into a nicely curved and invitingly deep glide.

*

I only caused a serious bank collapse once. It was years back when I was fishing the Pot River on Ron Moore's farm near Maclear. I was hauling myself over the lip of a steep overhang, bent on fetching my fly out of a tree. The bank collapsed, causing the demise of a lovely Hardy Featherweight fly reel and some damage to my pride. In hindsight I should have snapped the fly off, but as I recall I'd already lost a few flies in trees and this was probably one of those fancy ties you don't feel like losing.

Looking at the bigger picture, I don't tie many serious flies – by that I mean flies so time-consuming to construct that the last thing you want to do is sacrifice one. 'Good' flies should only be as fancy as really matters, and then completely expendable. Well, almost, what with the cost of hooks and fly-tying materials these days. The point is you don't want to regularly use flies that are so fancy that you feel like donning a black armband every time you lose one.

*

In most earthen banks in the Eastern Cape Highlands you see the entrance tunnels of martins' and kingfishers' nests – the Pied Kingfisher is common up here, but I see the occasional Giant Kingfisher and, from time to time and always fleetingly, the tiny Malachite Kingfisher that manages to look blue and gold at the same time. You might think fish would find a potential threat in such proximity to the front door of a kingfisher's nest, but if they do they obviously just live with it. Then again, in the hundreds of days I've spent on the rivers up here I can't remember seeing a kingfisher fly onto a perch and then disappear down a hole. Of course it must happen, but any proximity to bank-nesting kingfishers clearly doesn't affect a trout's choice of holding water; or else they don't understand the significance of holes in banks, which is probably more like the truth.

*

Sometimes I come across a honey of a run with a conveniently tall bank alongside it and think to myself, if I climb that bank I'll get a good take on what's going on under the surface. Then I'll study the bank and notice a tricky barbed-wire fence to cross, or a tangle of brambles or dead branches, or it's as steep as a mine shaft, and decide it looks too much like work, which always leads to the conclusion that I'm actually okay where I am. But there have been times when I've ended up fishless going through a promising run, looked up at a bank and thought I should have climbed it after all. I guess our hunger to catch better fish doesn't always trump our natural inclination to laziness.

*

There will be times when trout move into conveniently shallow secondary lies, when spotting them comes together quite easily when you're standing in the river. But in that emerald-tinted water typical of deeper lies in this part of the world, what you're looking for isn't always an obvious fish as much as just the occasional silver flash of light reflected off a deep-turning flank, or a fish showing only as a fleeting, gently-waving, darkly-linear form that's somehow in mild contrast to the swaying tapestry of the riverbed. This sounds vague, I know, but then that's exactly what it is, though over time you come to recognise the sub-surface signs that indicate a fish, and can more confidently call them for what they are. But the essential point about finding difficult fish like these is that it's always easier to do *looking down into the water from up on a bank.*

*

Some riverbanks are no more than low undulations along a river's edge, and some are really high, say three or four metres or more above the water. The useful ones are anywhere between the height of a garden hedge or the gutter on a single-storey house, but I've been on banks on a few streams when I'm three or four storeys above an almost sheer drop to the riverbed and get mildly giddy just looking down. From places like this you could make a killing, either actually locating fish or sizing up the structure of the riverbed, but I don't bother. I don't handle heights.

Chance spotting from above

On a visit to the Bokspruit River one afternoon a few years back, Tony Kietzman and I had fun dropping dry flies on unsuspecting trout holding in dainty runs, and we caught a heap of them, all small, some not much longer than a pencil. But I wasn't complaining because it was the sort of afternoon on the sort of river that perfectly suited the frame of mind I was in, the sort of day where if you'd later asked how many fish I'd caught I'd say, 'Ample,' and if you asked what size they were I'd say, 'Big enough to make us happy.'

The afternoon progressed to the point where I was done, and I climbed a small bank leading to my parked truck. Tony was throwing a few last casts into the run below me, wading in wavy, knee-deep water flowing over yellowish sandstone. I'd only been watching him for a minute when I spotted a decent trout. He was working up to it nicely so I said nothing, and two or three casts later the fish took his dry fly and bolted. It was the best trout of the day, all of fourteen, maybe fifteen inches, and Tony later said that the first he knew about that trout was when his dry fly went under. On the other hand, I'd no doubt been advantaged by the little elevation I had, though I can't say that I was really looking for trout at the time. From up there the trout just seemed to float into view.

I was glad I'd kept quiet about it. You never know how stage fright will freeze an angler's casting wrist when he's told there's a really good fish just ahead of him. It's undone me a few times.

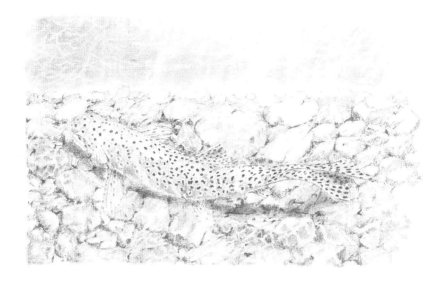

Stillwater banks

Some lakes have cosmically high vantage points, like the lovely bowl of water on the summit of a mountain that was once part of the Highland Lodge collection of lakes, a lake they called Mountain Dam, that had the features of a volcanic crater filled with water. I never saw more or bigger trout than I spotted one day here when I climbed the hillside that lifts steeply from one corner of the wall and runs for more or less a hundred metres towards the shallows.

It was mid-July and the lake was like crystal. From the hill we watched trout swim slowly in steady, seemingly aimless procession, and we guessed there wasn't one under six pounds. My friend Mark Yelland was with us; he spent a few hours trying for them off the side of the hill but couldn't get a take. Mind you, out in the float tubes we also had little by way of luck. The shallower water was covered in decaying, grey-coloured weed that broke into clouds of fine debris when you hooked into it. But there were deep, clear holes in the decomposing weed and we concentrated on those, and the water was so transparent you could see details on the lake bed five metres below you. I landed a bus of around seven pounds on a DDD, and moments later Billy de Jong caught a rainbow near on ten pounds. But beyond that, not a touch from the other three rods. Had the fish been feeding, who knows how many Mark would have hooked from his perch on that headland.

As an aside, the huge rainbow Billy caught happened to swim lazily past my float tube in full view a metre down, heading in Billy's general direction. All I had to do was 'talk him in', as it were. I shouted, 'Billy. Huge fish. Three o'clock. Throw short.' He hooked it first cast. There were no high banks involved in this catch.

Notes on banks and fishing above the Lindisfarne Bridge on the Sterkspruit River

I parked in the paddock above the Lindisfarne Bridge on Sarel Steenekamp's land, which covers both banks upstream and downstream of the bridge, and strolled over to inspect the water. The flow was strong and clear, and the river looked fresh. I drank coffee and set up my Boshoff 3-weight bamboo rod.

Burned grass crunched under my boots, the black tufts already green-tinged with new shoots. Between the patches of burned grass there were wildflowers, mainly white violets that on the black earth stood out like snowflakes. I saw mushrooms that may have been edible, I wasn't sure, but they brought to mind the old maxim, 'All mushrooms are edible. Some only once.' I left them alone.

I drifted a RAB through the first run, a clear, resinous place, and took two small trout from it, then got a brace upstream out of pocket water and another from a small pool above the pocket water. As the morning warmed, a few bugs hatched – at first small, grey-coloured duns, then larger, wheat-coloured duns – and then I saw the first trout rise. I hooked it in a basin of water the size of a dinner plate just off the bank.

A Cape Robin-chat with a twig in her beak perched briefly on a stone before flying into a thicket to add to her nest. Moments before, a pair of White-faced Whistling Duck swept over my head in silent formation. I suspected they were heading down the valley to the lake on *Birkhall*, where they aren't uncommon visitors.

Eventually I came to a long, deep-shelving pool, where years back I'd watched my good friend Mario Cesare catch a lovely trout we'd seen rising here. Strange how you remember a single trout, even years later. I worked up the deeper water on the left bank, using a nymph, letting it drift and tumble with the current, not bothering to add any movement, striking when the leader drew under. It was fun, and I took a few ten-inch trout and missed as many. There's never a shortage of trout in the back of this pool, but the long inlet flowing under a tall bank on the right is always more interesting and holds better fish.

I climbed the bank, which ran high and tight along the side of the river. From up there I had a bird's-eye view over the water. I searched the riverbed's mosaic of boulders and crevices, and gradually they became more detailed, as if opened by sunlight and by height. A deep channel of quicker-flowing water twisted out of sight on my bank. Impulsively I threw a cast up the channel, realising straight away that I wasn't sure what I'd do from up there if a decent fish took the fly, except to somehow scramble back down the bank to fight it in the river. It's the sort of cast you make without thinking. Or you make the cast out of plain curiosity; or because most water is somehow more tempting when you're above looking down on it than when you're in the water looking upstream. On the other hand, I think that throwing a cast is sometimes as compelling to fly fishers as pulling the trigger is to wing shooters.

The large RAB floated back along the edge of the channel, dancing on the threads of current. Somehow, from high above, the RAB looked bigger than it actually was, but I guess my unusual vantage point had a lot to do with the illusion. We're far more used to watching dry flies from a low angle.

A small trout slashed at the fly, briefly streaking the surface, hardly changing the fly's drift. The sharpness and brevity of the strike had all the hallmarks of the temptingly-big-dry-fly-drifting-over-an-excited-little-trout rise, the sort of flicking response to a fly that you recognise is the hallmark of an over-eager, four-inch trout.

I moved along the bank towards the inlet. I was lower now, and it was easy to get off the bank here. I spotted a trout. I dried the fly with a quick snap-cast aimed away from the water where the fish was holding. A tiny burst of silvery spray shook off the fly. It rode high on the surface again, drifted right over the fish, and a moment later was gone. I saw the leader tear away and briefly felt the weight of the fish, but under the bank the line locked solid. I lifted the rod, felt the rock-steady firmness, remembered the tangle of black roots along the water's edge down there, knew instantly what had happened, and broke the fly off with a crack.

I pulled off an arm's-length of fresh 6X to make a new tippet. A wind had picked up and the loose ends of nylon swirled, making it difficult to thread the knot. I changed to a nymph, a small, weighted Zak with a bright orange hotspot so fashionable these days, and dropped it into the same seam of water. It drifted a rod-length before it was taken, the tumbling fly clear to follow in the drift, the take so obvious it startled me. I set the hook, slid down the bank and landed a decent rainbow. The fish was iridescent, with spots like scatterings of charcoal. The trout shook in my grip, fins rigid, but when I removed the hook and opened my hand, as usual the fish froze for a second, then was gone like magic, lost in the liquid patina of the riverbed. This is one of the moments in fly fishing that I never tire of witnessing.

I climbed the bank again and walked to near the top of the run. At first I saw nothing, but after a few minutes two fish came into view – a smaller trout off to the left, sitting in a strangely exposed place over a shallow sheet of sandstone; the second, a bigger fish, holding to the far side of the main current less than a rod-length back from the smaller fish. I took a bead on the position of the smaller fish using a clump of overhanging grass for reference. The better fish was feeding, moving in and out of sight in the light and shadow of the river's flow. I waited and watched. The bigger trout darted across the run and chased off the minnow, then hung around for a few moments before slowly drifting back into deeper water. The smaller fish returned. The dynamics were interesting.

I climbed down the bank, slid silently into the river, then cautiously worked myself into position on a narrow shelf that fell off into deeper water. The challenge was to catch both fish.

I tied a tiny, match-head-sized poly yarn indicator to the tippet and set up a short drift just to my side of the larger fish, not wanting to get too close to the smaller trout. On the second drift, the indicator darted away and I immediately felt the weight of the trout and landed it. It was a cock fish, still in spawning colours and easily fourteen inches. When I released the fish, it shot downstream. I thought there was some good fortune in that and rested the run for five minutes.

I couldn't see the smaller fish in the shallow water, and it struck me that if I hadn't known there was a trout sitting there I wouldn't have bothered fishing this piece of water. I was glad I'd taken a bead on that tuft of grass. I lengthened the tippet, making it just long enough to feel I'd mildly overdone it, hoping to dampen the risk of drag, took off the indicator and changed to a dry fly. Given the shallowness of the lie, I tied on a small, dark CDC Midge and waited for the wind to drop.

The fly drifted a few moments in the wavy run and then it dipped. I landed the fish, a hen of around ten inches, a considerably lighter-coloured trout than any of the others I had taken that morning, and I wondered if this was partly due to the shallow, pale station it had chosen to take up.

I hooked two more small fish in the whitewater at the inlet to the pool; both threw the tiny, barbless dry fly on the first jump.

The wind strengthened, lifting swirling columns of dust. I left the stream above the whitewater and startled a trout from under my feet. As I grabbed hold of a bunch of grass to haul myself up the bank, my foot slipped and in a split second I had fallen in. It didn't feel too bad after the initial shock, but I was covered in mud. I cleaned off as best I could under a willow tree, where the sinuous shapes of fallen branches lay black and yellow in the grass, looking for all the world like a scattering of sleeping puff adders. With the worst of the mud off, I headed back to the truck.

I poured black coffee then carefully wiped each section of my rod with a wet rag. The cork handle was less easy to clean. I'd do that back home, properly, with soap and warm water. I stacked the two bamboo rod sections against a fence to dry in the sun, but each time I set them down the wind lifted them. They ended up resting safely enough on a cushion of grass so I left them there. My vest was also hanging out to dry on the fence. I threw an old carpet tile onto the ground and took off my boots, planting my wet feet on the small bit of carpet thinking, as I often do, that this is one of the best pieces of fly-fishing gear I own. Twenty minutes later I was threading up the hill to *Birkhall*. Driving past the lake below the farmhouse I saw that the White-faced Whistling Duck were indeed paying a visit.

*

I got to fish again one afternoon with Tony Kietzman. The Sterkspruit looked bright, and I used a dry fly that lifted enough trout not to get me wondering about changing to anything else. I would have brought up the subject of using banks, not that I think fishermen are split in their views on this, but we were engrossed in landing feisty rainbows that went up to twelve inches, some even fourteen. When we took a break for a cup of coffee, we chose a piece of high ground and sat under a tree alongside the stream. We were there long enough for me to get in a plug of sorts about the value of banks, and it was opportune that we actually did spot a fish in the water below us, although the moment would have shot up from just 'opportune' to 'profound' if it had been a lot bigger than the ones we were already catching so easily standing in the river. But in real life, of course, things don't often run the way they do in Hollywood film scripts. And anyway, the value of banks in fly fishing needed no more proof to either of us.

That evening I sat on the veranda writing my notes, adding a few words on the advantages of high banks, which was when the seeds for this chapter were sown. I sipped a beer while Basie worked on pieces of inch-thick steak that he seared this side then that over hot coals. Carien had laid out one of her signature salads; lettuce picked from the bed just outside her kitchen door, watercress from the stream running through her garden, chunks of pineapple, sliced onion, radishes, and a few stalks of celery. She prefers not to mix a salad. She lays out the ingredients separately; you decide what you want and help yourself. It's a useful approach and, along with grass-fed steak and a glass of red wine, I thought life couldn't get much better if I were a millionaire living high on the back of a hog somewhere in the Bahamas – until I thought, well, forget the Bahamas; life actually doesn't get much better than somewhere high on a bank of the Sterkspruit on *Birkhall*.

The Avon

CHAPTER 10

RETURN TO THE CHALKSTREAMS

If I try to think of the perfect trout river,
I know that it is a chalkstream.
CHARLES RANGELEY-WILSON, *CHALKSTREAM*

I was in London near the end of July, and I was again the guest of my friend Robin Renwick. We had three days set aside to visit the chalkstreams before we were booked to fly to Reykjavík in Iceland to fish for Atlantic salmon.

I'd taken a small room in a hotel in South Kensington – not an upmarket area, but not too shabby either, although I did ask whether it was safe to walk around alone at night and got a polite nod from the receptionist. There are places in London where you can't do that safely, and there's no harm in making sure about this kind of thing.

After I'd booked in, I had one of those gut-wrenching experiences that later, when things eventually turn out okay, can actually seem vaguely amusing. I was shown to my room by a young Polish lady.

The room was small – as in tiny and cramped. It made the cab on my fishing truck seem voluminous. The view out of the only window was of a brick wall that I could have leaned out and touched. And the room was hot as hell. I opened the window, looked at the wall, then politely asked the lady whether she couldn't find me another room. She said she'd see what she could do, but her shrug looked ominous. I packed my traveller's cheques, passport and air tickets into my carry-on suitcase, put my main case and the carry-on into the cupboard, and locked the room. I didn't forget to set the combination lock on the carry-on either, even though logic told me that a simple pocket knife could slit the bag open in a few seconds.

Then I took a cab to Farlows in Pall Mall to spend time kicking tyres in their fly-tying and book departments. The visit cost me a little money as usual, which hurt, given the wallet-throttling exchange rates South Africans live with these days, but I rationalised it by reminding myself that I wasn't exactly splashing out on hotels. Besides, I again got a good discount, and on the back of that, I stood myself to a good pub lunch and a pint of ale.

When I got back to my room at around four that afternoon, I unlocked the door, stepped in, opened the cupboard and found both my suitcases gone. I suddenly recalled, with horror, a few stories I'd heard of hotel rooms being broken into in the UK and Europe. I ran into the passage with a heart rate of 180 and bumped into a cleaner. She couldn't help, hadn't seen anything. In fact, she could hardly speak English. So I hurtled down three flights of stairs and breathlessly waited for the receptionist to finish booking in a tediously pedantic American couple, then sprang my story on the young man behind the desk.

'Let me see,' he said, glancing at the register. 'Ah, Natalia moved you to room 21. It looks over the park.'

'With my luggage?' I asked.

'Yes, with your luggage, sir,' he replied with a resigned look that said, 'What do you take us for?'

My son Robert and his wife Tammy arrived at the hotel that evening, both tired from a long day's work and a tedious drive across London in heavy traffic. We had a celebratory drink at the hotel, and I bought them dinner.

*

It was a year after my last chalkstream trip when I was on a steep learning curve that eventually developed into a level of moderate self-confidence on these rivers. I guess you would need two or three full seasons to get really sharp at fishing chalkstreams, and even then many veteran chalkstream anglers would still regard you as a novice. The truth is chalkstreams can be – often are – dead easy to fish, but soon enough you come across a fish, or end up on a tricky section of river, that cuts you down to size.

*

On the first day, Robert and I fished the River Test on the Kimbridge estate as guests of the owner, my friend Clay Brendish. Tammy drove us to Hampshire from London in perfect weather. Outside the village of Stockbridge we stopped under a blue, cloud-scattered sky to photograph huge sweeps of wheat that waved in the breeze like a sea of gold. It was one of the most dramatic landscapes I've ever seen in England, and we made the most of it with our cameras.

Kimbridge is a beautiful estate, and there was time to enjoy the scenery and a full English breakfast in Annie's, a small restaurant not a hundred metres from the banks of the Test. Then we strolled over to the Kimbridge clubhouse, where we tackled up in a lovely oak-beamed room full of the atmosphere of chalkstream fly fishing. It's known as the Granary, and maybe that's what it was in years gone by. There was an array of angling art on the walls, bookshelves filled with angling books and fly-fishing magazines, and a well-stocked glass-fronted drinks cabinet. Off the club room were the dressing rooms and showers. It was all a little lost on Tammy, but Rob and I have fished long enough to be impressed by creature comforts like these on fishing trips.

We began on a carrier of the Test, stalking along a smoothly mown bank with a 3-weight rod, a long leader and a RAB, until we spotted a decent rise from a fish that Robert hooked on his first cast. The drift took his dry fly straight over its nose. The trout gave him a real runaround, leaping a few times before he landed it – a four-pound brown by our estimation, if not by exact science. I did look through my vest for my tape measure, but I couldn't find it – as I often can't find many things in my vest – so we released the fish and shook hands on its weight.

Robert said, 'Dad, that's got to be my best brown. You can cast at the next one.'

I'd had as much pleasure watching him catch that fish as if I'd hooked it myself. But that's not something you can tell your son without sounding a little too sugary.

The carrier was rich with starwort and crowfoot weed-beds, and the trout were easy to spot, lying over the troughs of white chalk between the weed. We stuck with the RAB and each of us landed a few more trout, a mix of browns and rainbows. At midday, a big fish broke Robert – a timely cue to head for Annie's.

After lunch, we strolled to the Dun, which joins the Test on Clay's estate. The river was remarkable for its manicured, garden-like surroundings set against a leafy backdrop of tall trees, the neat gravel pathways and lichen-covered bridges. It had the air of a well-kept formal garden, but on a massive scale.

You can easily fish the river here without wading, which anyway isn't allowed on Kimbridge, because the banks are smooth and flat, and the trees are a long back-cast away. We worked up a meadow stretch of the Dun a few hundred metres long and as straight as a ruler before it disappeared around a corner into a stand of trees. The river was bathed in sunshine and flowing deep and clear. We caught a few trout, browns and rainbows, all on dry fly, because along with no wading, nymph fishing is also not allowed. We caught the fish in ways that were either predictably easy or predictably tough, depending on the situation of the fish. At times a trout would rise in a conveniently clear, perfectly situated spot upstream, and when we floated a fly roughly over its head and lifted into the rise with the right timing – just a little delay, or at least a delay long enough for the trout to turn down – we would hook it.

The afternoon was remarkable, though, for one particular fish, a blue trout that rose under an overhanging branch that Rob took on a delightful cast that sent his dry fly neatly over its nose. Blue trout are known to be terrific fighters, and this one proved it. I'd guess it was a shade over five pounds, and it took Robert a good twenty minutes to land. Up close, this trout was different to any I'd ever seen. It had very few spots, and they were small and pale. Its belly was silvery and its back was cobalt blue, almost the sparkling blue you see in some people's eyes. Its gill plates were flushed pale-pink, and the faintest hint of crimson ran along its flanks, but no more than a hint. Around the black of its pupils there was an attractive, pale-turquoise band with a thin aquamarine line above that. The rest of the eye-socket was surrounded in soft greys that varied in tone from pale to dark. It really was something else and, in its own way, attractive, if a little garish – but certainly nowhere near as pretty as your standard rainbow or brown trout.

Robert released the fish and it swam off lazily, so clear to see in the water that I wondered how these trout ever survive, in the same way I wonder how albino squirrels ever survive, at least to become adults. Yet they do. I've seen enough of them where I live in Cape Town to know that much, but it's still a minor marvel. Perhaps the blue trout are stocked when they are large enough to fend for themselves by dint of their power and weight. I'm not sure, and I'm not really concerned to find out.

*

We had tea at Annie's and, with the light turning treacle-coloured, I left Robert and Tammy to their cameras and strolled back up the right bank of the Dun. I had only made a few casts when an old, bottle-green Land Rover Defender drew up. Acquaintances from my previous trip stepped out, the two young Kimbridge river keepers. We exchanged greetings. They may just have come to make sure I wasn't using a nymph, but I doubted it. We chatted about the fishing and they mentioned their problems with poachers, mainly large, burly and brazen foreigners whom they couldn't match for size or aggression. I told them they needed my pal Billy de Jong for a week or two. He's built like a loose forward and specialises in making citizen's arrests, and he's not known for his gentle approach either. They asked me to mention him to Clay. I said I would. The Land Rover's engine started with a rattle and puff of blue smoke, and in a wink, they'd disappeared behind an avenue of trees.

*

What is it about old Land Rover Defenders that makes them just keep going like bulletproof warhorses, seeming somehow ageless despite their age? Most old cars just look sad, worn out, unreliable and, well, dated – but Defenders somehow don't really date. But then the model hasn't changed much in looks since the original models came off the production line more than 60 years back. It strikes me as a perfect example of why you don't want to fix something that works. Or it says a lot about some of the pitfalls of trying to keep up with high fashion.

*

I saw the ripples left by a trout rising on the far bank of the Dun, followed by another rise just two metres upstream of it. This time I saw the dorsal fin and tail of the fish break the surface. With the sun in my eyes I couldn't see either of these trout, and there were no insects on the water. But both rises had been deliberate and bold; no head showed and both fish left wide, slow-spreading rings, suggesting they were taking emergers. I changed to a size 16, dun-coloured Klinkhåmer. The river here was an easy cast wide, and its flow smoothly laminar, so the current was less of a problem than a help, in that you just needed to get the distance and the position of the fly right and the current would carry it as smooth as silk over the trout's head.

As it happened, my first cast was perfect, to within six inches of the target, and I saw the fish bulge under the fly. As it turned down, I struck. I was not expecting what followed. The trout tore off upstream at speed and with considerable power until the last of my 2-weight fly line disappeared and I was into backing. I should have been using my Sage ZXL 3-weight with my Hardy Featherweight reel rather than my Winston 2-weight and tiny Orvis CFO II, however elegant they may be. But the fish eventually slowed, and I was able to get fly line onto the reel by winding in as fast as I could walking backwards down the bank. It was a rainbow of twenty-two inches. And yes, over tea, I *had* found my tape measure.

The rest of the afternoon involved pleasant selective fishing, in that I cast only to rising trout. There was no shortage of them, and though most were modestly sized, they were all brightly coloured brown trout. They went off the Klinkhåmer for some reason; on a whim, I switched to a CDC One Feather Midge and hit the jackpot.

I found Robert and Tammy making the most of the late-afternoon light with cameras, and we strolled to the Granary, where we freshened up and signed the Kimbridge guestbook with a level of ceremony. Tammy drove us back to London on the M3 motorway, stopping once so we could stretch our legs and grab a cup of coffee. The coffee tasted like I imagined ersatz tasted, that acorn mix reputedly served to prisoners during World War II.

We were home by eight, and I stood the kids to dinner again in a nearby Turkish restaurant where, by contrast (and as expected), the coffee was excellent.

*

I always thought the River Test rises near the town of Overton in Hampshire, but it actually rises near the village of Ashe in North Hampshire, just a few kilometres from Overton. Why I'm telling you this is that the following day I was due to fish a beat described as the *upper* Test near Overton, and given that Overton is at least *close* to the source of this river, I assumed the Test would be a small stream rather than anything like a river. And that's what it was; shallow and as transparent as a glass of spring water.

The drive down from London with my host and good friend Frederick Mostert was through countryside similar to what I'd seen the previous day, except that as we neared Overton, a quaint, sprawling village, the countryside looked more rural and a few hills appeared. We were headed for Laverstoke Park, where Frederick had arranged a day's fishing on a section of the Test owned by an acquaintance of his, Jody Scheckter, the 1979 Formula One Drivers' Championship winner.

The entrance to his estate was imposing: large stone pillars with a gatekeeper's cottage alongside. Through the gates, a paved road wound across rolling parklands down to the river. We parked just beyond an old, iron-railed Victorian bridge that crossed this section of the Test roughly in the middle of the beat. While I stood on the bridge, the river slid silently under my feet and, just upstream, I spotted two fish, both grayling. To my left, pastures swept up to the Scheckters' manor house on the crest of a hill. It looked palatial, with tall columns at the entrance, set in a surrounding cluster of large trees. I recognised oaks, yews and elms. It was almost as impressive as the estate you may remember from *Downton Abbey*. And I'm not exaggerating. The house is a listed building dating back to 1710.

From the bridge looking downstream, the river ran in a gentle curve for about half a kilometre, before it flowed under the arches of an old red-clay-brick bridge. The bridge was no longer in use, but it was a perfect feature in the river's landscape, in a rustic, well-weathered way. Each of its three arches was about as wide as a fly rod; the water flowed through them less than a metre below.

In some places the riverbanks were eroded where retaining gabions had collapsed, allowing the river to break its banks, mostly on bends, where it was far wider and shallower. These broad sections were probably no more than a foot deep. Frederick said that although Jody was a conscientious, busy and dedicated organic beef farmer – besides beef, he also has a herd of Indian water buffalo that apparently produce a fine mozzarella cheese – he apparently isn't the slightest bit interested in fly fishing. So the fact that a lovely stretch of the Test, in obvious need of some immediate and ongoing maintenance, flowed through his property, was probably not high on his list of priorities. His section wasn't stocked and the weed wasn't cut, so it was, in every sense of the word, a wild, natural – untamed, if you like – piece of this noble chalkstream. The fishing is only by kind permission or invitation, so simple logic suggested that the stretch was not heavily fished.

We walked downstream as far as the clay-brick bridge, and I admired its beautiful symmetry, and how well it blended in with the stream and its leafy surrounds. The bridge's rust-red reflections danced on the surface of the water, hiding any chance of spotting fish, but directly across the stream and above the bridge, the water was transparent. I immediately spotted two trout. Frederick invited me to cast. I dropped a CDC One Feather Midge lightly on the water just above the leading fish. The brown trout lifted to the fly, but when it was no more than three inches away it spooked and fled, taking the other fish with it. We wondered if we had missed some flaw in my presentation, but it had seemed dead right to both of us. I have often had last-second refusals from trout, whether after a brief or lengthy inspection of the fly, and then for any number of reasons, but I have rarely seen a trout lift to a fly as if about to take it, then suddenly get such a fright that it bolted.

So I hit the usual default button. I lengthened my leader to around 20 feet, including a longer section of 7X tippet, and changed to a really small dry fly, a size 20 Para-RAB. Frederick did much the same.

The next pod of fish was holding in shallower water, and it included a few small grayling just behind the sprinkling of small trout. They looked as nervous as mice in a kitchen at night. Frederick's first cast was a little short, but his next reached the target. Again as the fly drifted into feeding range the fish fled – trout and grayling.

And so it went all morning, more or less, until we were back at the Victorian bridge with the iron rails, ready for lunch but without a single trout hooked, let alone netted. Some trout just spooked as the cast landed, a few looked so close to taking the fly that I readied myself to strike but, in the end, we didn't get a single take.

We stuck to the dry fly. I think you could say the river was too shallow for a nymph and, besides, we saw no sub-surface feeders and no hint of a hatch. I'd hoped that a few Blue-winged or Medium Olives would appear, but none did. Frederick had warned me the fishing would be tough. He hadn't fished this water often, but he said it had been tricky every time he had.

Just before lunch, we watched a trout of about sixteen inches lying still over a narrow ledge of chalk gravel not three metres away, the rhythmical opening and closing of its gill plates showing clearly as it breathed. I know a tough fish when I see it, and this one had all the credentials. Frederick persuaded me to try it. I moved slowly below the fish while he watched from behind cover. I threw a cast, stopping the moving fly line at mantelpiece height, the tiny dry fly dropping just ahead of the fish, as gently as a falling leaf. At that very instant, the trout spun around and made a darting run into a nearby weed-bed. There are times when you have to say there's no justice in fly fishing – or at least, if there is, that you don't fully understand the laws that apply to it.

*

It was some lunch that Frederick had brought: a Fortnum & Mason picnic hamper comprising biscuits, a variety of pâtés, a watercress salad, smoked salmon and a bottle of Chardonnay, all packed in a large wicker basket. Again I was reminded of the riverside lunches that make up my usual fare back home, lunches as far removed from this one as Saturn is from its furthermost moon.

Over lunch I wondered about all the refusals we'd had, and came to the conclusion, as you may have by now, that we were missing micro drag, with the emphasis on *micro*, meaning fractions of a millimetre of drag, no more. That's why I changed to a tiny size 18 RAB, and I'll argue that it worked, if only for a brief moment. But let me tell you the story.

The afternoon's fishing was interesting. The river narrowed upstream of the iron-railed bridge and became deeper, but the beds of starwort were thick, and finding holding spots in tightly woven weed-beds wasn't easy. I did find one fish in a hole against a bank, a fish of a pound or so, and it rose to the tiny, light-footed RAB, the fly dancing on its toes rather than hanging in the water. I thought the lighter footprint might help to neutralise the chance of drag and, for a moment, that fish was on, but the moment was brief.

Then suddenly the river was tree-lined, flowing under an embracing umbrella of bright green leaves, with rays of sunshine lighting the water in places where thin shafts of light pierced through the verdant surrounds. There was a foot bridge; below it, the river spilled over a low weir, where it tumbled into white bubbles before smoothing into a glide. Here, briefly, I had another fish on and so did Frederick, but that was all we saw before we started the gentle walk back to the car.

We poured coffee at the car, then sat on the iron bridge with our feet dangling above the river. We watched for half an hour and, when no fish showed, we slowly packed up and headed back to London. I can scarcely ever remember blanking on a more intriguing day's fishing, or in more delightful surroundings. I'd fish that beat any chance I got. It's by far the loveliest piece of trout stream I ever got skunked on.

*

It was interesting that we saw so many grayling this high on the Test. Remember, the Laverstoke Park section isn't far from the river's source. Oliver Kite, in his book *A Fisherman's Diary*, talks of a 'grayling line' where, below the line, grayling and trout are found, but above it there are mainly only trout and hardly any grayling. So the presence of so many grayling puzzled me. In fact, they outnumbered the trout. But then years back, fishing high on the Hampshire Bourne, we found grayling. Not one or two, but many. And just lifting your rod to cast to a holding trout often sent hordes of them fleeing upstream like the hounds of hell were after them. And it happened time and again. I'd opt to be above this so-called 'grayling line' anytime, and right up here we thought we would be. We were wrong. Or maybe Kite had it wrong.

To digress for a moment, there was something about this beat that would have made it a special place for my good friend Ed Herbst – and not just because it was an ultra-pretty piece of small-stream trout water with a decent head of wild browns in it, or that it ran in luxuriantly verdant landscapes, or that it's a stretch of possibly the most illustrious trout stream on the planet. It was all these things; but that's not the point. You see, Ed's been a Formula One racing fanatic for years, so the proximity to one of its former champions would naturally have added a novel dimension to his fishing here. And, so Frederick told me, behind his palatial home he has a shed full of his former Formula One cars.

Then there was a time when Ed really fancied a gin and tonic, and on special occasions his friends Sharland and Gavin Urquhart treated him to a bottle of Bombay Sapphire – top-quality stuff, perhaps the best gin there is.

Why am I telling you this? Well, a year after I'd fished here, the Bombay Sapphire company put up a new distillery right on the banks of the Test, immediately below the beat we'd just fished. Add that to its sublime small-stream qualities, together with its proximity to Formula One racing history, and you can see why it might have interested Ed more than any other small stream I can think of off-hand.

*

From my visit a year back, Roger Harrison's section of the upper Itchen in Hampshire held fond memories, so when Robin and I headed out of London to this piece of water the next day, I was long on anticipation. It was a perfect morning, the dome of sky becoming bluer as we travelled. The villages we passed through still had that sleepy, early-morning look about them, and by 10am, with the sky at its brightest blue, we were having tea on the Harrisons' lawn, along with Clay Brendish who had driven over from Kimbridge to join us. With only the gentlest of breezes blowing, I had high hopes for a hatch of mayfly.

Clay and Robin moved upstream, and I began fishing the river just above the Harrisons' garden. A decent trout showed its head near the far bank. I dropped a RAB close to it, but got no response. I had noticed tiny, dun-coloured mayflies hatching in small numbers, so I changed to one of my own patterns, a size 18 One Feather CDC Midge, because it just looked so buggy and so right. I caught that fish on the next cast, and stayed with my little midge imitation most of the morning, taking five more trout before

I reached the top of this beat of the upper Itchen. It's strictly catch-and-release water, so they all went back.

Clay walked past just as I was releasing a trout from a delightful stretch of water that seemed alive with rising fish, and I invited him to join me. We stood dead still, waist deep, almost leaning against the even pull of the current, waiting for a fish to show on the surface before we cast. I gave Clay one of my midge patterns, and we both took a decent brown on it. As we were debating whether to head out for lunch, a fish pushed a tiny dimple just upstream of us. Clay cast over the rise and hooked a pretty grayling of sixteen inches.

So this was just a morning on the Itchen, a morning that sounds so simple and not out of the ordinary, but a morning that you could wish might be the next morning for the rest of your life.

*

Over lunch, under the trees on the Harrisons' lawn, there was considerable interest in my midge pattern, and before long I had less than half-a-dozen left in my fly box. I'm not sure what the fish took the pattern for, but I assumed it must be a cripple or emerging mayfly because there was no sign of midges about. Roger said the small flies I'd seen coming off were probably Blue-winged Olives, though he added that midges weren't uncommon on his beat, especially on warm days.

*

I fished the carrier stream in the afternoon, reminded of my visit to this section a year before when I fluked two fish. I only got one on this occasion and, like the previous two fish I have landed on this tricky section, I again hooked this brown more by good luck than by skill. As usual there were few trout on show in the carrier, and I'd only seen three before I neared the end of the beat. Despite getting a few decent drifts over two fish, the trout kept their stations and kept looking down, never up. A third fish spooked as the midge pattern landed. What spooked it only that fish knows, because the fly seemed to land gently enough.

Then in a bathtub-sized lie in a bed of starwort, my fly snagged on a thin tendril of weed and I lifted the rod to free it. The fly briefly skated back towards me across a piece of open water when a brown of some size grabbed it and ended up in my net. I thought of changing to an adult caddis pattern seeing that the fish wanted movement, but, in the end, I stayed with the midge, twitching it gently in each drift through likely looking holding water, but it got no interest. It was the sort of situation where you can get too long on the theory of presentation, and develop a sort of tunnel vision based around the importance of a single incidental interlude.

The carrier ended in a short, treed-in section before rejoining the main river. Here in dappled shade, I found two trout on show, both holding deep, not a metre from each other. I took the trouble of photographing this brace of browns, and while I was selecting the settings and adjusting the focus on my camera, I happened to see, out of the corner of my eye, the white of a mouth as the better of the two fish turned to swallow a nymph. Moments later I left my Zak in its upper lip, just too quick and too sharp on the strike. The second fish, as I expected, had vanished.

Beyond the treed-in section, the river opened into what must be the most beautiful stretch on the whole of the upper Itchen. White-pebbled scoops scattered among emerald-coloured weed-beds; a stretch of the river that seemingly runs on forever, the clear water laced with patches of gently waving weed-beds that cradle the white troughs of typical chalkstream lies. And in most of these lies, or troughs if you like, there were fish, sometimes two or three or more. The stream was narrower here, with the slightest ripple on the surface, and the flow was quicker, so the dry fly carried nicely on the threads of the surface current. That made the fishing dead easy. I had just landed a brown, one among many I hooked and landed in this section, some of them weighty fish well over a pound, when I heard Robin's call. We would normally have fished until fading light saw us off, but Robin had to head back to London. We were booked on an early flight out of Heathrow to Reykjavík the following morning to hunt salmon in Iceland, a prospect that made leaving this lovely river a little easier to live with.

*

They say the upper Itchen is the best trout stream on earth, and you will wait a long while to hear me question that. But as I edited a draft of this chapter, I felt my writing was constrained, even matter-of-fact, when the actual living of it was nothing like that. I thought I was perhaps subconsciously taking on the typically understated view of life the English so naturally adopt. As I said, the truth is far from it. But in the writing of this, again those overdone 'a' words – 'awesome' and 'amazing' – came to mind, and I thought it best to avoid them. They'd do no real justice to this experience.

CHAPTER 11
ICELAND

The salmon runs are a visible symbol of life, death
and regeneration, plain for all to see and share...
If there is ever a time when the salmon no longer returns,
man will know he has failed again and moved one step
nearer to his own final disappearance.
RODERICK HAIG-BROWN, *FISHERMAN'S SPRING*

At Heathrow Airport, Robin Renwick and I each bought a bottle of The Singleton single malt whisky and a bottle of J&B from the duty-free liquor store, then joined a large group of anglers in the departure lounge. They were also on their way to fish for Atlantic salmon in Iceland. Most of them were heading for the East Rangá River, whereas we were going to fish the West Rangá – though, at the time, the difference was lost on me. Not only had I not been to Iceland, I'd never caught an Atlantic salmon.

It turned out that the West Rangá is a considerably bigger river than the East Rangá, and unlike the East, the West Rangá is actually a great big spring creek. Hard to believe. In fact, we crossed the

East Rangá on the bus drive down from Reykjavík and it looked cloudy, a dark shade of grey. People in the bus, all fly fishers heading for the West Rangá Lodge, started muttering something about a volcanic ash spill, and the information travelled through the bus like a poisonous virus because it concerned our own prospects on the West Rangá. It certainly stopped me dozing off on the ride south. As it happened, the West Rangá was clear and running beautifully, and we later heard that the fishing on the East Rangá stayed grim the entire six days we were in Iceland.

*

But to get back to Heathrow Airport for just a moment. I'd settled into my seat in the front row of an Icelandair Boeing 757, and was quickly getting used to the unaccustomed luxuries of travelling in the seats up front (like the sturdily built Nordic-looking air hostess who brought us Champagne and a newspaper), even if it was only a three-hour flight.

Suitably fortified, we took off, swept through a layer of low cloud and were soon enjoying an unhurried lunch in bright sunshine. It was interesting to find that the airline served South African wines with the meal – De Wetshof from the Robertson region – which was when I realised that the two bottles of Scotch I'd bought at Heathrow were still under the chair I'd been sitting on in the airport lounge. Was it an omen, I wondered?

*

Iceland suffered badly during the 2008 economic meltdown, and we saw signs of it in Reykjavík, where a few building sites, even two years later, still looked as though they'd been abandoned overnight midway through construction, with cranes and scaffolding in position around now decaying walls. The economic blows were followed by the eruption of a volcano that effectively closed European air traffic for two weeks, even though it was the lesser of the two volcanoes that could have erupted. The bigger one is Mount Hekla, equidistant from the lodge into which we were booked. I should mention the name of the volcano that erupted the year we were there, even if you won't be able to pronounce it, but I'm duty-bound to warn you that you could get arrested trying to say it out loud in a public place – Eyjafjallajökull.

Eyjafjallajökull erupted on 25 March 2010, and it and its nearby big brother volcano Mount Hekla were both still smoking when we fished there in early August that same year. In fact, I'd given up on this trip ever happening as I watched TV footage of the volcano back home, with atomic bomb-like ash clouds that hung around for a number of weeks and closed all air traffic. And seismologists had fears that it might erupt again.

*

From our lodge we could see Eyjafjallajökull about thirty kilometres to the south, an imposing mountain trailing a worrying wisp of white smoke like some giant chimney. On the bus there was talk about the risk of either of the two volcanoes near the lodge erupting again, and initially their proximity was vaguely disquieting. But after a while I didn't give them a passing thought. Neither, it seemed, did anyone else. It had nothing to do with good fishing eclipsing fears of imminent death from molten lava, or choking ash, or any sense of self-preservation. It merely boiled down to the fascinating proclivity we humans have to quickly coming to terms with something we can't do anything about.

It was the same when I was fishing for steelhead in northern British Columbia. Initially, whenever we got out of the drift boat for a pee, we were hyped up about running into grizzly bears, but later we weren't, though I never walked too deep into the riverbank foliage without thoughts of bears in the back of my mind. They are a risk, sure, but we somehow got used to the risk, or at least we rationalised our fear. One fellow in our party said the lava never got here when it erupted in March, so that's a good sign. 'Of what?' asked another.

It helps when you've finally come to the conclusion that there's not a lot you can do one way or another if a volcano a few kilometres away suddenly erupts and spews a few thousand tons of molten lava into the sky; likewise, there's not much you can do armed with a fly rod and a landing net if a grizzly decides he's had enough of you. They're the kind of threats where if you can't get on and live with the risks you shouldn't go there in the first place. I could also mention the hippos in the Okavango Delta, but I think my point is made.

*

The West Rangá is about a two-hour drive southeast of Reykjavík on the only major highway in the country, a ring road that covers the perimeter of the entire island. The West Rangá is almost totally a salmon river as far as the fly fishers are concerned, in the sense that all other salmonids are regarded as incidental catches and not what you came here for. On this river you're after salmon, full stop. Brown trout and sea trout were caught by some folk in our party, and I even heard of a brown of around six pounds being caught, and still nobody took much notice. I'd love to have hooked an Arctic char, but I didn't, and neither did anyone else. Which was strange, because I thought in a country this cold they would be plentiful. Our guide said that brown trout and char prefer the waters high in the mountains, where the browns reach double figures.

The salmon here average seven to eight pounds, but they can get to double figures. In their own way they really are beautiful fish – perhaps more aggressive-looking than trout, and really powerful. These are the fish you've come all the way here to catch. Or put differently, if you want to spend this kind of money catching brown trout, you should choose somewhere else – like the South Island of New Zealand or Tierra del Fuego in Argentina, where you could hire a guide, rent a helicopter, book into the best hotel and stay for a month, and still have plenty of change left over compared with the cost of a week's salmon fishing in Iceland. It's *not* inexpensive, and unless I was a guest, which I was, I would never have come closer to an Icelandic salmon river than Google Earth.

*

Travelling by road from Reykjavík to the West Rangá, unless I am dead wrong, would be one of the more dramatic experiences in your life. The landscapes are vast, beautiful and tundra-like, with strangely treeless sweeps of hilly and luxuriant grasslands dotted with brightly coloured wild flowers, turf-roofed crofts, countless sheep and shaggy-looking Icelandic horses no bigger than ponies. To the east, there was a distant hazy backdrop of snow-capped mountains. It was beautiful countryside, certainly, and parts had some grandeur and ruggedness, but there was a stark sameness about a lot of it that had me thinking Iceland could have been designed by a modern Nordic architect with a bent for vast, uncluttered spaces and the colour green. It was lovely, though, in the same way that the seeming endlessness of the Karoo makes it lovely. We were on the plains near the coast, but I believe the landscapes inland are far grander, more mountainous and rugged. And interesting to know: there are more than 10,000 waterfalls – in a country not much bigger than Ireland!

The West Rangá Lodge is a series of wooden cabins joined by boardwalks. They are spread around a large dining room and a bar that have an expansive view over the Home Pool, a wide stretch of the river from which at least two dozen salmon were hooked in the five days we were there. It was a comfortable, neat and cheerful place; in the late-evening darkness, the lights of Hella, a village less than a kilometre away, shimmered yellow on the water.

Our party was made up of a few Americans, a handful of Scots, and Englishmen, mainly Londoners. They were wealthy, influential and interesting people, and I didn't unearth a single snob among them. The food was good and the wines were excellent.

I quickly befriended a convivial old fellow from London, dressed each evening in the same rumpled tweed jacket. He had a mop of untidy grey hair, and he seemed to have fished everywhere other than the far side of the moon. But he was remarkably laid-back about all the fishing he'd done, and at the same time modest about it. Each night after dinner he insisted I share a Cuban cigar with him. We sat in the half-light outside on the veranda, talking and smoking and drinking red wine. He hardly ever mentioned his day or the fish he'd caught, other than in passing, but he always asked about mine. I gathered that he could find his way around most salmon rivers in Scotland and Norway, let alone Iceland, but I learned it all by deduction, by applying my mind to what he said as well as to what was left silent. For example, on fishing in Argentina, all I had to go on that he had actually fished there was his brief reference to countries with great sunsets, and Argentina being his best. And as for New Zealand, it was just a statement that he could live the rest of his life in a Maui motorhome, slowly travelling byroads, camping at night. He'd fished both the North and South Islands frequently. When I asked if he'd got any decent brown trout in the South Island of New Zealand, he tapped the ash off his cigar and said, 'Not enough.'

It also soon struck me that this group knew each other well, and that they had fished the West Rangá together many times. Coming cold into an established group of buddies can be daunting, but after the usual questions about what I did, where I lived and where I'd fished, they quickly lost interest – or wrote me off as no threat – and I was made to feel one of the party and welcome. The fact that I caught a heap of salmon was neither here nor there, because everyone in the party caught salmon, including the ladies. That's why they come to the West Rangá instead of going to other Atlantic salmon-fishing destinations. The East and West Rangá rivers are ridiculously productive, as good as the Ponoi in the Kola Peninsula, my tweed-jacketed friend let slip. And, being a spring creek, the West Rangá has the advantage of more constant levels.

It was also pretty clear that the routines set up for each day were sacred at the lodge, or maybe just non-negotiable, like the regimen of a boarding school – which is comfortable in a way, because you don't have to think much about any details before you go out fishing. It's done for you. All the anglers were paired up; Robin and I fished together. We left the lodge early each morning in our guide Rikki's ageing and noisy SUV for our allocated beats (there are ten on the Rangá). We were brought back around 11am for biscuits and coffee, then we left the lodge again for the next beat assigned to us, and fished until 1pm. After lunch we took a quick nap; by 3pm we were back on the river to fish two different beats until 9.30pm (10pm latest). Dinner was at 10.30pm, after which we chewed the fat over coffee and then headed for our rooms, by which time I needed no help getting to sleep.

*

We arrived at West Rangá Lodge in time for lunch, and after setting up rods we headed for the river. There were sixteen rods in our party, divided into eight groups. Robin and I drew the Rangá Falls beat for the first session, from 3pm to 6pm, and then Beat 3, nearer the mouth of the river, from 6pm to 10pm, when at this time of year it's almost still as light as it is at midday.

The West Rangá Falls are spectacular, so much so they've become a somewhat clichéd emblem for salmon fishing in this river. Every brochure or web page advertising the river, and all the magazine articles I ever read on fishing the West Rangá, have pictures of these falls. And they *are* stunning. They spill through fissures in a solid wall of black volcanic rock about 250 metres wide and about sixty high, sheets of white crashing into the emerald-coloured river below, where the water swirls in huge white throats and the air is laced in a perpetual layer of low-lying mist. Fifty metres below the falls seams of smooth, pale-green water appear in the river; another fifty metres below that the river is just fast and wide and impressive, full stop. To the left of the falls looking upstream is an old concrete fish ladder, and although I saw salmon leaping clear of the water below the falls, the ladder stayed empty. Each evening the water bailiff checked it to count the run of salmon, but from what we heard, the fish were not yet in – at least not in the same numbers they were at this time the previous year.

I followed Rikki's instructions and cast a big blue tube-fly into the boil near the foot of the falls. My attempts at Spey casting with a two-handed, 15' 9-weight Sage rod were clumsy, and the guide's instructions were hard to hear above the sound of the thundering water, but his body language was easy to read. The bright-green floating line swung at speed on the surface and, out of sheer habit, I fed line into the drift and tried to add a mend. Four or five seconds later, the line was dead straight and quivering way downstream of me in the powerful pull of the current. I lifted the line in a large arc and swung a long, clumsy, looping roll cast over my head and back into the boil. The line drifted out of the whitewater and ran into the lip of a smooth, green-coloured seam. Rikki – his full name is Ríkarður Hjálmarsson – had said just to lob the fly out, let it drift downstream under the slightest tension so you had a 'feel' of it but without drag (almost a contradiction in terms), then to kite the fly up when it swung out at the end of its drift. He added that if a salmon took the fly, not to strike. All of this in his charming Icelandic-accent-laced English while standing at the deafening foot of tumbling falls. It was like trying to follow a dissertation on the theory of quantum mechanics given by a professor mumbling in a foreign language.

On my second cast, I'd felt what I can only describe as a slow, deep 'weight' on the line, as if the fly was dragging heavily and, contrary to the advice I was given, I sunk the hook as hard as I could. A large fish cartwheeled out of the water, then took off with impressive strength – not straight, but always changing direction and using the current against its flanks. When Rikki sunk a net under it, the fish was still bucking violently. He posed briefly with the salmon for a photograph, as if he'd caught it himself, then pumped my hand with joy and said, 'See, I tell you zactly, and you listen right what I say. Not so?' I was warming to him. I decided not to admit that I didn't have a clue how I'd hooked the fish, because in the presence of his beaming joy I'd be raining on his parade.

This was the first Atlantic salmon of my life, and I let that reality drain warmly into my senses. It wasn't a big fish as far as salmon go, but that made little difference. It was like no other salmonid I'd ever hooked, beautiful in a silvery, opalescent yet understated way. I was about to suggest we release it, but before I could get the words out, Rikki despatched the salmon with a bone-crunching whack to its head and tossed it onto the grassy bank where it lay quivering among a scattering of bright-yellow flowers. I was mystified, but I wasn't going to say anything right then. I'd wait until we were away from the thunder of the falls.

Robin hooked a fresh, silver salmon, and then I hooked and landed a second, a far prettier and bigger fish than my first. It was much the same sort of take. The line just went 'heavy', but this time I waited, and sure enough the fish was well hooked, the reel was screaming, and I hadn't struck at all. I felt a sense of relief when it eventually bucked out of Rikki's net and was gone.

I had a third solid take but made the mistake of striking immediately, and that fish was also gone after being on for no more than a minute. Rikki, looking on, shook his head and tapped his temple with a finger as if to indicate he was dealing with a client who'd lost his marbles. We were below the falls far enough to hear each other speak. He just said, 'No strike, yes? How you say that in Eeenglish? Nooooo ssstriiike!' 'Oh,' I said, 'you mean I don't have to strike?' He gave me a wide grin, nodding at me, as if I'd at last seen the light.

There were eight other fish caught on this beat that day and later. Back at the lodge, they said the fishing had been slow!

*

I was using new gear – a pair of Simms waders and Patagonia boots, the soles of which, as you know, can potentially transmit diseases from one river system to another. I don't just mean Patagonia boots; any boots, and not just boots with felt soles either. I had collected my new gear from Robin in London because otherwise I'd have to have my boots and waders fumigated by a certified veterinarian. Even with new gear still in the box it came in, we had to show customs officials the purchase receipts when we entered Iceland. It's maybe something that should have happened in the South Island of New Zealand long before *didymo* nearly knocked out whole river systems down there. So I was comfortable with the precautions, even if I'm not usually comfortable around bureaucracy.

260

*

We visited each of the ten beats twice in the five days we were there, and each had a distinct character, despite it being the same river. Some sections were wide, slow and featureless; others were narrower, quicker and full of features such as seams, glides and rapids. I liked the water with features most, though in salmon fishing, they aren't necessarily the places that hold the biggest schools of fish or the better salmon.

Our flies were tube flies, some with cone heads, but all tied on lethal-looking treble hooks, around size 8 to 10. The popular patterns were the Frances flies, sometimes spelled Francis, in red or black. The Red Frances was the pattern I did best on, especially those that Rikki had tied, which were a city block ahead of the shop-bought ones issued by the lodge. Other popular patterns were the Blue Charm, the Collie Dog and the Sunray Shadow, which had a nice name but didn't do much for us in the water.

It seemed that the higher we got up the river the prettier it became, but Rikki had his favourite beats and he spared no words talking up these spots on the ride out to them. Beat 3 and the far bank at the Rangá Falls were two of his favourites. When we got to them, he would typically enthuse, 'Now you guys gonna catch plenty, plenty reeeeally big fish!' – claims always uttered with his arms widespread to give an indication of the size of the salmon he had in mind, forgetting his arm span was about equal to his height. He was a congenital optimist, and to him nothing was ever wrong about anything – rain was good for fishing, so was bright sunshine, even a little colour in the water; 'today' always looked good, 'tomorrow' was always going to be better; any fly was 'reaaaally good'; my rod was a honey; my casting was dead right, faultless in fact... And so it went on. Despite the communication gap – actually, his English was fine – he had a rare sense of fun and humour, and he knew how to handle a double-handed salmon rod in a way that was as sweet to watch as a Bolshoi ballerina. He had superb timing and rhythm, and I learned a lot just watching him load, swivel his body, swing and release with a long follow-through, the whole brief act done in smooth, seamless motion, the line shooting out long and as straight as a ruler.

In typical Rikki fashion, he also surprised me one day.

We were fishing the far bank at the Rangá Falls, that real hotspot of his, on a day when Rikki was glowing hot with optimism. I was throwing a longish line with a blood-red Frances tied to the tippet. He was standing a little way behind telling me I was going to catch a *beeeg* fish when a mink scurried past us and ran under a pile of rocks right alongside me. Rikki went ballistic, grabbed his cellphone and spoke animatedly on it for a few minutes, all the time his free hand moving this way and that to add emphasis to whatever he was saying. I couldn't make out a word.

'What the hell was that all about?' I asked.

'You wait and see,' he said smiling. 'It will be good! Meanwhile catch me a *beeeg* fish *pleeease*.'

Pretty soon two men arrived with a crowbar, a dog and a 12-gauge double-barrel shotgun. They pried the rocks loose one by one until the mink bolted and, with an ear-deafening bang, they blew it apart. It turned out that mink are real vermin in these rivers and there's an officially appointed mink hunter in each town who gets paid per skin. I was glad the mink hadn't bolted in my direction. That guy was mighty quick on the trigger. It took some time before the ringing deafness had left my ears, during which I didn't catch a *beeeg* fish.

To understand why they detest mink on the West Rangá, you have to understand that a few years back the salmon fishing on this river had all but petered out as a result of serious damage to the spawning beds way upstream. Most of it was the result of layers of volcanic ash getting deposited on the fine gravel. So, nowadays, the bigger hen fish that anglers catch are put into aluminium boxes and kept submerged at key points along the river. These fish are later stripped of their eggs in a fish farm on the upper reaches of the West Rangá, the eggs are fertilised, and when the progeny have grown into smolts, they are released back into the river. They will eventually go out to sea, and on their first return to spawn they come back up this same river as typically bright-silver, torpedo-like salmon called grilse. These were the fish we were mainly catching, but here and there we caught older salmon that were heavier, deeply coloured and more heavily spotted.

It's some operation they have here, and it's been a huge success on the West Rangá. Apparently, mink cause serious damage to this delicate biological chain, from wantonly attacking adult hen fish to eating the eggs. Hence the high-speed call-out of the shotgun-toting hit squad. They made Rikki's day. To add some more savour to it, I did catch a nice salmon as he had asked – sorry, instructed.

*

The West Rangá does look a lot like a giant spring creek. It flows clear, and the levels are pretty constant. Anywhere you park the car and approach the river, you come on a smooth-flowing, strangely silent river that leaves you with a keen sense of anticipation, because every beat of it just looks perfect for holding salmon. The water is ice-cold, and on average waist-deep (at most), though in places there are buckets in the volcanic riverbed rocks that are who knows how deep.

Before you wade in, you first look for salmon holding on the edges. Beginning early one morning on the beat just above the lodge, I was carefully walking down the riverbank searching some deep, emerald-green holes that had formed along the edges on this section. There wasn't the usual gentle slope into the river here. Rather this section had steep banks and a sheer drop to water that was flowing as smooth and as clear as an English chalkstream. The river was also narrow, no more than twenty metres wide and extremely deep. Rikki had warned me to move along the bank carefully, to keep my rod down and my eyes open. Then he disappeared downstream with Robin.

I *was* walking slowly, very slowly downstream, not more than a metre from the water, when I spotted something ahead that was dark and linear and very close to the bank. At first I thought it was a submerged log, but then I saw it weave gently in the current. It was a big salmon, and close – in fact, so close I could see from the kype that it was a cock fish. I was at a huge disadvantage being upstream because I was directly in its line of vision. But the bank downstream of me and adjacent the fish was densely overgrown with scrub trees, so I had to cast from where I was. I hadn't spooked the fish as yet, so I slowly sank to one knee and waited a full minute. Then I dropped a fly a few metres across and upstream of the fish. It was a sort of clumsy roll cast where I kept the rod as flat as I could. The line went out nicely enough, though I silently wished I had a conventional single-handed 9-weight fly rod with me. In this situation, the rod I had felt clumsy.

The fly sank and drifted in a smooth arc across the fish's nose. He took it in a sweep, or more like a sudden lunge, and I made the error of immediately striking. The fish shook his head, then bolted to the far side of the river where he leaped twice and seemed well hooked. But the hook lost its grip as he jumped a third time, and I cursed myself for striking. I'd guessed that salmon to be around fourteen pounds, an older fish no doubt, with at least two sea winters behind it.

Getting beyond the stand of scrub trees and still moving slowly, I spotted a second, smaller salmon holding in a similar spot fifty metres downstream, and I also hooked him solidly. By this time Rikki, who'd heard the commotion I made hooking the first fish, was alongside me. 'What I tell you!' he said beaming. I have never known a guide take more genuine pleasure in seeing his client catch a fish, but of course when I didn't, it felt almost as if I'd let him down.

Rikki helped me land that second salmon, a lovely nine-pound fish and, in a wave of contrite honesty, I confessed my sin of striking too early on the big fish I'd lost. He was more lenient than I expected. 'That always happens when you go too close,' he said. 'Maybe better you walked away from that *beeeg* fish first, to cast longer.' I got the message. Well, sort of.

That same session Robin took two beautiful salmon, with Rikki alongside him. They were a few hundred metres away, but I could hear Rikki hollering with delight. I'd landed three, the last of them the biggest salmon I got on the trip. All three were sight-fished.

*

There are a couple of things about the West Rangá that are worth sharing. As I said, the river normally slopes gently to the centre, and in most places you can wade right out to where you feel the seam of the central current dragging hard, though it starts to feel uncomfortably dangerous when the water gets to crotch level, and not worth the risk. You throw a floating line across and slightly downstream, keeping your rod low and horizontal, with the tip following the drift as you feed in line to keep the fly tumbling downstream with the current. You feel a slight tension come into the line as it tightens at the end of the drift and the current sends a mild vibration through the line and into the rod. That's probably the point where most salmon took our flies – as they swung up from the drift – though rarely a fish would take a fly just after it landed, which always felt fluky, and seemed to be considered unsporting. I'm not sure why. In fact, there were days when I was tempted to try a big DDD on these fish, but Rikki said to forget it. 'One fish for one hundred casts. Not worth it,' he said. I still have my doubts. I saw many salmon rising, though I was told that wasn't to insects.

I'm convinced that unless you're a good Spey caster, a single-handed rod would have got the job done more comfortably, certainly more efficiently in my case. Having said that, there wasn't a conventional single-handed rod to be seen. All the anglers were on Spey rods, and while some were pretty good Spey casters, from what I saw I'd say the majority weren't that crack at it.

There's a science to reading these rivers and to knowing where the fish are, but it's not a science you're going to pick up in five days, maybe not in five months. The guides obviously have a nose for it. Sometimes it's hard to understand why you are being told to fish in a particular place when other places look as good, or better. They talk about 'pools', but these are really lies in the conventional fly-fishing sense, though considerably bigger. The obvious pools, like the Home Pool in front of the lodge and the pool below the falls, *are* conventional pools, and they do attract a lot more fish than lies in shallower water, even the bigger, deeper ones.

Seeing fish moving is a comforting sign that you're in a hotspot. Salmon move up this river in pods, and occasionally they'll jump clear out of the water. That's the easiest part of working out where they are.

Other clues to fishy spots, other than obvious pools, I found a lot less understandable. For example, late one afternoon Rikki insisted we walk the extra mile to a place he had up his sleeve. The river was shallow here, and it split around a narrow island running about ten metres off the bank. The island was a few hundred metres long. We waded silently across the knee-deep strip of river, climbed onto the island, then, in a crouch, we walked silently and slowly downstream until Rikki was happy we were in the right spot. It felt a lot like we were stalking something, but the slender, shallow arm of river between the island and the bank didn't look like much to get excited about. In places, this arm of the river was no wider than a suburban side street. And it was shallow, and ridiculously clear.

'Okay, get in here, careful and slow, wade to the middle, then drift the fly close, close, close along the far bank, right where the reeds hang over,' Rikki said, speaking in a strangely serious whisper.

Then, suddenly, a couple of big salmon broke the surface.

'See that,' Rikki said excitedly, 'fish are coming through here! What I tell you?'

'They're just eating mayflies,' I teased him. 'I'll put on an Adams.'

But I did exactly as he said, though it wasn't a simple cast in that you can easily overcook a short throw at a narrow, reed-lined target with a heavy, two-handed fly rod – especially when the target is to your right and you're swinging the line from the left and back across in front of your chest. Again, I longed for a regular, single-handed fly rod, say an 8- or 9-weight Loomis, Sage or Orvis, it wouldn't matter. I landed the fly okay, about a metre from the reed bank, and fed line into the drift, feeling the tap-tap-tap through the drifting line as the fly began to bump riverbed stones. Near the end of the drift, the line took off. I mean, it really took off! I felt no slowing in the drift, no sudden unexplained heaviness as if the fly had hung up on a log, just a fly line that suddenly straightened at exactly the same time as the reel began to scream. I hit the fish hard as it was going away from me heading downstream, hoping Rikki never saw it. The salmon jumped as high as my chest; a big, beautiful, green-coloured salmon of about ten pounds. Rikki eventually netted it, singing, 'Hey lucky striker…' to the tune of 'Hey big spender…' Robin and I swapped places, and I realised Rikki must have picked up my sin.

Two or three drifts later, Robin hooked a salmon that jumped then fought strongly for the best part of ten minutes before Rikki could land it. And by the time we had reached the end of the island, we'd hooked five more big fish and kept three. Two had come off throwing the hook, despite neither of us striking, but Rikki was just beaming. He whistled a bright tune as we walked back to his truck. He swung the tailgate down and poured steaming coffee. Three handsome salmon lay in the grass alongside us. The rods were strapped onto a small rack on the bonnet of his SUV, the tips sticking far into the air over the back of the cab, making it look like a vehicle loaded with a rocket launcher in a rebel war. The thundering sound of its leaking exhaust added to the illusion of war. We boomed down the road, scattering flocks of geese in our path, Rikki again in full song.

We tried a section further downstream where the river was miles wide, almost a lake. A strong wind had sprung up, and although I moved a good fish, there was no encore to our island fishing. And we hadn't really expected any. We were late into camp that night, arriving well after 10pm, happy and pleasantly fished out.

*

The prettiest water on the West Rangá is far upstream of the lodge, on Beat 10, where the river flows through rolling green hills scattered with wild flowers. It is not as intimidatingly wide as the lower Rangá, and the river has an almost evenly laminar flow, like some streams on New Zealand's South Island. In fact, the whole scene reminded me a lot of New Zealand. But the river was broader than any I remember in that part of the world.

I walked off on my own and threw a line across the smooth flow. It drifted evenly for a few moments then stopped dead, and I was into a decent salmon. I got a second fish with my next cast. Both were smaller salmon. We lay back on the grassy bank drinking tea, and I thought the world wasn't a bad place right then. Robin hadn't fished. He'd decided to take a nap instead.

*

It's easy to develop a comfortable sense of complacency wading big rivers, but it pays to remember they're never entirely benign places. There was an afternoon on Home Pool, late into the day and late into the trip, when I was fishing alone, Robin and Rikki just in sight way upstream. I was wading the river, following a deep-water seam running along a shelf of rock. Ahead of me was a lovely sweep of smooth, green-tinged water, and a large salmon showed twice just out of casting range. I waded closer, stepping into what looked like a waist deep cavern of clear water running over a sandy bottom. It ended up being a lot deeper than it looked, and before I knew it the water was close to the lip of my waders. The pull of the current was strong, and I felt a mild wave of panic. I tried to turn, but the current wouldn't let me, so I waded backwards seemingly making progress up the sand bar to shallower water, but for each step I gained the sand collapsed under my boot and I had to start again. It felt a lot like being on a treadmill. In the end I had no option: I grabbed the top of my waders to seal them and floated off to where it looked like I'd hit some rocks in shallower water. I hit the shallower shelf in a much faster drift than I'd catered for, and with a surge of adrenaline, I had a sudden reminder of my own mortality – and a fair scoop of ice-cold water down my waders. Rikki had apparently been watching; he had warned both of us more than once about just this sort of risk-taking. I felt like a drowned rat when I got ashore, and I immediately started to peel off my waders. Rikki arrived, shaking his head and wagging his finger at me. He looked very much like a man who knew all along that he'd eventually have the last laugh. I guess he'd been thinking it was just a matter of time. And strangely, the same thought had occurred to me just the day before.

*

Over dinner one night, I sat next to a woman who had come along with her husband to fish in Iceland. They'd apparently had a good day. She told me her husband comes to the West Rangá Lodge every year to find himself. I've never thought you should go fishing to find yourself. Better to spend some time looking at what causes you to lose yourself, and do it as far away from a trout or salmon river as possible. You want to use fishing trips only to help you forget you were ever lost in the first place.

*

It was a sad moment, leaving the lodge and saying goodbye to Rikki. We had talked a lot about the mountain streams in Iceland that he told me were full of *beeeg* brown trout that take tiny dry flies. I wistfully said I would try to get back one day to fish them. We exchanged contact details, and he said he was hoping two nice clients would come in with the next group of fly fishers due that morning, when his relentless routine of guiding day after day, coming in for coffee and biscuits, netting fish, encouraging people, helping their casting, tying on flies and fetching those same flies off fences would begin all over again.

'Pray for me I not get two big assholes!' he said, laughing loudly.

I told him I hoped he got two pretty, nubile young blondes who were actually top-rate Alaskan fly-fishing guides and double-handed casting instructors taking a well-earned holiday.

'Hey, we can hope, yes,' he said, and waving a cheerful goodbye, shouted, 'And what means nubile, hey?'

'Ask your wife,' I shouted back.

(By way of interest, Rikki's wife was the head warden at a nearby men's prison at the time.)

*

The deal when you leave the lodge is you get a number of frozen and smoke-cured salmon calculated as a factor of the number of fish you landed. They handed us the frozen fish wrapped in paper as we were leaving the lodge. I noticed that despite being the beginner in the party, I'd surprisingly come pretty close to the top of the class. I was due two frozen and two smoke-cured salmon. I stuffed the frozen salmon at an angle into my suitcase and was only just able to close the zip. The smoked salmon we would apparently collect at Reykjavík airport, but for some reason they weren't ready when we got there. We were told not to worry, they would make a plan.

The frozen salmon added about fourteen pounds to my already heavy suitcase, making me vaguely worried that I'd be over the baggage weight limit when we checked in. But I was actually a lot more worried about entering Britain with undeclared fresh-frozen animal products from a foreign country. Robin said not to worry, to just look straight ahead and keep walking. We booked in without a hitch, had a pleasant flight and went through UK Customs as instructed, meaning looking straight ahead and just walking. I'm normally useless at looking innocent, always anticipating that polite tap on the shoulder and the 'Excuse me, sir. Would you mind stepping this way for a moment?', but I pulled this one off with the daring panache of a Colombian drug lord.

So I was back in London with two sizeable frozen salmon, and wondering what to do with them. My son Robert and his wife took one look at the fish, then pointed at the small freezer in their Dulwich home – and we all knew this wasn't going to work.

Then Robert had an idea. 'Dad, let's trade them!'

They often ate at their local pub, a cosy establishment in Dulwich called George Canning, not a ten-minute stroll from where they lived. We arrived there with the two frozen salmon wrapped in white butcher's paper just around lunch time. The chef, a young Australian, was busy and didn't seem interested in Rob's story about having two fresh Atlantic salmon, or that Rob was prepared to consider a deal.

'Okay, mate, drop that lot on the counter. I'll speak later. Just busy for the moment,' he said, frantically plating up dishes.

We ordered hamburgers, and were nearly done when the chef appeared wide-eyed with excitement at our table.

'You guys realise what these fish are?' he asked. 'Jeez, these are the freshest, most beautiful goddamn Atlantic salmon I ever saw. And I've been cooking for years!'

So a trade-off was done. Rob and Tammy would eat on the house at Canning's twice a week for a month. It seemed a good deal. We began that night with baked salmon, roast vegetables and a side plate of salad. A blackboard on the wall already announced in brightly chalked letters, 'Fresh-caught Atlantic salmon just in from Iceland!' with a pretty sketch of a steaming salmon dish below it. If I'd had some chalk, I'd have added a sketch of a smiling Rikki with his arms widespread.

*

All that was left was to somehow get myself back home without paying the large sum I had to cough up at the airport when I left Cape Town seven kilograms over the weight limit. This included the waders, boots, rods and fly vest (plus cameras of course) I'd taken to fish the chalkstreams before the trip to Iceland, but I'd left a lot of that with Rob when I flew to Iceland. So before leaving, we carefully weighed my luggage on their bathroom scale. I had to shed seven kilograms. I gave my old waders and boots to Rob, plus a fleece jacket and a few paperback novels I'd bought. But I was still overweight, which is where this story takes an interesting turn.

That evening we all had dinner in Covent Garden in London, and were joined by Tracy Eastman, a young South African friend working in the city. She mentioned she would be travelling to Cape Town the following week to visit her mother, and kindly offered to take my new Patagonia boots and waders with her. I don't know whether it was one of those offers you make and no sooner have said it than you wish you had bitten your tongue off, but to me it was like getting handed a lifeline. I accepted. And just as well, because even without the boots and waders, I left London only a fraction inside the weight limit.

Meanwhile some days later, Tracy, who is slightly built, was packing her bags in London to leave on her trip to Cape Town when she discovered a problem. She couldn't fit my wading boots into her suitcase. She tried everything, but a pair of size 10 boots takes up a lot of space. Not one to give up, she wore them – yes, size 10 boots on her size 5 feet – and she clumped through Heathrow Airport, fetching a lot of strange looks. She said it was the easiest thing taking them off at the security checkpoints. She just stepped out of them. Two days later she turned up at our home with my gear and, in return, Kathy and I took her and her mother out to lunch, though that didn't cost nearly as much as she'd saved me.

*

A week later, a courier company rang our gate bell. I signed for a big parcel that had come by air from Reykjavík. We opened it in the kitchen. Inside the layers of bubble wrap were sides of smoked Atlantic salmon. That's when it really came home to me that I'd been punching well above my financial fighting weight in Iceland. All I could do to repay Robin's generosity, and Clay's for that matter, was to invite them to come over to fish the Eastern Cape Highlands with me. Happily they both accepted. More about that trip later.

I left Iceland and England with a deep sense that most anglers are only too happy to share generously, and with memories of powerful rivers, pastoral streams, prodigious fish, and yes, a certain guide, of course – memories that will live with me forever.

CHAPTER 12

TROUT FLIES FOR RIVERS AND STREAMS – RANDOM THOUGHTS

A Southern fly fisherman's fly box, once opened, generally looks like an artist's palette that has been dipped in water: it is a collage of bright colours.
HARRY MIDDLETON, *IN THAT SWEET COUNTRY*

A few generalisations

I don't think there are any specific rules about flies for streams, whether they're small, fast-flowing mountain streams or meandering creeks, that generally don't hold good for bigger trout rivers. Having said that, most folk I fish with nowadays favour smaller patterns for both, though it's no hard-and-fast rule because I've too often seen large patterns, even *really* large dry fly patterns, fool small-stream trout.

In fact, a recent example was memorable enough to stay in my mind. I was fishing the upper Lourens outside Somerset West with Clem Booth and Robin Douglas. This is by anyone's definition a small stream. As we came to the lovely deep glide at the end of the beat, we saw a trout rise confidently. On a whim, I gave Clem a size 14 bright-yellow DDD, and he hooked a fish on it almost as soon as the fly landed. It leapt clear of the water and broke him. The only other yellow DDD I had was a size 10 dry fly meant for stillwaters and way too big for this stream. In fact, we had had some discussion about using it at all, but eventually I handed the fly to Clem and, bearing in mind its totally improbable size, wryly said to him, 'Now look, Clem, don't stuff this up.' He straight away hooked another rainbow, again within seconds of the fly landing, a fish this time all of fifteen inches, that leapt like a dog stung by a wasp – and, as you guessed, snapped him off.

After Robin had wiped the tears of laughter from his eyes, and Clem had lifted his head from its sorrowfully bowed position, I said that this little sequence had reinforced a long-held belief of mine about trying to second-guess small-stream trout – which is that you can't.

*

For smaller streams and rivers, the general entry-level fly size seems to have shrunk from size 14 to size 16, but with the range either side of that from size 22 (and even smaller in some hands) up to size 12, even bigger in other hands I know. And again, this trend to scale back on sizes is a trend on rivers, not only on streams, and especially on stillwaters in more experienced hands.

I happen to prefer fishing dry flies, but it's more personal preference than pragmatism. I like using them not because they're necessarily more effective, but because to me, a trout lifting to a dry fly strokes a few more pleasure zones than a trout snatching a sunken nymph. And on delicate streams, the 'plop' of a heavy nymph can spook fish, though not always irreversibly.

Then, I regard the advent of the CDC feathers as a kind of fly-tying epiphany, and for good reason. CDC presents lightly, looks buggy on the water, rides high, traps air and is versatile – never mind highly fashionable. The result is that new and creative CDC patterns pop up as frequently as mushrooms in the October veld, and in recent times, books have appeared devoted solely to CDC patterns. But there is good- and bad-quality CDC, dyed and undyed CDC, and large and small CDC feathers, and then tiny, ultra-soft CDC feathers called puffs, that have their uses in posts or wings or just to add life as a dubbed or spun thorax.

What to use: dry flies, emergers or nymphs?

It seems we change from dry flies or emergers to nymphs because we can't interest fish in dry flies or emergers on days when just catching a fish becomes more important than how we catch them. To most anglers, the dry fly is a sort of default setting, though it's set at different thresholds for each of us. Robin and another friend Stanton Hector, for example, both have a huge tolerance to not catching fish on a dry fly or an emerger, and still persevering or holding faith. My own setting is about one hour flat of concentrated hard work with no sign of a rise, before I change. My friend Billy de Jong's setting seems to be around three well-presented but unproductive casts, meaning his dry fly or emerger has run flawlessly, or drag-free, three times right over a trout that just rose. If that dry fly or emerger fails the test, then, in Billy's book, their passport is immediately revoked and nymphs are suddenly issued visas.

But for most of us, fishing dry flies is a personal but practical and pragmatic approach to getting a job done, free from anything like blind devotion or purism just for purism's sake. Actually, purism has nothing to do with it. Put differently, I happen to like fishing dry flies or emergers. I feel they add some poetry, and they are less likely, at least in good hands, to disturb fish than heavy nymphs. Sloppy casts aside, I almost feel it in my bones when to accept that a change to nymph is needed. It's not something that I can easily put into words unless I sight a trout cleanly feeding on nymphs.

One of the enigmas of fishing dry fly and emerger patterns is managing refusals. Frequently, the problem lies in the presentation, not the pattern, and here drag – especially micro-drag – is often the undetected enemy. Or the trout has somehow sensed you and is being cautious. Or it's being selective and you haven't matched up, or got the right whistle, as my late good friend Leo Rosettenstein often said.

But if it is a pattern problem, my vote is to rest the fish, change to a smaller, different dry fly or emerger, and reassess your approach to get the best drift over the fish. That often works for me, and makes a lot more sense than immediately changing to a nymph, weighted or unweighted.

And finally, a change of pattern is often motivated by plain intuition, one of the least explained aspects of presentation: unexplained because it is least understood, or it's dismissed as not being scientific. But the continual survival of mankind down the ages has, to a large extent, been dependent on man's evolution of protective and productive instincts. So, whatever you think about it, don't just write off the value of a whim or a hunch as being Lotto-type mumbo jumbo.

Nymphs
I'm probably not going to be able to tell you much about what nymph patterns we use on streams that you don't already know, other than that PTNs, Gold-ribbed Hare's Ears, Zaks and copper

wire nymphs in countless guises are all good, as long as they sink when they're supposed to. The slim outline of flies like Gary Glen-Young's G-Force nymph patterns with their silver or copper-lined clear glass beads, or MC Coetzer's nymph patterns, are advances I've taken note of as far as modern trends go, whatever that might mean. Like the trend to add hotspots or to use tungsten beads, or to use jig hooks to prevent snagging, which seems like an overkill on small streams but maybe not on rivers, even if some of the pools are suitably deep and mysterious. On big, especially robust freestone rivers, nymphs tied on jig hooks are, as the saying goes, horses of an altogether different colour.

Are the modern trends in nymph design worth using? If I had the time and the inclination, and if I found modern competition patterns aesthetically pleasing (to me, not the fish), or if what I currently use wasn't working, I'd be inclined to change. But read these as the views of someone stuck, if not in the dark ages, at least not in the modern, competitive, trend-setting era.

In correspondence with MC Coetzer, whose views I respect, I gleaned that he has always tried to snaffle the flies that worked for the best-performing individuals at international competitions. Early on he took note of the popularity of Czech-style nymph patterns, but was sharp enough to also note in some of the patterns he'd collected that 'their style was definitely *outdated*', to quote his words. These were bulky nymphs with a lot of *detail*, and detail, as MC says, is nowadays not considered to be important. And it shows in the almost bullet-like shapes, the sparseness of these patterns, and in the growing variety of hotspots, be these beads or blobs of bright dubbing of different sorts. And hotspots appear as relevant in terms of colour as in their precise positioning on modern nymphs. I now look at competition-style nymphs and have difficulty telling one from another; they all look so similar or play such minor variations on what appear to be extremely common themes that they are lost on me. The recently acclaimed Perdigon Nymph, a Spanish development for the heavily fished and fast-flowing streams in the Pyrenees, is a case in point. It looks more like a brightly coloured, well-sucked cough drop than a buggy nymph.

The Polish flies, MC said, have stayed pretty constant, at least at the time of writing this piece, and are often skinny and quite long versions of PTNs or Gold-Ribbed Hare's Ear patterns.

MC also commented that today few jig hooks are used, adding that the French believe a jig hook must only be tied on when you want the fly right on the bottom. For anywhere else in the column, the fly must be tied on a standard hook, because the French don't fancy the posture nymphs adopt when dressed on jig hooks.

MC spent some time fishing with Louis Jean Rauch in France in 2012, and rated him by far the most impressive fisherman he'd ever watched, from a fly-tying, casting, efficiency and accuracy perspective. Louis is one of the French master Pascal Cognard's regular fishing partners, and their patterns are similar. The interesting characteristic of Louis's patterns is the placement and subtlety of the hotspots. He believes the positioning is critical in heavily fished waters, where fish will refuse a fly with a coloured bead or with a hotspot *behind* the bead. Put simply, they've seen too many.

To depart from MC's insightful observations for a moment, to my own less-global insights, let me add that outside of nymph-pattern selection, which is clearly important and becomes all the more important on really heavily fished streams, the most critical thing is that nymphs are best fished as living insects, and mostly, but not always, under close scrutiny in a dead drift and at the right depth. At least until that doesn't work, when you want to add movement, such as lift, in the hope it will induce a take. This pays homage to the late Jim Leisenring, Oliver Kite, Frank Sawyer, Leonard M

Wright Jr and many others, who all came to the conclusion that induced movement in a fly has a trigger effect on trout.

The nymphs I favour are the ones I know from personal experience have worked, at least often enough to convince me that alternatives, though they might be interesting and offer theoretical advantages, as yet don't warrant a quantum shift in my thinking. So I rest with the Zak in all its guises, PTNs, Gold-ribbed Hare's Ears and, last but by no means least, the Brassie. This pattern I tie right down to size 22, using fine copper wire for the body and Hareline's Ice Dub, or ostrich herl, for the thorax, and I often use it as a dropper with a dry fly.

Having said all this, there's hardly a month that goes by where I'm not introduced to someone's latest panacea – his or her answer to all our nymph-pattern problems. So where is the truth? Well, the truth is that it is found, in elements or in parts, in *all* of this. Or else, the truth is that there is no absolute truth; that there are few wrong answers to modern or to long-since-accepted nymph patterns across the board. It's a comfortable state, because it leaves a sense of liberation. What's left is to concentrate on *how* you fish the nymph, and how well you can control its depth in the drift or its sink rate – or, put differently, how well you can control the fly.

A last word. I recently read *Nymphing: The New Way* by Jonathan White and Oscar Boatfield, published in 2016, all about French leader fishing for trout. In it, many modern nymph patterns from various masters are illustrated, and I sensed immediately the presence of the new trends in nymph patterns, for want of a better description. They all look similar: shorter-bodied, nearly uniformly beaded, hotspots on almost all of them, Coq de Leon tails far more common, and CDC collars more common than ever before. But, again, while these may be important developments, the real change in nymphing has come in how you *control* the nymph to present as a living insect as near to your quarry as it's possible to get.

Yet hotspots on nymphs still interest me, and I feel short of an answer. Drop back in time to the writings of Negley Farson in *Going Fishing*, published in 1942, and you'll read how he values the colour red in flies. I think I'm right in saying it was Farson's statement on the value of the colour red in artificial flies that got Tony Biggs, developer of the RAB, to try red thread on his now-iconic dry fly pattern – and the rest of that story is history. But wherein is the attraction? Is it just in the contrast, or is it some primordial neuro-circuitry that links bright reds, yellows and oranges with edible stuff, like trout eggs and maybe elements of freshwater crustaceans? And if it's just in the attention-drawing contrast, do we call nymphs with fluorescent orange beads or hotspots, attractor nymphs?

Dry flies and emergers

We can't avoid stating the obvious, namely that small-stream dry flies and emergers should present softly, have a buggy outline, and carry as few unnatural colours as possible. Modern teaching suggests they should be 'natural-looking scraps' rather than carefully modelled dry flies like, say, the Light Cahill. But good dry fly patterns *do* feed straight off the characteristics of the naturals they are meant to represent. These patterns end up being wispy, dull-coloured, delicate, often crippled, some in the process of emergence, others hatched, yet others returned to the water as spinners, but all so light that a gentle breeze carries them off. In modern terms, these characteristics are well captured with CDC feathers; Agostino Roncallo's brilliant Mirage dry fly is a perfect example of a mayfly dun imitation that is suggestive, light and delicate. Tied from a single CDC feather, it is a masterpiece of simplicity, and seeing it drift through a run, you're inclined to want to eat it yourself.

I tried the Mirage for the first time on the Sterkspruit, where it was brilliant, and Tony Kietzman and I used them that same trip on the trout in the upper Bokspruit, and caught fish all day – well, at least until our supply ran out. Then we went over to other patterns and, interestingly, we did just as well fishing versions of RABs, Philip Meyer's Para-RAB, a wolf spider imitation, and a CDC and Elk Hair Caddis, a pattern that I think the originator Al Troth would admit is a good variation of his original (or at least he'd admit it makes some kind of sense). I mention all this because it will give you an idea of what we are using these days on small, quick-flowing streams, both in the Western Cape and in the Eastern Cape Highlands.

The emergence of emergers

Looking at the evolution of modern floating patterns, it seems to me that the sea change has been in the development of a host of emergers, a notable example being the Para-RAB. They embrace the modern notion now popular among many fly fishers, that you should fish your flies *in* the surface film rather than *on* it, when, of course, the fly is then not a dry fly but an emerger. Homage is due for this bit of wisdom to people like Marjan Fratnik with his F-Fly, Hans van Klinken, Leon Links and others. And locally, homage is due to Philip Meyer who, in a sudden cascade of piscatorial wisdom, came up with the Para-RAB, one pattern I would now rarely fish a small stream without. My only contribution to his Para-RAB was the introduction some years ago of squirrel fibres to my standard RABs to add 'movement', although if you read back issues of the *Piscator* (I couldn't tell you what year, but I'd guess it was the late 1990s), I was tying a pattern I called a 'Halo-Hackle', not that far removed from the Para-RAB or at least edging towards it.

Today I would be inclined to include the Shuttlecock or Plume Tip CDC emerger patterns that Jeremy Lucas swears by, and those similar patterns Dave Wiltshire ties and calls Early Risers. They work predictably well, mainly because they cover so many bases emerger imitations demand and, as a bonus, they're simple to tie. Both Jeremy Lucas and Dave Wiltshire are experienced and capable UK-based fly fishers.

The common thread to CDC dry fly patterns and the Para-RABs and the Spiders is that you have to apply in writing to present them badly. They don't splash; they drift gently onto the water. You can't say that with as much certainty for standard or traditional dry flies like the Adams, and some hopper patterns (mind you, you might *want* those to splash to draw attention) that are invariably 'stiffer', carry more weight and, in some cases, offer greater wind resistance, or are a devil to tie.

One Feather CDC Midge

I fish my One Feather CDC Midge pattern a lot these days, a fly I designed after getting skunked during a hatch of mountain midges. Again, I prefer using natural, dun-coloured CDC to anything dyed, but it's such a scrap of a pattern that it really does need a post, otherwise it disappears as soon as it lands. So I add poly yarn or, nowadays, an off-white silicone-impregnated poly yarn post, a material that Leon Links sent me. I trim this down to the size of a match head, though even this minor departure from the appearance of the natural still worries me.

Generally, bright posts on dry flies don't concern me unless I am fishing a shallow, glassy run with spooky trout in it. Then I prefer no post.

Mayfly spinner patterns

Mention mayfly spinner patterns and I immediately think, 'the world's most underrated small-stream trout flies'. You need a couple of spinners. Again, I find a simple quill body with CDC wings tied spent works comfortably well. But there are a million other patterns, and your choice is probably as good as anyone else's.

The Elk Hair Caddis and its variant forms

What can you say about these patterns that hasn't already been said? It's a brilliant concept for a dry fly I'd never want to be without. It floats well, presents well and is a perfect dry fly for prospecting on freestone streams, caddis hatch or no caddis hatch.

Terrestrials

It's written in the scriptures that you leave terrestrials off any stream or river pattern list at your own peril, not so much because you come across that many terrestrials on the water or in stomach contents (with the exception of ants), but because you can't ignore a track record that's so good it shouts at you. The success of spider, hopper and ant and beetle patterns (floating or sunken) is compelling.

Beetles and ants

There are hundreds of different patterns, and every fly tier will tell you why his or her beetles or ants are good, maybe better than yours or anyone else's, and for a heap of nearly convincing reasons that at best are mainly specious or don't really matter. If you tie flies yourself, making up ant and beetle patterns doesn't need a university degree. And if you don't tie flies, just take yourself into a reputable fly store and pick a couple of patterns out of the bins blindfolded.

Floating beetle imitations have to join the terrestrial list as productive on small streams, and many local anglers have developed their own versions. I guess a common theme would be the use of foam bodies and metallic-green reflective materials to cover the abdomen. My own view is that on our small streams, outside of the willow-lined streams in the Barkly East district, the floating beetle takes a back seat to imitations of aquatic spiders and ant and hopper patterns.

Aquatic spider imitations

The realisation that the wolf spider is far more common than we thought began the development of aquatic spider imitations that are now justifiably among the most popular dry flies in common use on small streams throughout South Africa.

The first of the local spider imitation was Mark Mackereth's Caribou Spider. Leonard Flemming, Peter Brigg and Fred Steynberg have all since developed effective wolf spider imitations that float well and are extremely buggy. Bodies are of foam, and legs, again variable depending on who's tying it, are pheasant tail fibres, squirrel tail fibres or Hungarian Partridge fibres. Hackles, even halo-hackles, play an important role in stabilising the various patterns on the water and include various cock hackles, mainly dun, red or ginger, Egyptian Goose breast feathers and even CDC hackle fibres. Our aquatic spider imitations have been so well written up that to detail them again would not be productive, but I will include a few words from Peter Brigg on his latest version of the wolf spider at the end of this chapter.

Hoppers

As far as hoppers go, there are again countless patterns to choose from, but nothing has ever beaten Ed Herbst's Hopper in my own experience, just that they are a devil to tie.

Wet flies

Important, and among the prettiest and most traditional of all small-stream fly patterns, are the lovely soft-hackle wet flies, like the Snipe and Purple, popular in the UK from early times,and still popular today. One of the earliest exponents was T Pritt, who described the Snipe and Purple and similar patterns in his book *Yorkshire Trout Flies,* published in 1886. In the more modern idiom, the late Sylvester Nemes popularised this style of patterns in the

USA, beginning with his book *The Soft-Hackled Fly Addict* (1975). But if you really want to go into the deepest history, then a similar version appears in Charles Cotton's additions to Izaak Walton's *The Compleat Angler*, published way back in 1676.

There's a bunch of patterns I haven't mentioned, and should – like the Red Tag, just because it's so universally proven and effective, and yes, hiding my head, Woolly Buggers tied small. I know some people use them; I don't. It's not a matter of snobbishness, the unwarranted adoption of superior virtue, as Robert Traver neatly put it. It's a personal matter. I'm happy to go without catching fish after first trying them on a dry fly or emerger, and then on nymphs, terrestrials and even this limited range of wet flies, especially the soft-hackles, after which I'm happy to leave the fish in peace and move on. Catching fish just for the sake of catching them doesn't light my fuse. If it lights yours, that's fine by me.

Some irreducible tenets and the matter of size

As far as flies for rivers and streams go, you will get an earful of opinions and ideas on the subject depending on who you're talking to. I'm really no different, I guess, but having said that, there are a few unshakeable tenets.

The first is that small is good.

The second is that parachute patterns in all their guises are here to stay, and for a few good reasons.

Third, CDC feathers have been a revelation.

The fourth notion is that hotspots, including some really sophisticated new beads, on bullet-shaped, fast-sinking, no-clutter nymphs (in fact, often with lacquered UV-cured bodies, and as mentioned before, the Perdigon Nymphs are good examples), have increased the catch rate in sophisticated hands, while counterintuitively (and a blessing) 'standard' nymph patterns (read PTNs, Flashbacks, Gold-ribbed Hare's Ears, Zaks and so on) still keep working for most of us left languishing at less lofty heights on the piscatorial ladder of advancement.

Finally, you ignore terrestrials at your peril.

So my fly box is now a reductionist dream. All my flies are size 14 to 22, all are barbless, and the dry flies and emergers outweigh nymphs around three to one. There are a few favourite 'new' patterns, and we all have them. Mine is the One-Feather CDC Midge, which makes sense given the high population of mountain midges. After all, the net-winged midges in the *Blephariceridae* family are often referred to as mountain midges because they occur in abundance in fast-flowing, high-altitude streams.

Another essential is an all-purpose emerger, and to suggest emergence, as I have said, little beats the Para-RAB and its abundant variations, although Klinkhåmers and CDC Plume Tip emergers are probably equally effective, as is Hans Weilenmann's CDC Loop-Wing Emerger.

I match adult mayflies on streams with, among a few others, Agostino Roncallo's delicate Mirage dry fly (in black, olive or dun), and my terrestrials are Ed Herbst-type ants, beetles and hoppers.

My nymphs are PTNs, tied as Frank Sawyer suggested: the Zak in three guises – unweighted, with a brass bead or with a fluorescent-orange tungsten bead (too rarely used by me, perhaps) – and my 'quick-tie Zak', called the Easy Nymph, which has done well up in the Barkly East district and takes half the time a Zak takes to tie. I'll describe the tying of this and a few other key small-stream patterns later in the chapter.

Finally, my wet flies of choice would be North Country Spiders and the Red Tag.

Thoughts on Western Cape streams
I think it wise to add some thoughts on hatches, or insect prevalence, and fly patterns on our local streams.

According to Ed Herbst, there are two important but brief seasonal hatches that occur in early spring, from September to November. The insects are the net-winged midge (*Blephariceridae*) and the blackfly (*Simuliidae*). They both hatch in substantial numbers. On one occasion on the Elandspad River, the mountain midges – as they are also known – were so prolific that they looked like small, drifting patches of grey mist.

Traditionally, the net-winged midge would call for a Griffith's Gnat (invented by Andy Griffith), but Cape Town-based fly fishers have developed some interesting alternatives. A good imitation is my own One-Feather CDC Midge, but Darryl Lampert's HiVis CDC Midge is a better imitation. Says Darryl, 'The fluorescent red Antron post makes the pattern highly visible, a bonus when tied small or fished in tricky lighting conditions. The palmered CDC causes the pattern to sit on tiptoes, hiding the hook and providing a footprint of light which, to me, is a far better imitation of a dancing midge, or a mayfly, when seen from a trout's perspective. The natural movement of the CDC is obviously also a trigger and aids in a far gentler presentation when compared to conventionally hackled patterns.'

I have seen mating blackflies in their hundreds on the rocks, laying their eggs in little pink patches that quickly turn brown and resemble lichen. Thereafter the insects tumble into the water and can cause a frenzy of selective feeding. Despite this, there are no recognised patterns for the blackfly adult that I'm aware of.

Then there's a 'hatch' that is not a hatch at all, but the daily ovipositing flight of the female Darkening Dun mayfly (*Choroterpes nigrescens*). Most South African mayflies hatch at night, and many crawl onto rocks to emerge from their shucks, so significant mayfly hatches are rare and, in my experience, caddis hatches are even rarer.

The appearance of the egg-laying Darkening Dun mayfly is a happy exception and, usually around 10.30am, a stream devoid of rises can suddenly boil with cavorting trout. These are a most beautiful, tiny, ebony-black mayfly with cellophane-like wings.

The cause of the rise is mainly difficult to discern but, if you turn around and look downstream, the little spinners can be seen against the sun, rhythmically rising and falling as they fly upstream against the direction of the current, dipping down to brush their abdomens against the water surface to dislodge their eggs.

For the Darkening Dun mayfly hatch you need look no further than Agostino Roncallo's Mirage. It is a CDC equivalent of Harry Darbee's Two Feather Mayfly.

*

To round off on stream patterns, my guess is that Jeremy Lucas's Plume Tip (a CDC emerger) might well soar to greater heights – regardless of whether you're fishing for trout in rivers or streams.

The art of Impressionism and fly tying

I've been privileged to view numerous collections of Impressionist art in museums around the world, and I recall being particularly moved by a large Renoir my wife and I saw in Belgium. We spotted the painting from a distance, a scene of a group of people at a picnic in a riverside setting, with colourful boats in the foreground and glimpses of a typically French landscape in the background. It gave the immediate idea of a joyful gathering depicted in wonderful detail. But when I got closer to the painting, *there was no detail*. It was just a mix of broad brushstrokes of different colours that on close inspection didn't appear to portray anything. It was the illusionary use of paint on canvas that only sprang to life as you moved away from it. It was Impressionist art at its best.

So it should be with fly tying. We need to give the impression of an insect at a glance, even if it won't stand up to close scrutiny – because it doesn't need to. Try this experiment: on a size 20 barbless hook tie in three dun cock hackle fibres as tails. Leave them long and well separated. Dub a darkish, dun-coloured body and hackle the fly with a few turns of light dun hackle. Note: no wings, no ribbing. Will this simple pattern create the impression of a real bug? Well, attach it to your jacket near your shoulder. Many people will immediately take it for an insect, and some will even try to brush it off.

A few dressings you will find interesting and useful
1. The Easy Nymph, or 'Quick Tie' Zak
Add a brass bead (optional) to a size 12 to 16 hook and dress it with black 8/0 thread, then tie in a few wisps of dark cock or grizzly hackle for the tail. *Partially* strip three peacock herls of their flue and tie them in by their tips at the tail, together with a short length of copper wire. Spin the wire and peacock herl, and wrap them as a 'rope' to the thorax. Tie in a small-sized grizzly or black cock hackle here by its stem, having stripped the fibres off one side of the stem to reduce bulk. At the thorax add another peacock herl, this time leaving all its flue on, and again twist all these elements together (wire, peacock herls and hackle). Wind the 'rope' to the eye of the hook, or to the bead, and tie off.

On one trip to *Birkhall*, Billy de Jong and I tied up a few Easy Nymphs using an olive-dyed grizzly cape Billy owns, and we added a bright orange tungsten bead. We did well enough on this variation to believe it ought to have a name. We called it the Olive Easy. There's no end to our creative genius.

2. Pete's Spider
This is an important pattern because it captures the essential triggers of a wolf spider, and it's easier to tie than either the Flemming and Steynberg version. All three, by the way, use foam bodies, but vary somewhat in replicating the legs and the use of hackles and posts.

Peter Brigg told me he wanted to simplify the tying to exaggerate the trigger features, especially the legs and abdomen, and to improve durability. He initially settled on pheasant tail fibres for the legs, front and back. That changed to pheasant tail for the back legs, with the front legs replaced by squirrel tail fibres tied shorter than the back legs in a fan shape over the eye of the hook. Pete argues that these fibres provide a good profile from a trout's point of view, and they add to the pattern's general bugginess.

This is his step-by-step tying method:

'Using a light wire dry fly hook like the Grip 11011BL in either size 14 or 16, dress the shank with tying thread. (I use Gordon Griffiths 14/0 Sheer or UTC 70 in black.) Add a small bunch of squirrel tail fibres on top of the shank protruding over the hook eye, secure and trim the excess. Always leave about 2mm clear behind the eye for tying off later. Attach a piece of 2mm-thick, tan-coloured foam or Lava Lace foam pre-cut into a rectangle of approximately 10mm x 5mm to the hook at the bend. (The foam should be trimmed into a V at one end for ease of attaching at the tie-in point. Also, a drop of super glue helps to secure it tightly and avoid slipping.) Add a piece of white Antron or similar material at the tie-off point of the squirrel tail fibres as a sighter and to act as the parachute hackle post. Attach to the post a rust/ginger hackle. (This need not be a high-quality hackle, and one from a cheaper Indian or Chinese cape will do. It is simply for bugginess and profile rather than to help to float the fly.) At the tie-in point of the foam, add two strands of peacock herl and wind forward, tie off and trim excess about 2mm behind the base of the post. Fold the foam over the peacock on top of the shank, and tie off at the same point as the peacock. Secure and trim excess. In the previously mentioned 2mm gap, add two pheasant tail fibres each on either side for the back legs to protrude about 1 to 1½ times the length of the abdomen beyond the back of the abdomen.

(It is important to tie the legs in the gap behind the post to avoid complications when the parachute hackle is added and tied off.) Wind the hackle around the post with no more than three turns, secure and trim excess. (The hackle should be sparse and roughly 1½ times as wide as the gape of the hook.) Take the tying thread to the gap behind the hook eye, below the squirrel tail fibres, make a few turns and then, using your thumbnail at the base of the squirrel tail fibres, force the fibres into a fan shape and then whip finish. (I add a drop of UV resin at the base of the squirrel tail fibres to secure and maintain their fan shape over the eye.) Trim the post to the required length, and you are done.'

3. One-Feather CDC Midge

Keep this fly as simple to tie as possible. I've seen people trying to 'improve' it by adding tails (which the natural doesn't have), ribbing and even antennae. It makes no sense to me to add this level of detail because this is an imitation of a tiny insect, and it's good to remember that the view the trout gets of your artificial fished in a quick flowing run is from fractions of a second to two seconds at the most. Anyway, not enough time for a trout to appreciate niceties like ribbing or antennae. All that counts is to present an impression of the natural and perhaps to roughly match its colour, principles that should hold good for any pattern fished in quick water, no matter whether the water's gin-clear or not.

The net-winged or mountain midge is a tiny, delicate insect around 5mm in length, with extremely long legs that are at least twice the length of the body. They emerge in spring and live on vegetation near streams for two to three weeks before returning to mate and to lay eggs, when they often dance in small swarms that hover just above the water. Emergence is extremely rapid too, the insect using current flow to help it leave the pupal case.

As Ed Herbst put it in an article published in the *Piscator* of July 1992, if you bump into a hatch or mating flight of mountain midges and you don't have a matching pattern, you might as well be cherry picking.

Tie this fly on a light wire dry fly hook in size 16 to 18. I prefer the Tiemco 103 BL, which is a superb barbless, ultra-light wire dry fly hook. The equivalent hook sizes in this Tiemco model are 17 and 19. Select a medium-sized dun- or tan-coloured CDC feather. Dress the hook with fine black 10/0 Uni-Thread, moisten the feather tip with saliva and position it on top of the hook shank immediately above the bend. Make two loose wraps around the mid-stalk point, then gently and slowly pull the stalk of the feather back towards the eye of the hook until only a millimetre of the tip is left protruding at the tail end. Secure it here with two firm wraps of thread. Carry the thread forward to the thorax area, and tie in a post using a thin strip of orange or white Spirit River, or similar, poly yarn. Leave the post longish for the time being. Now twist the CDC feather and wrap it neatly and tightly around the shank to the post. Dub a small amount of black or peacock Hareline Ice Dub onto the thread and, with figure-of-eight wraps, cover the base of the post and the under-surface of the hook to suggest a thorax. Don't trim any loose Ice Dub fibres away. They add to the pattern's bugginess. Now carefully stroke the remaining CDC fibres away from the stalk and, holding the post firmly or after securing it in a gallows tool, put in one or two turns of the CDC feather around the base of the post. These fibres will act to stabilise the fly on the water; they also suggest the impression of an insect's legs. Tie off and trim.

The 'perfect state'

The whole business of fly selection can get complicated enough, so before reading this just remember that I'm not talking of spring creeks here or chalkstreams, or huge rivers with cavernous pools and waist-deep runs. I'm talking of small freestone streams that are mainly in the mountains, quick-flowing and a little turbulent at the run-ins, though in places they will open up a little into typically clear, slower-flowing and smoothly glassy glides.

Despite being clichéd, the old adage that it matters less *what* you fish than *how* and *where* you fish it still holds water, but only up to a point. What's missing is the importance of the flies we use giving the impression of a natural insect in size, outline and colour. When you get this right, you have pretty well achieved the 'perfect state' fly fishers continually strive for.

Why the 'perfect state'? Well, when the 'how' and 'where' we fish include the parameters around the nature of the pattern we fish, it will roughly hold that despite the few brief moments a small stream trout gets to inspect your fly, *it is very likely it will take it.*

The riddle of the ignored dry fly and educated hunches
But it does leave one interesting variable unaddressed. This concerns those occasions, and there are many, when a tried-and-tested dry fly or emerger pattern doesn't produce a fish where another floating pattern does. I can more easily understand a nymph working after an hour's blank fishing with a surface fly, but preference for one dry fly or emerger pattern over another is less easy to explain unless the reasons for it are obvious. And in my experience the same sort of selectivity doesn't happen nearly as often when you're fishing nymphs in small streams.

To get back to the surface patterns, let's suppose you haven't seen a rise in the stream in an hour, and you haven't seen a sign of a trout around your fly, and yet you still have enough confidence, say in your Para-RAB, to stick with it. But after another blank ten minutes you decide to change flies. The question is, to what? The obvious answer is to a nymph, but on a hunch, you pick another dry fly, like an Elk Hair Caddis, and suddenly you catch trout. How do you explain this? The short answer is, with great difficulty – unless there was a caddis hatch, and for argument's sake we'll say there wasn't.

It raises the question of how, on a given day, you can account for the effectiveness of one established dry fly or emerger pattern over another, again when there is no obvious reason to explain it. And the situation crops up often because there are a bunch of us who just like sticking to dry flies no matter what the trout are doing.

I'm not trying to provide an answer to this. I'm just raising an interesting point. I can understand trout taking a nymph when they're off dry flies, but to take one dry fly or emerger pattern when they steadfastly ignored another is not always easy to explain.

Knowledge by osmosis

What dry fly to change to in these situations is sometimes obvious; for example, you notice a hatch of duns and you can match it. But when there's nothing to give you a clue, your selection becomes an educated hunch. I say an 'educated hunch', because gradually over the years we absorb a lot of information – gain empirical knowledge, if you like – hanging around trout streams. Put differently, the longer we fish streams, the better our intuition gets – about, for example, which dry fly pattern to change to when the one you have on doesn't get as much as a passing nod. It's a bit like crossword puzzles. You have a few clues and enough general knowledge to eventually work out the answers.

Despite all the knowledge we build up by slow osmosis on streams, I notice that when conditions are slow, even seasoned anglers' opinions differ about pattern selection. Some will be right some of the time, and some will be wrong some of the time. Fortunately the trout soon let us know.

But I love the imponderable aspect of fly fishing; it's like solving riddles or trying to second-guess nature. For my money this is the beating heart of it all: the endless series of variables and deductions that serve to make our sport so endlessly puzzling at times and always so reliably appealing.

And I'll leave you with this quote on opinions, by Mark Twain in *Pudd'nhead Wilson's Calendar*: 'It were not least that we should all think alike; it is differences of opinion that makes horse-races.'

CHAPTER 13
DROUGHTS

The trout in the rivers are quick and wary, drawn to the cover of
rocky ledges and the coolness of the feeder streams and springs.
STEVE RAYMOND, *THE YEAR OF THE ANGLER*

As I write, late in 2016, we've had a serious two-year drought in
the Western Cape, and naturally it's taken a toll on the fishing. Not
in the way the sudden arrival of a cold east wind can ruin your
fishing, which is as quick as a light switch, but rather in the sense
of a gradual, incremental and insidious decline. To give you an idea
of its scale, people were comparing this drought to others, saying
things like 'This is the worst in living memory.' It's also when we
started hearing a few new metaphors, like a tadpole-throttling
drought or a duck-drying drought, even a frog-frying drought.
Robin Douglas and I often fish the stream that runs through the
Lourensford Estate outside Somerset West, and the manager of
the fishery, Gerhard Campion, mentioned to us this was the worst
drought recorded on the farm in a hundred years – and that was *a
year ago*. Since then things have got, well, frog-frying worse.

We're currently on Level 4B water restrictions in Cape Town. Swimming pools have dropped to unheard-of levels, gardens have slowly faded away, lawns have died, and only the plants my wife and I really cherish get any water, which we deliver by hand and not through a hosepipe. Hosepipes are banned.

At first, when we weren't really into this year's drought, though not quite out of the previous year's, Robin and I would arrive at the river and might comment on the level being low, or that we'd need 8X tippets, long leaders and tiny flies to catch fish and, of course, we'd fish gossamer-light and ridiculously cautiously. We'd take careful note of the telltale tracery left on sandbanks by receding water levels to see how far the stream had dropped since we were last there. Then, as the dry conditions persisted, the runs and pools shrank even further, fish became ultra-skittish, then sparse, until eventually we arrived at a point where the stream was no more than a fragile gully of rocks and stones seemingly covered by a sheet of clear glass. That's when trailing fronds of green algae appeared to complete the ominous picture and confirm our worst fears.

There was a time, before any temporarily relieving showers fell (and there were a few of those), when we would debate whether it was worth going out at all, and our decisions to go fishing were based more on sentiment and nostalgia than on the hope of actually catching fish. We started to reason that it was worth going if only because it had been so long since we had last put a foot in the river. We also occasionally reminded ourselves that if we didn't go fishing we wouldn't catch a fish for sure, and at the same time we understood that if we did go fishing it wouldn't matter that we didn't catch a fish either.

Then just the other day Robin called and said, 'Come on, let's go, even if it's just to look at the stream.' That was a first, and it was also when I realised our situation was pretty serious. We do still end up fishing occasionally – not so much to catch fish but because we both like being around water where trout live, even if we aren't sure they're there any more. Nostalgia is a strange reason to go fishing, but sometimes it fits – and it helps to ride out times like these.

But if the prospects for fly fishing the rivers and streams looked bleak, in a strange way it has never felt like a hopeless bleakness. Teasing light showers would fall from time to time. They were soaked up by the dry earth in a flash, but they offered transient relief to the streams. At least we aren't anywhere near where my favourite trout haunt, the Eastern Cape Highlands, was at the end of 2016, when a few rivers stopped running altogether, the Sterkspruit on *Birkhall* being one of them.

*

I've made two trips a year to the Barkly East District and, at times, the southern side of the Drakensberg around Maclear, for near on twenty years now – long enough to have become more an itinerant local than a casual visitor in the minds of some folk up there. Then in 2015, the drought bit in until the Sterkspruit had only the occasional deep, sea-green pools left. On *Birkhall*, Basie Vosloo told me he spotted a few big trout in these pools that he estimated were over ten pounds. None was caught, and I didn't make a trip that year. I also missed 2016, because there had been no relief and conditions were beyond miserable; they were dire, and it's a long way to drive from Cape Town just to look at empty riverbeds.

On the last day of 2015, I had a welcome call from my good friend Fred Steynberg. We exchanged season's greetings and naturally spoke about the weather – or, more pertinently, about the lack of rain. Fred lives in Rhodes and guides in the district. What he had to tell me about local conditions I found most interesting.

First, he confirmed that the situation was pretty cheerless, but that despite the conditions, two large trout had been taken on fly tackle, one of twenty-two and one of twenty-four inches, both from lower beats of the Bokspruit River. As I recall, *Knockwarren* was one of those beats. I found that encouraging news.

Fred is a remarkable naturalist and told me he'd noticed that a great number of yellowfish had over-wintered the year, not moving off downstream to warmer water as they usually do. Surely that had to relate to the dry weather and poor water flows.

He also spoke at length about the remarkable capacity trout have to survive the most hostile conditions and still appear, as if by magic, when the rivers return to normal.

And then, days after his call, rains came to Barkly East and surrounding districts, early in 2016. That's when I got two remarkable cellphone messages, each with a camera image, sent to me by Basie. They read:

The Sterkspruit River at 8.45am on 12 January 2016.

The Sterkspruit River at 9.45am on 12 January 2016, one hour later!

The first photograph shows the Sterkspruit bone-dry, just bare rocks, sticks and dry pebbles. The second photograph, taken from the same spot an hour later, shows the river a roaring highway of brown water.

More rain followed and there were even a few unseasonal falls of snow. It looked like the drought had broken and, much to our delight, there were reports of fingerling trout being sighted. The usual aquatic bugs were back and the fishing sort of picked up. Yellowfish appeared in numbers, and there was a real sense that the place was recovering.

And gradually, over the first and last few months of 2017, conditions improved to the point where I am thinking I must take the long road back to the Eastern Cape Highlands again, if only because it's been too long not seeing my friends in this area, too long away from those dramatic landscapes, too long without driving those endless dirt roads winding over high hills and down into deep valleys that cradle lovely riffle-surfaced rivers and butter-fat trout and yellowfish.

But I had seen this dryness, and recovery, all before. Years back – in October 1986, to be exact – I fished the Sterkspruit on *Birkhall* long before I knew Basie and Carien. I remember boulder-hopping up an almost-dry riverbed for hours, trawling nymphs through stagnant pools, seeing no sign of trout let alone catching one, until I suddenly came to a weir shaded by trees and full of cool, clear water. It felt like the quixotic discovery of an oasis. And there were trout in this man-made paradox, content in their protected, cold-water world. This same weir, on the boundary of the farms *Branksome* and *Broadford*, still held its water, and its fish, even at the bleakest low point of the district's recent drought. I know because I asked about it. And I still fish this weir every time I am in this part of the world, and I can't seem to blank on it, ever.

*

Of course, being anglers, we worry about our fishing prospects during dry times, and in moments of selfish intolerance we can curse when we see irrigation systems pulsing valuable jets of silvery water from fast-shrinking rivers onto crops. But we have to remember the old adage: where water flows, food grows. Irrigation water feeds the crops, and the crops feed livestock, and livestock puts bread on the farmer's table, pays the wages and the growing diesel bills. Dry spells or, even worse, full-blown droughts aren't easy on any of us, but the flora and fauna and the farmers carry the brunt of it.

*

One of the times I fished up on *Birkhall* was after a dry summer had gradually morphed through a dry winter and spring into a deep drought. It was November, and the days were clear-skied, dry and hot, the rivers as thin as silk. The usual afternoon build-up of promising clouds always made it seem like we were on the edge of a storm, but despite the odd roll of thunder, even brief lightning flashes, the clouds would eventually dissolve into the distance and disappear like phantoms. No rain fell. Rivers drew in on themselves and ran like glass, and you didn't catch fish unless you were very cautious or very lucky, or a combination of both – the sort of conditions where any good fish you happen to catch ploughs a deep furrow into your memory bank.

One brassy-skied morning on this trip, Basie took me to a high bank looking over a long pool on the Sterkspruit and showed me a school of yellowfish holding right at the back. It was a steep, virtually sheer-sided bank and the river ran in a tight loop ten metres below us. The pool was easily fifty metres long, flowing at a slow walking pace. The water was dark with depth where it ran against the steep bank, tailing away into an open, sandy-bottomed basin; just beyond the basin, water left the pool in a thin spread of shallow riffles. It was a long oasis in a drought, but it was promising.

The yellowfish were holding deep, only just visible as green, phantom-like shapes. As you spotted one and tried to follow it, it would somehow melt away and quickly be replaced by another that, in turn, also quickly disappeared. The fish were only easy to follow when they swam into the shallower water near the margins of the pool, maybe to feed, but they must have felt exposed and vulnerable in the clear water because they soon arrowed back into the cover of the misty depths.

That afternoon I fished for them. I walked up the riverbank to a position below the pool, slowed and crouched when I got near it. Well back from the edge, I cast a lightly weighted nymph upstream of the school, towards the inlet. I let the nymph drift, the fly visible for a while in the slow, clear current, snagging lightly at times until I freed it with a twitch, the fly dropping deeper and deeper until it swung into the sandy basin out of sight, the leader totally submerged, the nymph, by my guess, now static on the bottom among the yellowfish. I waited long seconds, then drew the nymph upwards off the riverbed: slowly, purposefully upwards. The tip of the floating fly line quivered suddenly as if a brief electric shock had passed through it. I lifted sharply. The fish bucked, then ran, arching this way and that, fighting deep in the misty-green water, visible only in momentary flashes of gold. I slowly worked the fish to the surface, then drew it to the edge over the pale sand where it gleamed like bronze.

I landed three more yellowfish, all around sixteen inches, each time resting the school for long minutes before casting again. The sun began to bake through my shirt, so I left the pool for the shady cover of a willow-lined section of river upstream and caught a few small trout. Later when a hatch came off and the sun was sinking, I returned to the pool to drift a dry fly over the yellows in the basin from an upstream position. A few nosed my small Elk Hair Caddis, and one or two took it hesitantly and predictably came off. So I tried a beaded Zak and hooked a heavy fish from waist-deep water. It streaked out of the pool and down through the shallow riffles with its back and dorsal fin clear out of the water, and was gone with the brief glint of a popping 7X tippet.

It had been testy, measured fishing, the best sort of fishing drought conditions can offer, or the best you can expect in the circumstances.

*

As South Africans, we tend to hold that we live in a part of the world where droughts are common enough to expect they will appear with fair regularity, which is probably more right than wrong, but not exactly scientific. Certainly, I don't think of fly fishing in fairy-tale terms, with streams flowing as pretty as freshly plucked peaches all season long. It doesn't work that way, here or anywhere else in the world – but if you average things out, I think it's not far off the mark to say that, given our African context and the steadily upward temperature trends globally, dry spells and droughts are gradually becoming more common, though the record books may prove me wrong.

I'm not sure if this is part-global warming, part-climate change, part-El Niño effect, all being, as I understand it, entirely separate phenomena. We might argue that it doesn't matter, and we may only be partly right, in the sense that if alone we can't do much about any of these changes, we can at least make known our collective support for the scientists who preach that climate change and global warming are largely our own fault. And although we seem to be at the eleventh hour with all this stuff, the progress of climate change is still to some measure stoppable, even if some of the changes it has brought are no longer entirely correctable.

*

The other day, Robin and I were up a mountain stream we occasionally fish. It was no more than a trickle and clear, and our approach was accordingly gentle and delicate, and fine and far off, as Charles Cotton nicely put it all those years ago. We missed a few trout, spotted even fewer, figured most had moved off downstream, and eventually opted for a scone with jam and cream and a cup of coffee on the veranda of a café overlooking a few bass ponds. It had been six weeks since the last rains had fallen in or near Cape Town, but that night the heavens opened and we had a downpour. The next day Robin sent me a photograph of the stream on Lourensford Estate, another wafer-thin stream we had given up on, more so after a serious bushfire had gutted the riverbanks. Overnight this forlorn little stream became a highway of tumbling water – but it didn't last long. Standing on the bank a few weeks later amid blackened sticks and ash, you could still smell the after-smoke of the bushfire. The river had shrunk further and was even lower than before the storm. But we tried it for an hour, fishing more in hope than out of true conviction, and we might have stayed longer had the sole of my wading boot not broken loose. I think we rose two small trout. But then, as I said, we were fishing more in hope – and hope, I realise, is the international currency most fly fishers learn to deal in soon enough.

In fact, it's the ability of streams to survive droughts, of fresh-water insect species to restore themselves, of trout to apparently endure the driest of times, of trees to bud and leaf again after bushfires, that serves to feed our sentiments of hope and to keep faith. I mean, the way things in the Sterkspruit came right after the woeful condition it was in you can only marvel at. But Fred Steynberg was right all along: the trout reappeared as if by magic.

And back home, just as we were beginning to believe the trout in a number of our lovelier but fast-shrinking smaller mountain streams actually hadn't survived, we had three or four days of cool rain in the Western Cape and the water levels rose. A week later I took a stroll along one of my favourite of these streams, and from a bank I saw trout – not many, but enough, among them a fish of fourteen inches. In raw times like these, there's as much pure joy in just seeing trout as there is in actually catching them.

309

The Bokspruit River

CHAPTER 14

RETURN TO BARKLY EAST

Fishing is not a sport I expect ever to exhaust or abandon. It has led me, and still leads me, into too many delights for that. Yet there are times now when I find myself wondering just what it is I am going to find, with the familiar tackle, in the familiar water, at a time made familiar by many past seasons.
RODERICK HAIG-BROWN, *FISHERMAN'S FALL*

This was a visit where the weather and the fish played along about as nicely as any fly fisher visiting this part of the world could hope for. It was March, but late March. The skies were domes of blue, sometimes laced with high cloud, the sort of skies that make landscape photographs come alive, and the rivers were just as pretty as the skies, running fine and clean enough to make for comfortable sighting and testy fishing. In the Sterkspruit the water was a cool, near-perfect 15°C, and for once the winds were just gentle breezes that mostly blew from the north in a helpful upstream direction. And, to add to the happy picture, you could already feel the mild chill the winds carried.

If I were to choose the best time of year to fish around Rhodes and Barkly East, it might well be from the middle to the end of March. In March the poplars and willows change subtly from a range of greens to biscuit and rust colours that gradually intensify to become the deep-yellow and red hues of late autumn, when the landscapes are so lavishly laced with colour you'll never drop your camera. But, of course, you pay for it with colder weather and falling streams.

Frosts arrive in April, and by May, if you haven't got a jacket on, it's not unusual to be fishing a river on a sunny day and still feel cold. And by then you have no choice; you're in chest waders unless your legs are bulletproof.

April and May are glorious months, but overall I'm happy to exchange their riotous colours for the less dramatic landscapes and the milder weather of March. Also, I'm happier not being in chest waders on rivers when I can. I've always seen them as a burden, even if they are more than just essential paraphernalia at times.

On the other hand, spring is also a pleasant time to visit, although the rivers and streams can be a touch low in September unless there's been winter snowfall or a few early showers. It's debatable, but I'd say October is better than November because November is the month when the summer storms begin, and instead of actually fishing, you can find yourself doing a lot of fly tying or driving slippery roads in the hope of finding fishable water in the upper reaches of some distant stream. So there's a tempting consistency to the fishing in March, when, as I said, the back end of the month, and going into early April, seems the best of it all, again given that conditions are right. But the weather's not something you can depend on here.

Having said all that, I've visited this part of the world nearly every month of the year and never found myself anything but pleased to be here, no matter what the conditions were like.

*

Many of my fishing friends and I have a way of overlooking the other side of the southern Drakensberg, meaning the rivers and streams around Ugie and Maclear. We do so not because they are any less exciting or less abundant or less pretty, but because, whichever way you look at it, the majority of anglers visiting this part of South Africa hail from Gauteng, the Western Cape and the Free State, and a trip to Maclear is that much further, with one of two road passes to negotiate.

If I were to do a little crusading, though, I would bite the bullet and recommend a visit to this part of the southern Drakensberg, because it's worth it. Streams like the Pot, the Little Pot, the Mooi, the Swith and the Wildebeest are gems. But with the growing bucket list of fly-fishing venues available nowadays, and with the limited free time most of us have, this is an area that gets missed too often, as does the nearby Somerset East district in the Karoo, where Alan and Annabelle Hobson run hosted fly-fishing opportunities that I'm told are remarkable.

*

But I digress. On this trip I was heading not for *Birkhall*, where I was later due to meet Billy de Jong and his family, but for Rhodes to visit my pal Ed Herbst. Ed had recently moved into Walkerbouts Inn as a permanent resident, where he had a fully equipped outside rondavel all to himself. The story of how he came to move from Cape Town to Rhodes is a long one, but I'll make it brief.

Ed contracted a rare neurological illness while he and his then-partner Jeanne were living in Vermont, a large sprawl of houses on the coast about eighty kilometres from Cape Town, where she had found 'the house of her dreams'. In the end it didn't really pan out that way for her, and when Ed's illness started to get a hold on him, they decided to move back to Cape Town and put their seaside house on the market. It stood unsold for many months, but finally, with Ed now barely able to make it up to the upstairs living area where they had a lovely view of the sea, they found a buyer. Then the actual cause of Ed's illness was discovered and treated, and his condition stabilised. That was a blessing, but a lot of damage had been done by then to Ed's nervous system, which left him pretty shaky on his pins and with a tremor in his hands. When the house sold, Ed and Jeanne moved to a rented cottage in the suburb of Pinelands in Cape Town.

Here it soon became clear that their relationship was not going to last, and they separated. A group of us, who rated ourselves among Ed's closest friends, decided that an option would be to move him away from Cape Town to Walkerbouts Inn in Rhodes, where he would at least be near the places he loved to fish, never mind that he couldn't get onto a river. We also figured that he would have a steady stream of like-minded visitors in the form of anglers staying at Walkerbouts Inn, or putting up in one of the rental cottages in the village. That was the theory behind it all, and Ed finally agreed to the relocation. The move happened smoothly, and initially things went well. But the reality was that despite the best efforts of the Walkerbouts staff, Ed was lonely and missing his friends, and found the cold weather a serious challenge.

So on this particular visit the first thing on my agenda was to call on Ed. I found him in residence, and we shared a gin and tonic looking over the town, reminiscing and reflecting. The following day I loaded him into my truck and we drove over to *Birkhall* to spend a night or two with Basie and Carien. I introduced a slight deviation into the plan and didn't take him straight to *Birkhall*; instead, I turned off just before the entrance to the farm onto a track I've got to know pretty well over the years. It winds down to a spot where I could park my truck a few metres from the banks of the Sterkspruit River. I set up a rod and line, and installed a canvas, fold-down camp stool on the edge of a pool in the shade of willow trees. With Ed steadying himself by holding on to my backpack, we threaded our way from the truck to the edge of the water. A few trout were rising, and Ed cast a Klinkhåmer at them, missed three and landed two, all without moving from the stool. They were rainbow trout about nine inches long.

It had been two years since Ed had last fished, and I was delighted. But in a sentiment that at first floored me, but that I later fully understood, Ed said he found the experience emotionally trying, in that it illustrated with painful nostalgia what he was once able to do with ease, freedom and pleasure, but no longer could, other than in circumstances as contrived as these. To the best of my knowledge he hasn't fished since. I guess it would be fair to say that Ed would love to fish again, but not at any price – meaning only if he could fish with the freedom he once had.

Billy was staying at *Birkhall* with his wife Maritza and their young son Barnie. The next morning I noticed Ed perched on a plastic garden chair out on the front lawn, taking obvious pleasure teaching Maritza and Barnie to cast. Billy and I sat on the veranda above them tying flies. We were both delighted onlookers.

*

I drove Ed back to Rhodes through the Bokspruit Valley. Along the way I stopped on the bridge that crosses the lower Bokspruit, with the farms *Eliasdale* and *Clefthill* on either side. There, in water as clear as it ever gets in the Bokspruit, I watched a decent-sized trout hunting insects. The fish was holding in about three feet of water and it was feeding actively. It would just lift its head or turn to the side to intercept drifting nymphs with slow, deliberate precision. But occasionally it would dart off in a sweeping arc like a hawk chasing prey, sometimes ending up facing directly downstream. I was fascinated to see just how visible the telltale white flash of its opening mouth was, even from twenty metres away. But then I was standing up on a bridge and, as I may have mentioned before, bridges make wonderful vantage points.

*

After dropping Ed I left with a heavy heart, and even back then, I felt a strong premonition that he'd soon be back in Cape Town. As winter approached it became clear that Ed's return was inevitable. He moved back that same year, after Steve Boshoff had located an ideal en-suite room for him in what was once the old Fairmead Hotel in Rondebosch, now a residence for older folk, where Ed has been remarkably happy ever since.

Two of Ed's friends stood head and shoulders above us all in what they did to get him to Rhodes and then to move him back again, including his huge library of assorted fly-fishing books and multiple suitcases filled with fly-tying stuff (and I'm not exaggerating). They were Sharland and Gavin Urquhart; without them, little would have been achieved. Well, certainly not as smoothly or as comfortably. They live in Cape Town and it's the unspoken view of many anglers that Sharland is the titular First Lady of South African fly fishing, given the considerable contributions she has made to the sport. Her husband Gavin is not a fly fisher at all, which makes his support of Sharland in her wide-ranging, pro-fly-fishing crusades and her parallel devotions to painting and gardening all the more noteworthy. Both are remarkably good people, straight out of the textbook definition of the term 'remarkably good', no matter how broadly you might choose to paint it.

*

I've heard the odd chirp from fly fishers who should know better, or don't know enough, that all the rivers in the Eastern Cape Highlands are the same, suggesting that once you've fished one, you've fished them all. In other words, your approach to the Bokspruit or the Sterkspruit or the Karringmelkspruit will differ little, and I suppose there is some truth in that. But I suspect it's a truth that holds good for freestone streams anywhere on earth.

There are differences in the rivers up here, sure, something I've come to appreciate in the many years I've visited this place, and they go well beyond just how you fish them, or the obvious differences in their particular topographies. Naturally, a river will change, sometimes considerably, from season to season, even from week to week or day to day, although, as I wrote elsewhere in this book, they never change in what I call their essence, meaning that each river has a particular atmosphere and a character that is somehow all its own, and which it retains no matter the weather or the season. You can't just wipe a river's atmosphere out, not least with a generalisation that goes along the lines of, 'When you've done one river in the Eastern Cape Highlands, you've done them all', any more than you can say the same of the chalkstreams of England, or the freestone streams or spring creeks of Montana, or the steelhead rivers of British Columbia's Skeena River system.

Of course, the same river and the way you fish it, will differ depending on whether you're on its lower or middle reaches, or high up near its source and, importantly, whether the water is low and diamond-clear, or full-flowing or slightly discoloured.

The Bell is a good example. You can't compare the *Glass Niven* or *Dunley* beats of this river with the stretches up on *Boarman's Chase* or *Ben Lawers*, neither in their topographies nor in the way you approach fishing them.

But Billy and I were staying at *Birkhall*, which has one of the best stretches of the Sterkspruit, so I want to focus on this river for a moment. All things being equal, and as I am on record saying in this book, it's probably the best trout stream in the district, though many will argue it lacks the charm of the Bokspruit, especially that river's upper reaches from *Brucedell* up through to *Gateshead*. That may be so, but in my experience the Sterkspruit consistently produces bigger and more robust rainbows than most, if not all, the rivers in this region. Possible exceptions are the Langkloof that flows by the side of the road from Barkly East to Elliot, then passes below the town to join the Kraai River, and the Karringmelkspruit, in a good season, near the town of Lady Grey.

Two Sterkspruit trophy trout are mounted on the wall of Basie's pub at *Birkhall*, and my inkling is that if Basie wanted to add to this collection he'd opt to fish the Sterkspruit rather than the Bokspruit or the Bell or the Riflespruit. Of course, if you are after trophies, then the Langkloof would also come into reckoning, as would the Kraai itself and, if conditions are good, also the Karringmelkspruit. I'm talking of those extraordinarily big fish that you might catch hereabouts maybe once or twice in a lifetime, river fish of seven to ten pounds. Your everyday 'good' fish from the Sterkspruit would not make a mounted trophy, but at sixteen to twenty inches they will rip backing off your reel, and they will take some trouble landing. There's not much more you can ask from a river. And to bag a real trophy fish you'd need to use weighted attractor flies fished in deep slots on a wet line. That's how it's been done before.

*

On this trip, Billy and I shared our time between fishing the river and drifting in float tubes on the lake immediately below the house, or fishing Basie's new lake in the mountains above it. We couldn't wait to try the new lake for a few good reasons: we'd both watched the wall being repaired; I'd made the happy discovery of fry and two small adult rainbow trout in the thread-like flow of the inlet stream; and we'd jointly persuaded Basie not to stock the lake when it filled, but to let the wild trout in the inlet stream do it for him.

The top lake was crystalline, and the day was bright. Malley, Billy's Jack Russell, was perched on the apron of his float tube, and we made straight for the inlet because we figured the flow of fresh water coming in would suit both fish and bugs. Also, the old streambed would act as a cool, deep-water canal, and the submerged vegetation would offer protection.

When we got there, the inlet looked just right: an inviting, pear-shaped spread of water no bigger than a bowling green, with a slight neck where it narrowed a little before opening into the general expanse of the lake itself. Looking down into the water from my tube I could make out the old streambed by following the rotting remains of the submerged ouhout trees that mapped its course. Even close to where the inlet stream first enters the lake, the water was deep and inviting. It was the sort of spot that stillwater trout just can't resist. It ticked all the boxes.

We'd only been there a few minutes when our rods bent into fish simultaneously. I felt a thud, then the typical head-shaking throb of a nice-sized fish, before it took off like a racehorse. It ran all the line off my reel, and was into my backing before I could check it.

Given our long association with this lake and its redevelopment, landing these two trout felt more like a special occasion than the usual call for mild celebration. They were like peas in a pod, both about three pounds, probably just over, wild-looking, perfectly shaped rainbows in excellent condition, with avocado-green backs, carmine flashes along their flanks and hints of orange on their gill plates. Were they getting ready to spawn? Lovely thought.

We were in an upland valley surrounded by seas of rolling grasslands that lifted in long sweeps into higher hills where blesbok and wildebeest grazed. Far to the north was the range of tall, blue mountains you see from just about anywhere you fish in the Eastern Cape Highlands. They turn the distant horizon into a spectacular backdrop; dominate it. We had always thought they were just a part of the southern Drakensberg or the Maluti Mountains, though for some reason the name Witteberg kept coming up. We also agreed that since both of us had always admired this range and had fished up here long enough, it was a little embarrassing to be searching for the name of these mountains.

To get back to the fishing: this is not a big lake, but it's not small. I guess it's about one-and-a-half hectares, which is a comfortable size to fish, in the sense that it's not so vast that you end up feeling slightly intimidated. Rather this lake felt cosily perfect, cradled in folding hillsides, somehow intimate, and that sense of intimacy lent to the pleasure we got fishing it. Anyway, that's just how some stillwaters work for me. Billy felt the same.

We were fishing a damselfly nymph imitation of sorts on floating lines and long, 15' leaders, leaving the fly line to bob on the waves until the nymph had sunk, and then putting in slow retrieves with the rod tip at a right angle to the line to absorb the shock of any takes. And there were plenty of them. I call the pattern a 'nymph' here, which the Red-Eyed Damsel certainly is, but I suppose you'd have to say the Hot-Spot Damsel Billy and I were using – his own invention – is as much an attractor as a nymph. It has an olive marabou tail, a body of two parts, the back half being hot-orange poly yarn that's teased-out, the front of the body wrapped in hare's ear dubbing. Then just behind the brass bead, Billy wraps two turns of spun hare's fur with long guard hairs that make a sort of hairy collar hackle. It's a pretty fly, and it worked well until we ran out of them.

It was the sort of fishing that was simple yet attractive and, in its own way, mildly addictive. There you are floating on near-transparent water, throwing out single casts (no false casts were needed), waiting for the fly to sink, slowly retrieving, knowing you're fishing a virgin pond seemingly full of wild trout that have bred up the little inlet stream you can see from your tube, and that the outcome of many casts is likely to be an exquisite hook-up. And yet, despite its predictability and its simplicity, the fishing never became boring. It was the sort of fishing that constantly holds you on the edge of pleasant anticipation. I could have sat in my tube catching those fish all day. We landed a dozen each. I eventually changed to a dry fly, a yellow DDD, out of interest and did well enough with it – two fish in two casts – for Billy to paddle over and take a few off me.

We lost a couple of fish on the take, and I had one snap me, not because the fish was that big, but because it was fast out of the blocks, and I was too sharp with my strike. Right near the end, Billy got a trout that might have pushed the scale over four pounds, but it fell off the hook right at the net.

I sampled the stomachs of a few fish and found a mix of pale-green chironomid larvae, dragonfly nymphs, tiny straw-coloured mayfly nymphs, alfalfa-green damselfly nymphs, a few water boatman and aquatic snails. There wasn't a bloodworm, the red version of the midge larva, in any of them, which I found interesting, because often they're usually so prolific in stillwaters.

*

I think it's worth putting in a brief note here on how the fishing in this lake has progressed since. The following year, 2014, I had to cancel my usual March trip to *Birkhall* for family reasons, and by the time October came around the Eastern Cape was in the throes of a throttling drought. The rivers ran in trickles, and the fishing was way off the mark. In 2015 and 2016 the drought was even worse, and I cancelled yet again. I haven't fished the lake since, but I get regular reports from Basie and, as I expected, the trout grew like stall-fed cattle and were six pounds and over by the end of 2014. Basie said he has hooked a few, but hasn't managed to land one. The lake was hardly fished during 2015, and in 2016 it was fished only occasionally by special guests who never kept a fish but said they'd guess the better ones were around seven pounds and that there was a nice mix of sizes, suggesting spawning had happened despite the drought years.

That evening Basie confirmed that the big range of mountains you see to the north of *Birkhall*, or from Rhodes for that matter, is the southern Drakensberg, and that *Birkhall* itself lies in the Witteberg Mountains, with his new lake high in the cradle of the Witteberg range, accounting, I guess, for the lake's spectacular setting and its sense of deep-mountain remoteness.

*

Later in the week, Billy and I spent a morning on the Sterkspruit. We started on dry flies and neither of us rose a fish, so we changed to weighted nymphs and probed the deeper slots. I used a Zak with a bright tungsten bead. We both got handsome eighteen-inch trout and a few others in the twelve-to-fifteen-inch range. The river was low and clear, and there were no hatches. Not a fish showed at the surface until around midday, when we suddenly spotted two trout rising in the same run. It was a section where the water runs shallow over bright, multicoloured pebbles so typical of this river. Some were deep-purple and shot through with traces of white; some were a lemon-ochre colour, and others as pink as ripe figs, ideal tapestries to hide shallow-lying trout. Billy caught the first on an Elk Hair Caddis, and I was about to cast at the second fish when I hesitated for a minute to unthread a simple tippet knot. Billy put his fly over the fish and hooked it.

'De Jong, you're poaching!' I said.

'Thought you'd be some time getting that knot undone, so I cast in case it went down,' he replied.

'Oh, really!'

'Honest,' he said, smiling, as he played the fish to the net, where it jumped and, if there was any justice in the world, would have come free. He landed the fish, and we agreed to settle the matter out of court. Besides, they were both smaller trout. But the deal was that I'd fish the next two runs, which I did, and landed a brace of equally small rainbows.

We caught a few more on the dry fly until the trout stopped rising and the river went dead. Even fishing the sunken nymph was unproductive. We decided to head out and were back at *Birkhall* for a late lunch a little before 3pm.

*

Carien and Basie eat their main meal of the day at lunchtime, a meal you don't want to miss if you happen to be asked to stay. There's something of a ritual to these lunches. After saying grace, Basie will carve a roast: a leg of lamb or a side of beef, or one of Carien's Cornish hens. There are bowls of rice and roast potatoes, often green beans and pumpkin, and always a fresh salad on the table. I'm not keen on dessert, but no lunch on *Birkhall* ends without one, frequently with a large jug of custard that I *am* keen on.

I've seen as many as ten people sitting around this table, often with occasional guests who just happened to drop by at the right time, but I've never had a meal here where there was anything like a shortage of food. In fact, at *Birkhall* there's no shortage of anything, especially not hospitality. And if by chance we're away on the river until late afternoon, Carien leaves plates of food for us in the warming drawer.

*

Talking of hospitality, one evening on this trip we were sitting on the veranda helping Basie with a braai. It had rained heavily that day, and Carien was not yet back from an errand she'd long since left on. She was nearly an hour late. It was dark when the headlights of her truck finally shone up the up the long driveway to the farmhouse, followed by a second set of lights. From the sound of the voices we heard after the distant banging of car doors, it was clear Carien had company. It turned out she'd come across a bunch of youngsters parked on the side of the road, totally lost and struggling to negotiate the muddy roads. Carien asked them to follow her back to *Birkhall* and invited them to stay the night.

They were Czech students touring South Africa on a shoestring budget in a bottom-of-the-range rental car, four of them, two girls, two boys, all in their early twenties. Only one spoke passable English. They had been blindly following GPS instructions en route from Bloemfontein to East London and had somehow ended up on a remote dirt road at night a few kilometres beyond *Birkhall* in what must have felt like the heart of darkest Africa. It's not the first time I've heard of a GPS getting the plot horribly wrong.

They walked from the darkness into the flood of the veranda's bright lights, carrying backpacks, looking bewildered and self-conscious, yet obviously relieved. After Basie's warm welcome they loosened up a little, then Carien led them away to freshen up. Hair brushed, looking neater and more relaxed, they joined us on the veranda for a drink, conversing as best they could through the services of one of their party who became translator. She did a good job, but here and there she got stuck on a few words, one of which was 'braai'. I figured they'd learn the meaning of that soon enough. Another was 'trout', which turned out to be 'pstruh' in Czech, if you should ever need to know it, though you might have some difficulty sliding the word off your tongue.

Thick steaks lined with a layer of yellow fat, lamb chops and Basie's homemade spicy sausage were sizzling on a grid perched low over the coals. The veranda was filled with the aroma of meat cooking, the classic aroma of a braai that, to my mind, is unparalleled when it comes to igniting an irresistible Pavlovian hunger response in the average South African brain. The meal was a banquet, and in snippets of after-dinner conversation, our visitors said they had never eaten better meat, or more of it. They left early the next morning in a flurry of hugs and kisses, with a heavy hamper of goodies for the road and, perhaps more importantly, a road map. They were clearly grateful recipients of the sort of spontaneous hospitality typical of *Birkhall*.

*

We had one of those delightful, laid-back mornings on the lake below the farmhouse, a lake well known to so many South African fly fishers. Billy put Maritza into a float tube, then spent time trying to get his four-year-old son to hook a trout from the bank. He would put out a cast and Barnie would put in a retrieve of sorts, his face lighting up at the merest hint of a take. There weren't many, but there was a moment when Barnie did have a fish on, and he shrieked with excitement until it got off. It was a wonderful family occasion, and thinking back on so many life stories I've heard or read of, it was the sort of thing Barnie will likely think back to one day and say, 'That moment changed my life,' or 'That's how I became a fly-fishing bum.' My own beginnings weren't much different, come to think of it, and it's an even bet yours were similar.

Billy and I fished again that afternoon, staggering down to the lake after a late lunch. It was a gentle afternoon with a prettily clouded sky that formed a perfect reflection of itself on the smooth surface of the water, so that when I looked across at Billy he seemed to be floating on clouds. Later there was a hatch of tiny *Caenis* mayflies, the insects rising on the southern bank in columns as thick and as grey as chimney smoke. We had noticed the occasional rise, presumably to their emerging nymphs, and had paddled in that direction. We hooked a few small fish on tiny mayfly nymph patterns, but later when the sun was about to drop under the hills, bigger trout began mopping up spinners. The trout were swimming with their backs above the surface gulping the bugs, sometimes with an audible, pneumatic-sounding 'plop'.

The secret here is to pick a fish and to lead it by a metre with a small spent-wing imitation. Or at least that's the theory of it. I had on a size 16 pattern, just a black thread body ribbed with nylon and a turn of pale-coloured CDC that I thought might be too big, but it was taken first cast, and that fish turned out to be the best of the day, a shade over five pounds.

We got a few more decent trout, and the fishing was just starting to feel strangely easy when the rises suddenly stopped, although the surface was still covered in spent mayflies and nothing about the weather had changed. We just put it down to another of fly fishing's mysteries, but we'd had six or seven fish each by the time we headed out. Billy lost a beautiful trout right near the end of the rise that ran so close to my float tube I could have netted it. It was a deep fish that ended the fight with two head-over-tail leaps.

I guessed it had snapped his tippet on the first leap.

That night it rained gently.

*

On the final morning, we lazily fished the lower beat of the Sterkspruit when the water was still a little misty from the rain, but the river was full of promise. We crossed the river to avoid having to cast with a stand of willow trees behind us. The water felt like ice. We ran beaded nymphs along banks bathed in buckets of shade, where we caught smaller rainbows. When we changed to heavier nymphs and drifted them through places where the water was deep and troubled enough to hide the telegraphing 'plop' of the landing fly, we caught better fish, each of us landing three of around fifteen inches. We were using upstream and across casts that we left to drift out until they were alongside or below us, with the fly deep. Most of the takes came as the fly swung up at the end of the drift, or when we lifted the rod tip at the end of a drift. It was the sort of fishing where the indicator eventually sinks and doesn't count for much unless it telegraphs a subtle, deep take, which occasionally it did.

You might ask how you know there's a fish on without seeing any movement in the indicator, or in the leader or fly line. Well, when a trout takes a fly swinging up after a long, deep drift, most times you've lost sight of the indicator and the leader, and often the tip of the fly line is sunk. As the line kites downstream it feels taut, can even vibrate a little, but the drift will still feel smooth. You suspect a take if the line suddenly feels 'heavy' or just begins to feel a fraction different in the drift. Then you strike. There's no way to describe this other than to say the feel of the drifting, or upward kiting line, suddenly changes. I know it's a clumsy explanation, but it's a situation I can't find the exact words for.

Come to think of it, this technique has a lot in common with steelhead fishing – other than steelhead fishing with a dry fly, which is an altogether different story because you will see the fish roll on the fly. Steelhead fishing with a wet fly or nymph just needs a lot more patience. It's sometimes said you'll put in a thousand casts for one fish. Look, it is grinding stuff, but it's not as tough as some anglers make out. If it was, steelhead fishing would have nothing like the remarkable cabal of dedicated devotees it currently enjoys.

*

There's a moment on every trip when you reel in for the last time, bite off the fly, seat it in your fly patch and hike out. It's never pleasant.

That afternoon I packed my fishing gear and loaded my truck. I left the next morning later than planned because Basie insisted on cooking a grand breakfast. We ate in the kitchen, just the two of us. I'd said goodbye to Carien earlier that morning, before she left to deliver a load of chickens, and had also said farewells to Maritza, Barnie and Billy before we went to bed.

One thing I've learnt about Basie over the years is that he's a perfectionist. So the omelettes he prepared that morning were, in typical style, elaborate and excellent. As were the Russian sausages he served. Basie makes his own, and they are the finest I've eaten anywhere. So the meal was more a minor banquet than a breakfast, with plenty of toast and marmalade and strong coffee.

Then, just as I was getting up to leave, Billy made a sleepy entrance into the kitchen, still in his pyjamas. I poured another cup of coffee. The night before I had told Billy I would be leaving at first light. If he didn't entirely believe me, he was at least good enough not to say as much, and he didn't look surprised to find me still perched in the kitchen well after 8am. We had a chat that boiled down to making tentative plans to fish again. It was well after 9am when I eventually threaded down *Birkhall*'s driveway, turned left, and was on the long road home. I had a flask of coffee and a packet of Carien's rusks on the passenger seat. I slipped a CD into the player. On long-distance road trips, I find gentle music eases tar fever. At the bottom of Basie's driveway, the odometer clicked over to 90,000 kilometres. Little did I know then, but this was going to be an interesting trip weather-wise.

I got the first real hint that it was as hot as hell outside when I stopped for diesel at a garage in Burgersdorp. I stepped out of the air-conditioned cab into an unexpected wall of heat that felt like a blast from the den of a dragon. Further along I dropped in at *Mount Melsetter* to say hello to Mike and Candy Ferrar. The temperature gauge on the dashboard read 41°C. I'd never seen it that high. I hadn't planned for any en-route accommodation, thinking I'd just see how far I got and take my chances, but Mike suggested I book in at a place in Graaff-Reinet that had air conditioning and a pool. He called and got me a room at a place called the Andries Stockenström Guest House. I arrived there with the temperature gauge reading 43°C, a little before 4pm. The tar was bubbling in the streets, there was a shimmering haze over everything, and there wasn't a hint of birdsong. This was heatwave stuff.

The guesthouse was charming, the main building dating back to 1819. I had a pleasant, outside room facing a tiny courtyard with a small pool. Even with the air conditioning on, it was hot inside. I had no swimming trunks, so I slid into the pool in my wading pants. There were two other adjoining rooms and within minutes an elderly fellow and his wife – both suitably clad for swimming – joined me. They were German tourists, a pleasant, outgoing couple who told me they were touring the country and having the holiday of a lifetime. They insisted on fetching me a beer from their room and we chatted, sipping our cold beers straight from the bottle, all three of us submerged to our chins in cool water.

Their ears pricked up when they heard I'd been on a fly-fishing trip. It turned out they both enjoyed fly fishing. I told them I had once fished the Wiese River in southern Germany, a lovely stream in the Black Forest. I mentioned the town of Lörrach. They knew it well, and said they often fished the Wiese. I spoke of the river's pretty brown trout and told them of my Swiss friend Leon Meier, who lived in Basel. He'd been my host many years back on a week's fishing in the Swiss Alps and some surrounding rivers in Germany, which I briefly wrote about in *Reflections on Fly Fishing*. I promised to post them a copy.

That night they joined me for dinner. The dining room was full, and it seemed that at least half the diners were foreign tourists. I had brought my fly boxes to the table. Bad move. Over the three-course meal I lost more flies to my new-found German friends than I'd lost in the previous week's fishing. The RABs and DDDs especially took their fancy.

After a full English breakfast, I was back on the highway the following morning. I stopped at midday in the tiny Karoo hamlet of Leeu-Gamka to top up with fuel. It was blisteringly hot. A huge truck pulled up in a patch of shade off the forecourt, rocking gently as it stopped with a long, hissing sigh of the air brakes. The driver climbed out dripping with sweat. He filled a large plastic bottle with tap water, took off his cap, leaned backwards, upended the bottle and poured the water over his head. I didn't blame him, but I did wonder at the wisdom of not providing long-haul drivers carrying valuable cargo with the simple comforts of an air-conditioned cabin.

I stopped as usual at Matjiesfontein for a cup of coffee and a thick slice of ham on crusty bread, and was home three hours later.

*

I had a phone call from Basie on 27 September 2015. He said the river was desperately low and not to think of coming up. He mentioned that my friend Brian Hammond had fished the Sterkspruit on *Birkhall*, where he had a good look at the biggest trout he'd ever seen in his life. At first he thought it was a yellowfish, but later realised it was a monster-sized rainbow. See what I mean about this river? Sadly he never caught it.

Basie called again a week later to say the Sterkspruit wasn't flowing, but trout were holding in the few deep, clear pools that still had water in them. He saw three fish in one of these pools that he said were well over ten pounds, then added, 'More like twelve pounds. Never seen bigger trout on *Birkhall* in all my life.'

It was tempting. But I stayed put in Cape Town.

CHAPTER 15

STREAM LUNCHES AND FISHING TRUCKS

It is possible to exaggerate and to be duped by gastronomic
nincompoops who write of gourmets with a sense of taste so
refined that they can tell whether a fish was caught under or
between the bridges, and can distinguish, by its superior flavour,
the thigh on which the partridge leans while asleep.'
ANGELO PELLEGRINI, *THE UNPREJUDICED PALATE*

It's interesting that relatively few angling writers – and I include myself – have had much to say about fly-fishing lunches. I suppose the reason is that lunches aren't high on the list of what's important to get across about any fishing trip, like where you fished, the conditions, the hatches, fish caught or lost, the techniques and flies that caught them, and, of course, whether any disasters struck. You could say that's the standard, almost formulaic template for most fly-fishing narratives. The downside is that some of the 'softer issues', like what you happened to eat, don't feature much, if at all.

If that's the case, why write this piece?

Well, after a close study of descriptive angling literature, and making a rough guess at what you could describe as the 'condition' of your typical angler, I came to the conclusion that in *not* writing about some of the 'softer' issues, such as memorable or disastrous on-stream lunches, we may be missing an interesting piece of the wider tapestry of fly fishing. Not the who with, how many, how big and on what fly bits, which are certainly interesting, but the less obvious issues that, when woven into a fishing narrative, can become the spice that livens the stew.

Some softer aspects of fly fishing already get a fair amount of attention from writers – like the landscapes, the flora and fauna, the idiosyncrasies of anglers (even, at times, their dogs), not to mention that hackneyed, all-too-often-asked question about why we fish in the first place which, to my mind, is a bit like asking why we breathe in and out.

I guess you could say that evening meals lend themselves more to angling prose than lunches, but they don't feature that much either. Which is strange because when a fishing day is done and a bunch of angling buddies find themselves under a star-studded night sky or around a cheerful log fire, you have the ingredients for the sort of engaging writing that most anglers would happily and easily identify with. I'm not excluding dinners in fancy lodges, but I'm thinking here more of the dinners a bunch of fishing pals rustle up, either in a camp or in those casual, self-catering fishing accommodations where you have the sole run of the place and can really let your hair down without being told not to come back again. Highland Lodge in the Eastern Cape Highlands is just such a place. For the purposes of this chapter, though, I want to stick to day-trip fishing lunches, always remembering that day fishing trips mostly kick off from your own front door.

What I take to eat on a day trip can depend on how lazy I feel and the route I'm going to use. So, for example, if I'm fishing in Somerset West with my buddy Robin Douglas or if I'm heading for the Smalblaar, I often stop at an Engen service station because there is one on each of these routes. Important, both have Wimpy outlets, and I'm a total convert to Wimpy burgers. I usually order two, eat one right there in my truck as a sort of late breakfast or, depending on the time of day, an early lunch, and stick the other one into the backpack to have later on the river. I occasionally buy a Wimpy toasted bacon-and-egg sandwich just to ring the changes, because, like the burgers, Wimpy bacon-and-egg sandwiches are in a class of their own. The coffee is a bonus, easily the best of all fast-food outlets and on a par with what you get from Starbucks, Vida or Wild Bean cafés. And no, I don't own shares in Wimpy.

But more often, I rustle up a sandwich at home, throw in an apple, a fruit juice or one of those tangy energy drinks that taste awful but apparently maintain your electrolyte balance. You know the ones. They come in those fly-tying-themed colours, like Krystal Flash-blue, Antron-orange, chartreuse-green, and what I can only describe as a sort of holographic tinsel-red.

I never buy shop-made sandwiches that come in neat plastic boxes. It's strange, because while I'm happy to pay upwards of R600 for half a premium-grade hackle cape, I'm reluctant to spend forty bucks on a boutique sandwich, partly because I choke at the price but mainly because they lean heavily towards exotic fillings (like roast chicken with avocado, mayo, smoky bacon or Caesar salad, or – my worst – bacon, jam and mature cheddar). They look nice, but with them sealed in plastic, you can't really tell what they'll taste like, although you see people lifting them off shelves, looking at them closely, then putting them back. What they're learning about the sandwich by peering at it at close quarters through a closed clear plastic box, I'm not sure. It's like what Robert Traver once wrote about what you can learn from wiggling fly rods in tackle shops. He said it was like seeing a woman's arm protruding from a car window: all you can really be sure of is that the window is open, certainly not which way she's signalling to turn.

Besides, I have niggling doubts about the wisdom of carrying cooked chicken or mayo up a river for three or four hours on a hot day, when the potential to poison yourself can't be brushed under the mat. I mean, why else do they keep them chilled in the first place?

*

My first memories of good fishing lunches were the ones Mark Mackereth, arguably the father of the dry fly on Western Cape trout streams, served on the Smalblaar. We did quite a few trips together in the mid-1960s, when I was a student and Mark was my mentor, and the Smalblaar was high on his list of good streams to fish. Back then it was the best trout stream in the province. I believe it still is.

We'd park at cement tables arranged under the trees that grew in a shady row just above Picnic Pool. Then we'd stroll down the side of the highway, climb in the stream, and fish back up what is now Beat 2. At midday we'd be back at the car, where Mark would set up his hamper on the table. Of course, the N1 was a lot safer then and less congested, and the National Roads Agency planted trees at picnic spots on highways and took the trouble to keep them neat and tidy.

Mark's lunches hardly varied: there was a side of tinned ham that he carved with a penknife and served on a plastic picnic plate along with Heinz potato salad and a cold beer. He liked to add a sense of occasion to these lunches, though the niceties of this passed over my head at the time. Years later, after I'd eaten my way through enough soggy sandwiches and overcooked hard-boiled eggs on a variety of rivers and lakes, I came to realise that one of the first true rituals of my fly-fishing life was the simple pleasure of enjoying the food and the sense of occasion that went with Mackereth's Smalblaar streamside lunches.

*

I don't know exactly when it was, but many years later, I fished the Injisuthi River in the central Drakensberg on the invitation of two older friends, Jim Luck and his wife Mary. By then I'd got to thinking that fly-fishing lunches warranted more than the casual planning I gave them, but on this trip I discovered they needn't be elaborate to be good. Mary had said not to worry about bringing lunch. Around midday she set up a hamper in the shade of a tree. She layered cottage cheese and sliced cucumber on plain cream crackers. We added salt and pepper to taste. That was it; an easy lunch assembled on the spot in minutes. When I'm stuck for time or feeling lazy, this is still a go-to river lunch for me, but later in life, when I got more affluent and fussier, I discovered you could turn this simple repast into a meal for a king by adding a slice or two of biltong.

*

John Beams, a great South African fly fisher of the 1960s and '70s, was a creature of habit. In all the years we fished together, his lunches hardly varied. He brought the tastiest sandwiches I can remember. They were made by his wife Hilda, and she didn't spare the horse, adding crisp bacon between two slices of buttered bread. Again, a simple repast, but unfailingly good, as I recall. Conversely, Jack Blackman, another well-known fly fisher in the 1970s, had his own ideas about fly-fishing lunches, and they too varied little from thick slices of buttered brown bread, a large tomato and a skinned raw onion, also large. He took alternative bites of tomato and raw onion as he ate the bread. Biting into a tomato is okay, but biting into a raw onion is my idea of challenging eating.

*

I remember a discussion with a friend some time back. I think it was Steve Boshoff, the bamboo-rod-making artist, but it doesn't matter. What matters is the conclusion we came to, which was that there are three unbeatable side dishes to any on-stream lunch: first, hard-boiled eggs, along with plenty of salt and pepper; second, cold pork sausages; and third, pickled gherkins. To me these ingredients go well beyond just defining basic needs. They reach the realms of delights of the palate.

*

Oliver Kite, like Mackereth, made an occasion of his streamside lunches and laced his insightful writings about chalkstream fly fishing with brief anecdotes about them. From this we learn, for example, that Kite had a liking for watercress sandwiches, tinned sardines, dandelion leaves picked from the riverbank, and sides of grilled sea-trout fillets. These 'victuals', as he called them, were washed down with either a stoup of cold ale, a pint of bitter or his homemade wine – often elderberry, sometimes golden plum, the bottle often secreted in the river to keep cool. These repasts were mainly slow-paced, woodsy, home-grown and now fashionably organic, but in one memorable and more celebratory lunch Kite describes 'putting away' champagne and a 'cold fowl' brought by a friend, followed by a prime melon, halved and packed with strawberries picked that morning and 'refreshed' with Cointreau!

His book *A Fisherman's Diary* is worth reading for the descriptions of his streamside lunches alone. Here's a passage from it:

'I picked some watercress from the clear water of a carrier, and ate it for my lunch with a hunk of my wife's fresh-baked bread, a few sardines and a stoop of ale... If Heaven is like this, some people have a lot to look forward to.'

*

When I do write about fishing lunches, I don't write with anywhere close to Kite's sense of occasion. I guess that's a matter of circumstance and the importance you place on this sort of thing, and mine has been lacking. If I jot down a few words about a lunch on a trip, it's because it struck me as that good at the time, or that bad, or because it was an experience in itself in one way or another.

I'll give you an example. We were fishing at Highland Lodge on a wet, windswept midwinter's day that was cold beyond description. The place is at high altitude and the wind seems to cut straight through you like frozen nails. I'd fished for around two hours before I beached my tube out of hunger, fatigue and hovering hypothermia (often all companion conditions in this place, by the way). And, to clinch it, the fish had stopped biting. I had already drained my flask of coffee, and eaten the sandwich I'd brought by mid-morning. So when I pulled in I was 'out of stock', as we say.

At Highland Lodge you can usually nip back to the house to get a bite and be back fishing in under half an hour, but this day we were visiting a new lake on the side of a high hill, and miles from base camp. Darryl Lampert was already ashore, leaning against his Land Rover. He'd probably come in for the same reasons I had: a combination of slow fishing, cold and hunger. I didn't say anything at the time, but you convey a lot of body language just by the way you step out of your float tube. Ever the survival tactician, Darryl loaned me a spare fleece shirt and fixed me a cup of instant chicken noodles soaked in hot water – well, warm water, actually, but eventually it did get the noodles to fill out. I stirred the mixture with a plastic spoon and added salt. It wasn't any highlight in my repertoire of outstanding fishing lunches, but it wasn't the lowest I'd sunk either. What I really could have done with was a steak sandwich and a mug of hot glühwein, but right then the noodles, though modest viands, as Kite would have said, were not only good, they felt a lot like they'd saved my life. You don't easily forget lunches like this, but equally, you maybe don't easily let yourself get this cold or this hungry too often either.

*

Many years ago, Tony Biggs and I were fishing the Bourne in Hampshire, and on the advice of the river keeper we left the stream at midday and strolled to the village pub in Hurstbourne Priors for lunch. Nobody took the slightest notice of us sitting there in our thigh waders. We had a leek-and-potato soup followed by a cottage pie, served with thick slices of bread and butter and a tall glass of ale. With a log fire burning, it all felt very homely and civilised, and again it was more an occasion than a plain fishing lunch.

That said, let me add that lunches I've had on chalkstreams have invariably been more worthy of a few lines than the lunches I've had on our rough-country freestone streams at home, where you hike in with what you've taken to eat, enjoy it under the shade of a tree, and later hike out with whatever's left over. But chalkstreams often flow through villages or alongside people's gardens, or through estates or alongside pubs, and there's plenty of opportunity to leave the river for a solid bite.

My son Robert and I were once fishing the River Test as guests on the Kimbridge estate. By midday we'd caught a nice mess of browns and then had lunch at Annie's, the little restaurant on this section of the river. I had a Ploughman's, with cheddar, brie and pickled onions, a crusty baguette and a side salad of freshly picked garden lettuce and watercress. I ordered a glass of white wine, a Chardonnay, that I chose from the wine list not for its merits as a pedigreed Chardonnay but because it came from South Africa. (The other wines were from Chile and Australia and, away from home, there's no price on loyalty.) It was a fine lunch and worthy of a few words, not only for the quality of the food and the prime location of the restaurant, but also for the company of my son on a fishing trip.

There is a restaurant that's even closer to the Test than Annie's: the Mayfly, a pub near Longparish in Hampshire. It's a well-known place with a wooden deck that juts out over the river. I ate here, again with my son, after we'd fished the Anton, a nearby chalkstream that drains into the Test just downstream from the Mayfly Inn. Below our table, brown trout milled around in anticipation of getting fed, which judging by their size they often did, although on this occasion the food they served was nowhere near as good as the view we had from the table we sat at right above the River Test.

*

The word *skaftin* probably won't mean anything to you, but it has meant a lot to me for many years fishing on *Birkhall*, when a certain kitchen maid, Angelina, used to prepare my lunch for the day's fishing. I always left her a healthy tip at the end of my stay because her *skaftins* were that good. Sadly for me, she eventually retired and left the farm. It was also general knowledge that I was a firm favourite of hers.

Skaftin comes from the Xhosa word *isikhafithini,* meaning a lunch box, *skaftin* being the simple phonetic interpretation I put on the word. Whatever, her *skaftins* were a delight. They comprised a series of buttered brown-bread sandwiches layered with wedges of raw onion and slices of cold roast beef or lamb, liberally laced with hot English mustard. She'd add a few small apples or an orange, sometimes a few thick slices of pineapple separately wrapped, and at least two fruit juices. The whole lot would be neatly sealed in tin foil and left waiting for my departure on the kitchen table.

The main point about *skaftins* was not so much that they were good to eat, and they certainly were, but that there was enough to feed a fly-fishing guide and two of his clients.

*

The lunches I've had in Roger and Victoria Harrison's garden top every high point in my life for this aspect of fly fishing, never mind that I was right on the banks of the upper Itchen, possibly the finest trout water in the world. One was particularly memorable.

342

The table was set with a checked green tablecloth under a tiny grove of apple trees only a short cast from the river. It was decked with silverware, linen napkins and shining wine glasses and bottles of fine French wines. It started with a salmon mousse topped with prawns on a bed of rocket and basil leaves, followed by a beef Wellington, and fruit salad and ice cream. Streamside lunches don't get much better than this – at least not where I normally go fishing. As I lay languishing after the feast in the shade of an apple tree, and hovering in postprandial paradise, I recalled a streamside lunch I once shared with Tony Kietzman for comparative reasons that will become abundantly clear.

It was on a day when my truck was parked in the paddock alongside the gorge section of the Sterkspruit on the farm *Branksome*. It was raining gently, and we were damp and cold. We were also dead hungry and, between us, we had an apple and a half-empty tin of baked beans left over from the previous day's fishing. We heated the beans on the tailgate of the truck, the tin perched on my tiny Primus stove, then shared the beans, taking turns to get them out of the can using a single teaspoon. When you're cold and damp and shivering badly, getting hot beans out of a can with a small spoon is like trying to thread wet spaghetti through a keyhole.

A beef Wellington on banks of the upper Itchen is very pleasing, not to mention civilised, but in a strange, roundabout sort of way, I suppose the end result of any streamside lunch is much the same. Put differently, if your head's in the right place, you can enjoy any kind of riverbank lunch, in the sense that after the meal, whatever it was, wherever it was, you mainly end up in the same space – suitably replete and ready for more fishing. The point is a little thin, I know; I'm just trying to say that, in many respects, all things are, if not entirely equal, at least relative to solving one simple common denominator – staving off the pangs of on-stream hunger.

And no, I don't know how we ended up with just one teaspoon that day, or just half a can of beans. Usually I have dozens of spoons, and if anything is lacking it's usually coffee, tea bags, powdered milk or sugar.

*

There was a lunch I had some years back on the Orange River near Douglas that I recall fondly, when our guides Jacques Marais and Etienne Rossouw cooked lamb chops very slowly on a wide metal grid propped up by carefully placed rocks. We were on the banks of the river under an azure sky. We had fished productively. It was the last day of our trip, and we sat well back from the coals in comfortable camp chairs in the shade of small trees. The coals, I was told, must be left to burn down to that uniform mix of fading pinks and greys. That's where they were when the meat got well salted and laid evenly on the grid. It sizzled and smoked, with never more than an occasional flicker of naked flame from the coals. The chops were only turned once. Then the meat was removed and allowed a long rest.

We ate with our hands. None of the other trappings that traditionally accompany most braais, like a salad, baked potatoes or bread rolls, were in evidence. It seemed they were seen as unnecessary distractions. We had the lamb chops and nothing else, and it was strangely quite enough. It's one school of thought, I guess, but since that streamside lunch on the banks of the Orange River went exactly along these lines, and took some beating, it's a school I would still happily subscribe to. You just focus on the meat. Nothing else. My wife says it lacks in some ways – 'in every other way', is actually what she said.

*

I find great comfort eating a fishing lunch off the tailgate of my truck, which has a lot to do with the fact that everything is near at hand, you can angle the truck to face out of the wind, and you also have immediate cover if it suddenly starts hailing. That's happened to me. But getting out of the wind is a big plus, especially on stillwaters where, if the wind isn't blowing, it usually means it's about to rain.

Of course, dropping the tailgate for lunch is relatively uncommon when you're fishing streams, because by lunchtime you're usually miles up- or downstream of the truck, hunting for the shade of a tree with a convenient rock to perch on. The tailgate mostly comes into its own at the start of the day – and at the end of it, when the sun is sinking, the legs are weary and strong coffee gets hauled out. It's also when you tend to find the tailgate piled under rod tubes, discarded waders, fly vests, nets, cameras and such. You can struggle to clear enough space to perch on to unlace your wading boots and pull off wet socks. It's nothing like the tailgate set for a sedate lunch.

It took a while, but stemming from all of the above, I've figured out that there are two items of fly-fishing gear we underrate – the simple camp stool and the carpet tile, both easily available at little cost. The carpet tile is, of course, to plant wet feet on after you've divested of boots and socks at the end of the day. It's either that or you tramp around with wet toes picking up dry dirt and grass.

Camp stools are especially useful if you happen to have lunch at the truck, which happens every time we fish a stillwater. The problem is the tailgate invariably gets too cramped to perch on. Then a camp stool can be a saviour. I have a small camp stool with no backrest and no armrests; it folds down flat for easy storage, has a strong canvas seat, and only weighs a few ounces. I shift it into the shade or into the lee of the wind alongside the truck to suit the conditions. I've converted many people to camp stools – and to carpet tiles, come to think of it. In fact, I don't know why they're not both for sale in fly shops, on prominent display up front, right alongside the latest rods and reels and the bins of fly patterns.

*

I have just figured out that since I wrote *Hunting Trout* I've owned four Toyota Hilux trucks – and only one was bought new and only one was sold with less than 150,000 kilometres on the clock. And every time, I've got emotional nearly to the point of tears trading them in. To me they all eventually get to fall under the heading of 'good friends' rather than just 'fishing trucks', and as I step out of one for the last time the memories flood back, and I feel waves of sadness and nostalgia, never mind a lot like a traitor. I'm not apologetic about these sentiments, either. After all, the truck has earned its stripes, taken me to far-flung places, brought me back, and left me with a kaleidoscope of memories of fishing trips, good and bad, and memories of a host of friendly gatherings around the tailgate brewing up coffee and arranging snacks, most often in the company of good friends, or at least like-minded folk.

The tailgate on a fishing truck as a gathering place should not be underestimated. Neither should you underestimate the habit a good truck has of becoming a fishing pal. Some days I talk to my truck – but not in front of other people. It's usually on long trips, when I'm alone, and when we could both do with a little company.

CHAPTER 16
THE DRY FLIES OF OLIVER KITE

There is no magic about it. It just happens to be an effective dry fly pattern when properly handled. Suitably presented, cocked on its hackles, with the tips fingering the surface of the water, it stands a very reasonable chance of deceiving fish, always provided they do not suspect the angler's presence and intentions.
OLIVER KITE, *A FISHERMAN'S DIARY: KITE'S IMPERIAL*

I spent some time a year or so back researching Oliver Kite's dry flies for an article destined for my website, and discovered that his patterns were generally poorly documented. Details in my fly-tying books were often scant, sometimes contradictory, occasionally plainly inaccurate. The exercise was like pulling teeth but I persisted, both out of stubbornness and inquisitiveness. Eventually I tied the patterns I wanted, photographed them and published the article on my website, even though it still asked a lot more questions than it fully answered.

So when I decided to include Kite's patterns in this book, my research had to start from scratch. I found a few nuggets in various publications but, in the end, I went back to Kite's own writings in *A Fisherman's Diary*, one of my all-time favourites. I read it again, carefully, from cover to cover. As various facts remained unclear, and as reference book after reference book failed to provide the answers I wanted, I turned to three friends, all knowledgeable chalkstream experts living in England: Bill Latham, Simon Cooper and Terry Lawton. They were extremely helpful – and also polite enough not to get annoyed with my endless queries, at least not outwardly so. Terry even went so far as to contact Frank Sawyer's son Tim on my behalf.

In time I had most of the facts I wanted, and could at last trust their veracity enough to include them in this book. But why include Kite's dry flies at all? Well, for interest's sake, but also for the sake of posterity – and I say that with all due regard to modesty. It's just that getting this stuff has taken hours and hours of long, slow-yielding research, and what I found has, I think, turned out to be historically relevant and, in many respects, important enough to warrant a more auspicious record than to only feature in the now-outdated article on my website.

The Americans have generally recorded their fly patterns, and much else around their fly-fishing history, pretty well. For example, the dry flies of the Catskill School are documented down to the last detail, both in outstanding books and in the archives of the Catskill Fly Fishing Center and Museum in New York state, where countless examples of fly patterns relevant to this great school of fly tying are kept as exhibits. Look, the Americans are a lot keener on this kind of thing; the English, I suspect, are more reserved. Outside of celebrating early anglers like Halford and Skues, and outside of a few good books covering various English fly-fishing histories and patterns, and perhaps outside of the Flyfishers' Club in London, UK angling and fly-tying history is less well recorded beyond the era of Walton, Halford and Skues. As far as Kite's dry flies go, this is certainly the case. By the way, I did write to the Flyfishers' Club asking whether they had any articles or papers by Kite, or any of his trout flies on show, and got a prompt and friendly reply from John Knott, the club's curator and archivist, sadly telling me they had none of Kite's dry flies.

Kite in context and a fly-fishing renaissance
Starting in the late 1960s and early '70s, there was something of a renaissance in South African fly fishing that followed the renaissance in the sport largely centred in America – a renaissance that, in many ways, is still ongoing. I say 'renaissance' but that's for want of a better word. Growth is too mild a term. Revolution isn't quite right either. That smacks of someone like Che Guevara coming into fly fishing to get rid of its lurking capitalists. Perhaps resurgence is the right word. Whatever, it was a time of great progress, plenty of new thinking and an exponential growth in the sport, and, as I said, American anglers, angling writers, fly tiers and tackle manufacturers were in the vanguard of it.

Initially, the role of the English was more muted, but with notable exceptions. Tom Ivens, Brian Clarke, John Goddard (Goddard Caddis), Brian Harris, Richard Walker and Arthur Cove all influenced our thinking to some or other degree. In fact, back in the 1970s, Tom Ivens's book *Still Water Fly Fishing* (1973) and Brian Clarke's work *The Pursuit of Stillwater Trout* (1975) made a huge impression on our approach to stillwater fly fishing in South Africa. And, as you would guess, Oliver Kite and Frank Sawyer influenced our upstream nymphing techniques, not least by describing the induced take, but also in the simplicity and effectiveness of their respective nymph patterns, the Bare Hook Nymph and the PTN.

Of course, long before the resurgence in the 1970s, Halford, Skues and James Mottram, et al, had begun to map the way of a trout with a fly for all mankind as far back as the late 19th and early 20th century. And around the same time, but across 'the pond', as they say, Theodore Gordon, George La Branche, Roy Steenrod and others were awakening Americans to the art and science of upstream dry fly fishing. Interestingly, Gordon was initially influenced by Halford's thinking on the dry fly, and for many years was in regular correspondence with Skues. And in 1950, Vincent Marinaro took the finer points of dry fly fishing ahead in leaps and bounds with his seminal work, *A Modern Dry Fly Code* – and then published another major work, *In the Ring of the Rise*, in 1977. This was at a time when another great American angler, writer and artist Ernest Schwiebert wrote *Matching the Hatch*, and became a household name with his much acclaimed book *Nymphs*, followed by his encyclopedic two-volume work *Trout*.

As for the influence of other American anglers from the 1970s onwards, Lee Wulff made a singular contribution worldwide, until his death in 1991. Charles Brooks unpacked nymphing in *Nymph Fishing for Larger Trout*, and Gary LaFontaine captivated us with works like *Caddisflies* and *Dry Fly – New Angles*. But a host of other American anglers also made significant inputs: John Betts introduced us to synthetic fly-tying materials, Doug Swisher and Carl Richards unpacked selectivity and emergers, and Gary Borger wrote, in my view, the best book of its genre, *Presentation*. Also in this mix were the likes of Datus Proper with *What the Trout Said* and Darrel Martin with *Fly Tying Materials* and, later, *Micropatterns*. Dave Whitlock contributed his *Guide to Aquatic Trout Foods*, George Griffiths (founder of Trout Unlimited) invented the Griffith's Gnat, and Al Troth designed the Elk Hair Caddis. And we could, I am sure, go on naming American pioneers for the next two pages.

The point is, the contributions of all these anglers, American and English, reached many of us fishing at the time in South Africa. In a way, you could say their works became part of our streamside scriptures. And the advances were diverse: apart from countless new books, there were improvements in fishing techniques and in tackle, a host of imaginative new fly patterns and inventive new fly-tying materials, and not least the commercial availability of quality genetic hackle from American breeders like Hoffman and Metz in the early 1970s.

More recently – well, in the past two decades or so – European influences, mainly French, Polish, Dutch, Swiss, Italian, Czech and Spanish, have enriched our fly-fishing techniques and our fly designs. Some anglers will tell you that the Europeans have had as much influence as the Americans and English ever did, but I'm not so sure about that. Besides, by the turn of this century, fly fishing was well down the road to becoming something of a global village, so advancements over the last twenty-odd years have anyway come from ever more wide-ranging and cosmopolitan sources.

Oliver Kite, the man

Kite was born in Monmouthshire in Wales on 27 November 1920, and died on the River Test from a heart attack on 15 June 1968. He had suffered from angina for many years, the illness starting while he was on overseas duty with the British Army in Australia. He returned to England in 1958, moving into Owl Cottage on High Street in the village of Netheravon – in fact, right across the road from Frank Sawyer. The Court Stretch of the River Avon was only a short stroll from his back door. But Kite fished nearly all the major chalkstreams of England, including the delightful Driffield Beck in Yorkshire, as well as countless rivers and streams in Wales, Scotland, France, Austria, Switzerland and Germany.

He is buried in the All Saints cemetery in Netheravon, in a churchyard dating back to the 11th century, and on a trip to Hampshire many years ago, I visited his grave and paid my respects to this great angler.

Kite's approach to fly fishing had a value all of its own. A large part of that value was in the simplification and economy that he brought to his angling, not to forget his inimitable writing style that conveyed his wise and often witty thoughts to many readers.

Kite's flies

It was from Kite's astute riverside observations that many of his fly patterns evolved, but the influence of people like Skues, Halford, Sawyer and others is evident in some. With the notable exception of Kite's Imperial, he is better known for his Bare Hook Nymph than for his dry flies. But he used dry fly patterns commonly, among them his Hawthorn Fly, imitating *Bibio marci* – an insect that begins to appear on UK streams from St Mark's Day (25 April) – his Sepia Dun, Apricot Spinner, Pale Evening Dun, and a pattern that he simply called 'My Mayfly'.

His references to fishing a pattern he called the Pheasant Tail Red Spinner and a pattern he calls a Black Gnat (Diptera family) are also fairly common, though the latter was probably not his own creation. In fact, I can find no dressing recorded at all for Kite's version of the Black Gnat, other than in *A Fisherman's Diary*, where he says, 'This magnificent fish (a 2½lb grayling) took a Black Gnat, which I dress with a black hackle slightly tinged with red.'

Kite used the Pheasant Tail Red Spinner when olive mayflies were on the water, and said it was 'as effective as Lunn's Particular' – high praise indeed in the world of chalkstream fly fishing. But it is in the tying of this pattern that I unearthed, and then solved, a minor mystery.

Kite's relative use of dry flies over nymphs is interesting. In five successive seasons, he records that he caught 951 trout, 551 on a nymph and 400 on his dry fly patterns. Of the 400 taken on dry flies, 128 were caught on the Pheasant Tail Red Spinner. More on this pattern later.

Kite's style and philosophies in tying the dry fly

There is a simplicity and sameness about Kite's dry flies that T Donald Overfield describes in his book *Famous Flies and Their Originators* as 'orthodox', and as 'leaving nothing to the craft that was not already known at the time'. Overfield believed, though, that Kite placed considerable store on 'movement', Kite being of the opinion that the 'fluttering fly' was frequently the one picked out by the trout. He also describes Kite as having a strong preference for long, stiff hackles that allowed the dry fly to 'land lightly on its points' and to ride high, on tiptoe as it were, on the surface, with the mobility gained from 'the breeze gently rocking the artificial to and fro'. Kite himself described this more eloquently: 'What deceives trout is lifelike movement. Put a dry fly on the surface, any decent pattern properly constructed with sharp hackles, and above all a decent thorax, and the stiff hackle points will finger the water as they rock in the lightest airs. There you have movement, life and deception.'

These principles resonate well with our long-standing subscription in South Africa to Tony Biggs's wide-hackled, sparsely tied RABs, a 'fluttering' kind of dry fly if there ever was one.

Now let me take you through Kite's main dry fly patterns.

Kite's Imperial

Kite developed this now classic dry fly pattern to imitate the large Dark Olive Mayfly, *Baetis rhodani*, but later also used it to imitate the Iron Blue Dun. In *A Fisherman's Diary*, he says, 'This much I know, that whether trout are eating olives, or iron blues, or both, they invariably accept an Imperial, the only dun pattern I carry (in early season).'

Later he writes, 'In practice, I nowadays use it whenever duns are on the water, be they olives, iron blues, blue-winged olives or anything else.' It certainly remained his most used dry fly, in

England, Wales and Europe, and a most effective pattern, judging by the number of trout and grayling he caught on it.

Peter Hayes, in his book *Fly Fishing Outside the Box*, importantly observes, 'But again there is a tremendously important element, in this case the flattened and humped thorax, which Kite was, I think, the first to incorporate in a dry fly. That alone has been enough to ensure consistent success for this pattern relative to the generality of un-humped (dry fly) patterns.'

Tying Kite's Imperial is taken from *A Fisherman's Diary*, and obviously refers to seasons in the United Kingdom.

Hook: Size 14 in early spring, 15 or 16 later in the season.

Tying silk: Purple.

Tail: Greyish-brown hackle fibres in early spring. Honey-dun later in the season.

Body: Four undyed heron primary herls.

Rib: Fine gold wire.

Thorax: Wraps of heron herls doubled and redoubled (in the Netheravon style).

Hackle: Honey-dun cock (tied just ahead of the humped thorax).

As mentioned, the doubled thorax is unique to many of Kite's dry flies. To form it, wrap the heron herls to around three to four millimetres behind the eye, depending on the size of the hook, trap them here with silk, then wind the wire ribbing up the herl body to around two to three millimetres from the end of the herl body. Now fold the ends of the heron herls that you've trapped on top of the hook shank with silk, back on top of themselves, and trap them with the wire ribbing. Wind the wire forward over the herls in the thorax area to where the herl body ends, and tie the wire off. Now pull the heron herls forward again to cover the thorax area and tie them off. Be certain that you leave enough space at the front of the hook shank for the hackle, and that you leave a prominent thorax of about two to three millimetres, again depending on the size of the hook.

In my view, this is a dry fly pattern right up there with the best of the classics from the Catskill School of fly tying. When I tied a few recently, I used the herl from heron primaries sent to me by my friend Bill Latham. He'd collected the feathers below a heronry on the banks of the River Avon, not far from where Kite had lived. Going to this level of detail is the kind of thing many fly tiers, myself included, find appealing; to others it's just a sign of some lurking obsessive disorder. I'm not sure I care. What I can tell you is this dry fly works a treat on small streams in the Western Cape.

The Hawthorn Fly

There are references in *A Fisherman's Diary* to the Hawthorn fly taking trout and grayling, and Kite describes tying the pattern after setting up his vice on an old ploughshare in a riverside field. He also describes this pattern's value on rivers other than chalkstreams in his book *Nymph Fishing in Practice*, where he had great success fishing it on the River Torridge in North Devon, and on various rivers in Wales. But Kite does not describe the dressing of this pattern, at least not in any detail. The detail comes from Donald Overfield's book, *Famous Flies and Their Originators*, as well as from Courtney Williams's book *A Dictionary of Trout Flies*.

Hook: Size 13 or 14. (No further detail is given.)

Tying silk: Black.

Tail: None.

Body: Peacock tied plump (or full).

Rib: Fine gold wire.

Hackle: Black cock.

This looks a very buggy dry fly. I have used it with success in Western Cape streams, irrespective of the fact that we don't get hawthorn flies in South Africa.

The Sepia Dun

The dressing is not given by Kite, but comes from *A Dictionary of Trout Flies* and from *Famous Flies and Their Originators*. It is primarily for imitating the Sepia Dun, *Leptophlebia marginata*. Sepia, a red-brown colour, is the predominant colour of this dun; it's a fairly common species in Ireland, the British Isles, Europe and the US. There are similar mayflies in South Africa (*Adenophlebia dislocans* is a fine example), New Zealand and Australia.

Overfield leaves out the fine gold wire rib in his book (an error on his part, I believe), but it is included by Courtney Williams.

Hook: Size 14 up-eye.

Tying silk: Dark-brown.

Tail: Dark-brown or black cock hackle fibres, or both, mixed.

Rib: Fine gold wire.

Body: Heron primary herls, doubled and redoubled at the thorax.

Hackle: Black cock.

I have also found this pattern quite effective on our local streams when we bump into hatches of this most beautiful, strangely fearless and camera-friendly mayfly, *Adenophlebia dislocans*.

The Apricot Spinner

Again, the dressing is not given by Kite, but it is in *A Dictionary of Trout Flies*, in *Trout Fly Recognition* by John Goddard, and in *Famous Flies and Their Originators*. This is the female spinner of the Pond Olive Mayfly (*Cloeon dipterum*), which has an apricot-coloured body.

Hook: Size 14.

Tying silk: Golden olive.

Tail: Pale yellowish-orange hackle fibres.

Body: Swan primary herls (duck primaries will do) dyed apricot, doubled and redoubled at the thorax. Effective substitutes are goose primaries, or apricot-coloured flat silk.

Rib: Fine gold wire.

Hackle: Pale-honey dun.

As an all-round spinner, you could probably get by with this, but spinner patterns to my mind need spent wings. This pattern is not conventional in today's interpretation of spinners – which is not to say it won't work.

The Pale Evening Dun

You will find this pattern in *Trout Fly Recognition*, in *A Dictionary of Trout Flies*, in *Famous Flies and Their Originators,* and in John Veniard's *A Further Guide to Fly Dressing*. It imitates a mayfly of the *Heptagenid* species found commonly in streams and rivers worldwide. Both Pale Evening Duns and Pale Morning Duns have equivalent species in South Africa, and in most countries around the world. These are, by far, the palest-coloured duns of all.

Hook: Size 15.

Tying silk: White.

Tail: Cream-coloured cock hackle fibres.

Body: Grey goose primary herls, doubled and redoubled at the thorax.

Rib: None.

Hackle: Cream cock.

Again, a useful pattern on South African streams.

My Mayfly

This is Kite's imitation of the most famous mayfly on earth, *Ephemera danica*. I found only two references to it in Kite's *A Fisherman's Diary*, the most important in the chapter 'Spring', where he fishes the Avon and is advised by the keeper, Les Sawyer 'to bring some mayflies, as there are still natural mayflies about'. Why he didn't use an Imperial is almost certainly because the mayfly Les Sawyer was referring to is the prince of all mayflies, *Ephemera danica*.

Kite gives his Mayfly dressing as follows:

Hook: Size 12 or 14.

Tying silk: Brown.
Whisks: Four of five pheasant centre tail herls.
Body: Dubbed mink fur.
Rib: Fine gold wire.
Hackle: Red in front and cream (or light ginger) behind.

The mink mentioned here is most likely American mink imported into the United Kingdom for farming. There are no natural mink in England, although there is a mink indigenous to Europe. Both species are variable in colour, anything from dark grey to sandy brown. Given the pale-straw colour and variegated body of *Ephemera danica*, I suspect Kite was using light-brown mink fur. An equivalent colour dubbing will, I am sure, not be noticed.

The Sedge Fly

There are a few references to the dressing for Kite's Sedge Fly, but none are greatly detailed. I've included this pattern, ascribed to Kite.
Hook: Size 12 or 14.
Tying silk: Brown.
Tail: None.
Body: Strands of pheasant tail herl.
Hackle: Dark-red cock hackle, palmered along the body.

A reference to a similar sedge pattern can be found in Datus Proper's *What the Trout Said*. Proper illustrates and describes high-floating sedge patterns, and lists the Palmer Sedge first, which is no more than a hook palmered with red cock hackle, although he suggests that a wing of rolled primary wing feather fibres or rolled hackled fibres can safely be added. Proper says the fly is hard to beat when fished as a skittering caddis.

GEM Skues's Little Red Sedge was also similar to Kite's Sedge, and used a palmered dark-red cock hackle, but with a wing of rolled hen pheasant breast fibres. This pattern may apparently have influenced Al Troth in creating his Elk Hair Caddis. But the history of winged caddisfly imitations goes way further back. *Tricóptero de León*, Spanish sedge patterns, used rolled Coq de Leon hackle fibres for wings as far back as the 1700s. Top grade CdL hackles are so beautiful, and so exquisitely barred, and so expensive, that we tend to only use them for tails on mayfly imitations, and then very sparingly.

Sawyer's and Kite's Pheasant Tail Red Spinner, the origin of the PTN and a minor mystery

I want to include both Oliver Kite's and Frank Sawyer's Pheasant Tail Red Spinner patterns, the latter being the dry fly that is accredited with giving the world its most ubiquitous nymph, the PTN. Later, I want to touch on Lunn's Particular, a real classic, to make this chapter more complete as far as great chalkstream dry flies go. For the same reason, I could also have added two other flies in the same league, the Greenwell's Glory and the Houghton Ruby, but that would have set me off on a long road, where knowing where to start is always a lot easier than knowing where to end.

Sawyer's Pheasant Tail Red Spinner

The pattern's history proved a real problem to unravel, but I finally cracked it. It is described as a wonderful imitation when olives are on the surface and, as I mentioned, Kite ranked it with Lunn's Particular. It's also an effective all-round dry fly when any spent mayflies with rust-coloured bodies are on the water.

In *A Fisherman's Diary*, Kite writes, 'I had on the Pheasant-tail Red Spinner (sic) which is the fly I fish as a matter of course on those rare occasions when I go out in the evening, until darkness dictates a change to the Sedge.'

However, Kite did not ascribe the pattern to himself, or to Sawyer. But to touch on that minor mystery, let's start with Sawyer's Pheasant Tail Red Spinner pattern that Overfield describes in

Famous Flies and Their Originators, and then at the same pattern as given in Terry Lawton's *Nymph Fishing: A History of the Art and Practice*. I didn't say all this wouldn't get a little complicated; that's often the way it pans out when you start researching the lineage of a fly pattern. It can be half the fun – and often only half the truth.

The pattern for Sawyer's Pheasant Tail Red Spinner in Overfield's book on page 160 records a few strange things. First, Overfield refers to the tail fibres as being white cock hackle, but then says, 'leaving pheasant tail fibres protruding to simulate tails'. Clearly an oversight.

The interesting part is that he describes building up a thorax of copper wire. Really? On a dry fly? Surely something wrong there.

Lawton's version, on the other hand, indicates red silk was used, the tail was white cock hackle, and the body and thorax were of pheasant tail fibres. He describes a dark-red hackle of the Rhode Island shade. He also makes the point that Kite noted the thorax was an essential feature of all Sawyer's dry fly patterns – and obviously also his famous PTN nymph pattern.

So I was in some doubt about Overfield's version, especially insofar as using copper wire instead of silk was concerned. In the end, I am more inclined to accept Lawton's interpretation.

What led me even more to this view is Sawyer's statement that this pattern evolved into the PTN. Remember, this makes it a historic pattern beyond words! Lawton in his book tells the story of Sawyer fishing a Pheasant Tail Red Spinner until the hackle disintegrated, and it still took trout as it sank. This, Sawyer himself said, was the origin of the PTN.

Sawyer made public the PTN's association with his Pheasant Tail Red Spinner dry fly in 1965. Overfield's book was first published in 1972, well after Sawyer's announcement. Is it possible, then, that Overfield mistakenly conflated the tying of the Pheasant Tail Red Spinner with that of the Pheasant Tail Nymph? I think he did. And there is an interesting footnote to the chapter in Lawton's book that deals with the origin of the PTN. It says, 'It was then a matter of having the imagination and understanding to transform the remains of a well-used dry fly into what was to become one of the world's most successful nymph patterns.'

To me this statement suggests that significant changes, not minor ones, were needed to transform the Pheasant Tail Red Spinner into the PTN. Were those changes not replacing the red tying silk with copper wire, using the tips of the pheasant fibres to represent the tails, twisting the pheasant tail fibres and copper wire together to form the body, and then using the wire itself to build up the thorax? I think so.

Finally, I went back to oracle Terry Lawton, who noted my doubts and sent my query on to Tim Sawyer, Frank Sawyer's son. Back came the reply. No copper wire was used. The thorax was built up of red tying silk and the tails were white cock hackle. I made the assumption that Sawyer would then cover the red silk with wraps of pheasant tail.

Lawton added that in the Robert Spaight-edited version of Kite's *Nymph Fishing in Practice*, there are dressings for a number of variations of the Pheasant Tail Red Spinner, and he emailed me a scanned version of the relevant pages. Spaight is a well-respected Lincolnshire fly dresser, and the pages made interesting reading. We've come this far, so let's round it off with insights from Spaight.

The (Generic) Pheasant Tail Red Spinner
The origin of this fly is open to some speculation. Eric Horsfall Turner, Peter Deane and Donald Overfield credit it to Frank Sawyer. Authors Geoffrey Bucknall and Sidney Vines credit it to Oliver Kite. Earlier versions certainly come from FM Halford and GEM Skues. Safe to say it's got a long history, and also safe to say, I believe, that Sawyer and Kite both adapted their own versions from the earlier patterns.

YET MORE SWEET DAYS

Spaight lists the dressings for what I believe are authentic versions of both Sawyer's and Kite's Pheasant Tail Red Spinners:

Sawyer's Pheasant Tail Red Spinner

Hook: Size 12 to 16.
Silk: Red.
Tail: White cock hackle fibres.
Body: Pheasant tail fibres.
Rib: None or red silk (my assumption).
Thorax: Red silk built up and covered with wraps of pheasant tail (again, my assumption).
Hackle: Medium-red game cock.

Note that there is no rib of wire or silk in Spaight's version. But if Sawyer's son spoke of the thorax being made up of wraps of red silk, it is most likely that his father used a rib of red silk as well.

Now we come to the last of Kite's dry flies that I want to include.

Kite's Pheasant Tail Red Spinner

Hook: Size 12 to 16.
Silk: Red.
Tail: White cock hackle fibres.
Body: Bright red silk, ribbed with pheasant tail fibres, doubled and redoubled at the thorax.
Hackle: Medium-red game cock.

So there you have it. And while you could say the jury is still out on some of this, for me the jury is no longer as out as it was.

Lunn's Particular

I mentioned that I would end the chapter with this pattern. Its only association with Kite is that he used it, and that he gave it high praise. It is also a most attractive chalkstream classic and an interestingly different dry fly pattern to tie, with its quill body and spent wings.

William Lunn was the first of three consecutive generations of Lunns who were head river keepers on the hallowed Houghton Club stretch of the River Test. He developed the pattern in 1917, and it rapidly became popular not only on the chalkstreams of Hampshire, but on trout streams worldwide. Lunn intended this pattern to represent the Medium Olive Spinner, but it makes a remarkably good imitation of many duns, and an excellent all-purpose dry fly.

Hook: Size 14 to 16.

Silk: Crimson to red.

Tail: Natural red cock hackle fibres.

Body: Natural red cock hackle quill.

Wing: Light-blue dun hackle tips, tied spent. (Some authors describe the wings as tied 'flat', others as 'semi-spent'.)

Hackle: Natural red cock.

A hesitant final word

My initial hesitation to include this chapter was partly because what I had researched at the time was incomplete and would require a lot of time to fix, if it was fixable at all. I also wondered whether all this detail would be rather too much for readers, more so because Kite is not a modern fly fisher, nor is he that well known in South Africa. But he was a supreme exponent of the arts of chalkstream nymphing and dry fly fishing, and there is no doubt about that at all. I did ask a few friends their view on including this chapter and got a thumbs-up from everyone, their rationale being that I had chapters on the chalkstreams and on Iceland, so the book already carried something of an international flavour. Other points made were that the chapter illustrates the importance of recording history, no matter that it's long-since-past history or not relevant to catching modern trout. Finally, Kite's dry fly patterns were elegant and attractive, and also effective and historically important.

One additional suggestion was that, since a number of fly tiers want to dress traditional or classic flies of whatever sort to textbook standards and specifications, this chapter would undoubtedly help them. And there are more than a few people in this league – fly tiers like Mike Valla with his traditional Catskill flies, and South Africans Ruhan Neethling, JP Gouws and Gordon van der Spuy, who spend hours dressing traditional salmon and Catskill dry fly patterns. Part is challenge, part is nostalgia, part is the pursuit of art – and a part perhaps borders on the obsessive, but who cares. I love this kind of challenge enough myself to fully understand it.

And since flies tied to these standards need patience, application and plenty of time, there's an unaccustomed sense of freedom bordering on pure self-indulgence when you sit behind a vice for hours on end for none of the usual reasons. Normally I'm behind my vice when I have a job to do, which mostly boils down to filling the yawning holes in my fly boxes; or maybe to tie up a few essential patterns for a special trip, something I always end up leaving to the last minute.

So, a few months ago, after I was more certain about the dressings, I took time out to re-tie the patterns in this chapter that I was initially unsure about, and then to the most exact specifications I could manage. I'm not going to say they turned out like Mike Valla's or Ruhan Neethling's masterpieces, but they were at least flies as true to the original dressings as I could get. I went the extra mile and enjoyed it. I did mention, for example, that the heron fibres I used to tie Kite's Imperial had come from a roost near where Kite himself might have sourced them; and I tried to match the hooks he would likely have used (I guessed the Mustad 94840 was close enough to the truth). It's not an up-eyed hook, but then Kite is quoted as saying that trout don't notice the difference.

Final words: while tying up the Kite collection, I ended up with a few extras flies that I occasionally fish on my local streams. They have caught trout, and I found that it felt good to pay homage to someone who mapped such a lovely course for us many years ago.

Bibliography for this chapter
David Collier, *Fly-Dressing* (David & Charles, 1975) • David Collier, *Fly-Dressing II* (David & Charles, 1982) • John Goddard, *Trout Fly Recognition*, p95-96 (A & C Black, 1966) • Peter Hayes, *Fly Fishing Outside the Box* (Coch-y-Bonddu Books, 2013) • Tony Hayter, *GEM Skues: The Man of the Nymph* (Robert Hale Limited, 2013) • Oliver Kite, *A Fisherman's Diary*, p31, 41, 132, 103 (Andre Deutsch, 1969) • Oliver Kite, *Nymph Fishing in Practice*, p46, 145 (Herbert Jenkins, 1969) • Terry Lawton, *Nymph Fishing: A History of the Art and Practice*, p71 (Stackpole Books, 2005) • John McDonald, *The Complete Fly Fisherman* – letters exchanged between Theodore Gordon and FM Halford, and between Gordon and GEM Skues (Jonathan Cape, 1949) • T Donald Overfield, *Famous Flies and Their Originators* (A & C Black, 1972) • Taff Price, *Fly Patterns: An International Guide* (Blandford, 1997) • Datus Proper, *What the Trout Said* (Nick Lyons Books, 1989) • Frank Sawyer, *Nymphs and the Trout* (A & C Black, 1977) • GEM Skues, *Side Lines, Side Lights and Reflections* (Fly Fisher's Classic Library, 1996) • Eric Horsfall Turner, *Angler's Cavalcade* (A & C Black, 1966) • A Courtney Williams, *A Dictionary of Trout Flies* (A & C Black, 1973) • John Veniard, *A Further Guide to Fly Dressing* (A & C Black, 1968)

The Willow Stream on Balloch

CHAPTER 17
VISITORS FROM OTHER CLIMES

Fly fishing, I have learned in forty-something years of obsessing over it, is simply too much fun to be taken seriously.
JAMES R BABB, *CROSSCURRENTS: A FLY FISHER'S PROGRESS*

Billy de Jong and I spent a quiet evening at a B&B in Colesberg so we could make the trip to Bloemfontein airport the next day in time to collect two of our friends flying in from London. It wasn't a cheap place to stay but it was comfortable, and the leg of lamb was predictably good, which is as you would expect when you're in the heart of the Karoo, the best sheep-farming area in the country, and paying lots of money for the rooms.

It was a fresh March morning as we drove out of Colesberg to meet Robin Renwick, who Billy and I have fished with a good deal in South Africa, and Clay Brendish, who was on his first visit to the Eastern Cape Highlands. He's fished around the world and I was quietly praying that conditions in the Rhodes area would hold or improve a little, because from what we'd heard the rivers were low and rainfall scarce. Then again, even if we battled to catch fish, it would be a new experience for both of them, and I felt pretty sure they'd be knocked out by the scenery and the hospitality of the Eastern Cape Highlands, two things you can always rely on.

Their plane arrived on time at 11am, and they trundled out with what seemed like enough gear to cover a month-long trip to Alaska. We shook hands, exchanged greetings, fielded questions on the weather and the fishing prospects, then loaded their gear into the back of my truck. Their baggage only just fitted because a large slice was already taken up by Billy's and my stuff, and neither of us travels that light. They had arrived on a Friday and were leaving the following Tuesday, so this was going to be a rushed trip. We planned to drop them back at the airport, and then spend another four days on *Birkhall* with Carien and Basie.

One more thing about my truck's crowded load bed: a week before the trip, Robin called from London to say he was having some wine and Cognac delivered to my house, and asked if I'd be kind enough to bring them to Rhodes. A day later I got home to an entrance hall seemingly filled with boxes, six to be exact, two of white wine (Springfield Estate's Life From Stone), two of red wine from the Hamilton Russell estate, one of the finest Hennessy Cognac, and a box of Vin de Constance, a delightful dessert wine from Klein Constantia. So yes, my truck was packed to the roof even before we collected our friends from the airport.

*

What we hadn't taken into account on the trip from Bloemfontein to *Balloch*, a guest farm in the New England District where we'd planned to spend the first night and a day's fishing, were the delays due to five stops on the road to Aliwal North. They were rebuilding the highway, rather than just repairing potholes and such, and the whole stretch was reduced to one lane. Initially, the idea was to get our guests to *Balloch* on the first day because it was closer than going all the way through to Rhodes, so we could cast a line that afternoon. In the end, we got to *Balloch* with darkness closing in, and had to shelve the idea of fishing. But at least there was still enough light to give our guests an idea of the grandeur of the scenery.

We were booked into Willowstream Cottage, on the banks of the stream that flows through the farm. The water level was down, but the stream looked good enough for a few fish. Margie and Graham Frost, the owners of *Balloch*, came across to meet our guests, stayed for a drink and left us with a leg of lamb in the oven and strawberries and cream in the fridge. Billy managed to lift a few boxes of liquor out of the back of the truck (he's still young and strong enough), and we talked and drank far too much to make the early start we'd planned for next day. But it was a pleasant evening. We had a fire going, Clay smoked a cigar, and Robin told us of his life as the UK's ambassador to South Africa and then to the USA. I discovered that night that nothing warms and numbs you quite the same way as neat Cognac sniffed and sipped from a wide-brimmed wine glass. So we got to bed late, but in that lovely, comfortable way that it just gets to be late on some nights on fishing trips. When we did all finally surface the next morning, Margie's staff were hovering around the dining room table putting the final touches to an English breakfast.

We fished the section below the falls in the morning, Robin and I going upstream after we'd dropped Billy and Clay on some good-looking water a kilometre or two below the cottage. The Willow is a small stream throughout its course on *Balloch*, notable for free-rising rainbows below the falls and some ethereal brown-trout fishing above it. When we collected Clay and Billy around lunchtime they looked hot and happy: they'd caught a few rainbows on dry flies, but the fish were mainly small, the best of them fourteen inches. None of the better trout had shown up. We'd done much the same.

After lunch we took our guests above the falls where the stream is tinier. This time Robin and Billy went upstream, and Clay and I walked a long way downstream along a vehicle track before climbing into the river. It's no more than a wispy brook, flowing through open grassland in the folds of high hills that give way to craggy cliffs and mountains with massive chunks of sandstone littered on the slopes. The stream was low and clear, and after an hour of gently threading tiny flies through glassy runs we hadn't caught much. Clay owns a lovely piece of the River Test near Stockbridge in Hampshire that he's been kind enough to let me fish over the years, so I wanted him to get a couple of decent brown trout, if only to prove that you can find lovely browns outside of English chalkstreams, even if his section of the Test is ten times wider than the one we were on, and the trout three times bigger.

Of course I'd raved to Clay about the Willow, the way South African fly fishers typically rave about our brown-trout streams, mainly because they're rare and because our stream-bred browns are so beautiful you can't help making a point of it. But he certainly was impressed with the rugged, sandstone grandeur of the valley, and I often caught him just staring up into the apricot-coloured buttresses that dwarf everything around you. The scenery is from the other side of Mars, it's that dramatic.

Later in the day, when our fortunes hadn't changed much for the good – we'd only had two or three unremarkable fish, even though they *were* pretty – I decided to follow a sheep track up the side of a hill while Clay was in the stream. The track cut back to a spot where I could look down onto a long, straight section. I spotted two nice fish about fifty metres ahead of Clay. They were holding deep and well back in the tail-end of two adjoining runs. I strolled down and told Clay where the fish were, and he did a neat job of catching both, confirming again the value of streams with high banks, though in this case, it was more a tall hillside than a high bank.

372

*

By late afternoon we had the truck loaded again and were heading for Rhodes on that lovely route that takes you high above the Joggem River Valley. This is where, if you happen to know the road, the hillsides and the riverbed are scattered with huge boulders, some of them the size of your house. It's a dramatic sight, so in my book this place always calls for a compulsory stop.

The view might be wonderful but it's an almost sheer drop to the river from many places, and looking down, the height and the size of the boulders, lying like they were poised to loosen any minute and roll into the river, can make your head spin. I'm speaking for myself on this, but I don't stand too close to the edge looking down into the Joggem River Valley. The scale of it alone makes me giddy.

*

When you have guests, you naturally want your plans to fall into place and run smoothly, and happily they did on this trip, aside from the general condition of the rivers, which were low, so the fishing was a little more testy than usual. It was also one of those years when smaller trout were abundant, though we caught enough good fish to settle my nerves – and Billy's. And Walkerbouts Inn was much enjoyed by Robin and Clay, as were the local folk they met and, of course, the village itself. As expected, the vast landscapes, the huge spaces, the domes of endless blue sky and the star-sprinkled night skies were the sort of sights people coming from London will always find remarkable.

I'd say if the trip had a downside it wasn't the lowness of the rivers as much as the long distances we had to drive getting to them. South African anglers are used to driving for hours on dirt roads to get to their fishing, but I don't think Clay and Robin expected

373

they'd be sitting quite as long as they did each day in a bumpy truck. I noticed, though, that they both enjoyed our frequent bridge stops, and the times we got out to aim binoculars at a high-soaring raptor or some rare endemic bird, like the Ground Woodpecker and the Drakensberg Rockjumper. I was hoping for an animal carcass near the roadside surrounded by feeding Cape Vultures, but that never happened. Come to think of it, I've only seen that three or four times in the many years I've been doing trips up here, and then I was always alone. And there's an irony in that, because seeing vultures close up, or watching their laboured downhill takeoffs and then the way they soar upwards so effortlessly on their long-spread wings, is always something you want to share.

*

Our first trip from the hotel was to *Gateshead*, and those of you who have done it will know the drive from Rhodes to *Gateshead* is a long, winding forty-five kilometres. Tony Kietzman had come along for the ride. The skies were leaden, and when we crossed the Bokspruit, the river looked low but fishable, if only on the edge of fishable. It certainly wasn't what we'd hoped for, meaning a plump stream looking just right. It could have done with a few more inches of flow to carry our drifting dry flies with more authority and to fill the better pockets with more holding water.

We parked on the banks of the river below the *Gateshead* cottage. It was windy and cold. I wondered if the dry fly would be any good, and resisted setting up a New Zealand rig because I know Robin hates using them. We did take a few small rainbows on the dry fly, but in the end, the better fish came to lightly weighted nymphs fished under tiny indicators. And, as always, we got the best fish by free-drifting the nymph through deeper runs, or swimming it exactly with the current through deep slots close to banks.

I hardly cast a fly, happy just to guide Robin and make sure he got a few fish. After all he has done for my own fishing over the years, I was glad I could put a little back into his. Fortunately, Robin has a lot of natural fish sense, so my guiding was more observing and suggesting than anything hands-on.

Upstream, Clay, Billy and Tony had a thin time to begin with, until the fish came on, and then they took a heap of small rainbows on dry flies.

Around midday the wind got stronger, and I could smell rain in the air. The clouds were now hanging like a dark bedspread on the mountains; we heard the first thud of thunder, followed by a gentle rumble that sounded far off. We were a long way upstream of the cottage by then, at least two or three kilometres from the truck, and I was about to suggest to Robin that common sense would have us take down our rods, hike up to the pony trail above the river and make our way back. But before I could get the words out, a jagged spike of lightning lit up the clouds, and a million kilowatts of electric energy hit the highest point, a hilltop, with a skull-numbing crack, not half a kilometre from us. The strike left a tall plume of dark smoke that lifted skywards in a mushroom-shaped cloud. Fortunately, no fire followed, but the column of smoke rose to at least fifty metres above the mountain. We didn't need a long debate to decide on plan A and, thirty minutes later, as we got back to the truck, heavy rain came slanting in. For a few minutes the water in the shallow runs danced white from the force of the large raindrops. Then, as fast as it had come, the rain blew away and the air smelled fresh, cold and earthy.

The lightning had also rattled the boys upstream. They were back before we had finished our coffee, and we all spoke about nothing other than lightning as we ate sandwiches alongside the truck. They'd heard the strike and saw the smoke, and like us, they didn't waste time taking down their rods and moving out.

With lightning around there's not much difference between the words *bold* and *stupid*. They mean the same thing in this weather. From long habit, as soon as I hear thunder, my default setting is to think the worst and get out. I don't try the bold and stupid setting any longer, though there was a time, when I was younger, when I'd hang around fishing until the last few moments – any of which, of course, could have been just that – or until sanity prevailed.

Then suddenly the clouds cleared, and the *Gateshead* mountain was lit yellow with sunlight. So we fished for an hour around the cottages, where we got a few decent fish, while I tried to keep the frightening concept of clear-air lightning out of my head.

*

I've had four close shaves with lightning, counting this one, and I can rattle off the names of the pals who were fishing with me, suggesting the events were of some magnitude. The people involved were John Beams, Hugh Huntley and Ivan Steytler. In John's case, we were making a run for it on a lake in the Inhlosane mountains in KwaZulu-Natal when lightning hit just ahead of us. It sounded like one of those thunderclap fireworks had gone off in my head.

With Hugh Huntley, we were easing through a gate on the farm *Briar Mains* in the foothills of the Drakensberg in KZN when a lightning bolt hit a rock the size of a wheelbarrow just beyond us.

The strike when I was out fishing with my old friend Ivan Steytler was the most spectacular. We were walking along a fence at the Old Dam in the Inhlosane, when the fence took a full hit. We weren't a rod-length from it, and I recall the air being thick with the smell of gunpowder. Both of us were left stone-deaf for a few minutes.

Thinking back on these three strikes, and the one with Robin at *Gateshead*, I should also say that while fishing I've probably had more close shaves with lightning than with snakes.

*

There is merit in treating evenings on fishing trips as events in their own right, and Walkerbouts Inn provided the ideal platform, with all our party seated at a brightly decked dinner table in a cosy ambience. Clay and Robin dress for dinner as if these occasions require a certain respect. We don't do that here in South Africa – well, not as much, or not as a rule, especially on fishing trips. I certainly don't dress for dinner with the pals with whom I fish. They'd get concerned if I did. But when I was with Robin and Clay fishing the chalkstreams in Hampshire, they always turned up for dinner in neatly pressed shirts and blazers. And in Iceland, all guests got dressed for evening dinner, including myself. No tie, though. I have limits.

By this visit I'd learnt about post-fishing dinner etiquette as far as Clay and Robin go, and took probably the last two neckties I own, two decent dress shirts and a jacket. In the end I didn't wear a tie. As I dressed, I wryly thought about the trips my pals and I have made to places like Highland Lodge or *Birkhall* or *Vrederus*, when we eat dinner in much the same clothes we fished in, save for a change of socks. Nowadays, quick-drying wading pants will have dried out by the time we get back to base, especially when the truck's heater is on, so most evenings we just stay in them. We may even sleep in them.

*

We spent a day fishing the Sterkspruit on *Birkhall* when the trout played along but the weather didn't. It was overcast again with a strong wind from the north, fortunately blowing upstream. The water was running clear and fine, but on a river like the Sterkspruit there are always plenty of deep slots that hold fish. With no hatches, and maybe also because of the wind, it just wasn't a dry fly day, but Robin got four decent fish from one long run fishing a Zak under an indicator and, on the off chance, I fished the same run again and picked up two more trout, one of them a sturdy fifteen-incher. And so the day went, with the wind getting so strong we decided to head for the small lake on *Birkhall*, the one below the farmhouse, to see if we could catch a few bigger fish off guard.

We were parked on the far side of the lake eating a late lunch when a White-breasted Cormorant, considered vermin to lake fly fishers, swept in and landed alongside a stand of reed beds against the wall of the lake. In a second Billy was out of the truck setting up his bow. We gave him no chance of hitting the small, moving target, especially not in a high wind. He crept into range behind the cover of the reeds. The target was at least twenty metres off, only the head and the thin neck visible. To make matters more testing, the bird would frequently dive for a few long seconds then pop up metres from where you expected to see it again. Finally Billy took aim, pulled the bowstring back until the bow bent deeply, then let loose. We saw the arrow fly through the air for a millisecond, and immediately the cormorant was upended. For a while the arrow floated with its red fletchings on the surface, but it drifted away on the wind. Billy spent ten minutes trying to get it back casting a fly at it. In the end, the arrow sank. Billy returned carrying the bird.

'That was the most remarkable bit of sharp-shooting I've ever seen,' Robin said.

Billy put it down to luck. We weren't convinced.

'I see the arrow refused your wet fly a few times,' I said to Billy. 'What pattern were you using?'

*

Under cloudy skies, we got in some pleasant fishing for the rest of the day on Basie's lake, taking a few decent fish on small flies, mainly midge imitations fished just below the surface, until the wind died, and the lake went as calm as a mill pond. Not a fish rose in the next thirty minutes, whereas just before they had been as cautiously busy at the surface as mice around a bread bin at night.

*

We fished the Bell the next day on *Glass Niven*. Robin and I hiked downstream from the bridge where I parked the truck in the shade of a willow tree just off the road. The water level was better than I expected, and Robin immediately had three good trout using a lightly weighted Zak, then broke off on a fourth fish that was clearly much bigger. It left a bulging boil on the surface. By the time we got back to the truck we'd enjoyed a fair morning's fishing. Billy and Clay had done equally well upstream.

During the afternoon on the lovely *Dunley* and *Malpas* beats of the Bell above Rhodes there was a caddis hatch, the insects as big as moths. Clay and Robin each got a dozen decent trout on Elk Hair Caddis patterns. This has to be one of the most universal and forgiving dry fly patterns around. I guess its equivalent nymph pattern would be the PTN or the Gold-ribbed Hare's Ear, and it's as good a prospecting pattern as it is when matching hatches.

There are few patterns you can really say that about with as much conviction, and when you can, it's a pattern that will be worth its place in your fly box.

*

A large drum of coals glowed like rubies on the lawn at Walkerbouts that evening. A bunch of us gathered around its warmth. We rubbed our hands held over the coals to keep warm. There were a few hotel guests along, and a scattering of Rhodes residents. It was a cold, windless evening, and the sky flushed a deep rouge-pink as the sun dipped behind the mountains. Wine flowed and our guests were in high spirits.

After dinner we moved back to the lawn where Clay lit his evening cigar. It was a clear night, the sky awash with a silver splash of stars. I can't remember many more spectacular night skies up here, and I've seen a few. It was windless enough to enjoy being around the fire, chatting. Clay even lit a second cigar, and after the last of the ash fell off that we toasted the stars with a Cognac and threaded slowly to bed.

*

The drive back to Bloemfontein was pleasant in that we got the inside track on internet-banking security from Clay who is an authority on the subject. In fact, his business did nothing else. It's clearly an interesting and challenging science, even in modern times, and it struck me that (a) you can never be too cautious with bank cards, and (b) those controlling these things can never say their work is done. Tomorrow invariably brings a new cluster of threats and yet more challenges.

We had a flask along in the truck and sipped coffee at all the road stops. There were five of them; we won two and lost three, meaning we at least passed through two without a mandatory coffee stop. It was a matter of luck.

Although their visit was short, Clay and Robin let us know they were interested in a return trip. They said a heap of good things about the trout in the Eastern Cape Highlands, and coming from Clay who owns a long stretch (in fact, the longest privately owned stretch) of the River Test, it said plenty about how much he'd enjoyed the visit. Robin, on the other hand, just loves South Africa and its fishing, no matter where, no matter what for.

We saw them off at the airport, then stopped at a delightful hamburger joint where we got burgers and chips and, unusual for places like this, a more than reasonable coffee. We had an uneventful drive back, arriving at *Birkhall* a little after 7pm when darkness was closing in. Basie was away on business but due back later that evening, and Carien had kindly kept dinner for us, thick slices of meat carved from a leg of lamb they'd had for lunch, served with cold roast potatoes and a salad. Robin had donated some of the leftover liquor to Dave Walker and we had kept the rest, so we weren't short of a glass of wine, or an after-dinner Cognac.

*

Our fishing felt a little flat after Robin and Clay had left, but we enjoyed the fact that things, like the number of fish we happened to catch on any particular day or how big the fish were, or what the weather was doing, now suddenly made little difference. On the river we could even park off in the shade of a tree and take a nap if we felt like it, or spend the morning tying flies rather than fishing. But these would have been scant rewards had both our guests not enjoyed themselves. Their trip had been a success because we didn't blank on a single day, no rods or legs were broken, and nobody got hit by lightning.

I did, on reflection, feel for the brave people who run fly-fishing trips professionally. The pressures on them must be relentless, week in and week out, and that pressure will come in any number of guises. Will your client catch a few decent fish – at least enough to make him happy with the arrangements? Will the weather hold? Will a client lose an important piece of gear, like a reel, a wallet or a passport? For us it was a lot easier because Robin and Clay are friends, not paying clients. That took much of the performance pressure off us, because when an angler isn't paying for the fishing he won't likely end up moaning if the fish are small, or if one day's thundery weather follows another.

But having said all that, looking after two people on rivers and lakes for five days is a responsibility, and it's also work, no matter how pleasant it all turns out in the end.

*

Our stay at *Birkhall* was relaxed and easy-going, a mix, as it turned out, of fly tying on the veranda, fishing the rivers and, for Billy, a spot of bow hunting in the hills behind the house. He got dressed in full camouflage kit, even daubed war paint on his face. He looked like a sniper from a Korean War movie, and he stalked the mountains from first light till mid-morning for two days in a row. Despite all this he never managed to get a shot at a wildebeest or a blesbok. He said they had eyes in the back of their head, and he never once got within the mandatory seventy-metre range he needed to let an arrow go before some animal blew his cover. I felt desperate for him given all the preparations and belly-crawling involved. It easily matches the complex machinations we fly fishers get up to, but at least we always get to cast a fly and we mainly catch a few fish.

We tried the Sterkspruit on *Birkhall* on the first day and did well under grey skies, and we also did well in the lake below the house, taking a few decent-sized rainbows. The weather never really lifted and heavy rain fell in the Sterkspruit catchment one night, which put the river out. So while Billy was up the mountain hunting, I took a slow drive up the Sterkspruit Valley, and found the river cloudy and unfishable all the way to its confluence with the Coldbrook. There I turned back. Had the Coldbrook not looked cloudy, I would have suggested to Billy that we fish it that afternoon.

The lake above *Birkhall* looked magnificent. Basie drove us up that afternoon in his Ford F150, a big, sturdy truck that gives a sense of being bulletproof. But while we were crossing what is normally a minor wetland we dropped up to the back axle in mud. The place had looked innocent enough, and in dry times it would be no more than a damp patch around a slow seep that drains off the mountainside. But after heavy rain it was a different story. It quickly sucked us in. Basie sent a message on his cellphone to get a tractor and, while we waited, I took a short hike up the inlet stream and wasn't surprised to find how well it was flowing and how fishable it looked, even if it's no wider than a city sidewalk.

Small fish were rising near the inlet, trout that had obviously left the tiny stream in which they had been spawned to take up residence in their new home. I thought wryly that in human terms that must have been like moving from a one-room apartment in the Bronx to an upmarket condominium in Manhattan. The water was clear, and I could easily make out the channels Basie had asked the contractor to excavate in the inlet shallows. We figured this would allow trout better access to the feeder stream for winter spawning, but it would also create deep, weed-free areas for us to fish.

The truck was well glued in mud, and as the tractor tried to drag the vehicle free, a sort of suction-effect formed under the chassis, pinning it down and slowing progress. I was expecting a sound like a Champagne cork popping when the F150 finally came unstuck, but it was more just a deep, mushy-sounding sigh.

*

The day before we left, we launched our float tubes on the lower *Birkhall* lake on a bright morning. A gentle breeze threw a ripple on the surface, and in no time smaller trout were taking our flies, dries and nymphs, on one of those days when it seemed clear that it didn't matter much what fly you had on because the fish were just dead hungry. They were trout shaped like little rain barrels and all around fourteen inches. I gently siphoned the stomach of one hen fish and found it packed with midge larvae. Most were your typically red bloodworms, but a few were pale-green larvae, some still alive and wriggling.

An hour later, by when we'd each taken plenty of young fish, Billy hooked a heavy rainbow in the shallows on a bloodworm imitation, a hen fish of around six pounds. He hooked another off virtually his next cast; while he was playing it, I hooked one that felt pretty good, also on a bloodworm. The fly line jolted to a stop in my slow retrieve, I struck, and the fish took off on a long run that took me deep into backing. Then it leapt clear of the water, but nowhere near where I thought it was. I reeled in as I paddled away from the fish furiously to regain contact, and when my fins hit firm ground I stood up and played the fish out in shallow water. Its condition was remarkable, but then this lake was one big soup kitchen. I didn't weigh the fish or measure it, but we agreed it was pushing seven pounds.

We left the water that morning when I could really only guess at the number of trout we'd caught. It was enough, though, to start feeling comfortably smug with our fishing skills and that sort of stuff. I came back to earth over a cup of coffee at the truck, and reminded Billy that my maiden aunt would probably have done pretty well on the day.

We left for lunch and to start the tedious task of packing.

*

It was a pleasant, gently paced stay. The weather had been awkward, but then we didn't know that the worst drought in living memory was about to grip this part of the world for the next two years.

The following morning we lazily packed up, then carefully went around checking we hadn't left anything. I was methodical and finally I confidently ticked the 'nothing left, all packed' box. We had a typical *Birkhall* breakfast and said our farewells to Carien and Basie. Then, slowly and sadly, the truck crunched down *Birkhall*'s driveway, shuddering at the thought of the big dose of tar fever waiting for us out there, just starting the 1,100-kilometre drive to Cape Town. It turned out to be a pleasant trip – in fact, one of the best I can remember – as good as you can hope for given that there is only so much to enjoy when you swap a lovely, river-filled place for endless stretches of monotonous tar. We were home before 9pm.

Somewhere en route my cellphone rang. It was Carien. She read out a list of the stuff we'd left behind. I thanked her. She laughed and said, 'Nothing changes!'

The Swith Stream

CHAPTER 18
FISHING ALONE

Nick did not like to fish with other men on the river.
Unless they were of your party, they spoiled it.
ERNEST HEMINGWAY, *BIG TWO-HEARTED RIVER*

The Sterkspruit below Lindisfarne Bridge

There are two gated paddocks on both sides of the road just before the Lindisfarne Bridge crosses the Sterkspruit River. The paddocks make convenient places to park if you plan to fish the stretches above and below the bridge, both interesting but dissimilar sections of river, and both private. The stream here has some gradient, with a mixed tapestry of quick riffles and runs and invitingly deep pockets along the banks, and there's a decent pool at the bridge, and even better ones just upstream of it around a corner of headland.

It was a Monday at about 3pm; a Monday that carried none of the barb you usually associate with the first day of the week, though on *Birkhall*, every day of the week feels barbless. The only barbed day is the one circled in my diary to remind me when I'm due to head home.

I parked the truck in one of the paddocks and dropped the tailgate. Swallows swung swift patterns over the pool below the bridge. Maybe I would be lucky and bump into a decent mayfly or caddis hatch, though a cold wind rippled my shirt and the sky was leaden, so hatches seemed unlikely. I strolled down to the bridge pool. I saw no insects and no rises, yet the swallows were hawking something off the surface with precision. Time and again their bills glanced the water in swooping flight. Whatever was hatching was that tiny I couldn't see it, but as my friend Hugh Huntley used to say, 'You can't fool a swallow. Just tie on something small, like size 26 small.' He used to add that fishing hatches like this if you could see your fly on a short cast it was probably too big.

I set up a bamboo rod, a sweet-casting Dugmore 3-weight, and in deference to the hint the swooping swallows offered, I tied on a size 18 One Feather CDC Midge. I didn't have any 26s.

By the time I was done, pale sunlight was filtering through gaps in the clouds, coating the stream in a silvery sheen. I crossed the river at the shallow outlet below the pool, then headed downstream, walking along a rocky bank, just far enough away from the water to keep my shadow off it. At the first bend, about a hundred metres below the bridge, I crossed the river again through cold, knee-deep water, hauled myself up a steep, earth bank, and continued walking downstream on a sheep path. From the path I kept half an eye on the river, stopping occasionally at the good spots to search the runs from up on the bank, using the willows to hide me. The river was flowing perfectly, and the water was clear enough to imagine I would spot trout easily if they were around.

I eventually found two fish holding near a bank. They would occasionally move out to take something in the current. I slid quietly into the stream below them, then waded into range and dropped the midge near the bank. It drifted quickly in the threads of current, its small orange post glowing in the half-light filtering through the branches. After a few decent but fruitless drifts, I changed to a small nymph and immediately hooked one of the fish I'd seen. I had no indicator on, but the leader moved so far and so fast, your maiden aunt wouldn't have missed the take. I sometimes don't bother with an indicator when I know where feeding fish are holding, when there's more than a hint of certainty to the outcome. I feel confident enough that I will read leader movement, or see the flash of a turning fish, or glimpse the white of its mouth.

I hooked the second trout, but it got off in one magnificent leap that left my leader partially stuck in clawing bramble branches growing along the riverbank.

I moved slowly upstream, wading on a sandbar that ran up the centre of a long stretch with deep pockets on both banks, pitching an unweighted nymph into likely spots, letting it drift, occasionally working the fly, and by the time I'd reached the bend where I'd crossed the river earlier, I had taken three more trout and missed a few. The first hour's fishing had been cold and windy, but pleasant. Settled on a convenient rock, I ate a sandwich and did some thinking. I could have done with company, but at least I wasn't talking to myself just yet. When you're alone on a river, talking to yourself isn't a sign you're going crazy. It's when you don't agree with what you say that you need to get worried.

*

Fishing alone, and this is a personal view, hasn't got much more going for it other than you are at least out fishing, which importantly means you aren't bored and you aren't working. I do know some people who prefer to fish alone (though my list isn't long), and they aren't real misanthropes either. I simply notice they fish a lot in their own company. Of interest, it seems the author and fly fisher Thomas McGuane enjoys fishing alone and, from what

I've read, so did Theodore Gordon, who was variously a hermit and the father of the American school of dry fly fishing.

I guess you could argue that the real solitary fishing experience favours your chances of slipping into a deep contemplation about the true meaning of life, though for me it doesn't. I tend to immerse myself in what I'm doing and don't easily lapse into any serious internal dialogue, say, about the parlous state of the world, the increasingly obvious indicators of my own mortality or the times I've really screwed up in life – which, come to think of it, may all be important reasons we go fishing in the first place. Angling has a nice way of wrapping you in a seemingly timeless, unthreatening present, like a temporary release from reality, but you don't need to be alone for that to happen. It even happens when you are fishing in company.

I suppose the most you could say for fishing alone is it lets you move at your own pace, be it slow to semi-comatose, or brisk and racy. There's no-one to tell you when to leave or that you can't take a nap, and fetching your own flies out of trees is better than fetching a pal's. These are mildly liberating virtues, but on balance, most of us – outside of the committed loners and the true misanthropes – would probably opt for company on a trout stream, if only because it's more pleasant to share an experience than to live it alone, and because who otherwise will believe you caught that hog from an impossible hole on a size 20 dry fly on a perfectly executed first cast?

The last thing I want to say in favour of fishing alone is that it's easier without company to take an unnoticed, self-indulgent nap. I don't only do this when the fishing's slow, or when I'm bored or recovering from a late night. I find that trout streams are soporific places, though they're more soporific when your night *was* a late one. I also find that the stitch and thread of nature is equally soporific, like the hypnotic humming of bees around flowers, so it's natural at times to choose a patch of shade-cooled grass, lie down, tilt your cap over your nose, fold your hands behind your head, shut your eyes, listen to the softly sibilant sounds of the sliding stream and just let sleep steal over you.

*

On this particular day I never did catch a hog from an impossible hole on a perfectly executed cast. But by the time I got back to the truck I had taken a few trout, one a really tidy fish of sixteen inches that I'd spotted sipping in a deep, couch-sized pocket of flat water on the side of a nice run. I took off the weighted nymph I was using, thinking the plop might spook the fish, and tied on a dry fly. On the first drift the trout missed the fly, a small Para-RAB, but it swallowed it boldly on the second.

I took my gear down, stowed my rod in its bag after carefully drying each section with a soft rag, and was just pouring coffee when the rain came down. It fell at a convenient angle so I could sit in the truck with the driver's side window wide open and not get wet. While I drank the coffee I enjoyed the pleasantly pungent, mulch-like smell that lifts off wet earth. The perfume of rainfall.

Then to the west there was a sudden break in the clouds, and sunlight flooded in that slowly turned into a soft, rouge-coloured sunset, which lit the distant hills and turned the bridge pool pink. But not a single trout rose. I swirled out my mug and was back in *Birkhall* in time for an early dinner; cold lamb and the remains of the sort of salad I'll never tire of – garden-grown lettuce, watercress picked from the furrow running through *Birkhall*, and thick slices of onion, tomato and pineapple.

The routines of Birkhall
I've got into a loose routine over the years on my visits to *Birkhall*. I'm up early, at about 6am. I pad into the kitchen, switch on the kettle, and add a heaped teaspoon of coffee to one of the mugs that

hang in the glass-fronted cupboard directly above the kettle. They are white mugs with big red polka dots on them. They have been in the kitchen ever since I can remember. I add farm milk, thick with cream, and a spoon of sugar. I sip the coffee and wait for Basie. Or else Basie has beaten me to it and he's there sucking on his pipe and exhaling clouds of blue smoke, his wet hair combed flat. The dogs are let out and they bark at the fading moon, the rising sun, whatever. They just bark. We talk farming or fishing, and then eat breakfast: eggs and bacon and sausages, toast and marmalade, more coffee. Then Basie is gone, Carien leaves on one of her endless errands, and I am alone. I have a hundred choices where to go fishing. Or I might write up my diary or set up my vice to tie flies on the veranda: perhaps a few more unweighted Easy Nymphs, or maybe a few Zaks with red-coloured glass beads, or One Feather CDC Midges, or RABs. Life here is richly coated with choices, all of them strung across lazy days that drift slowly by like sail ships in a light breeze.

On the Sterkspruit again
On Tuesday morning I decided to fish the Sterkspruit once more, for no better reason than there is a good stretch of it right below the farmhouse where I can park my truck close to the riverbank and be fishing with the minimum of hassle. Perhaps I just fish the Sterkspruit because when I'm alone I'm also less adventurous.

Whatever, this particular morning I pulled in under the shade of a willow, not more than a long cast from a lovely section of water upstream and down.

The river was fresh-looking, the morning sun reflecting off the serrated surface of a long riffle, making it dance with light. I set up my rod, this time a Boshoff bamboo, a 7' 9" 4-weight, and tied on a small size 16 Elk Hair Caddis, simply because it had come loose and was lying conveniently in my fly box. Besides, I thought, who knows, maybe it's an omen.

As a general rule, I find the fish in the Sterkspruit will often refuse large dry flies when they will rise to small-sized dries, something that applies to the middle reaches of the Bokspruit as well, though I've never really regarded my theory as more than something to bear in mind, nor have I come across anyone who backs it with equal conviction. Of course, once you believe smaller dry flies are the answer, your theory perpetuates itself because you end up never trying bigger dry flies, even though you know for sure that the truth lies somewhere in the middle; meaning that given the right day, both will work equally well or both will fail equally badly – or that if any rule in fishing is ever half-right some of the time, it is also half-wrong some of the time. In the end you just accept that angling is loaded with people's pet theories, and that most feed on shaky assumptions or some sort of homespun-wisdom, and that each of us pays homage to more than a few, including some of our own making. But on the Sterkspruit, I at least *usually* begin with a small dry fly pattern, meaning size 16.

I strolled downstream a long way and got into the river on a gravel bar circling below a run where sheets of smooth, pale-grey sandstone hang in a solid wall of rock running almost vertically along the far bank. I dropped the dry fly into the seam of current running close to the rock face, had a small trout on the first cast and another on the second, and that was pretty much the pattern – fish after fish, all small, all on an Elk Hair Caddis – until I reached the corner pool just a few yards below my parked truck. Here I found a poacher's rig, a forked stick, sunk into the earth. I pulled it out with some difficulty. Attached to it was a long piece of thick nylon with a large, bare hook tied on the end. The pool was alive with fish, and I guessed a poacher wouldn't really dent the population that much, even if he camped on this riverbank for a week. I broke the stick, cut up the nylon and stuffed it into my pocket. I took half a dozen rainbows on the dry fly without moving, the best around twelve inches.

Then I decided to rest the pool to try for a better fish on a deep-sunk nymph. I set up my camping chair in the shade of a willow and sipped coffee, as much from the need of it as to pass time. Around me the birdlife was busy and varied: a Bokmakierie was hawking in a nearby bush; a brace of Yellow-billed Duck swooped upstream; a Black-shouldered Kite hovered over a nearby field, holding dead still, only its wing tips trembling, seemingly attached to the sky by invisible threads. Then a tiny Malachite Kingfisher, as blue as a sapphire, perched for a brief moment on a branch on the far side of the river before it was gone like a brightly feathered arrow.

I rigged a small PTN below a weighted Zak, cast across the flow at the neck of the pool, and left the flies to sink and drift, flicking small mends into the line so that the core of the current washed the rig evenly downstream. At the end of the long drift, when the line had settled and was nearly static, I lifted the rod and was fast into a good fish of fifteen inches, easily the best of the day. It had taken the PTN.

From the corner pool, there's a dead-straight section of quick-flowing water for around two to three hundred metres, with riffles, pockets and deep little undercuts below the willows. I photographed this section of the river a day or two later when I was looking down onto it from a high point on the road that goes to Rhodes. The valley was flooded with early morning sunlight, the sky was a blue dome littered with plump pillows of white cloud, the river bright and resinous as barley candy. I took plenty of trouble over that photograph, and a large copy now hangs over the table in the *Birkhall* kitchen.

To fish this dead-straight section, I went back to a dry fly, a size 16 dun-coloured Mirage, one of Agostino Roncallo's patterns. It looked perfect on the water, riding just like a newly hatched mayfly, and it brought fish to the surface. Smaller trout took it with a hurried splash, but the better fish took it with a slow rise, and with an almost deliberate confidence. I find trout that rise unrushed and with assurance easier to catch; it's as if the deliberateness and confidence of these rises, the clear intent of them, somehow makes *you* more confident. You just have to remind yourself not to strike too soon or too sharply.

The rainbows I caught were in magnificent condition, something I've come to expect of the Sterkspruit's trout, regardless of the preceding season's weather. They weren't big by the benchmark up here, where sixteen- to twenty-inch fish are common enough. These were typically deep-sided trout, and strong and as iridescently coloured as the inside of an abalone shell. Even the little eight- and nine-inch fish were fat and chunky and as cheeky as terriers.

When I trudged back, I found the truck was still in the cool shade of the willow tree.

Coffee is something of an institution when I end a spell on a stream, and I poured the last of the flask into one of my pale-yellow enamel mugs that still carry a scratched and fading transfer of a trout in a net and the words, *Huntin, Fishin, Shootin – Rhodes Hotel*. Normally I'd be eking out the last of the coffee for two, maybe three people, which reminded me that's another advantage to fishing alone. You end up with coffee to spare.

By 2pm I was back at *Birkhall* with plans to spend the late afternoon on the upper section of *Branksome*, where the Sterkspruit runs through a poplar grove, flows under a bridge, and just above that, a pretty run ends in a weir of deep water. I only fish around three or four hundred metres of this stretch, from below the bridge to the weir, because the section is so full of features, structure and trout, it can easily soak up an entire afternoon. Near the end of the season, the river here is a tunnel of gold as the poplars and willows turn colour. In spring, it's a rush of greens, a cool, leafy place. You won't find many prettier sections of river water in this part of the world.

A wind had come in, blowing from the north, and slate-bellied cumulus clouds were piling up like fat cushions on the horizon. I hoped for rain, sure, but not quite at that moment. I walked down to the end of the poplars and began fishing up a wide reach of river that is more just riffles than runs, and the riffles are usually quite productive. The river is braided here, and it's never exactly the same two years in a row. Sometimes the better holding water is on the right bank, but some years the left bank is better.

There was no hatch and no interest in the dry fly, but the fish were keen on a nymph – small trout, eight to nine inches long – and I caught them dead-drifting short casts without an indicator. The strikes were typically bold jolts, so leader movement was easy to read. I say 'typically bold jolts', meaning that smaller trout somehow take a drifting nymph in quick water with a sharpness that is unlike the more measured, more subtle take of a bigger fish. Bigger fish don't jolt the leader as much as draw it under. But, of course, that's a guideline more than a hard rule.

In the slack water under the bridge I hooked a better trout. I checked the stomach contents: it was crammed with dark *Baetis* nymphs around size 16 to 20. I managed to take a photograph of the insects in the palm of my hand and a got a few shots of the fish in my net. Getting those photographs without help wasn't easy, and if it's a reason not to fish alone it's only a good one if you really are into cameras on rivers.

In the bubbly run below the weir, the fishing on the nymph was hectic, almost too good. I switched to a small DDD just for interest's sake, and that did nothing to slow down the action. There were a few twelve-inch fish in the mix, but most were smaller, though I can't say I enjoyed them any the less for it.

That night I spent a few minutes writing up my diary. At times it seems a chore, but the upside is that you get to relive your day, step by step, even question what you did or perhaps didn't do. And writing a diary the same night keeps me honest in a strangely roundabout way, in that the longer I take to write up the events of a day, the more I forget them and the more inclined I am to embellish things, or at least to paint a rosier picture.

The Coldbrook

I fished the upper Coldbrook stream alone one morning on the beat on Theuns Botha's farm, which starts under a buttress of tall, ochre-coloured cliffs that stretch for a few hundred metres. The bottom of the cliffs is made up of regular sandstone overhangs, but above the sandstone layer the cliffs are beautifully crenulated with long, apricot-coloured spires flecked with grey lichen. The whole effect is remarkably beautiful, the kind of backdrop fly-fishing photographers are drawn to like a magnet. One year we were there, a large raptor, its wings spread wide, appeared on the skyline floating just off the edge of the rock face, as if sent by God to purposefully gild the lily. Against the sun we couldn't be sure what the bird was; when we got a better view of it, we suspected it was a Long-crested Eagle. But I wouldn't have bet my house on it.

This far upstream, the Coldbrook is fine water, both in the literal and in the angling sense, meaning it is slender and see-through clear, and the fishing is good. It is as remote and as pretty a stream as you will find in this part of the world, though I'm happy to accept the upper Coldbrook may not be everybody's idea of great trout water. I know anglers who prefer rivers where the currents drag at their legs, and where they can bang out long casts with a chance of hooking trout over twenty inches. It comes down to personal preference.

The upper Coldbrook is best tackled with short casts, using the rod to make simple, Tenkara-style presentations that show only a few feet of fly line above the leader. There are a few long, mysteriously deep pools that you cover with conventional casts, but even in these, the trout won't average much over eight to ten inches. A fifteen- or sixteen-inch fish on this section is an occasion to pop the cork on a bottle of Champagne. As it happens, a few years ago I did indeed hook a trout of around sixteen inches up here. I was fishing with Phil Hills and Billy de Jong, and Champagne *did* come to mind, but only after we'd yelled and punched a few holes in the sky with our fists when I landed the trout.

So in the higher reaches, which aren't part of the Wild Trout Association (WTA) waters, this is a small stream, certainly no river, though I think of it as an Alaskan river in shrink-wrap and sometimes hold internal debates with myself on whether I've been any happier fishing anywhere else in the world than up this valley, at least on a good day with nice flows. There's a sense of compactness and completeness about a trout stream like this that has less to do with its depth and its flow, or the girth of its fish or the distance between its banks, and more to do with the fact that it is somehow perfect enough in itself to suck you in and saturate you in the tapestries and fragrances of its own kind of fishing – so much so, that in the moments I'm lucky enough to be on its banks, little else matters or gets to feel any better or more exciting. It's not something I can easily explain, but it boils down to the naturalness, the wildness, the remoteness, the beauty and the sparkle you find in some small streams that, when put all together, add up to a kind of perfection. And while you might get a few extra adrenaline jolts fishing in Alaska – not to mention jolts you might get through unexpected encounters with bears – I think most of us are happy fishing anywhere that's natural, beautiful and remote. Wherever that may be, I think you can only get happy up to a certain point, when happiness just can't escalate any more, no matter the size of the river you're on or the size of the trout you're catching. What would you call it? Maybe touching your fly-fishing-happiness threshold?

Last point. The WTA has a section of the Coldbrook, a beat just above the confluence with the Sterkspruit, that I have fished and found to be as charming as the private, upper beasts I write of here.

To get back to the fishing. The day was bright, and the Coldbrook looked easy and lovely. I splashed my truck through the drift where the stream flows over a narrow track that threads up this sparsely clad valley between hills covered with low scrub. I was parked near enough to the drift to hear the soft sound of the stream. I set up, swung under a fence, stepped into the back of a riffle and felt the cold water first heap against my legs, then run like fingers of ice through my boots. It would take ten minutes to get used to the sting, but when the day really warmed, the water would just feel pleasant and comforting.

The first run takes a sharp bend before spilling across the drift. I cast a Mirage dry fly into the run, the leader unfolded gracefully, and I sensed from the way the fly looked – sort of light and natural on the surface – that a fish would come to it. Just where the water deepened slightly, a really small trout took the fly in a swift rise and, on my second cast, another took it equally firmly. Both were small trout holding near the centre of the run, not under the tree-shaded bank where the main current ran deeper against the inside of the bend. So I drifted the fly tightly along the shadow, right under the grassy edge, hoping for a better fish. Nothing. I changed to a small, lightly weighted Zak, and when the leader held back for an instant, I had a fish, and later a second, both dark, fat and strong – and both, at ten inches, double the size of the first two I caught.

Then I noticed that I was talking to myself about the variable colours of stream trout. Not that it worried me. I think all anglers fishing alone are likely at some point to start talking to themselves. What I concluded in this discussion came as no revelation. I have come to the same conclusion a hundred times, and it goes along the lines that these last two fish were darker because they got less sunlight living under the shady bank, and they were fatter because the main seam of current flowed along that bank and carried more food to them.

When I finally got out of the stream, I'd taken plenty of fish. A couple were decent-sized trout, almost – but not quite – worth uncorking that bottle of Champagne for, and one was so heavily spotted I took a photograph of it held at arm's length. I also checked its stomach before releasing it. The contents were a rich soup of small, black *Baetis* nymphs, flying ants (also black), beetles, caddis pupae and one large dragonfly nymph. Yet this particular fish had taken a size 16 Mirage dry fly, a dun imitation, as if it had gone hungry all day.

That in itself was interesting from another point of view. Most of the fish I got took a dry fly or an emerger and yet, in the few stomachs I checked, I couldn't find an adult winged insect, with the exception of the ants I mentioned. Does that speak to some dietary preference that trout living in tiny, high-altitude freestone streams might have for winged insects whenever they can get at them, like mayfly duns or adult caddisflies or midges? It might. Or I should say, in a typical fly fishing-type answer to any imponderable, 'It depends.'

Our mayflies have briefer, less predictable hatching cycles than you find in American freestone streams or in the spring creeks and chalkstreams around the world. Although many mayfly species hatch at night and consequently go unnoticed by anglers, some hatch during the day, and no doubt make a juicy change in diet. I think that's a big part of what makes the dry fly so useful in this kind of mountain-stream setting – the appealing chance you give a trout to sup on the succulence of an adult mayfly and, with it, the chance for a nice change in diet.

The walk back along the dirt road to my truck took less than twenty minutes, yet I'd fished for three hours, covering two wide loops of the stream that eventually brought me to a fenced cattle-pen alongside the road where, if you imagine the letter 'S', all I had to do to get back was walk between the ends of the two curves of the 'S'. There was a satisfying sense of economy in this, in that actual fishing always beats hiking, especially at the end of a day. On the Smalblaar back home, when I fish Beat 2, I leave my truck at the weir and walk downstream along the highway, cross the little bridge over the Klip, a small tributary that can have trout in it at times, and then drop down a steep slope straight into the river. As beats go in the Western Cape, Beat 2 of the Smalblaar is long, a good five to six hours of hard going over boulders, the stream threaded with dragging currents – but at least when I'm done for the day, I can climb out of the river less than fifty metres from hot coffee and transport. It's the sort of arrangement that I smugly believe puts me nearer the top of the evolutionary ladder than the bottom, though I have to remind myself that when I was younger and fitter it didn't matter much either way.

On the walk back I was lost in thought, scuffing up dust with each step, hearing the steady, almost rhythmical, crunch of dry earth and stones under my boots, the rustle of dry grass, feeling the warm wind funnelling up through the valley. Dry grass, dust, stones, bare mountains, wind, cool water, trout. That's how it is up here; how we know it. These lean, parched landscapes may appear unlikely homes for trout, but trout have a long-established connectedness to them – even if the presence of these lovely fish up here still remains a little mysterious and even miraculous.

At the truck I poured coffee, opened a can of sardines and scribbled notes into the tiny wire-bound notepad I'd stuck in a pocket of my fly vest. I ate the sardines from the tin with the back of a knife, along with the few slices of pineapple and watercress that Carien had given me. It was a different lunch, but enjoyable. On the way out I called in on Theuns, but he and his family were away. Then I slipped a CD into the slot and had music all the way home.

Birkhall alone

There were occasional days during a stay one year on *Birkhall* when I had no choice but to fish alone, simply because when you're that near fishing it seems a sin to skip the chance just because you don't have a pal along. And when I'm staying there and not fishing, I constantly long to feel a fly rod in my hand, to see a line unfolding over the water, to savour the keen anticipation that comes with each drift and, of course, the delightful jolt of an occasional take, that sudden, exquisite moment that turns your blood electric.

Not much stands out about the two lone spells of fishing I did on this trip, other than for a morning on the Sterkspruit, when I saw a grasshopper land well ahead of me in the run I was fishing. It swirled in the currents, kicking circles in the water, floated right by me and a long way downstream until it was out of sight. A cast or two later, I took a solid trout on a deep-drifted Zak from the middle of the run the struggling grasshopper had just drifted through. In an obtuse way I hope my pal Ed Herbst reads a lot more into this than we all can rightfully claim to understand. He's an ant and hopper fanatic, and he sits on the sceptical side of the true value of Zak nymphs.

The second thing that stood out was not related to the fishing as much as to the simple joys of nature. I came to a promising run, loaded my fly rod to cast and immediately put up a Yellow-billed Duck that fled from the riverbank almost at my feet, dragging a wing in mock injury. Parting the grass, I found a well-concealed nest, still warm, with a cluster of cream-coloured eggs nestled in a bed of soft down. That discovery eclipsed any other that came my way that day. I have once before had a similar experience, when I was fishing with Tony Kietzman on *Branksome* in the gorge section. Both occasions were pattern perfect. When a Yellow-billed Duck suddenly leaves the riverbank dragging a wing in an unlikely upstream rush, all you have to ask yourself is where's she hidden her nest.

A jaunt to the Bokspruit

Let me end with a planned jaunt to the Bokspruit when I was due to fish with Mario Geldenhuys, a great rod builder and net maker, who at the last minute was unable to join me.

I fished the upper *Hillbury* beat of this lovely river alone, a beat that has a slightly different character to the higher beats of the Bokspruit in that the riverbed is more soft sand and gravel than hard sandstone and rocks.

I set up my rod, then discovered I'd left my fly box back at *Birkhall*. It didn't concern me because my fly patch was well stocked, although the flies obviously all had that awkward-shaped, buggy look that flies take on when they've been wet and left to dry on your vest patch over a few days, weeks or, in some cases, months.

The patch I use is the C&F model. It seals cleverly with a tight, plastic clip-down latch, and it's well ventilated. So while the flies didn't give the impression they'd just come off the vice, there at least wasn't any sign of rust around the hooks. I chose a RAB that looked like road kill, and in the first run I came to, a short, shallow, sandy-bottomed, unlikely-looking spot, I threw out a test cast to see how the fly would float – or more specifically, how it would look on the water. It was a crumpled mess, but an eleven-inch trout thought otherwise, swung out of nowhere and took it in a wink. Before the run came to an end I had taken three more trout on that same fly, and had christened it the 'Cripple RAB'.

And so the day went, with me changing flies only a couple of times, and then mainly from one 'Cripple RAB' to another, or to some other dry fly pattern that had once owned a pedigree but now looked like it permanently lived under bridges on the streets. They were all misshapen caricatures of the real thing but they never stopped working, no matter if they were once Elk Hairs, Para-RABs or Mirage dry flies. Maybe the fish were just hungry that day, or maybe we're missing the next great revelation in modern fly tying – 'The Theory of the Battered Fly'. After all, we all have cripple mayfly patterns in our boxes.

At midday, I sat on the bank in the fingers of shade thrown by a leafy willow, with a mug of coffee and a cheese-and-onion sandwich. I was debating in somewhat metaphysical terms, and allied to the potentially great 'cripple' revelation I referred to, the relative importance of precision and neatness in the flies we use, or, conversely, any added value that may be inherent in the very absence of it. I finally came to the conclusion that in some situations, namely fast-tumbling, freestone streams with a lot of wild trout in them, there could well be an advantage to using old, dried-out, untidy patterns, which probably comes down to trout preferring to take semi-hatched cripples because they're easier prey than mayfly duns just poised to take off on their maiden flight.

Then there is the less-convincing notion that untidiness in a fly might impart added movement or some additional trigger we may not have figured out yet. Would a regular, straight-from-the-vice RAB have done just as well on the day? I'm not sure, but the only way to find out would be to do a formal trial, where in the first month you only use flies that have dried over weeks on your fly patch, and then freshly tied flies for a month after that. But I suggest you keep it quiet. There's no knowing what people might start saying about you during that first month.

However interesting all this may be, I doubt that battered flies selected from your fly patch would consistently fool trout, especially not trout in the smooth-flowing, gin-clear waters of the world's pedigreed spring creeks, or those educated trout in testy chalkstreams like the upper Itchen or the Bourne. But it *is* food for thought, and I could have done with someone along with me just to offer an opinion. Alone in my musings, I jotted down some thoughts in my diary, but instead of making a few notes on a potentially enlightening new theory about the basics of attraction, I wrote a few words about the fickleness of trout.

The afternoon's fishing was equally interesting. Surface risers were absent, whereas in the morning, the occasional fish had spread rings on the surface. It may have been that the breeze had dropped or the steady buzz of bees added a kind of hypnotic lethargy, but the day became as still and quiet as a sleepy country village on a Sunday afternoon. Perhaps too still. After no response to the dry fly, I changed to a tatty Zak. A strip of loose peacock herl dangled awkwardly off its body. I left the fly as it was, and a short while later took a nice trout on it. After taking a few more, the fly was beyond shabby. The ribbing was loose and a long piece of black tying thread trailed from its thorax. Still, it took trout until it was in such poor shape that I'd lost confidence in it, or maybe thought the fly was that absurd that the whole exercise could turn into an uncomfortable mockery of the complex science of modern fly-pattern selection.

I was about to change to a less beaten-up Zak when, on a whim, I reeled in. It was well after 3pm and I'd had a decent day's fishing. I was also getting a little tired of my own company so, giving in to the sort of self-induced laziness that I suspect more easily conquers anglers who fish alone, I decided enough was enough and trudged back to my parked truck. With a companion along we would have probably fished out the rest of the day; the conditions clearly warranted it.

With an hour or two to spare, I drove across to Rhodes to visit Dave Walker. Chatting outside Walkerbouts Inn over a cold beer with half an eye on the hazy view of distant mountains, our conversation flowed along comfortably until the first signs of sunset warmed the western sky, then later flamed it into hot coals. The temperature dropped, and we moved inside. Three anglers were sitting at the pub, father and son along with the son's friend, all from upcountry. Naturally, they asked about my fishing, and later the discussion moved, as it inevitably does, to questions about what flies the trout were eating. With a suitably knowing look on my face, I answered honestly, 'Mainly cripples.'

The pub steadily filled with visiting anglers, and there was the usual cheerful background clamour of good-humoured banter, ever-expansive stories of fish lost or landed, the usual reflections on flies that worked and flies that didn't, stories of the day, stories from years back. A few village residents arrived, and later a couple of farmers, easily recognisable in shorts and khaki shirts, both big men with sun-scorched faces and hands that dwarfed their beer glasses. I noticed a few young anglers still wearing their caps with sunglasses perched rakishly on the brim, which is fly fishing's concession to modern fashion and as much a part of our dress code these days as the colourful blazers and scarves are part of the Oxford and Cambridge boat race. A fly box was brought out, the odd pattern selected, lifted to the light for careful scrutiny, admired, replaced. The talk turned to tackle, and someone left the pub to fetch a bamboo rod he'd recently inherited, while the steady procession of empty and refilled glasses fuelled the discourse. The rod arrived, a Hardy CC de France* in perfect nick, with dark Burgundy bindings on pale bamboo. It was admired and passed around as carefully as a loaded shotgun.

A short while later I stepped outside, called Carien and told her I wouldn't be driving back to *Birkhall* for dinner and would spend the night in Rhodes. I was enjoying the company. I got to thinking that a good collective noun for us fly anglers might be 'a communion of fly fishers'. Any takers?

---

* The Casting Club (CC) de France consisted of a group of anglers who met regularly at the Bois de Boulogne in Paris. Eventually, a regular casting tournament was arranged where extreme accuracy was required to drop a fly into small floating hoops set under overhanging branches alongside a wooded stream. Members of the club invited Hardy Brothers of Alnwick to design and produce a short, light bamboo rod suitable for this tournament. In 1910, JJ Hardy produced a 7' two-piece rod that weighed just over three ounces. He took it to the Casting Club de France, where he demonstrated precision casting. Hardy went on to market the rod commercially in 7', 8' and 9' lengths from 1911 to 1961.

CHAPTER 19
A MISCELLANY OF MUSINGS

I like the 'lawfulness' of the classic hatches, the technical problems of 'matching the hatch', accurate presentation, the avoidance of drag; but most, I think, I enjoy the incomparable rise, the abrupt opening of the stream, the dramatic splash, the electricity from stream, to eye, to hand.
NICK LYONS, *THE SEASONABLE ANGLER*

On fishing the dry fly with swallows and martins
We fished a local stream a short step ahead of a cold front. The wind was upstream, cold and gusty, the water temperature just 10°C, the trout scarce. But the upstream wind brought to mind a piece by Oliver Kite that I'd just read, where he said he felt blessed to have a downstream wind. I could only imagine that it had something to do with the wind not straightening the leader, leaving the tippet heaped a little, just enough to allow a longer drift before drag set in. It was an interesting observation, though, because we so often

preach the merits of an upstream breeze. You could argue that a gentle breeze doesn't matter much one way or another, but for the reasons I surmise from Kite's counterintuitive observation on the value of wind direction, we might be better off with a downstream zephyr. A downstream *wind* is a different thing.

There were various mayflies around (duns and imagos), including the very beautiful mayfly *Adenophlebia dislocans* of the *Leptophlebiidae* family, a bold, darkly-pied mayfly that you never find in great numbers, but when they are about their characteristic boldness is striking. They'll happily sit still for a close-up photo.

Early in the day, Brown-throated Martins flew over the river in loops so tight and fast my eye could hardly follow them. One suddenly appeared in my peripheral vision as a dusty-grey flash swooping at my dry fly and, with its suddenness, I struck, the way you strike instinctively at anything out of the ordinary and sudden on Cape trout streams. The strike snatched the fly away, but in a steep turn the bird was back, swooping at the run again in search of the bug. The fly pattern – not that it's important – happened to be one of Kite's Hawthorns. Or maybe the pattern was important, because I changed it just then and didn't raise another martin. The interlude brought to mind a stanza from a poem by DH Lawrence:

Dark air-life looping
Yet missing the pure loop…
A twitch, a twitter, an elastic shudder in flight
And serrated wings against the sky,
Like a glove, a black glove thrown up at the light,
And falling back.

Of course, Lawrence was writing here not of swallows but of bats, which spoils the story a little, though in the same poem he does refer to swallows:

Look up, and you see things flying
Between the day and the night;
Swallows with spools of dark thread sewing the shadows together.

Not four days after this encounter with martins I was back with Robin Douglas, this time on a little-known Western Cape mountain stream. Robin had never fished as far into the gorge as we went this day. I know the stream well, and the higher you climb the better-looking, the clearer and certainly the testier the runs and glides become.

The breeze was gently upstream, the flow was perfect and the fish were hungry. It was dry fly only. Wildflowers were out in profusion, and a scattering of those beautiful mayflies, *Adenophlebia dislocans*, showed up again, but this time no martins were sweeping the runs.

It was a fifty-fish day for us, and I'm not making that up. In fact, we might well have had more than fifty. Neither of us was counting. And we missed a heap of takes, and snapped off more than a few flies on our hair-fine tippets.

The next day Robin called to say he was hobbling around stiff and muscle-sore after the hike. I sympathised and told him I felt far worse.

A team of stillwater flies
Arthur Cove wrote a useful book on stillwater trout fishing, *My Way with Trout*. You will likely know of him. He was one of the most celebrated stillwater fly fishers of his time, and a pioneer and specialist on nymphing lakes.

In his book, Cove describes his version of the PTN, tied along the lines of Frank Sawyer's well-known nymph but with no tail and a thorax of dubbed rabbit underfur. Many describe the pattern as one of the most successful stillwater nymphs of all time; certainly it was on English reservoirs like Grafham and Rutland.

The book tells us that this fly was clearly well ahead of its time. But what interested me more was his categorical statement that a team of flies would out-fish a single fly in stillwaters under all circumstances. He mainly used three flies, and says he hardly ever lost a fish because the second or third fly snagged in weed. The only risk he mentions is a trout taking a free fly when you are already playing a fish on one of the other flies in the team, but that only happened, he says, on rare occasions in his lifetime of fishing.

His most interesting development was his Red Diddy, a bloodworm imitation, tied with a red rubber band fastened to the top of a hook shank with red thread. The secret was to shave away a small section of the rubber nearest the shank to give the rubber movement, almost a hinged effect.

On fishing stillwater patterns Cove says, and I quote:

There are few actual nymphs that are true swimmers, so most of us reservoir fishermen probably fish our imitations too fast anyway. I noticed that although the bloodworm lashed about a lot in the water they never made any real progress through it and, like most of the other non-swimming nymphs, they were really at the mercy of wind and drift.

Certainly food for thought. And cause to slow down retrieves.

On leaders and tippets and presenting the dry fly:
a series of compromises and an imponderable
The need for fine tippets at times, say 7X or 8X, is unquestionable, but they don't turn over well in windy conditions, especially fishing weighted nymphs or bushy dry flies. Heavier tippets, on the other hand, are more visible and technically more prone to induce drag. Long leaders, say 16 feet and over, again have advantages in many

situations, but they also don't turn over well in wind, and are obviously tricky to handle on tight streams.

So far so good, but what really intrigues me in this end-tackle stuff is the debate about floating the tippet for dry fly fishing. Some are for it, some against. For example, on the small mountain streams in the Western Cape, Ed Herbst always greased his tippet down to the fly because it made no sense to him to drown his dry fly as he pulled it out for the back cast, which is what happens when the tippet sinks. Ed has strong support for floating tippets from Peter Hayes, author of *Fly Fishing Outside the Box*, but many fly fishers hold the contrary view that dry fly tippets should sink.

Feeding into all this, I came on Roy Christie's rationale for tying flies with a parachute hackle at the bend of the hook, something he's since become known for internationally. Roy, now living back on his home waters in Northern Ireland, says, 'The design came into existence due to fish not eating floating flies while the tippet remained afloat attached to the dry fly. When the tippet sank four to six inches away from the fly, they would swim back over and eat the fly they had previously refused.'

This, Christie says, led him to design a floating nymph with the parachute hackle at the bend, which, in theory anyway, sinks the tippet on impact with the surface.

Personally, when I'm fishing dry flies, whether on freestone streams or chalkstreams, I never bother much whether the tippet floats or sinks. I suspect the most you can reliably advise on end tackle is to use fresh, good-quality, limp material, and then the longest leader and the finest tippet conditions will allow; where 'conditions' include the average size of the fish, the clarity of the water, and the strength and direction of the wind. After that, it all boils down to a series of compromises. That much is easy, but I suspect the floating versus the sinking dry fly tippet debate has far from run its course.

Observations learned from the old lady on the step

I want to digress for a moment, but bear with me because I think there's an important fly-fishing lesson here. It goes like this.

I walk my Jack Russell Polly every evening for about an hour through the streets of Newlands, the suburb where Kathy and I live in Cape Town, and I've got to know the streets pretty well. There's one particular spot where the road climbs a fairly steep hill that's 110 metres long. The road ends at the top of the hill in a T-junction. In the late afternoon, an old lady often (but not always) sits on the low front steps of her house at the apex of the T-junction, where she's looking directly down the hill. She sits about two metres behind a railed metal gate. She's almost always dressed in a purple-grey nightgown and she, and the steps of her house, are in deep shade by late afternoon when the sun is coming straight at me from behind Table Mountain. Why she chooses to sit alone in this strange place just staring down a mostly empty road I have no idea. But when I get to the bottom of the hill and turn into the road, I always look for her, because I marvel at how the shade, the face-brick exterior of her house, the metal railings of the gate and the drab, purple-grey nightgown she wears can totally camouflage her.

So it became a personal challenge to me to see whether I could see if the old lady was sitting on her steps behind the gate as soon as I entered her road 110 metres away. (Yes, I have paced this all out exactly. That's been a pivotal part of the exercise.)

At first, I often did not see her until I was less than forty metres away. But here's another essential point. She occasionally moves her hands. These are brief, rapid, wringing movements, but they stand out so much that even if I couldn't actually see her, I'd know she was there, even from as far as seventy-five metres away.

I became so intrigued with all this that on a walk with my wife Kathy I asked if she could see the old lady when we got to the bottom of the hill. She couldn't; not until she was thirty metres

414

away, when she saw the old lady's hands move. Nothing else had given her away up to that point.

Then Tony Kietzman visited us in Cape Town, and I took him on my walk specifically to find out whether he could see the old lady. As we turned the corner at the bottom of the hill, 110 metres from her, I looked up and immediately knew she was there. Tony could not see her. By now I was noticing that it wasn't only the movement of her hands that gave her away, but just the pale, contrasting colour of her hands. Tony only picked her up at around fifty metres away, when she moved her hands, and he was intrigued with the exercise.

Over three or four months I honed my skills at finding her, in much the same way that, over the years, my skills at finding trout have evolved and been honed. And it all comes down to deciphering abstract patterns of colour, light, shade and movement and reading these, or rather interpreting them, as a trout – or in this case, as an old lady behind a gate. This was something that at first I was unable to do and, months later, could do easily, even at 110 metres.

The message for anglers is simple: in clear streams, rapid movements of your hands or arms and the contrasting effect of light colours, especially the colour of your clothing, give you away to fish. I've seen people spook trout for exactly these reasons many, many times. In contrast, drab-coloured clothing, shade, the absence of sudden movements and the nature of a broken, neutrally coloured background will all serve to protect you.

Equally, if you are looking into a piece of water in the hope of finding a trout, look for movement, look for contrasting patterns, but above all, understand that *it takes time* to learn the visual messages each stream sends you, and it takes practice. In the case of the old lady, it took me four months or longer to fully interpret the meaning of the particular mosaic of shapes and shades and patterns and movements that now give her presence away to me so easily.

If you persist, as I did, you will become good at interpreting various visual images that, at first, have no meaning to you at all. I have learnt much from this mysterious old lady about the art and science of spotting trout. I now realise that when I see a trout that others can't see, the difference is that I am interpreting not a trout, but *patterns* I have learnt over years of application, years of searching riverbeds, and that what I'm seeing is mainly not anything like a plainly evident trout, or an old lady sitting on a step, but a particular combination of movement, shades of colour and contrasts, that mix in my mind and that, after years, my brain eventually interprets as a particular thing – a trout, or in her case, an old lady.

Abstract for sure. And that, as they say, is the lesson for the day.

Just recently she bought herself a salmon-pink nightgown. Kind of spoiled the fun. But I'm glad to see that, of late, she has returned to the old one.

So what has Wordsworth's poem 'Tintern Abbey' got to do with fly fishing?

I recently came across what I think is the best opening sentence in any book on fly fishing. It's from Steven Meyer's *San Juan River Chronicle: Personal Remembrances of One of America's Best-known Trout Streams*. Here's the sentence:

> My house rests on the border between two worlds – two worlds as different as ice and fire – that are connected to each other by clear running water and trout.

And that got me wondering about the best opening chapter of any fly-fishing book I've read. Not an easy call, but I ended up voting for Nick Lyons's *Bright Rivers: Celebrations of Rivers and Fly-fishing*. In the opening chapter 'Gray Streets, Bright Rivers', Lyons examines the value of his life on trout streams by comparing it to his life in New York, much as Wordsworth did in his haunting poem 'Lines Composed a Few Miles Above Tintern Abbey', when he used the peace and calm he'd experienced during his visits to the abbey on the restful banks of the River Wye to comfort himself during the five long years he spent in the 'din of towns and cities'.

It is a beautifully written piece, and in many ways Lyons, with equal grace and insight, sums up the predicament of fly fishers who must daily balance the wish to be set free on a trout stream or a seashore, against being stuck in a cramped, high-rise office or in mind-numbing city traffic.

To make his point, Lyons cleverly weaves in a few lines from Wordsworth's poem. But first, let's read what Nick has to say of his life in New York:

> I do not want the qualities of my soul unlocked only by this tense, cold, gray, noisy, gaudy, grubby place – full of energy and neurosis and art and anti-art and getting and spending – in which the business part of my life, at this time in my life, must necessarily be lived. I have other needs as well. I have other parts of my soul.

And then, in contradistinction, here are Lyons's thoughts on rivers and fishing:

> Nothing in the world so enlivens my spirit and emotion as the rivers I know. They are necessities. In their clear, swift or slow, generous or coy waters, I regain my powers; I find again those parts of myself that have been lost in the cities. Stillness. Patience. Green thoughts. Open eyes. Attachment. High drama. Earthiness. Wit. The Huck Finn I once was.

I catch the quick turn of a yellow-bellied trout in the lip of the current. Five trout in loose formation, in a pellucid backwater where I cannot get at them. A world. Many worlds.

> *...oft, in lonely rooms, and 'mid the din*
> *Of towns and cities...*

As Wordsworth said in 'Tintern Abbey', about the calming nature of the countryside he still felt, but no longer could actually live in,

> *...I have owed to them*
> *In hours of weariness, sensations sweet,*
> *Felt in the blood, and felt along the heart...*

Yes, I owe rivers that. And more.

Lyons is a wonderful writer. Paul Schullery, author of *American Fly Fishing: A History*, said of him, 'Nobody in the American history of fly fishing has had as positive an influence on the literature of fly fishing as he has.'

As for my own favourite rivers, well, they are to me the liquid temples from which I increasingly draw spiritual strength. I suspect the same might go for you.

And still the winds blew...
The weather in Cape Town was tourist-perfect for a few days, right up until Robin Douglas and I fished recently, when the doors that hold back the Cape's most ripping southeasters suddenly swung open, windows rattled, branches broke, leaves blew into the heavens, and the cerulean blue skies we'd briefly enjoyed turned smoky-grey and suggested rain was imminent. We went out anyway, onto the lower beats of the Lourens River, probably on the old premise that some fishing is better than none.

In time, the sun did come through and turned the sky a lovely blue that was shot through with the white lace of streaky clouds. But still the wind blew, straight downstream, so hard that even with short, sharp, tight-looped casts, our flies often landed well behind the tip of the fly line.

I thought of Ed Herbst when I saw *Simuliidae* (black fly) larvae on riverbed stones, the larvae leaning with the current in serried ranks like soldiers on parade. Wolf spiders scurried over the rocks (I still feel sure that, at times, trout take the Para-RAB for a water spider), swallows and martins swung circling loops over the stream, and the occasional fish rose. But in the unremitting wind, the fishing was hard-going, although we landed a few trout.

I tested the stomach contents of one fish and, as expected, *Baetis* mayfly nymphs were plentiful, as were adult black-fly larvae. But so were winged flying ants.

On a nearby rock we found hordes of adult black flies, and the shuck of a hatched dragonfly nymph at least two-and-a-half centimetres long. An imitation tied on a long-shank, size 8 hook would have worked, but we weren't that pressed for a fish at the time.

Try as I might, I could not get a trout to take any interest in Ed's latest black-fly larva pattern, which has a more pronounced waist than the natural, almost a Coke-bottle shape.

When we had threaded enough casts between brief lapses in the wind, had taken a few fish and had covered what felt like miles of water, we headed out to fish another section of the stream we thought might be more sheltered. On the ride over there, the tip of Robin's 2-weight Sage snapped, despite taking our rods apart and laying them in the back of the truck with what we thought was adequate care.

And still the wind blew, showering us in tumbling gusts of fine dust and leaf debris, wind so strong that at times we felt we could lean against it without falling over.

I must just add that if Ed's revised black-fly imitation went untouched on the day, it doesn't mean it isn't a promising pattern. I believe it is, and I will be posting a few to my pal Nick Taransky in

Australia and to Ian Douglas and Hugh Rosen, both in California, to spread the R&D net a little wider.

Fishing for stippled beauties with Andrew Fowler
Recently I fished with Andrew Fowler, who wrote the delightful book *Stippled Beauties: Seasons, Landscapes and Trout*. We were on a low, glassy stream under a cloudless sky. Because he was new to Cape waters I had hoped for better conditions; a few more inches of flow, less brightness, less of the sharp, gusty downstream breeze. (Breeze? It was actually wind, and it played havoc with our long leaders and ruled out any chance of using my delicate Sage 0-weight.)

But we had some moments straight from the mould of small-stream perfection, in that a few good trout were out feeding, dancing lightly, holding shallow over assorted mosaics of riverbed pebbles, the fish so clear to see and so ridiculously close that as we spotted them, we instinctively froze and held our breath.

We could easily have been skunked, but fortunately there were sporadic hatches – mountain midges and a tiny mayfly dun – so the fish were keen enough to come to the surface. By the time we called it quits, Andrew had landed half a dozen small trout, missed as many and lost a couple, one a real honey that snapped him off.

On our walk out, the fynbos was alive with wildflowers, including purple watsonias, blood-red ericas and butter-yellow irises. We are blessed in many different ways with our fishing in the Western Cape.

The value of purple
In search of a little angling communion, Robin Douglas and I sat around a table in his home recently, along with Ed Herbst and Gordon van der Spuy, and tied flies. I showed Robin how to wrap a Zak, and Gordon demonstrated a new dry fly pattern he calls

the Pardón de Meana, tied with CDC feathers and Coq de Leon hackle fibres. The pattern is a variation of one originally attributed to Luis Meana Baeza, a Spanish friend of Gordon's who is an expert on these rare and exquisite hackles.

But to return to the Zak, I am fussy about the way the Zak is tied because good ones outperform any other nymph I've ever used. Even the purple tinsel is important to me, the Fil Metallisé 4021, so I was intrigued the other day to read an article by Peter Gathercole about fishing a high-lying loch in Scotland where the trout 'crawled' all over his friend's fly – a Dabbler-style pattern with a tail of purple floss – while he couldn't seem to bless himself with a touch. He eventually borrowed one from his friend and immediately hooked fish.

Gathercole ends by saying that, although he had never been keen on using purple in a trout fly, this experience changed his mind!

Peter Gathercole, by the way, is also the author of three fly-tying books: *Fly Tying for Beginners, The Handbook of Fly Tying* and *The Fly-Tying Bible*.

The Sterkspruit on Birkhall

The other day I saw a photograph taken on the Sterkspruit River a year or two ago, and immediately recognised the run. I was fishing that exact spot a few years back, on a sunny day when the water was bright and the river low and extremely clear. A rainbow rose to my orange poly yarn indicator on the edge of a current seam, in no more than a foot of water.

There's no real revelation in that, except that I estimated the fish to be at least twenty inches. I had no small Yellow DDDs or egg patterns, but I did have a well-tied, brightly coloured hopper pattern after Ed Herbst's style. He may well have tied it himself. I rose the fish. It hovered long seconds under the fly, inspecting it, but in the end it took the hopper pattern, and I hooked it firmly. As it cartwheeled into the air, I confirmed my guess about its size. It was at least twenty inches, and then I lost it as I tried to check its downstream run for cover. There's no real revelation in that either.

The revelation was in the slow, languid rise of that fish and its sub-surface mix of glowing colours, because for a few exquisite and transitory moments, while it hung beneath the hopper, it was a silvery-green medley of liquid tones that briefly tinged pink in the sunlight. After sipping the fly, it took off with its beauty, downstream into the deepest seam of the current and was gone.

On a good day, there is such wonderful fish and such wonderful fishing in this river.

Tackling trickles

I fished last year with Robin Renwick on a hot day, the stream as low and glassy as I've ever seen it. Fortunately there was flow enough to carry our dry flies, and plenty of small rainbows rose to the tiny Para-RABs we fished on 20' leaders and 8X tippets. But we were mighty thankful for the upstream breeze. Without that helpful little zephyr, we might have closed shop and headed home.

I found two decent-sized rainbows that were so easy to see I cursed aloud for not bringing my camera. Robin fished over the first of them and got the fish to lift to his dry fly, but at the last moment it refused and darted off. The second fish, even bigger, was sitting out so clearly that it looked mildly ridiculous. I decided our best chance to get it was to change from the RAB to a small CDC dry fly, but when I looked up after changing the fly, it was gone. Maybe it caught a bit of rod-flash, or perhaps it was spooked by the shadow of a bird that just then chose to fly upstream.

These low, glassy, sighted-trout conditions always make me nervous. They demand technically bulletproof approaches. As a minimum, you need a long leader (18 to 20' ending in an 8 or even 10X tippet), and preferably a fresh, size 18 CDC dry fly (because they land so gently). If the trout is nymphing, I will trail the simplest size 20 nymph an arm's length below the dry fly. I have a standby. I cover a size 20 hook shank with black silk, rib it with ultra-fine wire and put a single turn of peacock herl behind the eye. I wet the nymph well before I cast so that there is no doubt it will sink the moment it lands on the water.

Later Robin took two nice trout, neither of them on a trailing nymph because he doesn't like the idea, but on a One Feather CDC Midge, and we left the stream counting our blessings.

A tenuous trickle of water…

Robin Douglas and I visited our favourite mountain stream the other day and, in the space of a morning's fishing, only managed to spook one trout all of six inches. The stream was a wafer-thin thread, a tenuous trickle of water, the result of relentless weeks of high temperatures, hot winds and no rain.

In places we could almost straddle the runs, and the waving emerald-green fronds of algae made wading potentially lethal.

We stuck to our task, stringing sneaky casts into miniaturised, shrunken spots, using long leaders and as much guile as we could.

Then a young man and his girlfriend appeared in the stream behind us, out on a romantic hike. We exchanged pleasantries then, with a cheerful wave, they left, walking straight through the run we were about to fish. That's when we sat back in the shade of a wild almond tree, ate lunch, retired the fishing and hiked out. It was the first time I've been totally skunked on a Cape stream in I don't know how long. At least the stones in the riverbed were still crawling with nymphs, despite the desperately thin flows. So, with a little rain, this stream and its trout will soon enough reinvent themselves to again illustrate one of nature's minor miracles.

Fishing stillwaters at a snail's pace

I found myself once again reading Paul Miller's delightful book *Secret Creek*. In one chapter, he deals with fishing the static midge pupa, or more correctly a team of them, which I found quite interesting. He first encountered the technique on Lake Eucumbene in New South Wales, Australia, in 2004, when the angler he was with took five fish on the static midge while everyone else struggled to land a single trout. His midge patterns were tiny and apparently 'insignificant looking' (just black thread on a size 12 to 16 hook, with a dubbed rabbit's fur collar), and the rig was simple as well. The three flies were tied five feet apart on a 16-foot fluorocarbon leader (I assume level), each fly hanging about eight inches or so off the leader. They were fished static in the wind drift and, when the drift was over, the top fly was 'dibbled' for a few moments on the surface before casting again. This apparently often provoked a take, and was the reason Miller suggested that a 10' rod would be useful for its added leverage.

The method is not new, and it remains deadly if executed well. I have tried to find the origins of it, but so far I haven't come up with an answer I trust. I suspect it was developed in the UK, likely in large reservoirs like Grafham, Rutland or Blagdon, and possibly by competition anglers. Or maybe it was just perfected by them.

There is one reference to the origins of fishing static midge pupa imitations, though, that I enjoyed, if only because I could have done it myself, at least back in the days when I still smoked. It's in Frank Sawyer's book *Nymphs and the Trout*, published in 1956. Apparently he'd cast out a small midge imitation and had then put his rod down in the grass on the bank to light a cigarette. He was about to take his first draw when he saw his fly line moving. He dropped the cigarette, hooked the fish, landed it, then had to stamp out the grass fire he'd started around his feet. But the incident had at least alerted him to the virtues of fishing the static midge.

Then by chance, Murray Pedder, a highly regarded South African fly tier, referred to a similar tactic with midges in an edition of *The Complete Fly Fisherman* magazine, where he advocated using an indicator (as do many UK writers on this subject), and said the method works best on windy days (I think possibly because the chop on the water imparts a gentle rise-and-fall movement to the flies) and in the cooler months. He described using slim, epoxy-coated buzzers (they sink quickly), and a Suspender Buzzer with a foam post to support the sunken fly.

In 2008, Darryl Lampert, Chris Bladen and I were fishing the lake on *Birkhall*. Chris and I were doing okay on damselfly and dragonfly nymph imitations, while way off in the distance, Darryl seemed to be doing well standing in waist-deep water. Chris and I eventually headed out in the late afternoon when rain came through, but Darryl stayed on. He arrived back at the farmhouse an hour later, when it was raining heavily and as black as coal outside. He was drenched to the bone and cold, but his broad smile told the whole story. He'd caught better fish than we had, and far more of them, nearly all on size 16 midge pupa imitations fished static.

One final observation from Paul Miller may be more important than we think. Fishing the static midge, he points out you obviously do far less casting; as a result, you spook fewer fish. I believe he's right. It's precisely why I limit my false casting on lakes. If I need distance, I false cast away from the water I'm going to fish next.

A moment of genius from a fine fly tier
Last week the rain washed out my fishing, and since then we've had such an unseasonably wet spell that a quote I once heard came to mind, where he says of the English weather, 'If you can see the

French coast, it means it is going to rain; if you can't see it, then it's already raining.'

Saturday's weather was small-stream perfect. I got a photograph of a big fish we've been watching for some time, but on this occasion we spooked him. Given his awkward lie, the odds are stacked in his favour, but in time I will catch him off-guard with a decent fly on the end of a good cast.

The rest of the day turned into what seemed like one missed take after another. The fish were in a half-hearted mood, the stream was low and challengingly clear, and we were a touch off our game.

Still, there was a new Carlin bamboo rod on display, a pretty Brodin landing net to admire that had a bug collecting net attached to the handle. And the landscapes were straight from heaven.

Even with the trout scarce, it strangely still didn't feel that the day's fly fishing with a couple of mates could get much better. And the fly that eventually got a few fish – and the most takes – was Agostino Roncallo's single CDC feather Mirage. This pattern, in my estimation, was a moment of genius from a fine Italian fly tier.

On bamboo

I don't own a forest of bamboo fly rods; far from it. But I cherish the few I have, as much for their smooth, full-feeling actions as for the inescapable fact that they're pretty – at least prettier than anything made from glass or graphite. But that's a personal view, I guess.

On the merits of bamboo, some people argue they are too heavy and too slow, and maybe too precious – or, put differently, too brittle. I recall a comment made by John Gierach, a true devotee of bamboo rods, when he wrote, 'One of the most often asked questions about any bamboo rod that's being used for its intended purpose is, *Aren't you scared you'll break it?* The answer is, *Yes.*'

Gierach, of course, meant that he loved the rod so much he wouldn't like to see it snapped; not that bamboo rods are more brittle or break more easily than graphite. In fact, they're stronger. I'm pretty hard on the bamboo rods I have, and so far I only ever broke one tip, and that was entirely due to my own carelessness. In the circumstances the tip would have snapped just the same if it were made of glass or graphite.

The other thing about bamboo is that it fits perfectly with the traditional ethos of fly fishing, in an organic kind of way that's important but hard to describe to anyone who doesn't share similar sentiments. The other day I wrote of the Swith Stream with this ethos in mind that went like this; 'The Swith is a deeply remote Eastern Cape trout stream, where the fish are so wild and natural that you'd have to dream up an excuse to plunk nymphs rather than small dry flies at them, preferably on a bamboo rod, if only just to keep faith with the perfect naturalness of the place.'

But in celebrating bamboo, let me get to the main point. Some years ago, my good friend Tom Lewin, who's psychotic about bamboo rods, was in Colorado with his wife Nikki, where they were lucky enough to meet Mike Clark, one of America's great rod makers, and a man whose work Tom greatly admires. He even got to fish a tiny creek with the great rod maker.

During this trip, and understanding her husband's obsession well enough, Nikki secretly ordered a rod from Mike Clark, planning for it to arrive (some years down the line, of course, because there's a waiting list) on the occasion of Tom's fiftieth birthday. The rod got here in time, and my runners tell me Tom was bowled over.

Some would say, 'What a gift'. I'd say, 'What a wife.'

CHAPTER 20

RIVERS AND STREAMS YOU CAN'T HELP LOVING

With rivers, as with good friends, you always feel better for a few hours in their presence; you always want to review your dialogue, years later, with a particular pool or riffle or bend, and to live back through the layers of experience. We have been to this river before and together. We have much to relive.

NICK LYONS, *BRIGHT RIVERS*

A while back, with a few idle moments on my hands, I did a mental count of the rivers and streams I've fished in South Africa, mainly for trout but also for yellowfish, and the total came to sixty-six. Of those, sixteen were in the Western Cape, twenty in KwaZulu-Natal, twelve in the Eastern Cape Highlands on the Rhodes side of the southern Drakensberg, eleven in the Eastern Cape on the Maclear side of the Drakensberg, roughly four in Mpumalanga, though that's likely to be an under-count, and one each in the Free State, the Northern Cape and North West Province. If I add three streams in Lesotho, the total is sixty-nine.

The exercise involved the kind of mind-searching that brought back some pleasant memories. I enjoyed diving around in my mind hunting up images of different waters and of the fish I caught in them, or lost, as the case may be. It also gave me the idea that I should pick a few streams for which I have a soft spot and write a few lines on them – so I did, and I ended up with an eclectic collection of thoughts and ideas about the rivers and streams I decided to include, though with nothing like any scholarly dissertations or any deep science on how to hook trout in them. In their selection I put some store in a few more abstract things that make the character of a trout stream what it is, like the surrounding landscapes, the flora and fauna, their potential to act as a fly-fishing classroom, the atmosphere of the stream, which might, in part at least, come from a its remoteness – though nowadays that's more often a pipe dream than anything like reality.

I was in mild conflict making these final choices, not so much over the streams I included as over those I didn't, since my general feeling about trout streams is that I like them all, which I have come to understand has nothing to do with how often I fish them or how big their trout get, or even how pretty they are – just that I feel a deeper sense of compatibility, for want of a better word, on some streams than on others. So this is by no means a complete list of the streams I love and could safely recommend to you. And, by the way, if I occasionally use the terms 'river' and 'stream' interchangeably (and I do), it's because I'm not exactly sure when a stream builds up enough of whatever it takes to safely be called a river, or when a river scales down enough to safely be called a stream.

*

The Greek philosopher Heraclitus of Ephesus said, 'You cannot step twice into the same river', which is one of those simple observations that Greek philosophers typically turn into something that sounds deeply profound. Certainly no river is quite the same from day to day, let alone from season to season, but in many ways that's not the full story, in that while a river might change cyclically for various reasons, mostly because of the weather and the seasons, it still retains a certain constancy, a certain 'feel', an underlying *character* if you like. This isn't the stream's day-to-day reality. It's more the mind's-eye image you keep of every river or stream, images that become a sort of embedded default setting for each stream and each river you've ever fished.

So, for example, if I think of the Smalblaar River in the Western Cape, I have an immediate picture of amber-coloured water flowing like glass in a cradle of smoky-purple peaks. If I think of the Mooi River in KwaZulu-Natal, I see a pastoral stream with apple-green holes under deep-cut banks, and willow trees, and cows grazing in nearby pastures. And there's something very pleasing about these images. For a start, they exclude the days when the river was too low to fish or too high, or the times when the fishing was blown apart by howling winds or slanting sleet or worse, or when the trout were like fussy accountants or plain impossible to catch.

So that's part of my broader thinking about rivers, and the images they conjure in my mind about their character, never mind that they change from day to day.

Sadly, some rivers, or sections of rivers, change substantially and lose their character because they've been damaged or polluted or neglected. Occasionally, though rarely these days, a river will change for the better, often through the efforts of a bunch of like-minded anglers who get together to restore it. A good example is the upper Umgeni in the Dargle Valley in KwaZulu-Natal. This stream, at least in its upper sections where there is good brown-trout fishing, was being throttled by the insidious advance of wattle trees, until my friend Andrew Fowler, along with the Natal Fly Fishers Club (of which he is now chairman), started to fix it. They have made substantial inroads.

Which reminds me of when I used to fish the upper Mooi River, only one valley removed from the Umgeni on the farm *Riverside*, and then occasionally on the section immediately above *Riverside* that runs through the Kamberg Nature Reserve. Both were lovely stretches of brown-trout water where the trout often came up for dry flies, especially early mornings and late afternoons. Happily, they are both *still* lovely stretches of brown-trout water, but there was a day years ago when we tried the section of this same river that flows into the nature reserve water and found it so choked with wattle and so dark and gloomy that we gave up. It had lost the feel and character of the Mooi, which seemed sad, because it was a cascade of dancing runs and plump glides with the potential to make a really fine little trout stream. Happily, it's a different story today. The wattles were removed, the stream's character is restored, the soul is salvaged, if you like, and I'm told the fishing's quite good – if you don't mind long hikes.

With all this in mind, let me get on with describing my choices. I'll try to capture their true character for you, never mind droughts or floods.

The Bokspruit on Gateshead, Eastern Cape

There's a settlers' cottage on *Gateshead*, dating back to the late 1800s, that Carien and Basie Vosloo run for people in search of the outdoors – but also for their good friends, and most of those are also looking for an escape from the assorted challenges of modern life and some fishing, which is the category I fall into. It's not that I dislike city life; in fact, I find parts of it quite pleasant, especially in a city like Cape Town with its mountain hikes, Newlands

Cricket Ground, outdoor coffee shops, convenience stores and leafy suburbs. But there is still traffic and throngs of busy people with the acquired impersonal attitudes and the ever-constant sense of rush that cities convey on us. At *Gateshead* there is silence, solitude and space, attributes most cities aren't exactly known for.

The dirt road up to the cottage follows the Bokspruit River Valley through typical grassland farming country with undulating hills and sandstone outcrops, and then it climbs a steep hill alongside a spectacular waterfall where the road is high enough to give you vertigo. A few kilometres further on from this waterfall, the road crosses two drifts that you have to negotiate carefully, because there are cavities in the concrete beds of the drifts, and during wet seasons the water will be lapping at your axles. Further on still, the road ends in tracks right at the front steps of the cottage, which is quite rare for roads into fishing cabins, even deep-country ones.

Naturally the cottage has a long history, which, depending who you talk to, includes ghosts, although so far none of us has seen one. The cottage has lime-washed stone walls, a black tin roof, a white-slatted veranda and a surrounding privet hedge out front with an adjoining spread of old, gnarled fruit trees – cherries and greengage plums – that in spring make a pretty picture of white and pink blossoms. The view from the cottage takes your eye to the stream, with glints of water and the reflections of clouds, then up into hills that rise steeply into the mountains that cup this valley like the folded arms of a giant. In autumn, the stream below the cottage is lined with tall Lombardy poplars that look like giant yellow candles. It's a peaceful, remote place – so remote that I've sometimes arrived here and thought I'd just as easily rest my feet on the veranda railings and do some soul searching as head off into the hills in search of trout.

Apart from the fishing and the scenery, the birdlife is special on *Gateshead*, with a few rare species that might or might not show up, which is part of what makes birding so absorbingly uncertain (much like fishing, come to think of it). So you might see a Drakensberg Rock-jumper or a Mountain Pipit or the Drakensberg Siskin, and if you do, you feel it's an event, because these species only occur in a thin band that includes this farm and a few surrounding slivers of Drakensberg countryside, and even then you won't see them reliably often. I've twice seen Bearded Vultures, and there's a pair of Black (now Verreaux's) Eagles. (Scientists changed their name a few years back, and the names of dozens of other birds for that matter, for reasons probably locked up in some taxonomic minutiae that, even if it makes sense scientifically, is still inconvenient and mildly irritating. Consider the poor Gymnogene, for example. It suddenly got the clumsy name of the African Harrier-hawk.) Anyway, these Black Eagles have nested on *Gateshead* for years. In fact, Basie pointed out the nesting site to me on one visit and, as if by divine intervention, a Black Eagle appeared above us and swung lazy loops across a pearly sky. What made this sighting even more special was that at the same time I noticed the fish rising madly in the stream below us, though you'd need to be a fisherman to see something significant in that.

There are at least fourteen kilometres of fishing on *Gateshead*, starting from below the cottage, where the stream is quite imposing. From there the fishing just goes on and on, right up into the mountains, until on the summit of the southern Drakensberg it turns into an unusual stretch of water that looks something like a high-altitude chalkstream. But I'll explain that later.

Most anglers would describe the water of *Gateshead* as perfect dry fly water, the more so the higher you hike up the valley above the cottage. And this stream certainly oozes dry fly qualities, at least as I understand them, meaning clear water, a good gradient with quick riffles that carry the dry fly nicely back to you, knee-deep, smooth-surfaced runs and plenty of protruding rocks that

Gateshead Cottage

leave inviting cushions of smooth water behind them. But if it's good dry fly water, which it is, it's also just a pretty stream to be on with a fly rod, no matter what you're fishing, which is maybe a more important thing to know about it. Anyway, good dry fly water is also good nymphing water, and you'll catch as many, if not more, trout here on nymphs than on dries, although you'll occasionally catch enough on whatever it was you were using to think you've mastered that particular technique. Enjoy the feeling. It usually doesn't last more than the rest of the week.

The decision to change from dry flies to nymphs can hurt a little up here, given most fly fishers have a sort of spiritual predilection for the dry fly, though a change to nymphs is easier when you are on seemingly endless water that is perfect for both – and no-one is watching. Generally, on water like this I fish dry flies until I doubt them, either because I haven't had a rise in an hour or because of refusals, or I've cast a heap of different dry fly patterns onto good-looking water that, one drift after another, produced nothing.

I often stick like glue to dry flies on *Gateshead*, not because they're predictably better or anything like consistently productive, but because the water looks so good for dry flies that I don't want to waste the chance. There's perhaps less logic in that than pure nostalgia – remember, I cut my eyeteeth fishing dry flies in the Western Cape. But I guess most anglers who've bothered to travel this far and end up this high on a clear mountain stream where the fish aren't that selective to begin with would feel much the same way. And I don't accord any additional virtue of purism to fishing dry flies, either. It's just another way of catching fish, although most anglers will tell you there's more poetry in it and that they prefer watching dainty dry flies drifting back to them than pieces of brightly coloured synthetic yarn – and I suppose there's something in that. In the end, it boils down to doing whatever puts the wind in your sails.

Some streams or sections of streams have such a good reputation with dry flies that you can feel strangely uneasy about fishing a nymph on them. The upper Bokspruit is one of those stretches; it's also one of the places where you start wondering what went wrong with your dry fly technique that you've ended up fishing a nymph.

There are a couple of interesting things you'll notice at *Gateshead*. First, much of the streambed is made up of sheets of dark basalt rock that have occasional deep faults running through them. These faults are either small and irrelevant, or deep and highly relevant because they hold trout. They appear as clear transitions in the river's colour, where the water turns from pale-amber where it's shallow to soft turquoise where it deepens, sometimes to a metre or more. Secondly, the higher you hike above the cottage, the better and more interesting the fishing gets, and I'll touch on the reasons for that in a moment. Finally, during daylight, hatches are relatively inconsistent and sparse, but I'm not an expert on the hatches at *Gateshead*, never mind that I'm also shaky on precise insect identification. But I've fished this stream and similar mountain streams in this area long enough to think it's safe to offer some broad observations. I'll summarise the hatches as best I can.

You get sporadic emergence of *Baetis* mayflies, small, dark-grey bugs that you'll mostly see early in the morning or at sundown, which is not to say they don't come off during the day. They do. Then there's the occasional hatch of caddisflies, smaller insects than the caddisflies you find in the pastoral waters downstream. They're tan- to light-grey bugs that dart erratically around the grassy edges, especially on mild evenings. Mountain midges appear from time to time, tiny, dust-coloured insects that typically flutter and dance over smooth slicks behind boulders like flecks of windblown ash. Hoppers and beetles arrive sporadically, and I once saw a hatch of small, black-bodied flying ants here, which, as it happened, never brought on the sort of crazy rise I'd expected.

From the hatches you can expect at *Gateshead*, and using simple empirical deductions, you can figure out a selection of dry fly patterns for this stream. I know that arguing fly selection is in the blood of most of us fly fishers, so I don't expect full agreement on my *Gateshead* pattern list. Nevertheless it goes something like this.

To cover *Baetis* hatches, an Adams (just to be provocatively old-fashioned for a moment), and small RABs; to cover emergers, a parachute Adams or a Para-RAB. The obvious choice for adult caddisflies would be an Elk Hair Caddis, or if you like an Elk Hair and CDC Caddis, and if mountain midges start fluttering around the surface, a One Feather CDC Midge will work. For terrestrials, any of the countless takes on ants, hoppers or beetles and, again from straight empirical experience, a yellow DDD. To match wolf spiders, Pete Briggs's or Leonard Flemming's ultra-buggy versions are both excellent patterns. All your flies would be from size 14 down to size 18, maybe even 20; and remember, all these patterns make good prospecting flies on quick-flowing, freestone streams as well, certainly in this country. In fact, I have hard evidence that RABs, Para-RABs, DDDs and the One Feather Midge work on more than a few overseas streams as well. For example, Ian Douglas, my good friend Robin's son, has had great success fishing Para-RABs in California. I've caught trout on RABs and my One Feather CDC Midge in the Test and the upper Itchen in Hampshire, and cutthroats (on RABs) in the Yellowstone River and a few brown trout in the South Island of New Zealand took close looks at a big, fat yellow DDD.

What I can say with some certainty about this list is that it won't let you down. But the question is whether fly-pattern selection matters that much on a stream like this. I think all you can say is it matters *less* than on streams where selective feeders are common, like in the chalkstreams of England or on the spring creeks in America. But bear in mind that the trout living at *Gateshead* have to be indiscriminate, opportunistic feeders just to survive. They can't afford to be fussy, given that food is relatively sparse. I also have my pet theory that adult insects, like a juicy mayfly dun, present an irresistible change of diet to mountain stream trout, but it's a theory that needs more research before it's anywhere near bulletproof.

In keeping with most of our freestone streams, trout get more food off the streambed than from the surface, so nymphs produce reliably well up here; as I said, probably more consistently well than dry flies, if you discount the fact that both will catch you heaps of the really small fish you find up here from season to season that have a go at anything.

Over the years I've used a variety of nymph patterns up here – PTNs, Gold-Ribbed Hare's Ears, Zaks (lightly weighted or unweighted) and Brassies, mainly in small sizes. They all work well enough, though I still can't tell you if one pattern works better up here than another. Honestly, I don't think it matters, though small nymphs, say in size 18, that sink quickly and have a discreet hotspot somewhere, like an hot-orange tungsten bead, strike a happy chord in my memories of nymphing *any* of the mountain streams in this area, and I can't ignore something like that.

*

I think the main reason the water gets better on *Gateshead* the further you hike upstream is that the gradient increases so the flow quickens, which results in a little more oxygen in the water and, importantly, more riffles, pockets and runs and fewer of those flat, uninteresting stretches that you find in the lower reaches. Pools get a little smaller the higher you hike, but they're often deceptively deep and predictably good. And the stream tumbles over many more waterfalls, where the white turbulence provides cover for the fish, especially during dry seasons when the flow is thin.

As you would expect, weather conditions affect the fishing here as much as on any water, except that with the steeper gradients up here there's better run-off, so after heavy rain the stream recovers faster than the more pastoral waters downstream. Then there's a fair amount of natural precipitation at night in the mountains, which helps support the flow, and there are plenty of those nutrient-rich seeps that drain off boggy hillsides and trickle into the stream through veld sprinkled with cow pats, so they end up like nature's equivalent of an intravenous feed.

I've seen this stream very low in dry seasons, when the fishing gets testy but not impossible. The levels drop until the water is just a sheet of glass, and the trout go on red alert – but they're still catchable if you stalk like a heron.

Whatever the weather, I can hardly recall anything bad enough that the stream wasn't actually fishable, whatever leap of faith that needed, except after a cloudburst in the mountains when the level can rise quickly enough to sweep you away. But leave it alone for a few days and it will run near-perfect again – meaning full, plump-looking and fresh.

Just a word on the trout here. On average they will be small, say nine to twelve inches, but sixteen-inch fish aren't uncommon and I've heard of anglers taking trout up to eighteen inches, occasionally on dry flies. Do I believe them? Yes, I do.

*

The Bokspruit on the summit is worth mentioning because it's a different sort of river. I only fished it twice, once with Ed Herbst when we got up there on horseback, and later with my friends Phil Hills and Ed Gerber, also when we got there on horseback. I remember a long stretch of silver water in a huge volcano-like bowl that disappeared around a far-off headland that I guessed must be fishable all the way to its source, wherever that may be – somewhere in spongy seeps that leech out of distant hillsides.

The stream up here is good in most ways a trout stream can be. It runs in gently rolling grassland in country that looks like a big, flat volcanic bowl, with slower-flowing, quieter water than in the steep hillsides below, which has a strangely luminous quality that's hard to describe other than to say, perhaps, that it reminded me of amber; in other words, resinous, or glowingly transparent. It's a smooth-surfaced, luminous stream, with colourful pebbles and rocks that shine brightly in the riverbed – and it's full of hungry trout. The rainbows we got were anything from six to ten inches and they were so pretty you had to believe only God could have put them there. They seemed like the easiest trout I'd ever caught. Thinking back on the fishing, I'd say it mattered little *where* you put your fly on this stream as long as it was just somewhere on the water.

All of this is a roundabout way of saying that I think you should visit this section, and if you do, opt to go on horseback. It's easier on the muscles in the thin air, and a lot more fun in a Western, cowboy-style kind of way.

By the way, I discovered that the farm on the summit isn't actually *Gateshead* any longer but *Albert Hall*; not that it's important when there isn't as much as a fence post in sight.

*

The *Gateshead* stretch of the Bokspruit won't be asking many deep questions of your technique or the fly patterns you choose, and there's a certain appealing freedom in that. But I guess if you want to make the fishing up here technical, well, there's nothing stopping you. Then I sometimes try to imagine where I'd go if I really wanted to fish alone, and I find *Gateshead* is always on my shortlist, not because I feel spiritually moved up here or because the landscapes and the fishing are so good, but because it's remote enough not to bring back reminders of the real world that, if I *was* fishing alone, I'd be trying hard to forget.

Finally, if I wanted to teach anyone the basics of small-stream dry fly fishing, this place is ideal. You would appreciate the beauty and maybe the solitude and, in time, say in an hour or two, your pupil would learn that even if a stream is high-lying, remote and full of small and innocent fish, it can still be delightfully challenging. And if the trout are naive, and they are, they're still street-smart. So you can't throw the basics out of the window, like gentle presentations, setting up drag-free drifts and keeping out of sight. I'd *start* with those three lessons first, because they are the pillars of the dry fly temple and your student must know them. In fact, I'd press them home for at least the first two hours. You can teach other stuff later, like striking sharply in the faster water, or how to quickly resurrect a soaked dry fly with short, sharp snap-casts that shake feathery puffs of dampness out of it. Later still, you could add a few of the details, like how to read the surface currents by following the bubble lines, and how to manage a dry fly that tumbles and sinks in swirling water when you somehow still have to watch the surface for any hint of a rise.

One of the things you won't be able to teach is how to throw tight roll casts with your back against bushes, because other than the first bit, there are no bushes on these banks. Failing that, this stream is the ultimate classroom, a flowing textbook of lessons rewarding enough to encourage a beginner, yet unforgiving enough to cut him to size. But if you just teach your pupil to present the fly gently, fish drag-free, stay out of sight, and at the same time keep an eye out for rare birds, you could say 'Amen' and close the lessons for the day.

The Bushman's River, Giant's Castle, KwaZulu-Natal

I haven't fished this river in years, but my head is still so filled with memories of its luxuriance and its brown trout, it feels like I fished it yesterday. And I still have friends who occasionally tramp its banks and send me emails and photographs, so in a way I feel I'm still fishing it, if only vicariously.

You can divide this river into two sections: bigger water downstream of a place called Snowflake Cottage that sits right on the banks of the river, and then thinner water upstream of the cottage and around the KwaZulu-Natal Parks Board's hutted camp on Giant's Castle Nature Reserve. Above the camp is where I stop knowing the river well, other than that it eventually forks into two fishable branches, the left one called the Tweedassiespruit, an ethereal but quite productive stream, that I occasionally fished. The other fork I don't know, and I should have explored it back when I had the chance. It was just that the river below the camp was so good we didn't bother much about fishing higher upstream, other than if storms had coloured the river. We also fished a tributary coming in way downstream of Snowflake Cottage called the Ushiyaki, but I never found the fishing in it as memorable as some people claimed it was.

The Bushman's is one of the true blue-ribbon brown-trout streams we have, right up there with the Mooi in the same province and the Witte and Witels rivers in the Western Cape. But what makes the Bushman's stand out is its proximity to the Drakensberg. The river seems to flow straight out of tall mountains, almost like an optical illusion, and you might find yourself fishing against a backdrop of snow-capped mountain peaks in winter or, in early autumn, standing on riverbanks splashed lilac and pink with the flowers of the Mexican cosmos, and not minding that these plants are alien imports from Australia.

Nothing much seems to have changed since I last fished it except for the occasional report that poaching may have reduced the number of fish. Whatever, the browns are apparently still daring, or shy and free-rising, or not, depending on their mood or on what hatches are coming off or which angler is reporting things. What is also constant is that these brown trout are typically butter-yellow and wild, and striking enough to imagine nature painted them this boldly just to show off a little.

I sometimes think back to the times when I stood in this river at the tail-end of some plump-looking run with the smoky-green water so inviting and so ripe you sort of just knew something would bite. I'd usually be throwing small, dark-coloured, almost black soft-hackle nymphs, drifting them along the undercuts or into the slack water behind boulders, or kiting them through riffles, keeping the line just tense enough to feel the mild vibrations of the currents. Back then conventional science preached that brown trout liked black flies, and that they mainly lived alongside banks or behind big rocks. That may have only been partly true, I know, but we caught enough fish from under banks and behind rocks on black flies to believe it was, and it soon became the gospel, and I still mostly believe it. I'm not thinking of traditional black wet-fly patterns like the Black Pennel or the Zulu, though they worked back then and must still work now – but flies like a small John Beams's Woolly Worm that in Tony Biggs's hands ended up less sophisticated and even more buggy. He tied them small on size 12 and 14 hooks, with a black seal's fur body sparsely palmered with black hackle ribbed with fine tinsel or wire, and left them unweighted, so the fly could swim and dance in the currents. It was that deadly a pattern, and a method of fishing, that we would have been better off not trying to improve it, but gradually this pattern morphed into a semi-traditional nymph that finally ended up near enough to a modern Zak.

The whole point of Biggs's take on the Black Woolly Worm was its simplicity, its lifelike movement and the absence of weight, balanced by its capacity to quickly absorb water, meaning that once it was soaked and sinking, it weaved in the current with the hackles giving it life. Tony avoided indicators, so when he hooked a fish we were never sure whether he'd seen the leader shiver or dart or if he'd just struck intuitively – which he often claimed was the case, and which just added to his reputation of being partly psychic and able to pluck trout like magic from thin air.

In my first book *My Way with a Trout*, I describe a trip when I caught a brown of eighteen inches in the Bushman's and then took a brace more that were not quite as big, but almost, and went on to miss a real hog, though this sort of fishing was far from the norm. Mostly the trout in the Bushman's averaged twelve to fourteen inches, which still makes the river good, and if you disagree I guess you're secretly fishing some brown-trout stream I haven't heard of and keeping quiet about it – not that I'd blame you.

As for browns holding near banks, it's a fact that they do, at least in KZN streams, though that's only true as far as it goes, meaning we did catch plenty from under the banks but mainly in broad daylight, and that held good for most brown-trout KZN streams we fished back then, like the middle and upper reaches of the Mooi, the Little Mooi and the Umgeni.

If the point about banks and brown trout is a no-brainer during the day, evenings are another story. As soon as the sun starts to settle, browns become anything but predictable in their lies, often moving out to feed in shallow runs – sometimes in ridiculously shallow runs. I know it's a generalisation, but even so, it's something you shouldn't sweep aside too lightly.

Late-afternoon hatches were a feature of fishing on this river, not only because they were fairly dependable but because they brought better fish out of hiding. I used RABs and traditional American dry flies, like the Adams, the Royal Wulff and variations of the Hendrickson, during evening rises on all brown-trout streams in this province, but I preferred using RABs because they were authentically local and the trout didn't ask many questions of them. If you don't know, my friend Tony Biggs invented the RAB, and we happened to fish the Bushman's together quite often. Thinking back, inventing the RAB was a moment of pure piscatorial genius, although Tony is not the sort of person to give himself much credit for developing a dry fly pattern that would be easy to tie, float well, look buggy and work on just about any mountain stream in the world. Such are the gifts of those chosen to be prophets among us.

The Holsloot River, Western Cape

The Holsloot runs inland of Rawsonville, a small town near Worcester in the Western Cape, and I include it to emphasise the suddenness of change, literally overnight, that you can occasionally see in a river. I'll come to the reason for it in this case in a moment.

The Holsloot starts as water released from the Stettynskloof Dam so, at least in part, this is a tailwater fishery. I say 'in part' because joining the water from the dam is a tributary stream, the Kaaimansgat, flowing in a typically pretty Cape kloof.

The future of the Holsloot is uncertain. During the 2017 season a devastating flood scoured the valley into a wide, featureless, rocky braid, the road into the valley was totally washed away at a culvert, and whenever I made enquiries about the river I was told its fishing was a thing of the past. I took it, for the time being anyway, as a sort of speculative truth, and as much as I disliked the notion I resigned myself to life without the Holsloot for a few years, and stayed clinging to the hope that this wonderful river would, through some sort of miracle, eventually be worth visiting again.

Well, three years later parts of it still aren't worth visiting, but a year or so ago a local angler was reported to have taken a few small trout from one of the upper beats, so I called him. He told me the lower sections of the streambed were scoured flat, the river wide and shallow and the banks treeless. But the upper beats were less affected and there were still a few small trout around up there.

So for my own peace of mind I revisited it. The changes left my jaw sagging. It was as if I was looking at another river altogether, certainly in its lower reaches. Out of curiosity I strolled to the beat I had loved most, Beat One. There were features I could still recognise as the Holsloot I knew, like the riverbed tapestry that is typically darker than most of the Western Cape streams, but equally as much of its character had gone. The bankside brush, which was always a feature of the Holsloot, was gone and I wondered if a wide, uninteresting stream, flowing in a wider, flat braid of surrounding rocks, is ever going to be a tree-lined, tight-flowing stream again. The upper reaches were, as my friend reported, more intact, more or less the old river I had known. But the river on this day was full and cold and I couldn't raise a trout.

*

The tailwater fishery bit may account for the fact that this river fished well when nearby trout streams were buckling under the heat of summer. But there was also a school of thought that suggested the erratic release of cooler water from the dam might account for the renowned unpredictability of this river's fishing or, more specifically, the well-known capriciousness of its trout. In high summer the fish in the Holsloot were definitely cushioned by the intermittent release of cool water, but that didn't fully explain why they unaccountably waxed so hot or cold. I always believed that some of the better-known tailwater fisheries of this world, like the Flaming Gorge section of Utah's Green River or the San Juan River in northern New Mexico, were more constant in flow, and more productive fisheries as a result. Certainly they both produce legendary trophy trout, and the tailwater factor is likely a big part of that growth. But if you read Steven Meyers' book *San Juan River Chronicle*, published in 1994, he describes outlet volumes from the Navajo Dam, built in the early 1960s, as variable, and argues that although the fishing in the San Juan seems to have been consistently good, there have been problems since the dam was built – due to increased rod pressure, sure, but also, he maintains, due to variable releases of water. He even has a chapter in the book titled *A River in Decline,* but nowhere did I read that the trout in the San Juan were as capricious as those in the Holsloot – difficult at times, yes, but largely dependable. I will leave the jury to chew on that.

*

The Holsloot was known for a mayfly fall, locally called the Holsloot Spinner: large, somewhat ponderous, predominantly soot-grey mayflies, probably of the *Leptophlebiidae* family, whose females carry a bright-yellow egg sac after mating. No two anglers' imitations of this spinner ever looked much alike to me, beyond being grey and having long, spent wings, meaning there was nothing like a chapter-and-verse go-to pattern at the time. Maybe that's because the appearance of the natural was nowhere near common or predictable, or for that matter well understood; anyway, according to the late AC Harrison, the Cape Piscatorial Society's former secretary who was a pundit on local entomology, these vast spinner falls most likely included at least three different species. What I know of these mayflies and their subsequent spinner falls is that they appeared later in summer rather than earlier, and then mainly in the fresh of morning or late on a mild afternoon, and that they could be dense enough to look like a fine mist rising off the water. If we came across one or two hatches in a season it was a lot, but we never visited the river without a few big spinner patterns that would roughly match something like a large, greyish, spent mayfly, if only not to risk tempting fate.

*

Anglers who visited the Holsloot regularly before the flood – and I was one of them – found the fishing characterised, as I mentioned, by the mysterious unpredictability of its trout. The fish could be forgiving and generous one hour, and strangely cloistered the next. There were days when I had a nagging feeling all the trout had been wiped out, a notion fed by an occasion some years back when the side of a mountain collapsed in a storm, slid into the river and knocked out the fishing for a year or more. I was camping up there the night it happened. That was obviously a rare event and mainly the Holsloot was just a consistently lovely river with predictably inconsistent trout, so that on one visit the fishing would be typically dull and on another, trout would suddenly appear all over the place and eat dry flies like candy, though that was rare enough to be remarkable. A good day on the Holsloot was mainly a five-to-six-fish day, where one, or maybe two of the fish you landed would go a shade over fourteen, maybe fifteen or even sixteen inches.

Near the dam the river forks to the left of the wall looking upstream, the right arm running up to the dam (with fishing all the way), the left arm becoming the Kaaimansgat. The unlikely name of this little tributary never put us off fishing it as much as the difficulty getting into it. It was heavily bushed for a few hundred metres before it opened up and became a charming stream. As you'd expect, it has stayed little fished and, as a result, remains fairly productive. I never fished it more than once or twice a season.

And then there are a couple of small feeder streams that flow into the Stettynskloof Dam itself that suggested huge potential when I first saw them but didn't deliver on the promise. Certainly we never saw a fish in what was good-looking water and all the reports I've had of the fishing in them have been equally bleak. It's strange, because I figure the trout in the dam must move up these streams to spawn in early winter, but who knows.

If you travel far enough up one of these streams, I'm not sure which one, you will eventually come across the remains of an Avro Shackleton Bomber in the streambed. Shackleton MR.3 registration 1718/K crashed on a routine exercise in atrocious weather at 3.05pm on 8 August 1963 with the loss of all 13 crew on board. The cause of the accident appears to have been the failure of sections of a rudder and aileron from severe icing and bad turbulence. Both parts sheared off the aircraft moments before Captain TH Sivertsen sent out his first and last Mayday transmission. The aircraft was off course, and the wreckage was only spotted by an air-force helicopter two days after the crash.

*

It's inevitable that a stream as rugged as the Holsloot will produce a few notable angling moments. I shared in one when I lost a Canadian guest for maybe forty tension-filled minutes until our paths eventually crossed more by chance than through my skills at tracking anglers lost in remote, rocky river braids lined with thick bush. I just wandered around shouting his name until I found him right where we'd last been together. He was sitting on a rock in the middle of the stream not looking the slightest bit worried. He thought I'd just gone off to do a little fishing on my own.

It was on this river that Andy Krajewski's girlfriend (later wife) Shirley was bitten on the calf by a puff adder as she was climbing out of Beat 6. She recovered fully and later told me that the scariest part of it wasn't the snake bite, but Andy's high-speed drive into town in his ancient VW Kombi on the fourteen kilometres of winding, tight-cornered dirt road, where in many places the riverbed is a sheer drop a few hundred metres below you.

My friend Roy Gordon was once fishing a beat with his son when they got to a pretty run where the stream flows alongside a sloping wall of granite. I know the spot well because we never missed climbing out here to spot trout off the convenient ledge it offers. Which is what Roy's son did. But he was back a few seconds later, looking pale. He said he'd run into a leopard; moments later, the leopard casually crossed the stream just ahead of them.

For all of its easy-to-lose-yourself-in ruggedness, the capricious nature of its trout, and the ominous presence of leopards and puff adders, it was a great fly stream, albeit not the kind I happily fished alone. Though there was a time when I did, mainly in my younger days, when I had the advantage of the blurred insight and sense of immortality that are the close companions of youth.

And I guess I somehow enjoyed fishing the Holsloot more because of its unpredictability, though that kind of contrary sentiment isn't easy to explain without sounding a little snooty.

I guess the fickle streak in trout is a big part of what makes them such sought-after game fish in the first place. (The other part is that they are far more beautiful than anyone can fully explain.)

*

Because of the river's unpredictability, I often started fishing on the Holsloot with a dry fly and dropper, my argument being that you were never sure what was going to be working on the day unless the fish happened to be rising. And it was a stream where you could bump into a sudden and prolific rise. Typically you would be fishing a flat, smooth, glassy run, usually on a clear day, when you may have taken a fish or two but couldn't see a trout anywhere ahead of you, when suddenly one or two would start rising right in front of you – and before you knew it you could be counting upwards of a dozen fish, some that looked fifteen inches or more, with plenty within easy casting range. Mostly the bugs they were rising to wouldn't hit you straight off, unless it was a nice big mayfly dun or caddisfly. But these intense rises were mostly to bugs so drab and so tiny you wondered why the fish bothered to eat them at all: insects like mountain midges, micro-caddis, and tiny, dull-coloured *Baetis* mayflies.

In this kind of sudden, spontaneous rise, you needed to do a couple of things quickly to catch fish. Like remain dead still, add more 7 or 8X tippet to the leader, try to identify the hatch, study the actual rise-form. I often changed to a pattern like a drab-looking mayfly or emerger imitation or a One Feather CDC Midge, as long as it was tiny, as in size 18 to 20. Then you needed to lay out a high-pitched cast that dropped onto the water as smooth as satin and landed *anywhere* near where you saw the last trout *closest* to you. And you needed to fish the cast right out, so that the fly drifted all the way back before you gently slid the line off the water to cast again. That way you didn't risk creasing the surface and putting the fish down, which was the other hallmark of these rises – the fish were easy to spook for reasons I never really understood.

If any of these patterns didn't bring me a take, my first change would be to a size 20 spinner. If that failed, I'd check again that the trout weren't taking emergers, and if not, I'd go to something like a small ant pattern fished with a quiet prayer, or to an equally small floating beetle. But there were hatches where the surface fly failed, when we often took fish on tiny size 20 nymphs, often Brassies. Mostly, though, dry flies or emergers worked okay; they were certainly the way to start, and going to a nymph was certainly the way to end.

Although these rising fish seemed bold, as I said, they were strangely nervous; it would take only one bad cast, one fly line lifted too sharply or a fly dragging badly, to bring the curtain down on the whole show. Why this should be I still don't know; nor do I know why when those big, soot-grey mayfly spinners appeared and flopped around like overloaded bombers, the trout would go nuts and you could catch fish after fish doing just about everything wrong and still not spook them. You get to wonder whether these fat mayflies didn't have some opiate-like stuff circulating in their veins that sent the trout on a temporary trip.

*

I've spent many years photographing trout in holding lies, partly to help other anglers spot fish but mainly because the challenge of it just got under my skin. And, to tell the truth, I never really managed to master the art. I've done most of this work on the Smalblaar River, the Molenaars section of the Smalblaar, the Elandspad and the Berg River before they built the dam, where the water was ridiculously clear and the trout were correspondingly easy to find.

But with its darker riverbed stones, the trout in the Holsloot were difficult to spot. You needed more time to scan the water, and you also needed a little luck – as in, you'd arrive at a suitably clear, flat-surfaced run just as a trout moved or decided to rise.

*

So that's the Holsloot, and I'm unhappy to be speaking in the past tense about it. It was fourteen kilometres of lovely trout water, with fish every bit as uncertain as the weather and big enough to please most fly fishers. Us anglers way down here on the southern tip of Africa live in the quiet hope that, in time, the Holsloot will return to the glories of its past. Some of it already has.

The Karringmelkspruit, Eastern Cape

The R58 highway crosses the Karringmelkspruit over a bridge sixteen kilometres outside the Eastern Cape town of Lady Grey, and upstream and downstream of that bridge there's around twenty kilometres of fishable trout river, most of it reasonably accessible. I know two of the lodges on this stream pretty well: Lupela Lodge, owned by Alf and Denise Ross, which is nearer the bridge; and the *Lammergeier Nature Reserve*, owned by the Isted family, which is well upstream of Lupela and has great accommodation in an old farmhouse called Ossa as well as a cottage right on the banks of the river called Woodlands. I'd say the *Lammergeier* stretch is the longer beat, not that it matters because the fishing – and the accommodation for that matter – are equally good on both.

Through most of its upper course the Karringmelkspruit is a rugged-looking river, flowing through landscapes that go back 200 million years to a part of our geological prehistory that left sheets of exposed sandstone to weather over aeons into tall buttresses, overhanging caves and cliffs that gradually cracked in places from high temperatures, dropping a litter of rocks the size of sheds onto the hillsides. Some of these rocks are so big you'd need ropes to climb them – not that you'd want to climb them, because this is not climbing country. The sandstone is too brittle and dangerous for it.

The Karringmelkspruit has a particular radiance, a golden glow that comes from light diffusing off the apricot-coloured sandstone of the riverbed. It's an interesting riverbed, a mix of basalt and sandstone that the river gradually scoured out in places to form deep, smooth-sided cavities. When you see their smoothly sculptured perfection and scan the jagged asymmetry of the surrounding rock formations, you start thinking about how the universe was formed, about volcanic forces and molten basalt lava, the relentless power of weathering, the demise of dinosaurs, things like that, and all in that brief flash of just 200 million years.

These riverbed cavities look a little like oversized buttermilk urns, which is what gave the river its name. Sometimes you'll come across sections where the river is wide, shallow and fast-flowing, true riffle water but running over smooth sheets of solid bedrock, yet you can still hook trout in these unlikely places because a few deep urns will provide holding water. The urn-like cavities show as darker water, and as your nymph drifts over them you get a lovely sense of expectation, which I suppose is not as profound as it sounds, because we *naturally* get a sense of expectation on *every* cast we make, other than those that land in trees. There are also a few great pools on this river big enough to launch a boat on, but I never worry much about them. I like fishing moving water.

*

The trout in the Karringmelkspruit are often confident feeders, meaning they will yank an indicator a metre or more in one sudden swoop, even in the thinnest water. And some of these fish will be big enough to surprise you – trout of sixteen to twenty inches plus, with girths to match. Well, almost. The point is that this is just a special river when it comes to finding strong, sizeable fish.

Some years back I climbed onto the roof of a small disused building known as the Cheese Factory right on the banks of the Karringmelkspruit just below the *Ossa* farmhouse. I'd got up there to scan the stream, and straight away spotted a sixteen-inch trout swinging gently in a seam of current in the middle of a run. The water was low and glass-clear. Then a second fish of easily twenty inches joined it. I watched them for a while; the bigger of the two fish rose so confidently that its dorsal fin broke the surface. I tried inching off the roof to get in a cast but they sensed me and bolted. This was a year when the Karringmelkspruit was paper-thin, and the fishing needed high caution, ultra-fine tippets and small flies – in fact, all the usual minimalist techniques for twitchy trout.

*

The first time I saw the Karringmelkspruit was way back in 1988, when we had come over Naude's Nek Pass from the KwaZulu-Natal side. I was with Hugh Huntley, Neil Hodges and Jake Alletson, on a trip that lasted longer than we'd planned because the fishing was far better than we imagined. We were in the VW Kombi Camper I'd bought second-hand when I thought I'd be spending a lot more time camping and fishing than I eventually actually could. We'd set up the car so we could stay overnight on riverbanks and survive in a degree of comfort, though we quickly realised that four people don't fit comfortably into a VW Camper. The vehicle was old and slow, rattled like a barrel of bolts and had a lot of things that didn't work – like the fridge, for a start.

But the Karringmelkspruit was special on that trip – exactly as a fellow by the name of Geoff Knipe had described it in an article he wrote years back for *Piscator*, the journal of the Cape Piscatorial Society. We fished the river below Lupela Lodge where we had enough water for a week's fishing, but we only had two days because we planned to visit other rivers in the area, like the Langkloof and the Kraai. What I remember from back then was a pretty, swirling, gushing, bush-lined stream, and that the fishing was easy, and plenty of its trout were happy to take dry flies, even when there wasn't a hatch. What we didn't know back then, and I only came to realise over the years, was that we'd caught the river in sublime condition. The level was perfect, it was sparklingly clear and fish of around ten and fourteen inches were all over the place. That's how serious love affairs with rivers begin – because after a start like that you'll forgive a river anything, forever.

Below the bridge over the R58 the Karringmelkspruit flows through a gorge – a gorge in the true sense of the word, not just a valley with steep hills on each side. Jake and I decided to hike into it on the second day. The going was tough. I'd never seen bigger boulders in a riverbed, other than in the Joggem Valley forty kilometres away to the east. We started fishing downstream, catching trout after trout, small fish on nymphs and dry flies, until we were within sight of the Cape Vulture colony we'd heard was pretty deep into the gorge. That's when we realised that we should have headed out an hour before. It was dark and cold when we arrived back at camp to our friends who were wrapped around a dancing fire. It felt like I'd arrived at the Ritz. A local farmer stopped by later and told us that trying to get to the vulture colony and back in a day was a bridge too far.

This is not one of the known laws of sensible angling, I know, but it ought to be, and it should go along these lines: when you are fishing in big boulder-ridden canyon-country, it's a lot easier climbing *over* boulders going *downstream* than climbing *up* them going *upstream*. The reason is obvious. In floods, the force of the water eventually tends to sweep everything into an angle facing downstream more than up. Well, more or less.

My friend Phil Hills tried the canyon some years back, in the sensible way, taking the gravel road that eventually crosses the river at the bottom end of the gorge where they pitched camp and fished each day just as far upstream as they wanted. He said it was spectacular, but the river was too low for the fishing to be good, though they landed a few decent trout. For the less faint-hearted, a great plan would be to start at the bottom of the gorge, camp overnight, and fish slowly right the way up to the national road bridge, camping out on the way through. Or you could do it the other way around. I guess it would take two or three days, depending on how carefully you fish canyon water and how good you are with boulders the size of two-car garages. But it's not something I'd do though without making elaborate precautionary rescue arrangements in advance.

Geoff Knipe also wrote about the gorge water on the Karringmelkspruit in Michael Salomon's *Freshwater Fishing in South Africa*. It was in April 1975, and Geoff was with a friend by the name of Alf Fulford. Like us, they miscalculated the time it would take to get out of the gorge and were trapped by darkness. They were saved by a fire they lit with, and I quote, 'the dry right-hand corner of a box of matches and a piece of toilet paper'. They had no food, and Knipe's clothes were wet through after he'd tried to cross the river. They had no jerseys or warm clothing – just thin shirts and jeans – and they spent an icy night warming their bodies next to the fire. Geoff also gives some interesting fishing stats on the trip. Just listen to this: one fish in every fifteen they caught was over two pounds, one in thirty-three was over three pounds, and his best fish was just over six pounds.

*

I've suffered a few disasters on fly-fishing trips, but so far never a true catastrophe. I'm discounting here things such as getting rained out, snowed in, flat tyres, truck sliding into muddy ditches, snapping fly rods, nearly standing on snakes and similar things, which are common enough. But there were two blots on fishing trips that qualified as minor catastrophes, and both happened on the Karringmelkspruit. The first was when my friend Jacques Rudolph, the cricketer, ripped his leg wide open on a barbed-wire fence, and the second was when I took a giddy tumble on this river.

With regards to Jacques's leg, I stitched it up that night, without anaesthetic, on the dining-room table in the *Ossa* farmhouse. He recovered.

The giddy fall happened when I was strolling along the riverbank watching a pair of buzzards flying in slow circles above my head and not looking where I was putting my feet. I remember seeing my rod cartwheel through the air before I actually hit the ground, and thinking, 'If I've broken anything, let it be my fly rod.' It was that serious. When the flashing lights stopped pulsing, I slowly got up. There were some scrapes and some blood, but I could still walk. I picked up my rod. It was lying intact, propped up against a bush as if I'd taken the trouble to put it there. Since then I don't walk on riverbanks when I'm looking at passing birds.

I remember John Gierach writing about a similar act of providence in his delightful book *The View from Rat Lake,* where his friend Koke Winter took a tumble watching Sand Cranes – only he ended up with a serious fracture. We both came to the same conclusion, though, about the inherent dangers of walking through rough country when you're not looking ahead – and I guess you should add the more insidious risk of negotiating barbed-wire fences with or without waders.

*

The Karringmelkspruit has been particularly kind to me from the time I took my son Robert and daughter Alison there, way back when they were both still at school, Alison only twelve and Robert in his early teens – and in the often perverse way fishing plays out, I haven't known the Karringmelkspruit produce that well since. One morning we fished a long run behind Woodlands Cottage where we were staying. I had rigged a Zak under a bright yarn indicator the size of my thumb, and so many fish pulled it under that in the end I didn't even have to shout for the kids to strike. They must have had half a dozen trout each, all between twelve and fourteen inches, and from the same run.

Which brings me to something AC Harrison once told me. He said the Karringmelkspruit was the finest trout stream in South Africa, and when I think back to when this stream is on form and bubbling just right through those crevassed hills, I don't much feel like arguing the point.

The Luzie and the Swith, Eastern Cape
The Swith was one of the streams that Ed Herbst and I didn't appreciate as much as we should have the first time we fished it. But back then we were new to the Maclear district of the southern Drakensberg, where trout streams are so common it was natural enough that we didn't get too carried away by just one of them. I've since fished a dozen streams in this district – that's an exact count, by the way – and it feels like there are as many I haven't fished as those I have, which is a comforting thing to say about any place you like visiting.

The Swith runs into the upper Luzie, which Sydney Hey describes with affection in *Rapture of the River*.

Ed and I fished the Luzie briefly back in the 1990s, when we were staying with Donie and Juan-Marie Naudé on their farm *Vrederus*. They have around five kilometres of it. Our first visit was to one of the lower beats of the Luzie, way below its junction with the Swith, and I remember we got there on a boulder-strewn track that felt like a vertical drop of a high wall straight into the valley. There were way too many wattle trees to make it feel anything like the stream Sydney Hey might remember, but as I recall the fishing was okay.

My next visit to the Luzie was at its junction with the Swith, again with Donie Naudé. We parked on a hillside looking down on the river, and it brought to mind that somewhat trite description of rivers as 'water from heaven'. And, yes, I accept there's also a little clichéd romanticism in that notion. But from the hill gazing down, the Luzie actually *did* look like water from heaven. Conditions were perfect, with the stream running fresh and the sun shining from a blue sky, and it was lovely. There were patches of whitewater, winking riffles that ran into the soft greens of runs and pools that were somehow still gorgeously transparent, smooth-surfaced glides, tempting pockets of slack water behind smoothly rounded boulders, swooping swallows that cut the sky like scythes over the stream. Donie couldn't remember when anyone had last fished here, at least not with a fly rod, so as you would imagine the fishing turned out to be good. I remember Ed losing a fish all of sixteen inches, and I hooked a few that easily made fourteen.

Ed said the only problem with this part of the Luzie was the bone-rattling track getting to it, which, if you think of it differently, will also likely remain its saving grace.

*

As I mentioned, my love of the Swith goes back years to when Ed and I first stopped at the tiny stone bridge carrying the gravel road from Rhodes to Maclear over Naude's Nek Pass, and then crossed over this bubbling little stream. Since then I can't resist stopping here; in fact, I can't remember when I ever drove over this stream without stopping. It's just one of those charming, quiet, trouty sort of places, a stream not much wider than a fly rod up here.

On our very first trip we spotted trout in the tiny pool above the bridge, panicky fish that shot under shadowy banks as soon as we leaned over the parapets. We considered putting a fly over them, but that ended in one of those uncomfortable ethical debates you get into whenever you feel tempted to fish private water that just happens to be conveniently remote. On our next trip a year later, when we were crossing this same little bridge and spotted these same little trout, we cracked, climbed into the stream and hooked a couple of fish under a cloud of guilt – and, of course, put them back, no doubt with a little affected moral rectitude. They were less than ten inches long and as pretty as you'd expect. Later on this trip we got permission to fish the stream officially.

Above the bridge the stream became a rivulet that soon dwindled into a series of barren pools trickling into one another over sheets of sun-baked bedrock. We found better water below the bridge, flowing through gently sloping grasslands, where the banks were lined in places with scrawny crack willows and ouhout trees (*Leucosidea sericea*), an indigenous evergreen scrub-like plant with smoky-green serrated leaves and brittle branches the colour of charcoal. They throw pools of shade over streams, attract bugs and grow in cold, misty areas, which no doubt accounts for their close association with trout – at least wherever I've been in this country.

The fish we caught that day had an amber, almost copper tint to them, and I briefly tried to convince Ed they might be a subspecies of cutthroat trout, though there was no sign of the carmine slash below the mandible or the salmon-pink fins. Ed had never caught a cutthroat, but many years back I caught a few in the Yellowstone

River in Montana, and in a some ways these little trout seemed to revive memories of them, though I might have just been romanticising a little, something that's easy to do when you're catching trout in a mountain stream that's new to you, feels remote enough to be on the edge of the Earth and is flowing so delicately it looks like a stream on tiptoes. By the time we'd got a dozen fish, I had to agree they weren't a strain of cutthroats at all; just a copper-coloured local breed of free-rising rainbows characterised more by an inclination to throw themselves recklessly at artificial dry flies than by any real resemblance to cutthroats.

We left the stream that afternoon not near to realising just what a great day's fishing we'd had and what a gem we'd unearthed, but that kind of deep insight often only strikes you years later when you've fished a heap more streams that were far less attractive and caught fewer trout in them that were nowhere near as hungry and not half as pretty.

The best of the Swith is on John and Amanda Jordaan's farm *Höningskloof*, where it runs through spectacular, rugged countryside; in fact, it's a toss-up whether the fishing is more special than the scenery here, and it's good when you can say that about a place. The stream flows through typical sandstone country with ochre-coloured ramparts and steep-sloping hillsides, the riverbanks lined with the once ubiquitous crack willow and ouhout trees.

This part of the Swith is lovely water, clear and quick, and in sunlight the scarlet-red fibrils of crack willow roots shine up through the water like spilled blood. The trout aren't as copper-coloured down here but they're still pretty, and they're wild and obligingly free-rising.

If there's a downside to fishing the Swith, it's maybe that some days it's too easy. Okay, I've been in this valley when the fishing was tough, but not often, and mainly because it had rained for days or else it hadn't rained in months. I've been cold here, when,

462

as you'd expect, the fish were moody; and on rare occasions it's been hot enough to take a swim – when the fish were obviously equally moody. But overall, I've found a predictable constancy to this stream in ways we anglers believe count – like enough trout that are just forgiving enough, dependable dry fly fishing and good nymphing when the fish aren't rising, and all of it wrapped in an appealing sense of remoteness. It's the kind of stream where you can end up wondering if you're out fishing or simply idling around a riverbank in deep meditation.

And notice I haven't used the words 'big trout' once. It's another of the streams I know where you don't miss catching big fish, though you can't deny they'd be a pleasant addition to the absorbingly minimalist fly fishing. I've caught a couple of 'nice' trout here, meaning twelve- to fourteen-inch fish, and I don't remember suffering any pangs of remorse about not hooking a sixteen-incher. (I haven't fished the river often enough to quite swear there aren't any sixteen-inch trout around, though experience leads me to believe that if there are, there won't be many.)

*

Downstream of the first shallow drift that John Jordaan confidently crosses in his battered Toyota Land Cruiser (it had over a million clicks on the clock the last time I was in it), there's a rock painting worth seeing. To get to it, John drives through the Swith in his truck, a manoeuvre that seems impossible and potentially lethal, until two more similar river crossings later you are way downstream. He parks the truck in a narrow pasture running on the edge of the stream, and from there it's a short walk up to the site.

The cave is alive with art but it's the centrepiece that's remarkable; a painting around two metres off the ground and maybe twenty centimetres by ten. At first glance, the painted figure looks like a hermaphrodite holding a bow, with breasts and what appears to be a penis. Years back I sent a few photographs of the painting to a local San art expert, Dawn Greene. She replied, 'The white figure is male, I would say, and not hermaphrodite. I'm unsure as to whether those are breasts – could be his quiver and bag, or there's another painting superimposed. I would need to see it to be more definitive. It is similar to later depictions of ritual specialists. The relatively detailed facial features suggests the painter may have been depicting a ritual. If it is quite a large painting, it would support this.'

Whatever the explanation, this painting is worth seeing – and believe me, the trip in is an experience.

*

I've had a few of those crazy sequences lately where you get up before sunrise to be at the airport for an early flight to Joburg to attend a meeting, then find yourself back at the airport for the return flight and eventually get home long after dark. The best I can say about airports, never mind days crammed with meeting schedules, is that as rushed and chaotic as they usually are, they do remind me of all that's good about the slow-paced tranquillity of the secluded places I know, like the Swith – and that I should count all these places as a heaven-sent blessings.

The Upper Wildebeest River, Eastern Cape

The Upper Wildebeest is tiny, even by small-stream standards, but it makes up for its size by being among the most beautiful trout streams in the district, not in the sense that the stream itself is that beautiful, but because the surrounding landscapes are grand and striking and frame it perfectly. I normally fish it from the Ugie side, Ugie being a small town on the edge of some good trout fishing in this part of the Eastern Cape. From Ugie, you travel through pine plantations to get to it, but by the time you're heading up the dirt road that eventually goes over Bastervoetpad Pass to Barkly East, the stream is alongside you and the pines are long since behind.

It's rough-hewn countryside, with boulders scattered on grassy hill slopes that rise up to marmalade-coloured sandstone overhangs and tall spires that reach into the sky. In fact, it's not unlike the terrain around the Karringmelkspruit or the Joggem Valley, or the drive up to the Kloppershoekspruit. They're striking landscapes. You see them a lot in the Eastern Cape Highlands anywhere near high mountains, and they're so typical of this whole area that you can start taking them for granted, even after just a few hours of fishing; after a day or two you might hardly notice the countryside at all, until somebody looks around and reminds you just how beautiful and wonderful it all is.

There's another way to get into this stream, and that's on Bastervoetpad Pass from the Barkly East side, but that depends on the pass being open to traffic, which it mostly isn't, either due to the poor condition of the road or bad weather on the escarpment.

I was with my friends Tony Kietzman and Lloyd Rennie the only time I've travelled over the pass. It was a day when the view was seemingly endless, with mountain ranges running in rows like the ribs of our planet until they gradually dissolved into the blue haziness of the horizon. I recall that we stopped at places where springs dripped into fern-covered gullies strung with wildflowers, including orchids, and that we spent time studying them and gazing out over the mountains, drinking in the view, never mind that we were supposed to be heading for some good small-stream fishing. But Tony is keen on wildflowers, orchids in particular, and we were so spellbound by the views that stopping now and again to take it all in somehow felt right. I remember the road twisting down the steep slope of the Drakensberg until the surrounding hills gradually flattened and the drop-offs into the valley became less intimidatingly sheer, and suddenly we were driving alongside the headwaters of the Wildebeest and mildly surprised by its sudden appearance. I've visited this stretch more than a few times, but this was the only trip where I'd got there over the pass.

I can't exactly remember how the fishing went, only that it was a typical small-stream day, the kind I never tire of – clear water, a few staircase waterfalls, long, knee-deep, rock-studded runs with bubble lines drifting slowly through them, short stretches of serrated riffles where your dry fly could really dance, pools no bigger than Persian rugs – the kind of words that would of course fit a hundred other streams. And there would have been the usual snagging on bushes and plenty of trout that rose flashily but missed the fly altogether, sometimes twice, even three times, and a few places where you spot trout in clear pools that suddenly empty as soon as soon as you lift your rod. The fish would otherwise have been predictably naive and hungry, so naturally, as on many small streams, we would begin to believe we could catch them at will, which is always only partly true, because small-stream trout mainly won't rise unless the drift is clean, and as long as they haven't spotted you. When the drift is okay and you're out of sight, they come up like arrows, and some will take the fly and leap clean out of the water in one seamless movement. I don't know how they do it.

The fish would have been cold to the touch, stiff with electric shudders in our hands, and predictably pretty, a palette of pearly blues and greens and rose pinks and sunset orange, all wondrously spotted. We wouldn't remember how many we'd released, because it was usually be enough to confuse any attempt to actually keep score. A few hooked fish would have darted into craggy corners to sit tight, as small-stream trout so often do, and we'd have waded across, felt between the rocks for the cold softness of the fish, then felt with fingers for the fly and gently freed it. And the better ones wouldn't have been much over ten inches, not that it matters, because we mostly leave streams like this with the feeling that there's another way of looking at fly fishing altogether, a way that doesn't need anything like big fish in it to paint a perfect picture.

For the record, I *can* tell you we were fishing barbless flies and that I was using my 0-weight Sage SPL, which paints a fly line so lightly and flexes so effortlessly to the tug and throb of small-stream trout that you have to believe that whoever designed it was not only mighty clever, but had in mind a stream exactly like this one. It still has to be the best small-stream fly rod ever made.

Anyway, as we rattled back on the long road home with the sun sinking ahead of us, I mentioned that it was a pity Bastervoetpad was so often closed to traffic, and Tony replied that he didn't mind because it would help keep other anglers out. Strange how we fly fishers arrive at a remote stream and in the space of a few hours feel as though we partially own it, or at least want to keep its fishing secret. That's not because we worry that sooner or later some visiting angler will turn out to be a hard-nosed property developer with who knows what ideas in mind, but because we know that fishing like this is always tenuous and fragile and won't take much pressure, never mind that we'd just found it so delightfully abundant.

LIST OF FLY ILLUSTRATIONS

ACKNOWLEDGEMENTS

The first proofreading of my manuscript was undertaken by a man who has an eye for errors like a hawk has for mice. He is Dean Riphagen, in my view one of the most discerning fly fishers this country has produced. Additional editing came from my dear friend Dulcie Brandon-Kirby, a musician, novelist and consummate wordsmith who, by happy chance, also enjoys fly fishing. Dulcie and Dean were both involved in editing *Hunting Trout*, and I was particularly fortunate to rekindle this partnership.

Then angling bibliophile Paul Curtis cast his critical eye over the book and was kind enough to give it a pass mark, along with countless valuable suggestions and a cover blurb. Thank you Paul.

I thank Duncan Brown for the flattering foreword he wrote. He is the author of *Are Trout South African?*, a professor of English, and the Dean of the Faculty of Arts at the University of the Western Cape – a gentle academic with a fine eye for words and a deep love of fly fishing.

I thank Tudor Caradoc-Davies for his astute guidance and for connecting me to Tim Richman of Burnet Media, who found enough in my writings to consider publishing this book – and then, having agreed to go ahead, had the patience to listen to my interminable nitpicking around the many idiosyncratic practices we fly fishers visit on any serious prose concerning our precious pursuit. I sense he put his heart and soul into this book, and I was very fortunate to have met him as well as his appointed graphic artist Simon Richardson, who survived yet more of my lofty idiosyncrasies in coming up with a lovely cover. Then I thank Ania Rokita, who did a wonderful job of beating my stumbling syntax into shape. I suspect she would make a good fly fisher; more particularly, a good dry fly fisher on testy water.

I thank Basie and Carien Vosloo of *Birkhall*, who are more part of my family now than just good friends, for giving me so much fishing; Robin Douglas, the best river companion ever; Ed Herbst, the world's most indefatigable fly-fishing intellectual; Robin Renwick, who opened the chalkstreams of Hampshire to me, as well as the salmon of Iceland; and Billy de Jong, who trudged countless river miles with me, sharing our dual love of fish and fishing and of cameras near flowing water.

I thank my wife Kathy, who created the comfortable space in which it was possible to write a book like this, and my beautiful and talented daughter Alison for her help with the layout.

I thank my many fly-fishing friends who were steadfast while I lived the writing of this book, and who were valuable in their inspiration or in their advice or just in their companionship, on stream or otherwise. Without them there would be no story to tell. In alphabetical order, they include:
Terry Andrews, Wolf Avni, Roger Bart, Vicky and Luke Bell (Highland Lodge), Tony Biggs, Chris Bladen, Sarah and Jonathan Bolton, Clem Booth (London, UK), Gary Borger (USA), Stephen Boshoff, Gary Herman Botes, Theuns Botha, Clay Brendish (River Test, Kimbridge, Hampshire), Peter Brigg, Korrie Broos, Sheena Carnie, Greg Carstens, Mario Cesare, MC Coetzer, Gerrit Compion (*Lourensford Estate*), Simon Cooper (Nether Wallop, Hampshire), Ian Cox, Laurence Davies, Hansjörg Dietiker (Zürich, Switzerland), Miles Divett, Ian Douglas (California, USA), Keith Douglas, John Dreyer (Sydney, Australia), Stephen Dugmore, Mike and Candy Ferrar (*Mount Melsetter*), Leonard Flemming, Andrew Fowler, Margie and Graham Frost (Willow Stream, *Balloch*),

Shaun Futter, Agostino Gaglio, Mario Geldenhuys, Gary Glen-Young, JP Gouws, Mike Harker, Roger and Victoria Harrison (Upper Itchen, Itchen Stoke Mill, Hampshire), Stanton Hector, Philip and Caitlin Hills, Ríkarður Hjálmarsson (Iceland), Alan and Annabelle Hobson (Somerset East), the Isted family (*Lammergeier Nature Reserve*, Lady Grey), PJ and Lizelle Jacobs, John and Barbara Jellis, Amanda and John Jordaan (Swith Stream, *Höningskloof*), Barry Kent (Florida, USA), Tony Kietzman, Angelo Komis, Mark Krige, Darryl Lampert, Bill Latham (Hampshire), Arno Laubscher, Gerhard Laubscher, Terry Lawton (Norfolk), Tom Lewin, Leon Links (the Netherlands), Nick Lyons (New York, USA), AD Maddox (Livingston, Montana, USA), Andrew McKenzie (Sydney, Australia), Mike McKeown, Philip Meyer, Sean Mills, Zane Mirfin (Nelson, New Zealand), Ritchie Morris, Frederick Mostert (London), Alan Myburgh (Western Australia), Juan-Marie and Donie Naudé (*Vrederus*), Ruhan Neethling, Jim Read, Gerhard Redpath, John Robinson, Tim Rolston, Agostino Roncallo (Genoa, Italy), Hugh Rosen (La Jolla, California, USA), Alf and Denise Ross (Lupela Lodge, Lady Grey), Jay Smit, Al Spaeth, Graeme Steart, Fred Steynberg, Pieter Taljaard, Nick Taransky (New South Wales, Australia), Warwick Tarboton, Marcel Terblanche, John Thoabala, Craig Thom, Platon Trakoshis, Bruce Truter, Sharland and Gavin Urquhart, Gordon van der Spuy, Hans van Klinken (the Netherlands), Richard Viedge, Dave Walker (Walkerbouts Inn and the Wild Trout Association, Rhodes), Lyndon Webb (Victoria, Australia), Joan Wulff (New York, USA), John Yelland, Mark Yelland and Matt Zilliox (Oregon, USA).

Tom Sutcliffe
April 2019

Printed in Great Britain
by Amazon